RURAL DEVELOPMENT IN INDIA
Policies and Programmes

Abdul Azeez NP
S. M. Jawed Akhtar

KALPAZ

ISBN : 9789351281528

Price : ₹ 950

First Published, 2016

Published by :

Kalpaz Publications
C-30, Satyawati Nagar,
Delhi-110052
Ph. : 9212142040
E-mail: kalpaz@hotmail.com

Printed at : G. Print Process, Delhi

Cataloging in Publication Data--DK
Courtesy: D.K. Agencies (P) Ltd.
<docinfo@dkagencies.com>

Rural development in India / Abdul Azeez NP, SM Javed Akhtar.
pages cm
Contributed articles.
ISBN 9789351281528

1. Rural development--India. 2. Rural development--Government policy--India. I. Azeez, N. P. Abdul, editor. II. Akhtar, S. M. Jawed, editor.

HN690.Z9C6 2015 DDC 307.14120954 23

Contents

Contributors 7

Preface 9

1. Geographical Indications and Rural Development in India: A Survey
   Ruchi Sharma 13
2. Rural Treasures: Traditional Knowledge, Innovations and Best Practices (With focus on Western Rajasthan)
   Trilok Kumar Jain 29
3. Challenges and Barriers in Rural Development in India and Beyond: A Regional Outlook
   Najmudheen, T 35
4. Role of Agriculture Sector in Sustainable Development of India
   Shaukat Ali 61
5. Agricultural Credit and Agricultural Development in India.
   Kaberi Sarkar and *Sebak Kumar Jana* 81
6. Demand for Agricultural Credit: A Financial Inclusion Perspective
   S. M. Jawed Akhtar and *Saba Parveen* 101
7. Demographic Dividend in India: Addressing Education and Skill Development.
   Anup K. Mishra, Santosh K. Singh 117
8. Inclusive Growth of Self-Help Groups in India
   Jasmin Treesa T.J. 133
9. Factors Affecting Child Health: A Study of Respondent Mothers and their Children's Health in Rural West Bengal
   Paramita Roy and *Arunangshu Mondal* 141
10. Role of Credit and Banking of Rural Development in Agriculture Sector *Ms. Sony S. Hiremath* 161
11. Rural Credit Market and Village Economies
    H. R. Prajapati 165
12. A Review of Financial Inclusion Initiatives for Rural Development-Issues, Challenges and Recommendations
    Sonam Agrawal 183
13. Interest Free Micro Finance for Financial Inclusion and Rural Development.
    Manzoor, K. 193
14. A Peep into Past Rural Self-Employment Programmes Initiated by the Government of India
    Dr Shankar Chatterjee 207

15. Employment Structure in Kerala with a Special Preference to Palakkad District
Sasi, C 223

16. MGNREGP: A Programme for Inclusive Growth and Development: An Assessment
Aboobacker Sidheeque K.P 231

17. Empowering Women through Education: A Rural Indian Perspective
Ismail Thamarasseri 245

18. Kudumbasree-The Self Help Group Model Poverty Alleviation Programme in Kerala
Dr K. Baby 255

19. A Study on Constraints Faced by Elected Women Representatives under Panchayati Raj Institutions (PRI) in Empowerment Process, West Midnapore District, West Bengal
Ria Sarkar 271

20. People's Participation and Decentralised Planning in Kerala. A Revisit: Case Study of Two Village Panchayats
Dr.E.M.Thomas 301

21. Local Governance and Solid Waste Management in Kerala : Case Study of a Municipality in Kerala
Justin Thomas 317

22. A Study on Consumer Awareness among Rural Households with Special Reference to Palakkad District
Savithri, K.B 329

23. An Overview of Integrated Child Development Scheme (ICDS) on the Nutritional Status of Children in the Rural Areas of Kerala
Dr N. Karunakaran 341

24. A Study on the Health Status of the Scheduled Castes in Palakkad District, Kerala
Nisha T.A. 353

25. Gender Disparity in Rural Poverty: A Sociological Evidences and Issues in Kerala.
Jafar K. 363

26. Death Rate and Infant Mortality Rate in Mysuru District: A Spatial Analysis
Sowmyashree K.L and *Pradeep Kumar* 377

27. Pradhan Mantri Jan DhanYojana (PMJDY): A Myth about Financial Inclusion for Rural India
Rasananda Panda, Shailendra Patil and *Anushree Karani* 383

Index 397

Contributors

1. **Aboobacker Sidheeque K.P.,** Assistant Professor on contract, LBS College of Engineering, Kasaragod, Kerala.
2. **Anup K. Mishra,** Assistant Professor in Economics, DAV, PG, College, Banaras Hindu University, Varanasi, UP.
3. **Anushree Karani** - Research Assistant, General Management Area, MICA, Ahmedabad.
4. **Arunangshu Mondal,** Coordinator, Child-Fund India Project, Prayatn Sanstha, Pratapgarh, U.P.
5. **Dr K. Baby,** Assistant Professor, Department of Economics, Govt. College, Chittur, Palakkad, Kerala.
6. **Jafar K.,** Sociology / Anthropology Investigator KIRTADS, Calicut, Kerala.
7. **Dr E.M.Thomas,** Associate Professor, Department of Economics, Christ College, Irinjalakuda, Kerala.
8. **Dr Shankar Chatterjee,** Associate Professor, National Institute of Rural Development (NIRD) &PR, Hyderabad.
9. **Dr N. Karunakaran,** Head of the Department, PG Department of Economics, EKNM Government College Elerithattu, Elerithattu – Post, Nilishwar – Via, Kasaragod – Dist, Kerala, India.
10. **H. R. Prajapati,** CSEP/SSS, Central University of Gujarat.
11. **Ismail Thamarasseri,** Assistant Professor, Department of Education, Central University of Kashmir, Srinagar, Jammu & Kashmir.
12. **JasminTreesa T.J,** M Phil Scholar, C.B.M. College, Kovaipudur, Coimbatore, Tamil Nadu.
13. **Justin Thomas,** IV Sem. MA Economics, Christ College, Irinjalakuda, Kerala.
14. **Kaberi Sarkar,** Associate Professor in Economics, Gobardanga Hindu College, Gobardanga, West Bengal.
15. **Manzoor. K.,** Research Scholar in Economics, University of Kannur, Kerala.
16. **Najmudheen. T,** Research Scholar, Department of Political Science, Aligarh Muslim University, Aligarh.
17. **Nisha T.A,** Research Scholar in Economics, St Thomas College, Thrissur, Calicut University, Kerala.
18. **Paramita Roy,** Associate Professor, Dept. of Social Work. Visva-Bharati, Sriniketan.
19. **Pradeep Kumar, K,** Research Scholar, D.O.S in Geography, University of Mysore, Manasagangotri, Mysuru.

20. **Rasananda Panda**, Professor of Economics, General Management Area, MICA, Ahmedabad.
21. **Ria Sarkar**, Master of Science, Ramakrishna Mission Vivekananda University, Belur Math, Ramakrishna Mission Ashrama, Narendrapur, Kolkata, West Bengal.
22. **Ruchi Sharma**, Assistant Professor of Economics, Department of Humanities and Social Sciences, Indian Institute of Technology Indore, M-Block, IET, DAVV Campus, Khandwa Road, Indore, India.
23. **Saba Parveen**, Junior Research Fellow, Department of Economics, Aligarh Muslim University, Aligarh, 202002, U.P., India
24. **Santosh K. Singh**, Ph.D. in Economics, FSS, Banaras Hindu University, Varanasi.
25. **Savithri, K.B**, Guest Lecturer, Sreekrishnapuram V T B College, Mannampatta, Palakkad, Kerala, India.
26. **Sebak Kumar Jana,** Associate Professor in Economics, Vidyasagar University, Midnapore, West Bengal.
27. **Shailendra Patil**, Student, MICA, Ahmedabad.
28. **Shaukat Ali**, Assistant Professor, Vishveshwarya Group of Institution, Greater Noida, Phase-2.
29. **Sonam Agrawal**, MBA, Department of Business Administration, FMSR, Aligarh Muslim University, Aligarh.
30. **Sony S. Hiremath**, Research Scholar, Department of Management, Karnataka State Women's University, Vijayapura.
31. **Smt. Sowmyashree K.L**, Research Scholar, D.O.S in Geography, University of Mysore, Manasagangotri, Mysuru.
32. **S. M. Jawed Akhtar**, Associate Professor, Department of Economics, Aligarh Muslim University, Aligarh, 202002, U.P., India.
33. **Trilok Kumar Jain**, Professor, Department of Economics, Manipal University, Jaipur.

Preface

The notion of rural development has been conceived in diverse ways by researchers, ranging from thinking of it as a set of goals and programmes to a well-knit strategy, approach or even an ideology. If you go through the relevant literature, you will realize that its scope and content are nebulous and do not have well-accepted analytical boundaries. Rural development which simply connotes the development of rural base that is agriculture, in course of time assumed a newer meaning and has been approached from different angles. It has been defined as "a strategy designed to improve the economic and social life of a specific group of people-the rural poor. It involves extending the benefits of development to the poorest among those who seek a livelihood in the rural areas. The group includes small - scale farmers, tenants and landless".

Development of rural areas and the rural people has been the primary concern of the economic planning and development process of the country. The subject of rural development has gained widespread appeal in recent years. This is largely a result of the way issues regarding development themselves began to be perceived. During the post-World War II era, development theorists became increasingly dissatisfied with the way traditional concepts of development emphasized growth and neglected important issues related to distributive justice and other dimensions of development. The interest in rural development is partly an offshoot of such disenchantment and also on account of the growing realization of the centrality of rural development in facilitating the process of overall development.

Rural development became a planning concern as it became clear that the strategies adopted in developing countries remained largely ineffective in alleviating poverty and inequalities in rural areas. It became increasingly clear that apart from an effort to increase agricultural and industrial production, it was also necessary to address directly the problems of education, health services and employment and to attack the problem of poverty in rural area. The increasing interest in rural development is a result of the realization that a systematic effort is necessary to create better living conditions in the rural areas where the vast majority of populations of developing countries reside.

During the 1950s and 1960s, development policy makers sought to increase productivity and per capita incomes through advances in the manufacturing sector. In the realm of agricultural production, growth in output during the first two decades after independence was achieved mainly by increasing the area under cultivation, supported by expansion in public investment in supporting infrastructure. It was soon realized, however, that the gains from these methods reached, to a large extent, only a small minority - mainly those who were already better off and privileged. In fact, the gains made as a result of these efforts are believed to have further accentuated inequality in incomes in rural areas. By the 1970s it became clear that there were serious problems in the way the issues and problems of development were being tackled. In particular, the hope that the problems of unemployment and poverty in rural areas would get addressed adequately was certainly not realized.

Historically, it has been observed that industrialization and the advancement of economies in western societies was linked to major economic changes in the rural society. The industrial revolution in England, as also in many other countries in Europe, and the maturing of Japanese industry among others, were all preceded by far reaching changes in agrarian societies. Land reforms and other legislative reforms were instrumental in bringing about a change in rural economies in many of these countries. Industrial growth and modernization were accompanied by increased productivity in the agricultural sector and urbanization. In many cases, access to colonies was a critical input in their economic advancement. Also, large male migration from Europe was very helpful in relocating surplus labour. For instance, it is well documented that over 40 million people emigrated from Europe during 1870 to 1914 alone. As a result of all these factors these societies were able to reduce poverty and increase the role of non-agricultural activities in their economies.

On the other hand, in large parts of the developing world, these conditions have not been brought about. The impact that rural development strategies can have in these countries, in the absence of those prerequisite changes, cannot be underestimated. It is also clear that the patterns of economic transformation in developed countries cannot be replicated as the historical circumstances in the developing countries are quite different from those prevailing then in the former cases. The upshot of all this is that well formulated and clearly focused strategies of rural development are a must in the developing world.

It is clear that rural development, in its all dimensions, is sine qua non for a strong and vibrating nation like India which aspires for becoming a super power in the world. It is also true that no nation can survive if it ignores its vast human potential in general process and women in particular because development is above all a human process and not just a mechanical or technological change. Development does not mean the construction of physical structure, installation of huge machines or going for latest technology. The aim of development should be to sub-serve the needs of human beings, enrich the quality of life, both individual and collective in either area – rural or urban. Mere development of urban area will lead to a cancerous growth in country, consequences of which will be fatal. Rural development in a predominantly rural country like ours is of paramount importance. Creation of more and employment/work opportunities for women in on-going schemes / projects and exploring new avenues for their engagement in economically gainful activities will go a long way in ameliorating rural India. No doubt, formulation and implementation of various rural development schemes/ programmes have touched many a milestone, yet a lot remain still to be done. Let us hope for a bright future for rural India and rural women.

This edited book examines the basic issues, problems, policies, programmes and prospects of rural development in India. We are grateful to the contributors of all the papers for their valuable contributions and also grateful to several of my teachers, colleagues, friends and students for their encouragement at various stages of the preparation of this book. Last but not the least, I thank to the editorial and production teams at Gyan Publication, New Delhi for the cooperation and help to publish this book in an elegant manner.

Dr.Abdul Azeez. N.P

Dr. S.M. Jawed Akhtar

1
Geographical Indications and Rural Development in India: A Survey

Ruchi Sharma

1. Introduction

Natural resources are assets occurring in nature that can be used for economic production or consumption (Glossary of Environment Statistics, 1997). They are sub-divided into four categories: mineral and energy resources, soil resources, water resources and biological resources. The local population utilises resources occurring in nature for their economic gains that become part and parcel of the diverse culture of a country. Many practises using such resources develop over a period of time through the human interaction. In terms of agro-based resources, a country may enjoy some unique features due to climate, soil, terrain and any other environmental characteristics that may be reflected in the goods produced in the particular region. For instance, Darjeeling tea, which according to the official website is, "tea, which on when brewed, has a distinct, naturally occurring aroma and taste" and is grown in the designated area. It is pertinent for an economy having such resources to be able to commercialise those. Such commercialisation will help in the development of the local communities involved. For the commercialisation of resources, the state may provide for an institutional mechanism under Geographical Indication (GI henceforth), that is a type of intellectual property right (IPR[1]). GI, according to the World Intellectual Property Right Organisation (WIPO henceforth), "is a sign used on goods that have a specific geographical origin and possess qualities, reputation or characteristics that are essentially attributable to that origin". Such rights built the reputation of the goods in the national and international market and allow the producers to earn rent through the differentiation of the product. The most widely used example of such rent earned is by the producers of Champagne which is a well known GI''. Indication of source (IS)" and "Appellation of Origin (AO)" are alternative mechanism available that also associate a good with a geographical region. However, the protection granted under IS and AO varies from GI. Literature espouses GI as a channel for rural development as a community commercialises its specific resources and distribute the gains amongst its members. The process of establishing GI and ensuring that it leads to the development of the community is rather complex. It requires establishing transparent institutional framework and ensuring the flow of the benefits to each member involved in the value chain.

GI like other intellectual property rights (IPRs) are territorial in nature, that is, the level and conditions of protection are determined by national laws and enforcement institutions. The need for international protection of IPRs became evident when foreign exhibitors refused to attend International Exhibition of Inventions in Vienna in 1873 (WIPO, 2005). These exhibitors had fear that their ideas would be stolen and exploited commercially in other countries. These apprehensions have grown over the last century with increase in the international trade. IPRs along with GI became part of international agreements with Paris Convention (1883). Following this there were many developments at international level that lead to the establishment of WIPO in 1970.[2] WIPO became a specialised agency of United Nations (UN) in 1974 to administer IPRs related matters. Currently, WIPO administers 24 treaties covering various types and aspects of IPRs. These treaties do not require its member states to stipulate similar standards of protection in their domestic legislations covering different IPRs. Developed countries, especially US and EU in the context of GI, intended to set minimum standards of protection for IPRs across countries through WIPO. These initiatives were thwarted because of the opposition from developing countries (the South) at WIPO (Drahos, 2002). Developed countries then shifted the forum for IPRs related talks from WIPO to General Agreement on Tariffs and Trade (GATT). According to Adolf (2001), GATT offered following advantages over WIPO: (i) access to developing countries' product markets in return of IPRs, (ii) ability to use cross-sectoral retaliation under Dispute Settlement Mechanism in case of dispute and, (iii) participation from large number of countries. Drahos (2002) established that IPRs entered the arena of multilateral agreements with the introduction of "Agreement on Trade Related Aspects of Intellectual Property Rights" (TRIPs) under the aegis of World Trade Organisation (WTO) due to extensive efforts on the part of developed countries. GI is also a part of international agreement under Article 22, though earlier there were a few international treaties that covered IS and AO.

In order to comply with the requirements of the TRIPs agreement, India formulated law to protect GI in the country. India is also actively involved in the ongoing negotiations at WTO with respect to GI along with the other issues. It shows that the policymaker consider GI as a significant institutional framework that may be developed for the benefit of the rural population. This paper aims to review the current situation regarding GI in India and identify the areas that require further development in making GI as a tool for the rural development. The first section of the paper gives details about the GI, its definition and the economic rationale behind these rights. The second section focuses on the international developments with respect to GI and current debate regarding the same. The third section gives details about the current status of GI protection in India along with the data on the GIs protected in the country. The fourth section reviews the studies undertaken to gauge the impact of GI protection in India. Based on the review, this section brings forth the future course of research work that needs to be undertaken and identifies the factors that need to be considered to ensure that GI act as a tool for the rural development.

2. Section I: Geographical Indication

A GI is a sign used on goods that have a specific geographical origin and posses qualities or a reputation that are due to that place of origin. Most commonly, a GI consists of the name of the place of origin of the goods. Agricultural products typically have qualities that derive from the place of production and are influenced by specific local factors, such as climate and soil. GI may be used for wide variety of agricultural products, such as, "Tuscany" for olive oil produced in a specific area of Italy (protected, for example, in Italy by Law No. 169 of February 5, 1992), or "Roquefort" for cheese produced in France (protected, for example, in the European Union under regulation (EC) No. 2081/92 and in the United States under US (Certification Registration Mark No. 571.798). The use of GI is not limited to agricultural products. They may also highlight specific qualities of a product which are due to human factors that can be found in the place of origin of the product, such as specific manufacturing skills and traditions, in a village, town, a region or a country. An example for the latter is "Swiss Watch" that is perceived as a GI in many countries for watches made in Switzerland. The protection granted under GI falls under the category of positive protection as against the preventive protection. The legal means that defend the reputation of the producers against unfair protection and basic labeling rules is referred to as preventive protection (Larson, 2007). The key difference between the positive protection and preventive protection is that the former require registration with no such restriction for the preventive protection.

The mechanism of GI works in the following way. Consider a local area where a certain type of strawberries are produced and due to the specific characteristics of the soil there is a sweetness that is not found in the strawberries produced in any other place in the world. All the producers intending to reap benefits occurring due to the special characteristics may form a cooperative organisation. As an organisation they may file an application for the grant of GI. Considering that the GI is granted, the organisation now needs to spend resources on the advertisement of the product nationally as well as internationally. The grant of GI ensures that the product is differentiated from the other products in the market and allows the producers to earn premium on the same by charging a higher price. It also helps consumers who will know what they are buying and will save them from counterfeit. It is evident that the meagre grant of GI will not be sufficient to ensure the profits to the producers. There is a need to advertise the product (locally and globally), to built the reputation of the product in market, to undertake the quality control among all the producers[3], and to keep an eye on the fake products (locally and globally) including taking legal action if the need arises. The initial filling may also be done by a government agency for instance in India, Textile ministry is very active in filling GIs. As mentioned earlier that all IPRs are territorial in nature, GI protection has to be taken in individual country where the producers intend to sell the product.

The economic rationale behind providing GI protection is the market failure due to asymmetric information in the market transactions where a consumer may not be able to observe all the features of the product. Market failure predominantly occurs in case of "experience goods" and "credence goods". For such products, the consumers are at the risk of being cheated and mislead into buying low quality product. Specifically, if the consumer intends to buy a product produced in a particular geographical area and all the producers claims so it will impossible for the consumer to differentiate the product. Thus, producers need to signal the quality of the product to the consumer by building reputation that is a costly and time consuming process. Moreover, there is still an uncertainty that the competitors may free ride on the reputation by unfair means. Empirical research shows that the producers who built reputation may earn premium on the price of the product to the extent of 10 per cent for origin-guaranteed products (WTO, 2004)[5]. The legal institution of GI provides protection to all the producers who produce in the

3. As every producer will have the incentive to free ride on the reputation.
4. Goods can be classified into three types, based on the degree of information available to consumers while purchasing the goods, namely search goods, experience goods and credence goods (Nelson, 1970). The consumer can determine the quality before the purchase of search goods. In case of experience goods, only after purchase a consumer can ascertain the quality of the product. However, for credence goods it is not possible to gauge the quality of the product. Such classification may differ across consumers as well for the different attributes of the goods (Rangnekar, 2004).
5. The premium earned based on the reputation also depends on factors including market size, demand elasticity, availability of substitutes, and promotion of the product (Correa, 2002).

designated area as their product enjoys certain characteristics or reputation attributed to the geographical area. For instance, in case of Darjeeling tea all the producer may use the GI and earn premium. As mentioned earlier, producers may create an association or an organisation that will ensure that the standards of the product are maintained by the participants.

IS and AO also provide protection similar to GI albeit with a few variations. According to WIPO (2011), IS (indication of source) means any expression or sign used to indicate that a product or service originates in a country, region or a specific place. The primary difference between IS and GI is that if the latter is attached to a product, it must have a quality, reputation or some other characteristics that are essentially attributable to that geographical origin. IS, however, does not have such requirement. AO (appellation of origin) is used on products that have a specific quality that is exclusively or essentially due to the geographical environment in which the product is produced. It is noteworthy that in case of GI even reputation associated with the product may lead to grant of GI whereas for AO physical characteristics of the product due to geography including human and natural factors must be present. It is evident that in terms of protection, GI is less restrictive than AO and limited as compared to IS. The coverage of GI in the TRIPS agreement marked a major step forward in the multilateral protection of geographical denomination and for the first time that a truly international forum attempted to lay down rules and obligations for GIs.

Table 1: Major International Conventions for GI Protection Prior to TRIPs

Conventions	*Agency*	*Coverage*
Paris Convention	WIPO	Includes indication of source and appellation of origin.
Madrid Convention	WIPO	For the repression of false and deceptive indication of source on goods.
Lisbon Convention	WIPO	For the protection of appellation of origin and their industrial registration.

3. Section II: TRIPs and GI

As mentioned earlier, IPRs are territorial in nature, that is, the level and conditions of protection are determined by national laws and enforcement institutions. However, TRIPs agreement under WTO internationalised the IPRs provisions at the domestic level including GI. According to *Article 22.1*, GIs are "indications which identify a goods originating in the territory of a

Member, or a region or locality in that territory, where a given quality, reputation or other characteristics of the goods is essentially attributable to its GI."

TRIPS agreement requires that Members shall provide the legal means for interested parties to prevent "the use of any means in the designation or presentation of a goods that indicates or suggests that the goods in question originates in a geographical area other than the true place of origin in a manner which misleads the public as to the geographical origin of the good." Member should refuse or invalidate the registration of a trademark which constitute or consist of GI with respect to goods not originating in the territory indicated, in case the use of such an indication in the trademark may mislead the public about the true place of origin as per *Article 22.3* of TRIPs. GI are different from the trademark as the former helps consumers to identify a product that is produced in a certain place and has certain characteristics that are due to that place of production. GI can be used by all producers who make their products in the place designated by a GI and whose products share typical qualities. On the contrary, trademark distinguishes products of one commercial undertaking from that of another commercial undertaking. It can be used by a single producer who owns that trademark. In some countries, for instance, the US trademark laws provide GI protection that is compatible with the TRIPs requirement. The conflict between the two types of protection arises as geographical name may not be distinctive and trademark laws might require distinctiveness as a pre-requisite for the grant of protection. Consequently, courts have refused the grant of protection under a geographical name. The protection in a few cases is given under "collective trademark" that is granted to an association of producers, manufacturers or service providers. TRIPs agreement attempts to resolve the conflict between GI and trademark laws by letting the Members determine the kind of protection they intend to grant in the domestic laws.

TRIPS Agreement provides a additional protection to wines or spirits under *Article 23.1*. The additional protection includes provision for the legal means by the Members States for interested parties "to prevent use of a GI", identifying wines and spirits, "not originating in the place indicated by the GI in question". Such protection has been extended "even where the true origin of the goods is indicated or the GI is used in translation or accompanied by expressions such as "kind", "type", "style", "imitation" or the "like". Thus, "Champagne style sparkling wine, Made in the USA" would be prohibited even though this is clearly not deceptive (Watal, 2001, p. 268). Moreover, it also provides protection against use of the word on non-related product for instance, "Champagne" for grape juice produced in Mahabaleshwar. The discussion on the issue of "extension" that is to bring other goods in the ambit of extensive protection is currently underway in the ongoing Doha round of trade talks of WTO.

Article 23.2 of the TRIPS Agreement establishes that, the registration of a trademark for wines or spirits which contain or consists of GI identifying wines or spirits shall be refused or invalidated with respect to such wines or spirits not having this origin. This could be provided if a Member legislation so permits or at the request of an interested party. *Article 23.3* of the TRIPS Agreement specifically cover the cases of homonymous GI for wines, whose use does not falsely represent to the public that the goods originate in another territory as provided in *Article 22.4* of the TRIPS Agreement. The problem of homonymous GIs may arise in case a place in the previous colonies is named after a place in home country of the colonial power. TRIPs agreement requires that both indications must be protected and Members must determine the conditions necessary to differentiate homonymous indication for wines. In doing so, they must ensure that consumers are not misled and that producers concerned are treated equitably. *Article 23.4* of the TRIPS Agreement provides for the establishment of a multilateral system of the notification and registration of the GI for wines and spirits. Such a system is destined to facilitate the protection of GIs for wines and spirits.

Article 23.4 of the TRIPS Agreement states "In order to facilitate the protection of GI for wines, negotiation should be undertaken in the Council for TRIPS concerning the establishment of a multilateral system of notification and registration of GI for wines eligible for protection in those Members participating in the system". Regarding this, Paragraph 18 of Doha Ministerial Declaration states "we agree to negotiate the establishment of a multilateral system of notification and registration of GI for wines and spirits by the Fifth Session of the Ministerial Conference" in 2003 (in Mexico).

The second issue related to GI revolves around whether to provide more extensive protection to all other goods as provided to wines and spirits. The EU, that hosts the largest number of GIs and developing countries are arguing a case for such extension and the United States, which, in many product areas, is mostly a 'consumer' of such indications and prefers relatively weak levels of protection. A WTO report (WT/GC/W/633, 2011, p. 4) on the discussions on GI issues in the Doha round notes that "delegations continued to voice the divergent views that have characterised this debate, with no convergence evident on the specific question of extension of *Article 23* coverage: some Members continued to argue for extension of *Article 23* protection to all products; others maintained that this was undesirable and created unreasonable burdens. It was clarified that trademark systems were legitimate forms of protecting GIs, in line with the general principle that Members are entitled to choose their own means of implementing their TRIPS obligations. Extension proponents sought guarantees that the trademark system could and would protect their GIs at the higher level for all goods.

Discussions clarified that GI extension did not mean that existing exceptions under the TRIPS Agreement, such as for generic terms and prior trademark rights, would cease to apply. This discussion underscored the benefits of understanding more fully the scope of protection that applies at a practical level under different national systems". It is noteworthy that in case of GI, the north-north and south-south debate is more predominant as countries are paring per their specific requirements. For instance, India, along with the EU, China, Kenya, Mauritius, Nigeria, Pakistan, the Slovak Republic, Slovenia, Sri Lanka, Switzerland, Thailand and Turkey are arguing for an 'extension' of the ambit of *Article 23* to cover all categories of goods. On the other hand, the US, Australia, New Zealand, Canada, Argentina, Chile, Guatemala, Uruguay are strongly opposed to the 'extension'. Das (2009) noted that though India is in favour of "extension", the stance is not in favour of multilateral register as the country does not have significant number of GIs.

4. Section III: GIs in India

The initiatives to exploit GI potential began when Department of Industrial Promotion and Policy under Ministry of Commerce and Industry established a system of GI protection with the enactment of the Goods (Registration and Protection) Act, 1999 that was notified in the Gazette of India on December 30, 1999, the rules were notified on March 8, 2002 and the Act came into force in September 2003. The primary motivation behind the act was to meet the implementation deadline of TRIPs. The GI Act is being administered by the Controller General of Patents, Designs and Trade Marks who is the Registrar of GIs. An Intellectual Property Appellate Board (IPAB) has been set up at Chennai to hear appeals against the decisions of Registrar of Trademarks, GIs and the Controller of Patents.

In India, before the enactment of this legislation, GIs were protected indirectly (i) under the consumer protection acts; (ii) through passing off[6] actions in courts; and (iii) through certification trade marks (Das, 2007). India enacted the GI Act in order to comply with the TRIPs agreement under its WTO obligations. However, GI protection granted in India is a step ahead of TRIPs in terms of higher level of protection (*Article 23.1* of TRIPs) that is not restricted to wines and spirits and extends to other goods (*Article 23.1* of TRIPs). It is noteworthy that though stricter protection is provided by India, other WTO Members may not grant such a protection which opens the window for their misappropriation in the international arena. Watal (2001) noted that the implementation of the GI across countries is varied in comparison to the other obligations under TRIPs. According to the GI Act (1 (3)(e), "geographical indication", in relation to goods, means an indication which identifies such goods as agricultural goods, natural goods or manufactured goods as originating, or manufactured in the territory of a country, or a region or locality in that territory, where a given quality, reputation or other characteristic of such goods is essentially attributable to its geographical origin and in case where such goods are manufactured goods one of the activities of either the production or of processing or preparation of the goods concerned takes place in such territory, region or locality, as the case may be". As evident from the last sentences, for manufactured goods, the Indian act has stringent requirement as compared to TRIPs. The Act explains that any name which is not the name of a country, region or locality of that country shall also be considered as the geographical indication. This gives flexibility to include names like "Basmati". According to 1 (3)(f), "goods" means any agricultural, natural or manufactured goods or any goods of handicraft or of industry and includes food stuff. This definition is in addition to the TRIPs.

The GI Act of India establishes a system of registration that gives the validity to the indication *prima facie*. The Act identifies 34 classes across which the goods can be identified for the registration process. Further, it allows for multiple classification of a goods, for instance, "Pochampally Ikat" is registered under three classes (Das, 2009). The Indian Act distinguishes between registered proprietor and authorised user. According to the Act, "registered proprietor" in relation to a geographical indication, means any association of persons or of producers or any organisation for the time being entered in the register as proprietor of the geographical indication" (1(3)(n)). Further, any person claiming to be the producer of the goods in respect of which a geographical indication has been registered under section 16 "may apply in writing to the Registrar in the prescribed manner for registering him as an authorised user of such geographical indication", (17(1)). This approach allows the producers that enter late to be part of the association after the registration (Das, 2009).

After the enactment of the GI Act, the registration activity picked up pace after 2003[7]. All domestic GI applications since 2003 can be classified into registered (206), going through pre-examination (62), advertised (22) or under examination (54). A couple of applications have been refused as well including Basmati Rice and Banjara Handicrafts and Mirror Work. Table 2 gives the year-wise details of the GIs registered in India till 2012.

7. Appendix I gives the detailed registration process under the GI act of India.

Table 2: Number of GI Registered in India on the Basis of Date of Filling

Year	*Total No. of GIs Registered*
2003	3
2004	13
2005	20
2006	30
2007	39
2008	25
2009	32
2010	24
2011	13
2012	7
Total	**207**

Author's calculations based on data available at GI Registry, Chennai. Interestingly, many applications from countries like Italy, France, Poland, Spain, Sweden, Mexico, Cyprus, Czech Republic, Austria, Ireland, Germany, and Greece are filed and are also under examination (14) and pre-examination (112). In total there are 132 applications of which six are registered.

Though the number of GI applications in India has been increasing, most of these applications are from the handicraft class.[8] Figure 1 shows that agriculture class has received small number of registrations. One possible explanation for this could be the spread of producers over a large area and problems associated with the cooperation. In case of handicraft, mostly a community or limited families are involved in a particular art and it is relatively easy for those to come together for a common goal. In terms of the economic theory, the problem can be found with the free riding problem where once the rights are granted other may want to join to reap the benefit but not during the process of registration. Note that, once granted GI becomes a collective goods for the producers located in the specified region.

All the registered GIs in India are categorised in to four categories namely, (i) agriculture, (ii) foodstuff, (iii) handicrafts and (iv) manufactured goods. The details show that among the total there are 48 in agriculture goods, four in food stuff including Dharwad Pedha, Bikaneri Bhujia, Hyderabad Halem and Tirupati Laddu, 145 in handicrafts and nine in manufactured goods. In terms of states, Karnataka has maximum of 32 registrations followed by Tamil Nadu as given in Table 3.

8. Appendix II gives the details of the GIs registered with the Registry at Chennai.

Table 3: State-wise GI Registration

Sr. No.	*State*	*No. Registered GIs*
1	Andhra Pradesh	12
2	Assam	3
3	Bihar	5
4	Chhattisgarh	5
5	Goa	1
6	Gujarat	9
7	Himachal Pradesh	6
8	Jammu & Kashmir	6
9	Karnataka	32
10	Kerala	21
11	Madhya Pradesh	6
12	Maharashtra	10
13	Manipur	3
14	Nagaland	1
15	Odisha	15
16	Pondicherry	2
17	Punjab, Haryana & Rajasthan	1
18	Rajasthan	9
19	Tamil Nadu	24
20	Telangana	11
21	Uttar Pradesh	15
22	West Bengal	9

5. GIs and Rural Development

There is a fundamental difference between GI and other intellectual property rights particularly trademarks that offer similar protection to the consumer. GI creates a collective monopoly that can be enjoyed by all the producers in a particular area unlike other IPRs like trademark or patent where monopoly rights are granted to an individual producer. GI is therefore a tool through which a rural community can differentiate their product from the others. GIs are not private property in a sense similar to other IPRs as they cannot be bought, sold, or transferred (Rangnekar, 2009). The role of GI in rural development is indirect and requires considerable planning and efforts on part of the state to ensure that the economic gains from GI trickles down. Larson (2007) has reviewed GI cases from the developed and developing countries and made following suggestions that will help in the development of GI as an instrument for rural development: (i) adequate provisions to ensure that the production is localised, (ii) need to be precise about the product description and quality criterion, (iii) legal status and legitimacy to the governing body that should be involved in production practices, market management, legal protection of GI in other countries, compliance inspection, technical control and research, (iv) a clear rural development policy and (v) regulation of the labelling. These factors ensure that an enabling environment is created whereby rural community can participate in the process and gain economically. In the context of the developing countries, Larson (2007) found that although there is evidence of economic benefit from GI protection in the developing countries the distribution of the same to the rural community remains elusive. Larson (2007) noted that developing countries face various problems in ensuring GI as a developmental institution including, small scale of production, orientation towards self-consumption, non-democratic governance structure, market segmentation, non-existing regulatory authority and owning of the GI rights by state.

In case of India, Das (2009) has performed case study for the GI taken on "Pochampally Ikat" and "Chanderi Fabric". These studies have shown mild economic gains to the weaver after the GI has been attributed. The studies further reveal that though the GI was initially undertaken by the government bodies, it was only after the co-operation with the self help groups and weaver organisation that the benefits could reach the weaver. Das (2009) noted that the producers of GI confronts major challenges including the registration in foreign jurisdiction, enforcement of the rights at national and international level and building brand image locally as well globally. Note that all these factors require financial resources and therefore support from the state at least in the initial stages. Jena and Grote (2012) show that though Basmati rice is not a GI, it still enjoys premium over non-Basmati rice and increases the income of the farmers.

6. Section V: Conclusion

GI as a tool for rural development has a long way to go. In India, the process though initiated under the compulsion to abide by the TRIPs requirements is beginning to generate some benefits. The state, however has to play a significant role in order to establish GI as a tool for rural development. The first step in that direction is to spread awareness about GI across the country. Following which in order to deal with the free riders problem of the collective action, state also has to take initiative in registering the GI. Later, there is a need to collaborate with the producers associations and ensure that the quality of the goods is maintained. There is a need to develop marketing strategy at centre or state level whereby the products can be advertised globally or in the potential market. The role of state will also be important in registering GIs in foreign jurisdiction. Moreover, there is a need to conduct more studies at the state level to (i) identify the potential goods that can be registered as GI and (ii) to analyse the impact of the existing GIs. The latter studies will help in identifying the bottlenecks if any that are restricting the benefits to accrue to the rural community and therefore will further help in improving the working of GIs.

References

1. Adolf, H. 2001. "Trade Related Aspects of Intellectual Property Rights and Developing Countries." *The Developing Economies*, 39 (1): 49-84.
2. Correa, C. 2002. "Protection of Geographical Indications in Caricom Countries."www.crnm.org/index.php?option=com_docman&task=doc...82 (accessed March 1, 2011).
3. Das, K. 2009. "Socioeconomic Implications of Protecting Geographical Indications in India". http://wtocentre.iift.ac.in/Papers/GI_Paper_CWS_August%2009_Revised.pdf(accessed February 26, 2011).
4. Das, K. 2007. ''Protection of Geographical Indications: An Overview of Select Issues with Particular Reference to India". Working Paper 8, Centre for Trade & Development (Centad), New Delhi, 2007.Available at: http://www.centad.org/download/WorkingPaper_FinalPDF_4June07.pdf(accessed February 26, 2011).
5. Drahos, P. 2002. "Developing Countries and International Intellectual Property Standard-setting". Study Paper No. 8 Commission on Intellectual Property Rights. http://www.iprcommission.org/graphic/documents/study_papers.htm(accessed December 13, 2005).
6. Glossary of Environment Statistics. 1997.http://stats.oecd.org/glossary/detail.asp?ID=1740(accessed March 1, 2011).
7. Jena, P.R. and U. Grote. "Impact Evaluation of Traditional Basmati Rice Cultivation in Uttarakhand State of Northern India: What Implications Does it Hold for Geographical Indications?" *World Development*, 40 (9) 1895-1907.

8. Larson, J. 2007. "Relevance of Geographical Indication and Designation of Origin for the sustainable use of genetic resources". http://www.underutilized-species.org/Documents/PUBLICATIONS/gi_larson_lr.pdf (accessed March 2, 2011).

9. Nelson, P. 1970. "Information and Consumer Behaviour." *Journal of Political Economy*, 78 (March-April) 311-329.

10. Rangnekar, D. 2004. "The Socio Economics of Geographical Indications: A Review of Empirical Evidence from Europe", UNCTAD†ICTSD Project on IPRs and Sustainable Development, Geneva, Switzerland.

11. Watal, J. 2001. 'Intellectual Property Rights in the WTO and Developing Countries'. The Hague: Kluwer Law International.

12. World Intellectual Property Rights Organization. 2011. www.wipo.org.

13. World Trade Organization. 2011. Document WT/GC/W/633, www.wto.org/english/tratop_e/dda_e/chair_texts11_e/dg_trips_e.doc(accessed February 28, 2011).

Appendix I

Following steps are involved in the registration of a GI''.

1. **Filing of an application** by the association of persons or producers or any organisation or authority.
2. **Preliminary scrutiny and examination** by the examiner for any deficiencies. The applicant should within 1 month of the communication in this regard should remedy the same. The content of statement of case is assessed by a consultative group of experts versed on the subject and they ascertain the correctness of particulars furnished. Thereafter an Examination Report is issued.
3. **Show cause notice is issued** if the Registrar has any objection to the application, he will communicate such objection. The applicant must respond within two months or apply for a hearing. The decision is duly communicated and if the applicant wishes to appeal, he may within 1 month make a request.The Registrar is also empowered to withdraw an application, if it is accepted in error, after giving an opportunity of being heard.
4. Every application, within 3 months of acceptance shall be **Published in the GIs Journal**.
5. Any person can file a notice of opposition **within 3 months (extendable by another month on request which has to be filed before**

3 months) opposing the GI application published in the Journal. The registrar shall serve a copy of the notice on the applicant and **within 2 months** the applicant shall sent a copy of the counterstatement. If he/she does not do this, he/she shall be deemed to have abandoned the application. Where the counter-statement has been filed, the registrar shall serve a copy on the person giving the notice of opposition. Thereafter, both sides will lead their respective evidences by way of affidavit and supporting documents. A date for hearing of the case will be fixed thereafter.

6. Where an application for a GI has been accepted, the registrar shall register the GI. If registered the date of filing of the application shall be deemed to be the date of registration. The registrar shall issue to the applicant a certificate with the seal of the GIs registry.
7. A registered GI shall be **valid for 10 years** and **can be renewed** on payment of renewal fee.
8. Additional protection for notified goods is provided in the Act.
9. Any person aggrieved by an order or decision may appeal to the intellectual property appellate board (IPAB) within three months.

Source: GI Registry, Chennai.

2

Rural Treasures: Traditional Knowledge, Innovations and Best Practices (With focus on Western Rajasthan)

Trilok Kumar Jain

1. Introduction

Rajasthan is the largest State of India with a land area of 3,42,239 Sq. Km. and population 56.47 million of which 43.26 million population is rural and 13.20 million urban (as per the provisional results of the Census of India 2001). It has only one per cent water resources whereas total area is 10.41 per cent and total population is five per cent of the entire country. 12 districts of the State, which comprise of 60 per cent of the area fall within the Great Indian Desert or Thar where 64 per cent of its population resides, despite scanty rainfall with all its variation, timing and intensity. This is the most populous desert in the World.

It has a distinct physiography on account of the existence of oldest mountain ranges i.e., Aravalli which divides the whole State into two major India watersheds i.e., the Ganga basin in the eastern side and Luni basin in the western slopes. The Aravalli hills also demarcate the State into two distinct climatic regions i.e., semi-arid lying in the East of the Aravalli and the arid region lying in the West. The Western desert region has extremities of temperature, high velocity of wind and very low humidity.

60 per cent area of the State is desert having very low density of population and rainfall. Rajasthan has the lowest population density (165 persons/km) as compared to the national average (274 persons/km) and the highest percentage of rural population (77.12 per cent) showing that the State is still predominantly rural. 75 per cent people depend on agriculture and animal husbandry for their livelihood. In the desert area, which is 60 per cent of the total area of the State, the mainstay of the people for livelihood is animal husbandry.

For various reasons, it still remains a socially and economically backward State. Sex ratio is 922 female/1000 male, literacy rate is 61.03 per cent but female literacy rate is 44.34 Percent, infant mortality is 79 per thousand live births, maternal mortality is 677 per lakh live births and crude birth rate is 28.33 per thousand which is very high. Per capita income is Rs 7932 (93-94 as base) as compared to Rs 10254 at national level.

Recurrent droughts, poor resource base for economic development, per capita higher cost of development due to desert areas with very low density of population, low levels of literacy particularly among women, a very high rate of population growth and scarcity of water make the task of socio-economic development a formidable one as compared to many other States in the country. Administratively the State is divided into 32 Districts and 241 Tehsils. It has 32 Zila Parishads and 237 Panchayat samities. Out of 32 Districts, 12 Districts are in the desert area.

Modern science and technology has enabled progress in this region and now there is Indira Gandhi Canal, which has completely changed the life-style, agriculture practices and the social life of the people. The rural areas are transforming, however, with the progress, there is also a loss of the rich traditional practices, which have now disappeared with the arrival of modern practices.

Rural Rajasthan had solutions to many problems. In spite of limited resources, the people have innovated and evolved many technologies, which are useful as well as sustainable. The important issues that the people of rural areas face and their solutions are discussed below:

(a) Health related issues
(b) Education related issues
(c) Employment generation related issues
(d) Infrastructure related issues
(e) Access related issues
(f) Monsoon and agriculture
(g) Animal husbandry

A detailed discussion on these issues is presented below:

Health related issues: Almost all the areas in rural Rajasthan have health related problems. The desert areas have particular problems. The villages are dispersed and there are no nearby hospitals/dispensaries. There are immediate requirements for the rural areas:

There should be training/information guidance to the rural volunteers and Anganwadi workers etc. with regard to health management. There should be mobile dispensaries/hospitals, which should visit villages regularly and should be available at a call (like the facility of 108). These mobile dispensaries should have video conferencing facilities so that the best doctors may be contacted as per requirements.

Rajasthan has many traditional food practices, which are good for the health of people. These traditional practices (like Methi Laddu) are now disappearing. There is a need to document, preserve and promote such traditional practices.

There are many doctors, who settle down in villages after retirement (for example, Dr NM Duggar settled down in Village Sherera and thereafter the village has completely changed. Please read the complete story for details[1]). Such doctors, who voluntarily settle down in villages should be supported and there should be some support system from the government to motivate them.

People of Rajasthan used many herbal drugs, which were locally available, easy to use and had no side effects. These herbs were very effective and were very conveniently available. However, with the arrival of modern medicine system, people have switched over to the new system. We have lost the rich knowledge base and rich treasure of practices, which people had.

Education related issues: Traditionally Rajasthan had very rich traditional education system. There were Gyanshalas, Gurukuls, Poshala and other such institutions in villages and cities. There used to be a system of education which was blended with religious education. However, the modern education system has completely obliterated the traditional system. Now Education is a major issue in Rajasthan. Most of the government schools have inadequate infrastructure and lack of required motivation among the staff. There is a need to appoint the local person from each village as the teacher, who may be given support through visiting teachers, mobile vans and modern infrastructure support. Urmul Trust and many such NGOs started short duration compact programmes on education. Such programmes should be popularised. The programme of Urmul Trust was a six month residential programme and it was a very impact making programme.

Employment generation related issues: Rajasthan has always tried to solve the issues relating to employment through community involvement, collective initiatives and other community based initiatives. Whenever there would be drought (there are frequent draughts in Rajasthan), the kings and the rich people used to start construction and other work to enable people to get employed (these were the practices which were prevailing 60-70 years ago). However, today, the government programmes (like NAREGA) have taken up strongholds. The traditional community based practices have now disappeared. However, due to emphasis on government jobs and government backed programmes, the traditional practices and collective entrepreneurial practices of people have now disappeared.

Infrastructure related issues: Rajasthan has always faced hardships due to infrastructure issues. There are still inadequate facilities for transport, energy, water, sanitation and other amenities. The people of Rajasthan have generally evolved resource sharing to overcome these hardships. Whenever the people would move from one place to another, they would use larger transport system and move in a group (for example, they use camel cart with about 4-7 persons). They have innovated and created many innovative practices with regard to use of water (for example, in Rajasthan water storage was a major contribution of women. In every 30-40 km distance you will find one village with name ending DESAR – which denotes that ladies have prepared some pond / bawdi (water storage) at that place and therefore that place is having a name ending DESAR. Examples are Kodamdesar, Rajaldesar etc.). Such practices are now getting extinct.

Access related issues: There were many barriers in Rajasthan due to caste or other such orthodox practices. However, Rajasthan, had always had a very intricate system of information sharing. Women would get information as quickly as men. The information sharing process was through communication channels and communication media. There were many practices like Pata System (In Bikaner, there would be a wooden platform in every locality, where people will gather in the evening and share information).

Monsoon and agriculture: People of Rajasthan had developed knowledge base about monsoon, rains, water and related issues. They would very accurately predict rains based on some symptoms. (for example, if a bird is trying to dig itself in sand, it would indicate possibility of rains in near future). Such indicators and predictors were developed through generations. However, now we are losing all such treasures. Rajasthan had very rich organic agriculture practices, which required very less water and which ensured that the crop was able to survive extremes of weather. However, most of these rich practices are now lost. Modern fertilizers and pesticides have replaced all such knowledge base.

Animal husbandry: Rajasthan has very rich heritage of animal husbandry. There used to be a cow/buffalo/goat in every home. This practice has helped people in recovering from sever difficulties. There was a constant source of support, food and belonging. However, such practices are disappearing now. In modern buildings animal husbandry is not at all possible. This is a practice which was the backbone of the economy of Rajasthan and we shall regret loosing this practice. There were many castes, which totally depended on animals (for example, Gujars were the people, who used to rear cows). Instead of animal loving population, we have now people who are willing to set up slaughter houses everywhere.

Innovations and knowledge base: People in rural areas have evolved technologies, instruments, knowledge base and practices, which have enabled them to survive all hardships. In spite of no rains for years, they could survive and could also enable their animals to survive. They had evolved practices, which ensured that there would be maximum possible conservation of natural resources. However, we are loosing all such knowledge, technologies and practices. There is an urgent need to document such practices at least.

Observations

Modern progress has enabled us to progress. However, there are some rich treasures, which we are losing. Based on the insights and discussions, the author contends that there is a need to set up a centre to document traditional knowdge and practices. Such centre should be set up preferably in cities like Jaisalmer, Barmer or Bikaner, which are very rich in such practices. These areas are the core of the desert regions. The hardships of desert has enabled people to survive with limited water and other essential amenities. Such practices will help us in survival in the future, when there will be shortage of drinking water.

NOTE: Author has witnessed the plight of poverty and hardships through many NGOs in various capacities in rural areas of Western Rajasthan. The interactions with the rural people has given the writer some insights relating to rural issues. The author is not against modern science, technology and progress. However, the author tries to present that there are many traditional practices, innovations and skills which we are losing due to modern development. The author shares observations on these in this article. The credit for all these observations should go to the rural people, who have openly shared their knowledge, expertise and experiences.The author is grateful to NGOs like Urmul Trust, Bikaner Vikas Samiti, Bal Vikas Samiti etc., which have enabled the author to see the rural areas very closely during last two decades.

Refereance

1. Read the complete story (The doctor who adopted village life to serve the community) at : http://www.iuemag.com/february2014/di/the-doctor.php.

3

Challenges and Barriers in Rural Development in India and Beyond: A Regional Outlook

Najmudheen T

1. Introduction

Rural areas constitute a larger part of the world. About three-fourth of the total population of the world are living in these areas. So that rural development is central to the development efforts of any nation. In the developing countries of Asia, particularly South Asian countries, the large segments of the rural population are poor. Rural development is, therefore, concerned with improving and transforming the economic and social life of the rural poor, and in this, the basic human services are critically important.[1] The rural development generally refers to the process of improving the quality of life and economic welfare of people living in relatively isolated and sparsely populated areas. A substantial volume of assistance has been provided to rural authorities by government and non-governmental agencies for the development of key areas like agriculture, food security, natural resources management, economic development, banking, habitation, health, sanitation, education, employments and so on. In fact, a nation can be strong and prosperous only when all villages are freed from backwardness and poverty.

The term rural development is the overall development of rural areas to improve the quality of life of rural people. And it is a process leading to sustainable improvement in the quality of life of rural people, especially the poor. In India, out of a total population of 121 crores, 83.3 crores live in rural areas.[2] Thus, nearly 70 per cent of the India's population lives in rural areas. These rural populations can be characterised by mass poverty, low levels of literacy and income, high level of unemployment, and poor nutrition and health status. The Ministry of Rural Development in India is the apex body for formulating policies, regulations and acts pertaining to the development of the rural sector. Agriculture, handicrafts, fisheries, poultry, and diary are the primary contributors to the rural business and the economy. In order to tackle the specific problems, a number of rural development programmes are being implemented to create opportunities for improvement of the quality of life of these rural people. The rural development programmes intend to reduce the poverty and unemployment, to improve the health and educational status and to fulfil the basic needs such as food, shelter and clothing of the rural population. To improve the conditions of rural people, Government of India launched some schemes through the Planning Commission of India such as Mahatma Gandhi National Rural Employment Guarantee Act (MGNREGA), Rastriya Sama Vikas Yojana (RSVY), Indira Awas Yojana (IAY), Sampoorna Grameen Rozgar Yojana (SGRY), Integrated Tribal Development Project (ITDP), Pradhan Mantri Gram SadakYojana (PMGSY), Integrated Child Development Services (ICDS), Development of Women and Children in Rural Areas (DWCRA), etc. All these schemes are aimed to reduce the gap between rural and urban people, which would help reduce imbalances and speed up the development process. Despite the richness of rural development programmes, the questions of 'adequacy', 'reachability and 'accessibility' remain still unanswered. The condition of rural development beyond India is also not better.

Notwithstanding some impressive economic growth, the challenges and barriers in rural development in South Asia region continues to be a stark reality for a large number of households. Despite several successful policy interventions by governments, the number of malnourished children and adults remain alarmingly high in the region–higher than those in Sub-Saharan Africa. Agriculture continues to be a very important livelihood option for a vast majority of rural population, even though the sector's contribution to the economy is shrinking. The regional rural development barriers stem from challenges ranging from environmental problems, poverty, hunger and lack of access to basic healthcare and education, unemployment, socioeconomic inequality, corruption, resulting from many layers social exclusion.

In the Twenty first Century, equally important stumbling block in the way to rapid socio-economic development in the countries of the South Asian region, especially India, is undoubtedly the illiteracy in general and the adult-illiteracy in particular. In spite of a tremendous growth in the number of educational institutions in India in the last five decades, the problem has remained unresolved. Almost 18 to 20 per cent children are never enrolled, and among those enrolled in the proportion of children not reaching the secondary school certificate level is more than 80 per cent, which is indicative of the fact that there is very heavy drop-out on the way.

Literacy, skill development, and education of the teeming masses of rural South Asia is the real problem of region's rural development. In sum and substance, these under-privileged masses are that section of South Asian population which suffers from several social, economic, religious and other barriers, and whose per capita income is so low that there is not only no scope for savings but the energies consumed in physical labour are often not recouped fully. It believes that the greatest resource of social and economic development of a vast and highly populated country like India is its teeming masses. In other words, human resource development is the key factor for the socio-economic development of India. Unfortunately, India's performance in the matter of education and skill development of the under-privileged masses cannot be considered satisfactory. The gulf between the privileged and the under-privileged has only widened. The another more worrying is the fact that in spite of a steady rise in the literacy rate, the actual number of illiterates is simultaneously increasing.

Apart from these issues, there are many other challenges and barriers in the rural development of India and beyond such as human health problem, poverty, unemployment, food crisis, water constraints, environmental issue, climate change, and so on. The growing economy with a vibrant service sector has not been able to absorb surplus labour force from agriculture due to the low levels of literacy and skills they possess. The divide between farm and non-farm income levels has been increasing. Despite numerous rural programmes and policies initiated by countries in the region, the accomplishment of rural development credibility still challenging in South Asia. In the backdrop of the increasing uneasy condition of rural development, the present study is a modest attempt to explore the major challenges and barriers in rural development in India and beyond. Such a regional outlook gives a better understanding to assess the real problems of rural development in South Asia. Which subsequently helps to formulate adequate measures to overcome the increasing challenges and barriers in rural development. This study also examines the conceptual clarification of 'rural development' comprehensively. Among several potential future challenges and barriers in rural development in the region, the paper highlighted the importance of preventive measures to tackle all these issues.

2. Conceptual Framework of Rural Development

The term 'Rural Development' is a subset of the broader term 'development'. Development is a universally cherished goal of individuals, families, communities and nations all over the world. Development is also natural in the sense that all forms of life on planet earth have an inherent urge to survive and develop. Given these two attributes, that is, its universal supremacy as a goal and its natural occurrence, development deserves a scientific study and analysis. Hence, it is not surprising that the subject of development has been studied by scholars of all faiths, ideologies and disciplines.[3] The aims of development spelled out in 1970s in the preamble of the international development strategy for second United Nations Development decade indicates that the ultimate purpose of development is to provide increasing opportunities to all people to better life.[4]

Similarly, Rural Development is a process, which aims at improving the well being and self realisation of people living outside the urbanised areas through a collective process. According to UNO, Rural Development is a process of change, by which the efforts of the people themselves are united, those of government authorities to improve their economic, social and cultural conditions of communities into the life of the nation and to enable them to contribute fully to the national programme. Rural Development is a process of bringing change among rural community from the traditional way of living to a progressive way of living. It is also expressed as a movement for progress.

The term rural development connotes overall development of rural areas with a view to improve the quality of life of rural people. In this sense, it is a comprehensive and multidimensional concept, and encompasses the development of agriculture and allied activities; village and cottage industries; crafts; socio-economic infrastructure, community services and facilities and, above all, the human resources in rural areas. In other terms, rural development can be conceptualised as a process, a phenomenon, a strategy and a discipline. As a process, it implies the engagement of individuals, communities and nations in pursuit of their cherished goals over time. As a phenomenon, rural development is the end result of interactions between various physical, technological, economic, socio-cultural and institutional factors. As a strategy, it is designed to improve the economic and social well-being of a specific group of people, that is, the rural poor. As a discipline, it is multidisciplinary in nature, representing an intersection of agricultural, social, behavioural, engineering and management sciences.[5]

It can also say that, rural development is a strategy to enable a specific group of people, poor rural women and men, to gain for themselves and their children more of what they want and need. It involves helping the poorest among those who seek a livelihood in the rural areas to demand and control more of the benefits of rural development. The group includes small scale farmers, tenants and the landless.[6] Conceptually, there are some basic elements in rural development, such as basic necessities of life, self-respect and freedom, which need to briefly mentioned here.

Basic Necessities of Life: People have certain basic needs, without which it would be impossible (or very difficult) for them to survive. The basic necessities include food, clothes, shelter, basic literacy, primary healthcare, and security of life and property. When any one or all of them are absent or in critically short supply, it may state that a condition of 'absolute under development' exists. Provision of basic necessities of life for everybody is the primary responsibility of all economies, whether they are capitalist, socialist or mixed. In this sense, it may claim that economic growth (increased per capita availability of basic necessities) is a necessary condition for the improvement of the 'quality of life' of rural people, which is rural development.[7]

Self-respect: Every person and every nation seek some sort of self-respect, dignity or honour. Absence or denial of self-respect indicates lack of development.[8]

Freedom: In this context, freedom refers to political or ideological freedom, economic freedom and freedom from social servitude. As long as a society is bound by the servitude of men to nature, ignorance, other men, institutions and dogmatic beliefs, it cannot claim to have achieved the goal of 'development'. Servitude in any form reflects a state of under development.[9]

In this context, it is essential to bring about a more equitable distribution of income and wealth for promoting both social justice and efficiency of production, raise substantially the level of employment, achieve a greater degree of income security and expand and improve facilities for education, health, nutrition, housing and social welfare and safeguard the environment.[10]

Thus, rural development is a dynamic process, which is mainly concerned with the rural areas. These include agricultural growth, putting up of economic and social infrastructure, fair wages as also housing and house sites for the landless, village planning, public health, education and functional literacy, communication etc.

3. Assessing Rural Development in India

In the twenty first century, rural development has attracted the attention of social reformers, economists, politicians and the like because three-fourths of India's populations live in rural areas.[11] With the increasing population, demand for basic needs has been steeply rising during the past five decades in most of the developing countries. The growing populations need food, clothing, shelter, fuel and fodder for their livestock. The predominant rural character of India's national economy is reflected in the very high proportion of the population living in the rural areas; it was 89 per cent in 1901, 83 per cent in 1951, 80 per cent in 1971, 76 per cent in 1981 and 70 per cent in 1991 with more than 500 million people living in rural areas.[12] As per the 2011 census, in India, over 70 per cent of the people are living in rural areas[13] who neither have adequate land holdings nor alternate service opportunities to produce or procure these commodities. In the absence of adequate employment opportunities, the rural people are unable to generate enough wages to sustain their livelihood.

India's growth story in various sectors like industry, services, mining, and power, particularly since the dawn of the new millennium, though impressive, has not been inclusive one. Whereas urban areas have developed fast, the rural areas still lack the basic infrastructure of connectivity, marketing and adequate means of employment generation. Although efforts have been made to bring about a socio-economic transformation in India, with an integrated approach towards improving the quality of life of rural poor, these have not been able to cut much ice.[14]

Poverty remains a major issue with our huge populations living in rural areas, particularly in the BMARU states of Bihar, Jharkhand, Madhya Pradesh, Rajasthan and Uttar Pradesh. In addition to low income, problems of violent conflicts, food insecurity, illiteracy, ill health, unemployment, gender inequality, unhygienic living etc. are various aspects of rural society.[15]

The Ministry of Rural Development, Government of India, plays a pivotal role in the overall development strategy of the country, especially in the development and welfare activities in the rural areas. The vision and mission of the Ministry aim for sustainable and inclusive growth of rural India through a multipronged strategy for eradication of poverty by increasing livelihood opportunities, providing a social safety net and developing infrastructure for growth. It aims to improve quality of life in rural India and to correct the developmental imbalances. As one delves deeper into the history of development strategies in the country, one begins to realise that India's approach to rural development has undergone a paradigm shift, i.e., from 'top-down' to 'bottom-up' approach. In the beginning, India's approach to the development agenda in general and that of rural development in particular was 'top-down' in nature. This implied, all developmental decisions were taken/ monitored/ implemented centrally. The main thrust for development was laid on agriculture, industry, communication, education, health and allied sectors. In short, India's approach to rural development, initially, was one of centralising.

Eventually, India's strategy for development underwent a historic shift in the 1990s, that is, from the policy of 'centralisation' to one of 'decentralisation'. The historic shift came with the realisation that accelerated development can be provided only if governmental efforts are adequately supplemented by direct and indirect involvement of people at the grass root level. The idea is to inject a 'bottom-up' approach to the developmental journey that will make the cycle of development participatory and will ensure that the fruits of economic reform are proportionately shared by all sections of societies. The Constitution has placed enormous power, accountability and responsibility on the Panchayats to formulate and execute various programmes of economic development and social justice in rural areas. Undoubtedly, a plethora of centrally sponsored schemes are being implemented directly/ indirectly through Panchayats on many aspects including health, education, income generation, drinking water, housing and roads. The programmes like Pradhan Mantri Gramdoya Yojana (PMGY), Mahatma Gandhi National Rural Employment Guarantee Act (MGNREGA), Bharat Nirman Programme,

Sarva Shikshya Abhiyan (SSA), Total Sanitation Campaign and National Health Mission (NHM) are a few such initiatives.

As one looks at the number, richness, volume and vastness of these programmes and approaches the concrete reality in rural areas, one encounters a huge gap between policy and their successful translation. Despite the richness of programmes, the questions of 'adequacy', 'reach ability, and 'accessibility' remain still unanswered. For instance, SSA has not succeeded to address the issue of basic infrastructure in elementary schools. NHM has not succeeded in resolving the challenges such as malnutrition, epidemics, infant and maternal mortality that the nation is grappling with. The ability to provide safe drinking water to every household in rural areas continues to be a difficult proposition. Similarly, MGNREGA does not come as a panacea to poverty and the problem of livelihood in rural India. Besides, studies indicate that women's political empowerment though the policy of reservation in Panchayatiraj has become mere tokenistic than substantive. These anomalies are symptomatic of the fact that even the policy of decentralisation, that is, that of the 'bottom-up' approach which has been India's current approach to rural development in the twenty-first century is not free from its own share of inadequacies.

It is therefore imperative to analyse the prevailing conditions and draw strategies for rural development to make the country's growth broad based. It is equally essential to bring about a more equitable distribution of income and wealth, promote social justice, raise substantially the level of employment and improve facilities for education, healthcare, housing, food security and social welfare among the rural masses. Any strategy for rural development must involve the people themselves and their institutions at all levels. To fortify the participants and bring social change, India needs to adopt a multi-pronged strategy since it has varied regions, communities, people, languages and resources.[16]

4. Challenges and Barriers in Rural Development

India is emerging as a major power with the economy registering high growth rates and its cities and urban centres beginning to display marks of affluence. Yet, there is no uniform development, the rural hinterland not being able to march in tandem with urban India. Rural development in India has had a checkered history; more than a third, i.e., over 2000 million rural people subsist in poverty in the 1990s. Agrarian reform, begun in the 1950s, appears an unfinished and long overdue task. As each era passes by, the shape of the problem transforms without solution. Technological change promised freedom from hunger, but the reach of technology has been severely restricted by myopic policy visions and resource constraints. The direct anti-poverty

often invisible and unawareness of the impact of malnutrition (death, disease and low intelligence). Malnutrition undermines economic growth and economic costs are substantial. Individuals lose lifetime earnings because of malnutrition and a country can lose income. Though South Asia fares better than Sub-Saharan Africa in terms of various determinants of food security (viz., poverty, per-capita income, percapita dietary energy supply, etc.), it has a worse record in terms of outcomes such as malnutrition.

As per the report of Syed Rifaat Hussain, the proliferation of AIDS, the "fourth ranking cause of death in the world," has the potential to "destroy social and economic development and break down social and governance structures." Furthermore, "the impact of the epidemic aggravates the vulnerabilities of the weakest groups in society, including women, children and the poor." Approximately 5.1 million people in India, 74,000 people in Pakistan and 61,000 people in Nepal have been infected, making South Asia "home to the second highest number of people living with HIV/AIDS, around 13 per cent of the world total". The US National Intelligence Council estimated in 2008 that India's HIV/AIDS patients would increase "from 5.1 million to 20 million by 2010"[23]. Since India shares a porous border with its neighbours, cross-border movement of infected patients poses severe threats to Bangladesh, Bhutan, Nepal, Pakistan, and Sri Lanka. As mentioned above this region accounts for more than half of the world's undernourished children, one reflection of the fact that 'the burden of this human deprivation falls heavily on children and women' in the region[24]. The absence of basic health systems throughout the region has had disturbing ramifications for maternal health as well. In South Asia, shortfalls in health services, compounded by systemic poverty and malnutrition, result in one of the highest maternal mortality rates in the world[25].

The role of public health services must give preventive health care equal emphasis as curative health care. People should be empowered through education and awareness to participate in managing preventive health care related to environmental sanitation and hygiene[26]. Emerging animal epidemics, such as the present bird flu, swine flu, so on also needs to be seen as a threat to rural livelihoods rather than just a threat to urban people.

4.2. Poverty

Poverty is pervasive and its effects are deep and profound. Poverty is a major challenge to rural development in South Asia, where it is not only all-encompassing, but also distributed disproportionately across regions and socio-economic groups, with women, minorities, people belonging to lower castes, casual and migrant labourers, youth and the unemployed as its main victims. It has been estimated that one-third of the population of the South

Asian region is chronically poor, which means that they face several forms of deprivation throughout their lives and are most likely to pass it on to their future generations. Roughly 40 per cent of the world's poor live in South Asia, where poverty is basically a rural problem[27].

As far as Indian poverty is concerned, one-third of the world's poor live in India, and there are more poor people in India alone than in the whole of Sub-Saharan Africa. Indian poverty is predominantly rural, where landless labourers and casual workers are the worst off economic group. Scheduled Castes and Tribes, women and female-headed families, old people, female and children face more deprivation than others. The rural poor are primarily those with limited ownership of assets— including land. The vast majority of the rural poor in India is engaged in agriculture (including fishery and livestock), either as agricultural wage labourers or marginal farmers.

The common factor that cuts across all the countries in the region is penury. Poverty continues to intensify due to increasing militarism, environmental degradation, the lack of democratic governance and processes and the exclusion of groups of people on the basis of class, caste, gender, disability, age, race and religion. Poverty and an appalling inequality between the rich and poor are also causative factors for socio-political tension, armed insurgencies, gender discrimination, violence and child labour.

Poverty is an extremely complex phenomenon, which manifests itself in a range of overlapping and interwoven economic, political and social deprivations. These include lack of assets, low income levels, hunger, poor health, insecurity, physical and psychological hardship, social exclusion, degradation and discrimination, and political powerlessness and dis-articulation. The fact is that the victims are always the rural people. Despite numerous national policies and social programmes have been initiated to prevent poverty by different countries, the intensity of poverty still hunting South Asian rural masses.

4.3. Unemployment

Unemployment is another challenging issue in rural development of South Asia. Economic growth of a country depends upon the skills of its people and the application of knowledge, inherited or acquired by them. Optimum utilisation of human resources undoubtedly leads to a considerable degree of economic development of a country. Unemployed human resources signify that a section of the society is without any source of income. Unemployment occurs when a person who is actively searching for employment is unable to find work. Unemployment is often used as a measure of the health of the economy. The most frequently cited measures of unemployment are the unemployment rate. This is the number of unemployed persons divided by the number of people in the labour force. South Asia faces rising unemployment in the face of sustained economic growth.

The South Asian region is home to 1.4 billion people, constituting 22.2 per cent of the world population. Despite being rich in human resources and sophisticated technical skills, yet the number of people unemployed climbed to new heights in 2005. Generally, unemployment means an economic active person without any employment. In this region, labour markets continued to suffer from rates of informal/agricultural employment where jobs are poorly paid and unprotected. Furthermore, most rural people of the region are employed in the agricultural sector that makes them vulnerable to climatic conditions. In South Asia, the region with the highest vulnerable employment rate in 2011 (at 77.7 per cent), 51 per cent of workers were from the agricultural sector.[28] The growing youth population would also require new jobs to be gainfully employed. According to the International Labour Organisation report over 12 million new jobs will be required each year in South Asia.[29] In other words, productive capacity is inadequate to create a sufficient number of jobs. This is a chronic phenomenon. According to the World Bank (WB), despite the high rate of economic growth in South Asia region over an extended period, the region also has the world's largest concentration of poor—more that 500 million people live on less than $1.25 a day.[30]

Unemployment is one of the most acute problems facing the region's youth today. Young people aged between 15 and 24 account for one-fifth of South Asia's population, while half of the region remains unemployed. According to the latest International Labour Organisation (ILO) report, Global Employment Trends 2014: The risk of a jobless recovery, the youth unemployment rate in South Asia reached 10.2 per cent compared with 2.5 per cent of the adult population.[31] In this way, the problem of unemployment is not diminishing but increasing over time and became a major task before rural development of all South Asian governments.

4.4. Food and Water Issues

The problem of food and water security is a growing rural development issue in South Asia. The food insecurity is a gigantic problem in front of the world population. Food insecurity exists when people are undernourished as a result of the physical unavailability of food, their lack of social or economic access to adequate food, and inadequate food utilisation. It may be happening at, individual, household, and regional levels. In spite of the reaching horizon of economic development, people are struggling for the survival of their daily life[32] as at least 25,000 die people every day due to lack of proper diets. Nearly 852 million people in the world are victims of vicious cycle of maturation and chronic hunger. It was a period of the last 30 years when 70 per cent enhance was in the world population, world agriculture produced 17 per cent more calories per person today.[33] At the global level, 33 countries have been recognised most vulnerable where the undernourishment prevalence rate is over 35 per cent. Over 60 per cent of the world's undernourished people live in Asia, and a quarter in Africa. The South Asian region is home to more chronically food insecure people than any other region in the world. Poverty is the main cause of food insecurity and hunger. Poor people in the world do not have sufficient land to grow, or to purchase enough food.[34]

Since the population of India has been rising sharply in comparison with the food grain production; the problem of the food crisis is also accelerating day by day. In the absence of adequate and balanced food, many people in India have been suffering from hunger and malnutrition. India has experimented several programmes for improving food security e.g. Public Distribution Services (PDS), Integrated Child Development Services (ICDS), Mid-day Meals Programme, Provision of health facilities, Employment Targeted Programmes. But India has still not been completely able to solve the problem of chronic food insecurity.

Unlike in Europe and Southeast Asia, economic growth has not been matched by significant improvements in social indicators in South Asia, with the exception of Sri Lanka. In 2005, South Asia was home to 44 per cent of the world's nearly 1.4 billion poorest people[35] and contained the largest number of the world's hungry – nearly 350 million. The food and financial crises of 2007 and 2008 have increased these numbers. Moreover, unlike during the Green Revolution in the 1970s, agriculture no longer contributes as greatly to income. Agriculture now accounts for less than a fifth of the GDP in South Asian countries, yet it still contains more than half of their labour force.[36] Agriculture in South Asia is caught in a low equilibrium trap with low productivity of staples, supply shortfalls, high prices, low returns to farmers and area diversification, results a threat to food security.[37]

Food security in South Asia is significantly determined by access to food by the poor in the region. The recent global food crisis and the increase in world food prices have brought forward the food security concerns to the forefront in South Asia, especially because besides the urban population, a large majority of rural people in South Asia are net buyers of food. About 70 to 80 per cent of the rural households in South Asia are net buyers of main food items, such as rice and wheat. Further, since formost households (and especially for the poor households) the expenditure on food is close to 50 per cent of the total expenditure, food price volatility could in principle have significant adverse implications.

Substantial increases in food prices are forcing governments and development agencies in the region to reassess the policies for agriculture, food security, and international trade that they have pursued over the past three decades. In South Asia, food costs constitute the major portion of the average household expenditure. If food prices continue to rise without a matching increase in salaries and incomes of people at the bottom of the economic ladder, it is estimated that approximately 100 million people could be pushed back into poverty, generating a host of political, social, economic and environmental challenges.[38]

Along with the issues related to food, access to safe drinking water and sharing of water resources between the countries in South Asia have become matters of critical importance in rural development. In many regional countries, water services are inadequate and do not meet minimum standards for safe drinking water. Nearly 63 per cent of the region's population has no access to sanitation facilities, while 11 per cent of the population does not have access to safe drinking water. Most South Asian countries are also plagued by water pollution and declining water quality and groundwater levels. The pollution caused by widespread construction and infrastructure projects is not confined to individual countries, but affects the entire region.[39] The impact of climate change also perceived as a threat to food and water security in South Asia as its sensing erratic weather patterns, swinging from prolonged droughts to heavy rainfall causing flash floods and landslides and directly impacting on agriculture and food supply in most South Asian region. This region is also highly vulnerable to the effects of climate change in particular due to potential melting of glaciers and inundation of low lying islands and coastal areas. Increased glacier melts would initially cause flooding, but would eventually lead to reduced water flows in major regional rivers.[40] All these challenges and barriers would have severe implications on food and water security which subsequently undermine the fruitful rural development of the region.

5. Environmental Disaster and Climate Change

Environmental disaster and climate change is another rural development concern of South Asia today. Other than terrorism, a large number of people have been killed or displaced in the environmental disasters over the last one decade. Although the exact reason for these frequent weather extremes are still the subject of debate and investigation, the fact remains that these have posed a serious challenge to states in South Asia. India is highly vulnerable to climate-related disasters. The Natural Hazards Risk Atlas 2011 compiled by the World Bank and other international agencies ranks India in the highest risk category along with six other countries (Mexico, the Philippines, Turkey, Indonesia, Italy, and Canada). Hydro meteorological disasters are the most devastating and commonly occurring disasters throughout the world, comprising more than two-thirds of all major disasters. According to the National Commission on Floods, the area prone to floods in the country was about 40 million hectares, out of which 80 per cent, i.e., estimated 32 million hectares could be provided a reasonable degree of protection. A major strategy to increased flood resilience is to improve drainage. Rural development schemes are designed to improve drainage in low-lying or flat areas, to strengthen embankments and make drainage lines (starting from higher-order streams in the catchment area) more effective in discharging excessive runoff. In India, around 68 per cent of the country is prone to drought in varying degrees. In 2002, India witnessed a severe drought which affected 300 million people, 150 million cattle and reduced food grain production by 29 million tons. The entire country was declared drought-hit in the years 1966, 1972, 1979, 1987 and 2002[41].

This region, home to about 1.5 billion people, nearly a third of whom are still living in poverty, faces a major challenge in achieving rapid economic growth to reduce poverty and attaining other Millennium Development Goals in an era of accentuated risks posed by environmental disaster and global climate change. The impacts of climate change are likely to result in huge economic, social, and environmental damage to South Asian countries, compromising their growth potential and poverty reduction efforts. Countries in the greater Himalayas region—which includes Bangladesh, Bhutan, northern India, and Nepal—are facing the increased frequency and magnitude of extreme weather events resulting in flooding, landslides, damage to property and infrastructure, devastation of agricultural crops, reduction of hydro power generation, and negative impact on human health. The coastal areas of Bangladesh, India, the Maldives, and Sri Lanka are at high risk from the projected sea level rise that may cause displacement of human settlements, salt water intrusion, loss of agricultural land and wetlands, and a negative impact on tourism and fisheries[42].

South Asia is very vulnerable to natural calamities such as earthquakes and flooding. Typhoons, cyclones, floods and other water-related disasters are on the rise, according to a World Bank evaluation, increasing by as much as five times in 2010 alone, with tremendous loss of life, livelihoods and property. Severe flooding in 2007 along the Ganges and Brahmaputra rivers affected over 13 million people in Bangladesh; flooding in Pakistan in 2010 severely affected 20 million people. India has likewise suffered numerous events of extreme rainfall, flooding and droughts. The economic cost of the 2007 floods in Bangladesh was over US$1 billion; in Pakistan it was nearly US$10 billion. The degree of human suffering has been immeasurable. Millions of tons of food lost to crop and land damage have added unknown numbers of food security-related deaths to the thousands of deaths due to the actual flooding and its consequences, including disease[43].

According to Rifaat Hussain, "South Asia is among the world's most vulnerable regions to both natural and man-made disasters. Over the last 25 years, disasters have killed nearly half a million people in South Asia" and "inflicted colossal financial damages worth US $59 (billion).[44]" The South Asia Disaster Report 2008 states that "South Asia recorded 128 natural disaster events between 2006 and 2008. 93 per cent of these were of hydro meteorological origin. 86 incidences of flooding were reported, with nearly 8000 lives lost. India had by far the highest number of disaster events, but flooding in Bangladesh claimed the most lives."[45] The importance of environmental security is not confined to man-made and natural disasters, but also is reflected in issues of environmental degradation and sustainability. Hussain reports that, South Asia as a region is characterised by extremely high environmental stress resulting from floods, scarcity of water, high urban population density, energy shortages, deforestation, and air pollution.[46]

The global climate change and its potential impact on agriculture can perhaps be considered as a truly long-term challenge to the food security. As far as climate change is concerned, South Asia is considered to be highly vulnerable to the effects of it.[47] This is a particularly important challenge and barrier in rural development of South Asia given the greater significance of agriculture in this region and its dependence of rural people. Climate change could have adverse effects on crop yields and hence lead to the deterioration of food availability. Large scale changes in the food production could lead to price volatility and hence affect the access to food for the poor house-holds. Climate change will have significant impact on the spread of diseases and thus could influence the food utilisation by the households. Climate change could manifest through changes in the frequency and severity of climate extreme events such as droughts, floods and cyclones.The impacts due to these events could have an influence on the vulnerability aspect of food security. Thus, climate change can in principle affect all the four dimensions of food security.

Thus, climate change is a challenge and barrier in rural development. It affects the rural poor more, because they reside in geographically and environmentally marginal environments with poor infrastructure such as roads. Shifts in temperature as well as extreme and erratic weather with floods and droughts affect more drastically their livelihoods, including crop production. Although the rural poor have the least capacity to manage shocks, they are mostly uncovered by risk management structures.

States in the region have over the last two decades acknowledged climate change and its impacts as having grave consequences for their people, particularly in the shape of changing rainfall patterns and the consequences for agricultural sectors, the risk posed by rising sea levels in coastal cities, and the devastation which would follow the increase in the intensity and incidence of natural disasters such as cyclones, droughts, floods, heat waves and rain storms. Regional developing countries are particularly vulnerable to climate change due to high population density, poverty, and lack of resources for adaptation. The region exhibits a broad range of extremes: in topography, from the tallest mountains to the largest deltas to atolls barely above level; in precipitation, from arid lands to vast plains subject to unpredictable flooding; and in the environment, from glacial to tropical. Climate change projections for South Asia by the Intergovernmental Panel on Climate Change indicate that warming is likely to be above the global average, that monsoon rainfall is likely to increase, and that an increase in the frequency of intense precipitation events is likely. Climate change impacts in the South Asian countries are therefore numerous and multifaceted. They face a huge challenge to deal with climate change impacts and avoid greater social, economic, and environmental damages.[48] Because a large portion of regional people are living in rural areas.

One of the greatest impacts of climate change in the region is predicted to be the decline in water resources. Climate change is also seen as a threat to agricultural yields and livelihoods in South Asia. According to the World Bank, around 70 per cent of the region's population lives in rural areas, and accounts for 75 per cent of South Asians living in poverty.[49] Agriculture is the form of livelihood for the majority of these people, employing 60 per cent of the work force.[50] The Symposium on Climate Change and Food Security in 2008 portrayed the significance of this regional threat by stating that "Climate change has multi-dimensional effects on the agricultural-systems in South Asia, including increases in temperature, decline in fresh water availability, sea level rise, glacial melting in the Himalayas, the frequency and magnitude of natural disasters and shifting of cropping zones."[51] According to the fourth assessment by the Intergovernmental Panel on Climate Change (2007), future projections on climate change indicate that South Asia will experience increasing temperatures in the twenty first century.[52] leading to adverse effects on ecology, which in turn will exacerbate threats to human security in rural areas.

South Asian countries like Nepal, Bhutan, Pakistan, Sri Lanka, and India are mainly agrarian economies, and depend heavily on the climate cycles for good harvests of the various crops they grow, such as rice, wheat, jute, sugarcane, and other cereals and pulses. Thus, climate change is perceived as threatening food and water security in the region, as well as livelihoods and the way of life of the majority of rural people who inhabit it.[53] The livelihoods of subsistence farmers and fishermen in South Asia are endangered due to soil degradation, droughts, desertification, drying up of rivers and increases in salinity of fresh water resources. River erosion and increases in the severity of storms and flooding will cause large scale urban migration, creating upward pressure on housing, infrastructure and employment and may be a cause for conflict.[54] Climate change is, thus expected to exacerbate the existing vulnerabilities in South Asia, leading to the further depletion of scarce food and water resources, augmenting migration and increasing the number of internally displaced people. Unless all the countries in South Asia make collective efforts to protect the ecosystem, environmental disasters are likely to continue. However, cooperation in terms of sharing flood data, early warning systems, managing the post-flood situation will certainly reduce human suffering especially in rural lives of the region.

6. Conclusion

As discussed in this paper the South Asian regional countries, especially India faces too many rural challenges and barriers nowadays. Although urban problems seem to be getting more attention than the rural challenges, there is as much a problem in the rural areas as in the urban. That is why "after a period of neglect to bring back rural development in the centre of the development agenda."[55] Ignoring this statement is dangerous because dealing with the situation is critical in tackling current global development challenges. Most of the resources needed for fulfilling the growing demands for global food, water and energy come from the rural areas.[56] The population problems in urban areas originate from the movement of people from the rural areas. The world's poorest populations also live in these rural areas. This makes rural development as much an important agenda as urban development.

South Asia, home to 1.4 billion peoples, needs to carry out major reforms in rural areas to achieve high levels of human development. This region has made substantial progress in agricultural production, but this has been "neither adequate nor equitable enough to reduce the region's huge backlog of poverty." The regional rural insecurities emerge from challenges ranging from, environmental problems, poverty, hunger and lack of access to basic healthcare and education, to political violence and oppression, corruption, and socio-economic inequality resulting from 'many layers of social exclusion: religious, linguistic, gender, access to land/occupation, zaats/kinship/caste-like structures among others, particularly in countries like India, Pakistan, Nepal, Bangladesh and Sri Lanka. Despite impressive economic growth over the last couples of decades, South Asia continues to have the largest number of the poorest people in the world-more than 600 million.[57]

The need of the hour is to strengthen the localised elected base in contrast to the appointed authority. Government intervention should not only improve the incomes of the poor, but their bargaining power vis-à-vis the moneylenders, landlords and bureaucracy. Such empowering measures which merely act as doles and don't enable the poor to stand on their own legs or fight for their rights. Empowerment is good in itself, leads to higher incomes, checks corruption and arbitrary use of power. In the past this was sought to be achieved through land reforms; unfortunately, it appears to be closed chapter now.[58]

The ultimate goal should be to achieve rural prosperity through the participatory development process. This will be possible only if the individual and the community become the focal point of development. No development is possible without bestowing the real decision-making power on the community. Such empowerment has to be an essential ingredient in all our planning and implementation of programmes. This will call for large-scale promotion of strong and viable self-help groups, community-based interest groups, user groups and genuinely strengthening the civil society movement. Merely devolving the community at the grass-roots level will not yield the desired results. The strengthening of the PRIs should be looked upon only as a means to achieve the ultimate end of empowerment of the community. Hence, a strong organic linkage between the formal structures of the government and PRIs on the one hand and the informal structures of NGOs and Community Based Organisations (CBOs) on the other has to be vigorously pursued and promoted.[59] Access to safe drinking water and a healthy environment have to a fundamental right of every citizen in rural development.

It is needs to mention here that if the region were to emerge as a civilised and a benevolent democracy in the twenty first century, the democratic government must accept the challenge of wiping off illiteracy from its surface. The backlog from the outgoing century will have to be dealt with separately while a new strategy of compulsory primary and elementary education for every baby born in the twenty-first century must be devised and forcefully implemented by all countries in the region. The most important problem is that of a general parental in difference and their need to employ child-labour for supplementing family incomes to ward off hunger and food-insecurity. There is no easy solution to this problem, though concentration on female education may reduce it in the coming one to two decades. Considerable stepping up of public investment in primary education is called for. Urgent measures to increase the quantum of national savings are called for which could be gainfully invested in primary and elementary education in the region. Moreover the demand for social consumption in the fields of education and health will come down which may enable the planners and administrators to raise efficiency of these social service sectors.

While the changing tastes and preferences of rapidly urbanising population would demand high value agricultural products, the South Asian agriculture dominated by the small holder farmers with low resource and skill set is increasingly going to find it difficult to diversify. While a conventional development argument supports rural to urban migration as part of the natural development process, the evidence from South Asia suggests that there is more of what could be referred as distress migration of people moving to urban areas as the livelihood opportunities are drying-up in agriculture and at the same time other sectors are unable to absorb the labour due to low skills possessed by them. This does not auger well for the food security situation in the region.

The recent global food crisis highlighted the fragility of food security in the region. Food price volatility and its effect on access to food could get further aggravated by in the coming years as the governments grapple with a variety of responses often chosen due to domestic political compulsions.These and other features of South Asian agriculture, such as declining investment in agriculture, small holder nature of farming in the region, declining productivity and considerable regional differences necessitate urgent policy responses to effectively address the food insecurity concerns of the region and facilitate choice of alternative livelihood options by the rural population.

Smallholder farmers should be supported through various interventions, including promotion of index-based insurance for addressing risk and uncertainty, facilitation of Information and Communication Technology intervention to improve access to information, and encouraging farmer associations to increase the bargaining power of the small holder farmers. Creation of regional food reserve (with limited size) in South Asia promotes cross-country cooperation and serves as a buffer in the years of food grain shortfall. Empowering women by giving them land as well as facilitating rights to produce food would go a long way in addressing food insecurity in the region. It is well endorsed that for effectively tackling food security concerns the public policy must integrate responses to food access and food utilisation also. It is important to recognise the relevance of integration of another kind, wherein policy responses to different stresses are not viewed in isolation but to the extent possible in an integrated manner. Such an integrated approach would increase the probability of selecting response strategies that are complementary in nature.

Meanwhile, the efficacy and potential of the cooperative movement in addressing the problems of rural India stand proved. Since rural development essentially encompasses a multi-disciplinary approach, there must be an inbuilt mechanism to involve people's representation in the conceptualisation, planning, and management of any rural development programme, particularly relating to crop production, water conservation and minor irrigation. The developmental challenge in rural India is not about making a choice between the imperatives of industrial development and the compelling need for agricultural growth; it is essentially about helping the rural sector realise its own potential for development by using the gains of modern science and technology and industrial development as such. It does not make good economic or political sense to reduce the whole issue to one of a choice between one sector or the other. The country has to strive for growth with a human face that is socially equitable and regionally balanced, where all the sectors and the entire population partake of the fruits of our growing economy.[60]

Rural development in India has witnessed several changes over the years in its emphasis, approaches, strategies and programmes. It has assumed a new dimension and perspectives as a consequence. Rural development can be richer and more meaningful only through the participation of clienteles of development. Just as implementation is the touchstone for planning, people's participation is the centre-piece in rural development. People's participation is one of the foremost pre-requisites of development process both from procedural and philosophical perspectives. For the development planners and administrators it is important to solicit the participation of different groups of rural people, to make the plans participatory.

Regional country, especially India stands at a turning point that has the potential to bring rural India into the mainstream of economic development. No challenges come without opportunities. This country has an unparalleled opportunity to harness the maturity in its economic system, the technological advancements brought about by the Infotech revolution, and the potential of a global market to bring in a new dimension of development in rural India. There is an unmistakable realisation and emphatic acknowledgment not only in India but also beyond that if the twenty-first century is going to be the Asian century, then India will be playing a pivotal role in making that happen. For that, it has to carry on board India's large rural populace as well to actualise the dream of developing the nation. The wheels of industry and commerce could rotate smoothly only with a strong agriculture and prosperous rural hinterland.

Despite concerted efforts have been initiated by the regional countries through several plans and measures to alleviate poverty in rural South Asia, there still remains much more to be done to bring prosperity in the lives of the people in rural areas. At present, technology dissemination is uneven and slow in the rural areas. Good efforts of organisations developing technologies, devices and products for rural areas could not yield high success. Experiences of many developed countries suggest that technological development fuelled by demand has a higher dissemination rate. However, in South Asian region, technology developers in rural areas have been catering to the needs (with small improvement), rather than creating demand. There is no industry linkage machinery to create demand-based-technology market for rural communities. Besides, there is also an imbalance between strategies and effective management programmes. Propagation of technology/schemes for rural development is slow and there is a lacking in wider participation of different stakeholders. An ideal approach may, therefore, include the government, Panchayats, village personals, researchers, industries, NGOs and private companies to not only help in reducing this imbalance, but also to have a multiplier effect on the overall economy.

Rural development practice needs varieties of alternative approaches that practitioners can depend on –in the course of delivering results. This study argues that a comprehensive approach should be promoted and implemented in order to attain sustainable rural development results. Similarly, the removal of the rural development challenges and barriers will accelerate the process of rural development in India and beyond. The role of SAARC as a regional organisation, governmental and non-governmental organisations in this regard is, indeed, commendable and vitally important. But much remains to be done.

Notes and References

1. Anjani Kumar Singh, (2008), "Paradigm Shifting in Rural Development," in *Rural Development in India*, (eds.), K.R Gupta and Prasenji Maiti, Vol. 3, Atlantic Publishers, New Delhi, p. 180.
2. See Census of India, 2011, Available at http://censusindia.gov.in/2011-common/CensusDataSummary.html
3. Katar Singh, (2009), *Rural Development: Principles, Policies and Management*, Third Edition, Sage Publications, New Delhi, p. 2.
4. Anjani Kumar Singh, (2008), "Paradigm Shifting in Rural Development," in *Rural Development in India,* (eds.), K. R. Gupta and Prasenji Maiti, Vol. 3, Atlantic Publishers, New Delhi, p. 180.
5. Katar Singh, (2009), *Rural Development: Principles, Policies and Management*, Third Edition, Sage Publications, New Delhi, 2009, p. 3.
6. *Ibid.*
7. *Ibid*, p. 4.
8. *Ibid.*
9. *Ibid.*

10. Anjani Kumar Singh (2008), "Paradigm Shifting in Rural Development," in *Rural Development in India,* (eds.), K. R. Gupta and Prasenji Maiti, Vol. 3, Atlantic Publishers, New Delhi, p. 180.
11. K.R. Gupta and Prasenji Maiti (eds.), (2008), *Rural Development in India,* Atlantic Publishers, New Delhi, p. v.
12. Anjani Kumar Singh, (2008), "Paradigm Shifting in Rural Development," in *Rural Development in India*, (eds.), K. R. Gupta and Prasenji Maiti, Vol. 3, Atlantic Publishers, New Delhi, p. 181.
13. *The Hindu*, July 15, 2011.
14. K. R. Gupta and Prasenji Maiti (eds.), (2008), *Rural Development in India,* Atlantic Publishers, New Delhi, p. v.
15. *Ibid.*
16. *Ibid.*
17. Somnath Chatterjee, (2007), "The Developmental Challenge in Rural India," *The Hindu*, April 4, 2007.
18. *Ibid.*
19. M.L. Dhawan, (2005), *Rural Development Priorities*, Isha Books, Delhi, p. 151.
20. *Ibid*, pp. 151-52.
21. Vibhuti Hate and Seth Gannon, (2010), "Public Health in South Asia", A Report of the CSIS Global Health Policy Centre, Center for Strategic & International Studies, Washington, DC, July, p. 1.
22. Vibhuti Hate and Seth Gannon, (2010), "Public Health in South Asia", A Report of the CSIS Global Health Policy Centre, Center for Strategic & International Studies, Washington, DC, July, p. 4.
23. Syed Rifaat Hussain, (2008), "Non Traditional Security (NTS) Challenges in South Asia", Consortium of Non-Traditional Security Studies in Asia, pp. 2–3, available at http://www.rsisntsasia.org/resources/publications/policy-briefs/inaugural-meeting/rcss.doc
24. Monika Barthwal-Datta, (2012), *Understanding Security Practices in South Asia: Securitization Theory and the role of non-state actors*, Routledge, New York, 2012, p.148.
25. Vibhuti Hate and Seth Gannon, (2010), "Public Health in South Asia", A Report of the CSIS Global Health Policy Centre, Center for Strategic & International Studies, Washington, DC, July, p. 3.
26. M.L. Dhawan, (2005), *Rural Development Priorities*, Isha Books, Delhi, p. 152.

27. Ganesh Thapa, (2004), "Rural Poverty Reduction Strategy for South Asia", Paper Presented at an International Conference on Ten Years of Australian South Asian Research Centre organised at the Australian National University, Canberra, From 27-28, p.1.
28. "Global Labour Market situation", *International Labour Organisation*, p. 44. available at http://www.ilo.org/wcmsp5/groups/public/—dgreports/—dcomm/publ/documents/publication/wcms_171681.pdf,
29. "Global Labour Market Situation", *International Labour Organization*, p. 35, available at http://www.ilo.org/wcmsp5/groups/public/—dgreports/—dcomm/ publ/documents/publication/wcms_171681.pdf
30. "South Asia: Regional Strategy Update 2012", The World Bank, available at http://web.worldbank.org/WBSITE/EXTERNAL/COUNTRIES/SOUTHASIAEXT/0,,contentMDK:21265405~menuPK:2298227~pagePK:146736~piPK:146830~the Site PK: 223547,00.html.
31. Krishna Kumar VR, (2014), "South Asia Faces Youth Job Crisis," *Asia Weekly*, China Daily Asia, Friday, October 24, p.1, available http://epaper.chinadailyasia.com/asia-weekly/article-3467.html.
32. Ali, M. (2009). *Geography of Agricultural Marketing-At Grass Roots Levels*, Pacific Publication, Delhi.
33. FAO, 2002 and 2006 FAO (2002-2006), "The State of Food insecurity in the World-2001", *Food and Agricultural Organization*, Rome, http://www.fao.org. and FAO (2006), "The State of Food Insecurity in the World 2006 Eradicating World Hunger -taking stock ten years after the World Food Summit", http://www.fao.org.
34. FAO (2006), "The State of Food Insecurity in the World 2006 Eradicating World Hunger -taking stock ten years after the World Food Summit," http://www.fao.org. also see Roa, C.H.H. (2005), *Agriculture Food Security, Poverty and Environment*, Oxford University Press, New Delhi.
35. Chen, Shaobua, and Martin Ravallion, (2008), "The developing world is poorer than we thought, but no less successful in the fight against poverty", Policy Research Working Paper, Development Research Group, Washington DC, World Bank, August.
36. Tushaar Shah and Uma Lele, (2011), "Climate Change, Food and Water Security in South Asia: Critical Issues and Cooperative Strategies in an Age of Increased Risk and Uncertainty", A Global Water Partnership (GWP), and International Water Management Institute (IWMI) Workshop, 23-24 February, Colombo, Sri Lanka, p. 3.

37. S.S. Kalamkar, (2014), "Food Security in South Asia", in *South Asia in the Globalized World*, ed., C. Vinodan, New Century Publications, New Delhi, p. 57.

38. Farooq Sobhan, (2103), "Cooperative Security Framework in South Asia: A Bangladeshi Perspective'', in *Cooperative Security Framework for South Asia*, ed., Nihar Nayak, IDSA, New Delhi, Pentagon Press, p. 36.

39. Farooq Sobhan, (2013), "Cooperative Security Framework in South Asia: A Bangladeshi Perspective", in *Cooperative Security Framework for South Asia*, ed., Nihar Nayak, IDSA, New Delhi, Pentagon Press, pp. 36-37.

40. Nirupama Rao, (2011), South Asia 2020: Moving towards Cooperation or Conflict, in *SOUTH ASIA Envisioning a Regional Future*, (ed.), Smruti S Pattanaik, IDSA, Pentagon Security International, New Delhi, p. 8.

41. *Ministry of Agriculture* (2009): "Manual for Drought Management," New Delhi , 2009.

42. Mahfuz Ahmed and Suphachol Suphachalasai, (2014), Assessing the Costs of Climate Change and Adaptation in South Asia, *Asian Development Bank*, Philippines, p. xii.

43. Tushaar Shah and Uma Lele, (2011), "Climate Change, Food and Water Security in South Asia: Critical Issues and Cooperative Strategies in an Age of Increased Risk and Uncertainty", A Global Water Partnership (GWP), and International Water Management Institute (IWMI) Workshop, 23-24 February, Colombo, Sri Lanka, p. 3.

44. Syed Rifaat Hussain, (2008), "Non Traditional Security (NTS) Challenges in South Asia", Consortium of Non-Traditional Security Studies in Asia, pp. 2–3, available at http://www.rsisntsasia.org/resources/publications/policy-briefs/inauguralmeeting/rcss.doc

45. TharukaDissanaike, (2009), "South Asia Disaster Report: Special Copenhagen Issue", Bourton on Dunsmore, available at http://practicalaction.org/docs/region_south_asia/south-asia-disasterreport-copenhagen.pdf

46. Syed Rifaat Hussain, (2008), "Non Traditional Security (NTS) Challenges in South Asia", Consortium of Non-Traditional Security Studies in Asia, pp. 2–3, available at http://www.rsisntsasia.org/resources/publications/policy-briefs/inauguralmeeting/rcss.doc

47. U. Kelker and S. Bhadwal, (2008), "South Asia Regional Study on Climate Change, Impacts and Adaptations: Implications for Human

Development", Paper Prepared by TERI and Human Development Report Office, 2007/08, p. 4, available at: http://hrd,undp.org/en/reports/global/hdr2007/08

48. Mahfuz Ahmed and Suphachol Suphachalasai, (2014), "Assessing the Costs of Climate Change and Adaptation in South Asia," *Asian Development Bank*, Philippines, p. vii.

49. "Climate Change and South Asia: Rural lives and Livelihoods of Millions at Risk", (2007), *World Bank*, 30 Nov. 2007, available at: http://web.worldbank.org/WBSITE/EXTERNAL/COUNTRIES/SOUTHASIAEXT/0,contentMDK:21571064¬pagePK:146736¬piPK:146830¬theSitePK:223547,00.HTML

50. *Ibid.*

51. R. Lal et al., (2011), *Climate Change and Food Security in South Asia*, Springer, New York.

52. "Fourth Assessment Report: Climate Change 2007", (2007), Intergovernmental Panel on Climate Change.

53. Monika Barthwal-Datta, (2012), *Understanding Security Practices in South Asia: Securitization Theory and the role of non-state actors,* Routledge, New York, p. 44.

54. "Assessing the Evidence: Environment, Climate Change and Migration in Bangladesh", (2010), *International Organization for Migration.*

55. Remark made by the Secretary General of the UN ECOSOC session 2003, in Geneva, Switzerland.

56. Magel, H. (2006), "Changing FIG –model for a changing world," Farewell speech at the FIG Handover Ceremony in Münster, Germany, 2 December. www.fig.net/council/council_2003_2006/magel-papers/munster_magel_eng.pdf

57. A. Kumar, (2010), "A Review of Human Development Trends in South Asia: 1990-2009", Human Development Research Paper 2010/44, *UNDP*, November, p. 28, available at http://hdr.undp.org/en/reports/global/hdr2010/paper/HDRP_2010_44.pdf

58. Anjani Kumar Singh, (2008), "Paradigm Shifting in Rural Development," in *Rural Development in India*, (eds.), K.R. Gupta and Prasenji Maiti, Vol. 3, Atlantic Publishers, New Delhi, p. 187.

59. *Ibid*, pp. 188-89.

60. Somnath Chatterjee, (2007), "The Developmental Challenge in Rural India," *The Hindu*, April 4.

4
Role of Agriculture Sector in Sustainable Development of India

Shaukat Ali

1. Introduction

Agriculture occupies the most important position in Indian economy, as it is one of the largest private enterprises in India, which continues to dominate the change in economy through its link of various sectors of production and markets. The role of agriculture sector in India can be seen through its contribution to GDP (Gross Domestic Product), employment and sustainable economic development of the country. Agriculture contributes to 14 per cent of the nation's GDP, about 11 per cent of its exports, nearly half of the population still depends on agriculture as its principal source of income and it is a source of raw material for a large number of industries. Accelerating the growth of agriculture production is therefore necessary not only to achieve an overall GDP target of eight per cent during the 12th Plan and meet the rising demand for food but also to increase incomes of those who depend on agriculture to ensure inclusiveness. The sustainable agricultural development of any country depends upon the judicious mix of their available natural resources. In fact agriculture determines the fate of the country like India where about two-third of the population still lives in rural India with agriculture as their livelihood, in spite of the increasing urbanisation that has been taking place since many decades. Therefore if agriculture does not develop, it will be really bad for the economy as the fall of agriculture growth not only affects employment but GDP too, thus increasing poverty. The larger objective for the improvement of agriculture sector can be realised through rapid growth of agriculture which depends upon the increase of the area of cultivation, cropping intensity and productivity.

The sustainable agricultural development will be possible if we address certain important issues such as, changes various agricultural policies of the government that influence the domestic inter-sectoral terms of trade which has impact on some policies such as monitory, exchange rate and trade that are transmitted to the agriculture sector. There are many questions regarding the Indian agriculture sector in present scenario i.e., whether trade policy and devaluation of rupee help in raising agricultural exports ? how the aggregate crop output and terms of trade have influenced rural poverty and real agricultural wages of unskilled workers over the period? The analysis and appropriate solution to these issues must be addressed properly which has contributed significantly for the sustainable development of India. Thus, agricultural productivity can be increased by two ways. First, increasing output by efficient utilisation of available resources, second increasing output by variation of input. The first method is better with respect to productivity and sustainability. But due to increasing population, this method cannot provide a permanent solution. Thus, we can go for the second method which may potentially cause environmental degradation and affect economic sustainability. There, fore there is a need to tackle the various dimensions of sustainable agricultural development.

The issues of sustainable development in agriculture sector can be discussed under three broad types of farming systems *viz.*, traditional production system, modern agriculture system and sustainable agriculture system. We can compare them across three important dimensions such as ecological, economic and social sustainability. Ecological Sustainability: generally the traditional and conventional farm practices are not ecologically sustainable. It misuses natural resources, reducing soil fertility, causes soil erosion and affects global climatic change. On the other hand, sustainable agriculture system has some advantages over traditional one. It improves soil fertility by using advance technology to maintain the growth rate of this sector. Secondly, sustainable agriculture practices have the ability to retain and store rain water. Thirdly, sustainable agriculture practices consist in mix cropping system which produces diversified crops. Fourthly, it also reduces the use of hazardous chemicals and pests as excessive use of chemicals, pesticides and fertilizers badly affect the local ecology, health as well as population as a whole. Lastly, conventional agriculture system produces green house gases in many ways. Like reducing the amount of carbon store in the soil and in vegetation through the production of methane in irrigated field and produce artificial fertilizer. But by adopting sustainable agricultural system we can easily overcome this problem.

A sustainable agriculture system is economically viable, whereas the conventional agriculture practices involve more economic risk for the long term. Sometimes governments are inclined to view export oriented production systems which are more important than supplying the domestic demands. Focusing on exports alone, involves certain hidden costs like transportation costs, as well as local food security is also at risk. Therefore, Policies should address domestic demands too, particularly in food security which is equally important to the visible trade balance. It is a misconception that specific commodities promise high economic returns. But market production implies certain risks as markets are fickle and change quickly. Cheap foreign food may sweep into the national market, leaving Indian farmers without a market. Thus, as a World Trade Organisation's signatory, the government of India is under-pressure to deregulate and open its economy to the world market so that it cannot protect its farmers behind tariff walls. On the other hand, the main source of employment to rural people is farming. Trends towards specialisation and mechanisation may increase with narrowly measured "efficiency" which reduces employment. Therefore the welfare costs of unemployment must be taken into account while designing National agricultural support programmes. Sustainable agriculture, with its emphasis on small scale, labour intensive activities, helps to overcome these problems. Social sustainability in farming techniques is related to the ideas of social acceptability and justice. Development cannot be sustainable unless it reduces poverty. The government must find ways to enable the rural poor people to benefit from agricultural development. Social injustice will prevail unless some sections of the society is neglected from development opportunities. But robust system of social sustainability can bridge the gap of "haves" and ''have-nots''. Many new technologies fail to become applicable in agriculture sector due to the lack of acceptability by the local society. Sustainable agriculture practices are useful because these are based on local, social customs, norms and traditions etc. Local people are more likely to accept and adopt them. Moreover, sustainable agriculture practices are based on traditional knowledge and local innovations. Local people have the knowledge about their environment crops and livestock.

Traditional agriculture is more gender oriented, where women bear more burdens in terms of labour. Sustainable agriculture system ensures that the burden and benefits are shared equitably between both genders. Secondly, conventional farming focuses on few commodities. But sustainable agriculture system improves food security by improving quality and nutritional value of food, by producing more ranges of products throughout the years. Traditional farming practices are also driven by the caste and wealth oriented people. The rich and higher castes are benefitted more, whereas the poor and lower castes are left out. Sustainable agriculture attempts to ensure equal participation which recognises the voice and speech of every individual.

2. Literature Review

We will present a brief review of existing literature on growth pattern of agriculture sector. In this study we come across various explanations about the pattern of the contribution of agricultural growth in sustainable development of India.

Evenson, *et. al.* (1999) found that India has one of the largest public agricultural Research establishments, to be developed. The important factors that contributed in the growth process of Indian agricultural sectors are economic liberalisation policies of government since 1991, budgetary constraints and declining return on public research. It is also suggested that public investment in agricultural research have had impact on the growth of Total Factorial Productivity (TFP) in the Indian crop sectors.

Mishra, *et. al.* (2003) found that the changes in various policies of government influenced the domestic inter-sectoral terms of trade. These changes have impacts on some policies such as, monetary, exchange rate and trade, which are transmitted to the agricultural sectors. Secondly, trade policy and devaluation of rupees among others helped in raising agricultural exports. It is also suggested that aggregate crop output and terms of trade have influenced the rural poverty and real agricultural wages of unskilled workers over the period of time.

Rao (2003) explained that the slowing down agricultural growth in the post-reform period, in spite of favourable macroeconomic environment is neglecting the reforms which directly affect agriculture. The reform agenda of agriculture is based on a frame-work of a two-pronged strategy, first to release the initiative of enterprises for farmers in the private sector by removing restriction on agricultural trade, processing etc, secondly, to facilitate adequate supply response to the incentives for the farmers. It can be done by strengthening infrastructure, agricultural research, extension and delivery of credit while protecting the environment.

Lotter (2003) suggested that the organic crop system performs better than conventionally managed crop systems during extreme climate of both drought and excessive rainfall. The writer pointed out the example of Ronald Farming System Trial. In the 20/ Rodale Farming Systems Trial, organic and a conventional crop rotation were compared; the organic crop systems performed significantly better in four years out of five years of moderate drought. In the severe drought year of 1999, three out of the four crop comparisons (LEG soybean, MNR soybean and MNR maize) resulted in significantly better yields in the organic systems than the conventional. The LEG maize treatment yielded significantly less than the CNV due to weed pressure. Demonstrating the skills in managing weeds is an important part of organic farming. The scholar also pointed out various evidences which indicate that the better water holding capacity of organically managed soils is likely a key mechanism for better yields during water deficits. Water harvest is important for groundwater recharge which was significantly better in the organic systems in the severe drought year over a five year period. Organic crop management techniques will be valuable resources in an era of climatic variability, providing soil and crop characteristics that can better buffer environmental extremes.

Vyas (2003) concluded that the relationship between poverty and sustainable development are closely related to each other. The main features of Indian agriculture system, its sources of growth and problems can add value in sustainable development of this sector. The issues of poverty and food security should also consider while formulating economic reforms policies in agriculture sector. The initiatives should be taken to improve its productivity, through effective policies which increases profitability will ultimately maintain sustainability in major farming systems.

Virmani (2004) found that the fundamental objective of economic policy is to generate equitable economic growth and to increase well being of all citizens.Thus, the timing and sequencing recommendation were based on a qualitative ordering of reforms in terms of the cost-benefits ratio of different policy action where cost includes the risk of failure, which is arising from underdeveloped markets and possible sabotage by vested interests of poor countries. It is also suggested that the problems and policies are related to different sectors such as agriculture, industry, power and urban development. It is also highlighted that certain important issues that have been at the centre of public debate, are recent adoption of value added tax, capital account convertibility, FDI in India which will play a valuable role in the sustainable development of this sector.

Ruel, *et al.* (2005) highlighted those five areas of action plan which bring rural India on a higher growth trajectory that would reduce hunger, malnutrition and unemployment at a much faster pace than has been the case so far. These areas are increasing investment in rural infrastructure, reorientation of social safety nets, mega irrigation schemes, liberalised marketing system and trade liberalisation in agriculture; these five areas of actions are interlinked and can work best if they are pursued in conjunction.

Puttaswamaiah (2005) observed that the agriculture sector, world over, has experienced a phenomenal growth since the mid-twentieth century. The growth driven by Green Revolution technology has made a significant change on aggregate supply of food grains, ensuring food security to the growing population. It is also suggested that the next stage of agricultural growth, however, may face serious challenges in terms of sustainability; whereas the main problem faced by the developing countries in the south pertains to sustainability of resource use, on the other hand in the north is over-use of chemical inputs. These problems led to increase awareness, and it was felt to move from the input intensive agriculture sector persuaded during the Green Revolution phase to sustainable farming in different parts of the country.

Mittal (2006) observed that the sustainability issue of crop productivity is fast emerging. Agricultural productivity was high during 1980s, but has not been sustained during 1990s. Therefore, proper applications of technology in production can increase productivity. It is also highlighted that the examination of important issues related to the trends in the agricultural productivity with reference to individual crops growth in the major states of India. The temporal and spatial variations in the productivity status of major crops in India can be analysed by using the TFPG (Total Factoral Productivity Growth) estimates and its sustainability.

Mahindra (2008) observed that in the last two decades of economic reforms there is an achievement in the economic growth but inequalities and exclusion in Indian agriculture, poverty and human development continuously increased. In this regard it is emphasised that there is a need for economic reforms with equitable development. This is based on key inter-related elements of inclusive growth that is agriculture, poverty, food security and employment, social sector and regional disparity. Thus, it is also suggested that growth and equity objective should be pursued simultaneously.

Mittal (2008) observed that the future demand projection of agricultural products like rice, wheat, total cereals, pulses, edible oil, oil seeds and sugar/ sugarcane is increasing due to the growth in population and per capita income. On the supply side production is constrained by low yield growths. Therefore the future demand-supply gap can be fulfilled by appropriate policy framework. It is also suggested that to meet the future food requirements, the need base policy should be laid down, in order to increase productivity in agriculture sector through public investment in irrigation, development of infrastructure, research and extension.

Gulati (2009) found that the research investment and its impact on agricultural productivity, growth and resource allocation is widely acclaimed. Micro-dimension of technological changes such as fertiliser response in dry land areas, pest and irrigation management, small farm considerations, and supply response led to the significant contributions in the area of agricultural economics, which ultimately maintain the agricultural development in the country. Thus, it is suggested that for the advancement of agricultural economics, the institutional development is also essential to sustain agricultural development.

Amutha (2010) observed that the new opportunities are opening the eyes of farmers, development workers, researchers and policy-makers. They can now see the potential and importance of these practices not only to their direct economic interest but also as the basis of further intensification and ecological sustainability. Research has an important role to play. Bankers should think of how best they can provide incentives and credits accessible to poor farmers and women in order to make investment possible in dry land farming. It is also suggested that the farming will continue to change. The key to sustainable agriculture is the capacity of farmers and all other factors in agricultural development, as well as the wider society, to learn, experiment, adapt and cooperate in an effective way. Therefore, it is concluded that the small farm management will improve productivity, profitability and sustainability of the farming system that can go a long way to ensure all round sustainability.

Chinai (2012) pointed out that the agricultural policies of India are responsible for the sustainable growth of the sector. Some policies supported the growth of this sector but on the other hand other policies did not do the same. As the 'Green Revolution' of the 1960s and 1970s brought a boost to India's food grain production, and pride in achieving 'self-sufficiency'. Despite that, the country's malnutrition crisis continues to deepen, statistics reveals that more than half of Indian children of small age face a debilitating future and 50 per cent of the 2.1 million annual deaths of children under five years of age, because of malnutrition. Over 60 per cent of Indian women, irrespective of class, are anemic. Small farmers are unable to practice viable farming due to some factors such as the absence of knowledge related to sustainable farming technology; lack of infrastructure such as storage, transport, roads, access to indigenous seeds and markets. In 1990s, when India adopted economic reforms policies (known as Structural Adjustment Programme or SAP), government withdrew the agriculture subsidies and reduced the number of people receiving subsidised food. This intention is evident, for instance, in the imposition of targets that who will access the Public Distribution System, ultimately leaving out thousands of genuinely poor people. At the same time corporations are clamouring to supply fortified, supplementary and packaged food through the national food programmes. Therefore, it is also suggested that India's development policies are increasingly focused on exploitation of natural resources such as minerals, forests and rivers on an industrial scale. This form of development is pushing communities into poverty, turning them into ecological refugees and urban migrants who are vulnerable to malnutrition. 'Development Projects' in four Indian states have displaced at least 1.6 million people, says the Action Aid Report, 2010. While other developing countries have quickly learnt the right lessons and rectified their policy failures. According to the report, India has yet to comprehend the fallacy of its current development model. It urgently needs to draw from the experiences of other Southern Hemisphere countries that are demonstrating success.

After, a perusal of the different reviews of prominent scholars, it is found that the government policies have to perform adequate role in bringing and maintaining agricultural growth which plays a prominent role in sustainable development of India. However, it can be achieved by formulating and implementing the policies that have lead to reform. Some of the important policies, argued by some scholars in this regard, were "Green Revolution" (1960s-1970s), economic reform policies or structural adjustment programme

(1990s), support for advocacy and training to health initiative (SATHI, 2009) on nutritional crises in Maharashtra, that boosted India's foodgrain production.

It is also found from the scholar views that proper application of technology to extract and utilise the agricultural resources is also needed to improve the sector. Paraduman Kumar and Surabhi Mittal (2006) said the agricultural productivity was high during 1980s, could not remain the same during 1980s due to the lack of proper application of technology in production. Temporal and spatial in the productivity status of major crops should be analysed by using TFPG (Total factoral productivity growth). But it is still needed to find that in spite of lack of reformed base policies, and application of technology, agriculture sectors contributed significantly in sustainable growth. Some major crops make this country self-reliant in case of foodgrain, exports, employment, raw materials for different industries etc. Thus, this paper highlights the sustainable growth of some major crops like wheat, rice, maize and cotton, which has contributed significantly in the sustainable development of India. By this article efforts have been made to highlight certain unidentified areas in this regard to gain better insights.

3. Methodology

The data is collected from secondary sources. The main sources are the State of Indian Agriculture (2011-2012 to 2012-2013), Government of India, Ministry of Agriculture, Department of Agriculture and Cooperation, Directorate of Economics and Statistics, New Delhi. Out of total Indian agricultural crops, only four major crops i.e. Wheat, Rice, Cotton and Maize were selected. Their performance has been analysed in relation to the occupied areas, production and yield rate over the period of two plan periods i.e., 10th plan (2002-03 to 2006-07) and 11th plan (2007-08 to 2011-2012). Out of four major crops the performance of Rice and Cotton is measured in terms of their exports over the period of three years (2009-10 to 2011-12) in relation to quantity in tonnes and value in Rupees. The performance of Wheat and Rice is analysed too, in terms of their contribution in Foodgrains. Production, procurement and procurement as percentage of production of wheat and rice over the period of six years from 2006-2007 to 2011-2012 has been also analysed. The data is analysed using percentage analyses.

4. Objectives of the Paper

(a) To know the role and contribution of agricultural sector in the sustainable development of India.

(b) To know the causes of lack of sustainability in agricultural sector.

(c) To analyse the growth rate of agricultural sector.

(d) To find out the ways and means to sustain the production of agriculture sector.

4. Result and Discussion

All India average Annual Growth Rate of Area, Production and Yield rate of four major selected crops in percentage of two plan period i.e. 10th Plan (2002-03 to 2006 to 07) and 11th Plan (2007-08 to 2011-12) is given in the Table 1. Comparisons are made on the basis of their relative performance in ralation to occupied Area, Production, Yield rate and the share of each products out of total cereals in case of Wheat, Rice and Maize but in case of Cotton, individually its performance is measured over the period of time. This can be highlighted by the following figures 1, 2, 3, 4, 5, 6.

Table 1: All India Average Annual Growth Rates of Area, Production and Yield of Principal Crops (Per cent)

Crops/ Crops	*Average Annual Growth per cent 10th Plan 2002-2003 to 2006-2007*			*AverageAnnual Growth per cent 11th Plan 2007-2008 to 2011-2012*			
Group	Area	Production	Yield	Area	Production		Yield
Rice	-0.39	1.25		1.17	0.18	2.69	2.41
Wheat	1.3	1.11		-0.32	1.31	4.64	3.29
Maize	3.77	4.02		-0.15	2.16	8.9	6.47
Total							
Cereals	0.07	1.21		0.74	-0.03	3.79	3.76
Cotton	0.57	20.01		19.4	5.97	10.46	3.93

Source: *Directorate of Economics & Statistics, Ministry of Agriculture.*

Growth Rates of Area, Production and Yield Rate of Rice in Two Plan Period

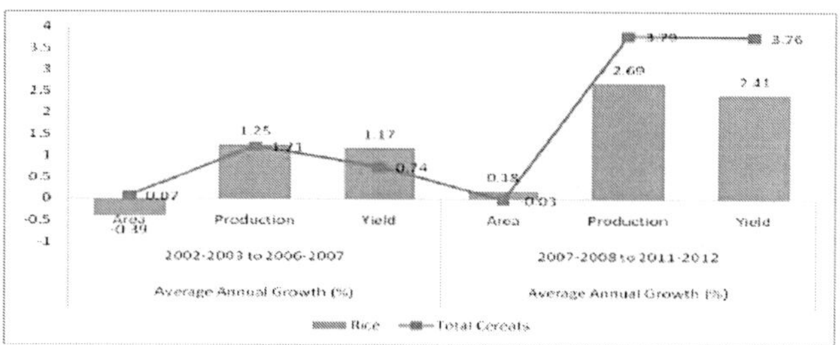

Source: *Directorate of Economics & Statistics, Ministry of Agriculture.*

Figure 1

Total area occupied by the rice during 11th Plan is 0.18 per cent followed by the 10th Plan which was in negative (-0.39 per cent) and its production was increased to 1.25 per cent from 10th plan to 2.69 per cent in 11th Plan period which is more than two times of the previous plan. Subsequently, yield rate in the two periods of the same product is more than two times as it was increased to 1.17 per cent from 10th Plan to 2.41 per cent in 11th Plan period (Refer to Table 1).

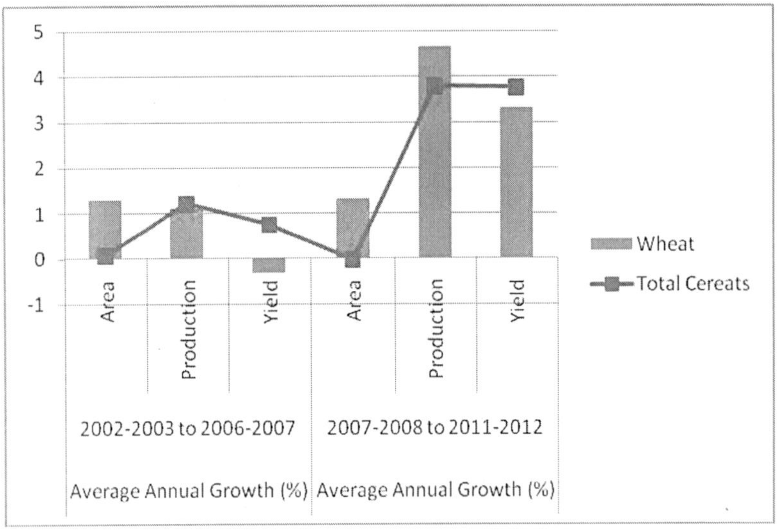

Fig. 1. Growth Rates of Area, Production and Yield of Wheat in Two Plan

Source: Directorate of Economics & Statistics, Ministry of Agriculture.

Figure 2

Total area occupied by wheat was 1.3 per cent in the 10th Plan period was increased to 1.31 per cent in 12th Plan period. Subsequently the production of the same product in the 10th Plan period was 1.11 per cent which increased to 2.64 per cent, approximately more than four times in the 12th Plan period. In the mean time yield rate of this product was 3.29 per cent in during 12th Plan which was in negative (-0.32) in the preceding period (Refer to Table 1).

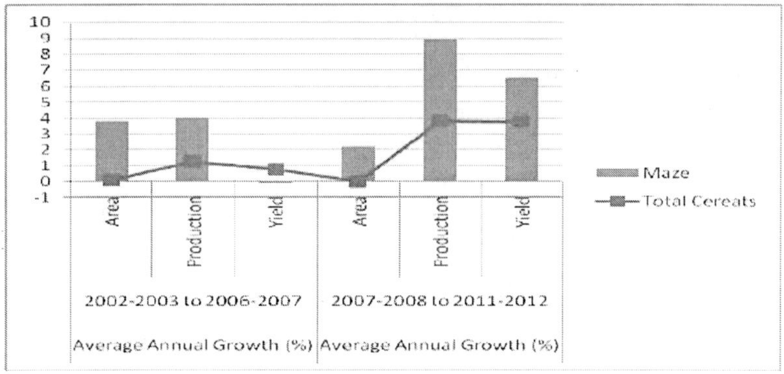

Fig.2. Growth Rates of Area, Production and Yield of Maize in the Two Plan Periods.

Source: Directorate of Economics & Statistics, Ministry of Agriculture.

Figure 3

In case of maize the total occupied area during 11th Plan decreased from 3.77 per cent to 2.16 per cent from 10th Plan period. But the production increased to 4.02 per cent from 10th Plan to 8.9 per cent in 11th Plan period which was more than two times. Subsequently, the yield rate was in negative during 10th Plan period noticed as –0.15 per cent which tremendously increased to 6.47 per cent during 11th Plan (Refer to Table 1).

Crop-Specific Growth

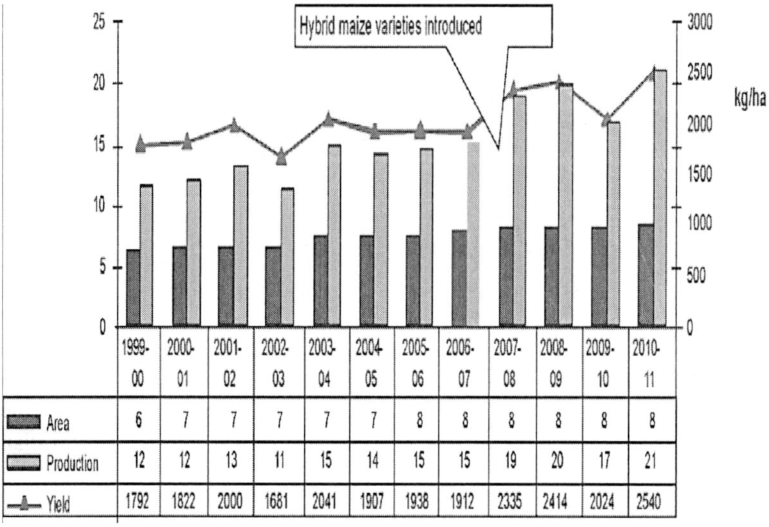

	1999-00	2000-01	2001-02	2002-03	2003-04	2004-05	2005-06	2006-07	2007-08	2008-09	2009-10	2010-11
Area	6	7	7	7	7	7	8	8	8	8	8	8
Production	12	12	13	11	15	14	15	15	19	20	17	21
Yield	1792	1822	2000	1681	2041	1907	1938	1912	2335	2414	2024	2540

Fig. 3. Area, Production & Yield of Hybrid Maize

Source: Directorate of Economics & Statistics, Ministry of Agriculture.

Figure 4

From Fig. 4 it shows that the areas as well as production of hybrid Maize is increasing. This finally indicates that the yield rates are also increasing in the same direction as shown in the above Fig. 4. In the year 2002-03, it has been observed that the production per hectare is 11million tonnes, but in the year 2010-11 it has increased near about more than two times that is 21 million tonnes. Similarly, yield rate increases to from 1681 kg per hectare in the year 2002-03 to 2540 kg per hectare in the year 2010-11. So there is significant change in the yield rate of Maize followed by the changes in the area and productions.

This incremental ratio of maize highlighted its contribution in the sustainable development of Indian crops over the period of time. Growth is depending on some important factors such as introduction of hybrid varieties, application of HYV (High Yielding Varieties) technology in agriculture sector, expansion of irrigation facilities, credit facilities to the farmers, land reform policies, agricultural prices as well as marketing facilities for the agricultural products.

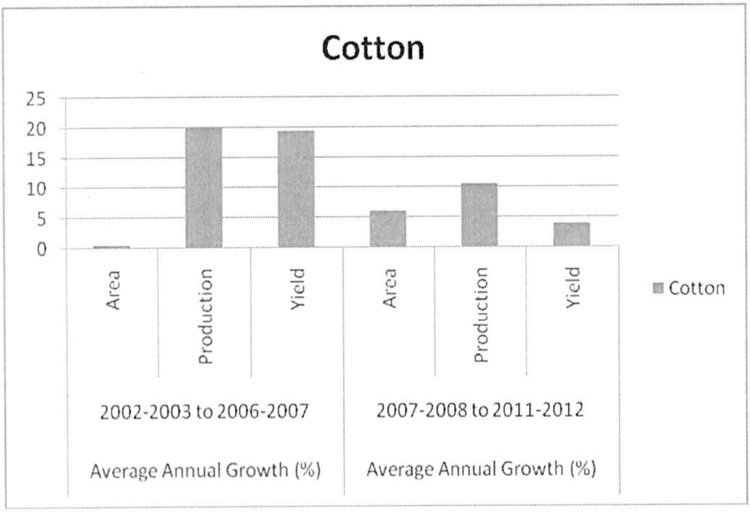

Fig. 4 : Growth Rates of Area, Production and Yield of Cotton in the Two Plans

Source: Directorate of Economics & Statistics, Ministry of Agriculture.

Figure 5

Total area occupied by cotton was 0.57 per cent during 10th Plan which increased to 5.97 per cent in 11th Plan. On the other side production was 20.01 per cent during 10th Plan period which was quite better but could not retain it in the 11th plan and it reduced to 10.46 per cent. Same way the yield rate was also decreasing gradually more than six times. During 10th plan its yield rate was 19.4 per cent which reduced to 3.93 per cent in the 11th Plan period (Refer to Table 1).

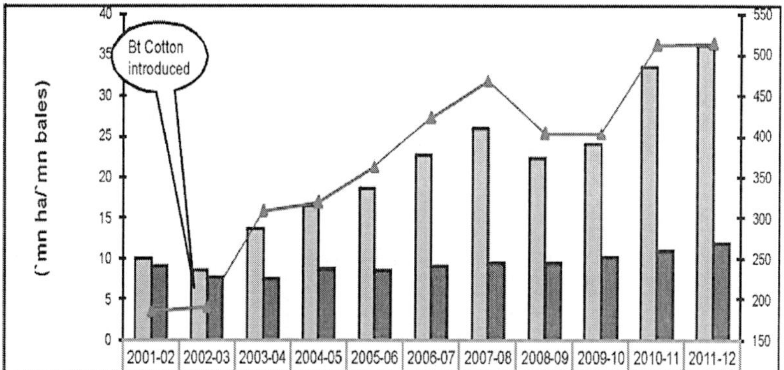

	2001-02	2002-03	2003-04	2004-05	2005-06	2006-07	2007-08	2008-09	2009-10	2010-11	2011-12
Production	10	9	14	16	18	23	26	22	24	33	34
Area	9	8	8	9	9	9	9	9	10	11	12
Yield	186	191	307	318	362	421	467	403	403	499	476

Fig. 5 : Area, Production and Yield Rates of hybrid Bt Cotton

Sources: Directorate of Economics & Statistics, Ministry of Agriculture.

Figure 6

From Fig. 6 it has been observed that the area as well as production increases in the year 2004-05, which leads to increase in the yield rate of production of cotton . In the same year the production per hectare was 16 million tonnes which tremendously increased in the year 2011-12, 34 million tonnes per hectare. Similarly yield rate of cotton increases in the ratio of 318 kg/hectare to 476 kg/hectare in the 2011-12. The biggest increase in the growth rate of yields in the two periods is with the introduction of Bt Cotton in 2002. By 2011-12 almost 90 per cent of the Cotton area is covered under Bt Cotton, production has more than doubled (compared to 2002-03), yields have gone up by almost 70 per cent, and export potential for more than Rs 10 thousand crore worth of raw cotton has been created.

Therefore, this significant change in the yield rate of cotton contributed importantly in the sustainable development of Indian crops, which plays a vital role in the sustainable development of India. The growth of cotton also depends on the same factors which contributed to the growth of maize i.e., introduction of hybrid varieties, application of HYV (High Yielding Varieties) technology in agriculture sector, expansion of irrigation facilities, credit facilities to the farmers, land reform policies, agricultural prices as well as marketing facilities for the agricultural products. This incremental ratio of Bt cotton highlighted its contribution in the sustainable development of Indian crops over the period of time, which has contributed significantly for the sustainable of the country.

Contribution of Rice and Cotton in Total Agricultural Exported Crops in terms of Percentage

Agricultural exports increased from Rs 120 thousand crore in 2010-11 to Rs 187 thousand crore in financial year 2011-12 registering a growth of nearly 55 per cent. Increase in value of agricultural exports during 2011-12 was primarily on account of higher exports of cotton, marine products, guar gum meal, basmati and non-basmati rice, meat and meat preparations, spices, and oil meals. During the same period export of tobacco, dairy poultry products, sugar and molasses registered a decline. In 2011-12 in comparison 2010-11 the share of Agricultural exports in total exports increased from 10.47 per cent to 12.81 per cent.

Out of four major selected crops in this paper only two major crops that are Rice and Cotton contributed significantly among the top major exported crops of India. The raw cotton inclusive waste was 13,58,000 tonnes in terms of quantity was exported during 2009-2010 which declined to 12,58,000 tonnes during 2010-2011 but in terms of value it increased to Rs 9537 crore from 2009-2010 to 12981 crore during 2010-2011. In the year 2011-2012 the exports of the same crop increased both in terms of quantity and value. Quantity increased to 12,58,000 tonnes from 2010-2011 to 20,13,000 tonnes in the year 2011-2012. In terms of value it was Rs 12981 crore during 2010-2011 which increased to Rs 21623 crore which is almost double in the year 2011-2012.

In case of basmati rice the quantity was increasing to 2017000 tonnes from 2009-2010 to 2186000 tonnes during 2010-2011.This quantity further increased to 1,54,50,000 tonnes in the year 2011-2012. On the other hand, the value of the same crop was Rs 10890 crore during 2009-2010 which reduced to Rs 10582 crore during 2010-2011 but it increased to Rs 15450 crores during 2011-2012.

In case of rice other than basmati the quantity was 1,40,000 tonnes during 2009-2010 which reduced to 96,000 tonnes in the year 2010-2012 but it tremendously increased in the year 2011-2012 (to 40,99,000 tonnes). Same way the value reduced too during 2009-2010 to 2010-2011from Rs 365 crores to Rs 220 crores. But it also increased tremendously from Rs 220 crores to Rs 8668 during 2010-2011 to 2011-2012 which is almost 40 times than the preceding year.

See the annexure Table 1 on page 26.

Production, Procurement and Procurement as percentage of Production of Wheat and Rice over the period of six years (2006-2007 to 2011-2012)

The main objectives of food management are procurement of foodgrains from farmers at remunerative prices, distribution of foodgrains to consumers, particularly the vulnerable sections of society at affordable prices and maintenance of buffer stock for food security and price stability. The Central Government extends price support to paddy, coarse grains and wheat through the FCI and State Agencies. All the foodgrains conforming to the prescribed specifications offered for sale at specified centres are bought by the public procurement agencies at the Minimum Support Price (MSP) inclusive of bonus announced, if any. The farmers have the option to sell their produce to FCI/ State Agencies at the MSP or in the open market as is advantageous to them. Government procurements of wheat and paddy during the last few years are shown in Fig.1(b) at annexure on page 26.

In recent years there has been a high procurement as percentage of production of rice and wheat mainly because of high production and surpluses of several agricultural commodities even in deficit states like Bihar, Assam, Eastern U.P. which have started generating surpluses of certain cereals. The excessive built up of stocks with FCI has been posing problems of storages which have high carrying costs. The excessive procurement by government has also not letting the private trade to play its role particularly in respect of two major cereals, namely wheat and rice that account for over 75 per cent of total foodgrain production in the country.

Thus, the growth rates of these products contribute significantly in food grain. For example, the production, procurement and procurement as percentage of production of wheat increased from 14.7 Per cent in 2006-2007 to 40.6 Per cent in 2011-2012 see annexure fig. no.1 (b) on page no.26 thus it increased near about three times in these five years.

In case of rice the production, procurement and procurement as percentage of production of rice also increased to 26.9 per cent from 2006-2007 to 39 per cent in 2011-12. See the annexure Fig. 1(a) on page 27.

Thus, as per the analyses of four major crops in terms of the production and contribution in foodgrain and exports in two Plan period (10th and 11th), it is found that more or less production of agricultural crops is increasing over the period of time. Consequently it strengthens the country in terms of foodgrain and exports of some major crops, particularly Basmati rice and Cotton. Moreover it will lead to increase foreign exchange reserve in the country. Therefore in a nutshell it can be undoubtedly said that the agriculture sector plays a leading role in the sustainable development of India because certain important measures have been taken by the government such as application of HIV technology in agriculture sector, expansion of irrigation facilities, credit facilities to the farmers, land reform policies, agricultural prices as well as marketing facilities for the crops.

Conclusion

As per the analysis of the finding, it is observed that the overall growth performance of agriculture sector has been fluctuating across the plan period among the selected crops under study. The production and yield rate of rice, wheat is increasing in relation to their occupied areas in 10th Plan period in comparison to 11th Plan. On the other side the yield rate of cotton is decreasing in 11th Plan period than in 11th Plan. But the performance of Bt cotton and hybrid maize is positive as their production and yield rate, both are increasing in relation to the occupied areas than the general cotton. Similarly in exports, the share of rice and cotton is increasing over the period of time. In case of food grain the rice and wheat has been playing an important role to make this country self-reliant as their contributions are also increasing gradually during the selected time under study. Consequently the overall positive performance of agriculture sector is not only restricted to its contribution in GDP, but also it has far reaching ability to impact on poverty alleviation and rural development. Several areas should be taken into consideration for the growth of agricultural crops, such as enhancing public sector investment in research apart from effective transfer of technology along with institutional reforms in the research to make it more accountable, conservation of land, water and biological resources, development of rainfed agriculture, the development of minor irrigation, timely and adequate availability of inputs, support for marketing information, increase flow of credit particularly to the small and marginal farmers.

Achievements of foodgrain and nutrition security and alleviation of poverty and unemployment on a sustainable basis also depend on the efficient use of natural resources (land/soil, water, agri-biodiversity and climate). Inefficient use and mismanagement of productive resources, especially land, water, energy and agrochemicals has vastly reduced fertility and damaged the physical, chemical and biological properties of the soil. The availability of land for agriculture purposes has already its limit.

The transition from traditional to high value agriculture growth will be primarily driven by private investment, which is three fourth of total investment in agriculture. However, this may happen rapidly and smoothly, if government policy acts as a catalyst by providing greater investment in R&D, roads and public irrigation.

Thus, the visionary role of agriculture sector depends on some important factors, like efficient markets at home, freers trades, comparative advantages, environmental sustainability. The agriculture sector calls for major reforms, from marketing to investment and institutional change, especially in water management, new technology, land markets and creation of efficient value chain. Now the time has come to see the potential importance of these practices not only for their economic interest but also as the basis of intensification and ecological sustainability. Therefore to conclude, it can be said that there should be fine tune balance between government policies and agricultural productivity. Government policies should be revised and reformed as per the requirements of agriculture sector, especially with regard to small-farm management practices in order to improve productivity, profitability and sustainability of the farming system which in turn contribute significantly to the overall sustainable development of India.

Annexure

Table 1: India's top 10 agricultural exports

Sl. No.	Item	2009-10		2010-11		2011-12		Percent change in Value during 2010-11 over 2009-10	Percent change in Value during 2011-12 over 2010-11
		Qty.	Value	Qty.	Value	Qty.	Value		
1	Cotton Raw incl. waste	1358	9537	1258	12961	2013	21623	36.1	66.6
2	Marine products	710	9999	801	11548	1032	16588	15.5	43.6
3	Guargum Meal	218	1138	408	2806	707	16557	147.7	482.9
4	Rice Basmati	2017	10890	2186	10582	3212	15450	-2.8	46.0
5	Meat & Preparations		6206		8776		14111	39.6	60.8
6	Spices	663	6157	749	7870	931	13176	27.8	67.4
7	Oil Meals	4671	7832	6798	10846	7436	11762	38.5	8.4
8	Sugar	45	110	3241	10339	2747	8779	9299.1	-15.1
9	Rice (other than Basmati)	140	365	96	220	4099	8668	-39.7	3840.0
10	Other cereals	2892	2973	3188	3596	4072	5479	21.0	52.4

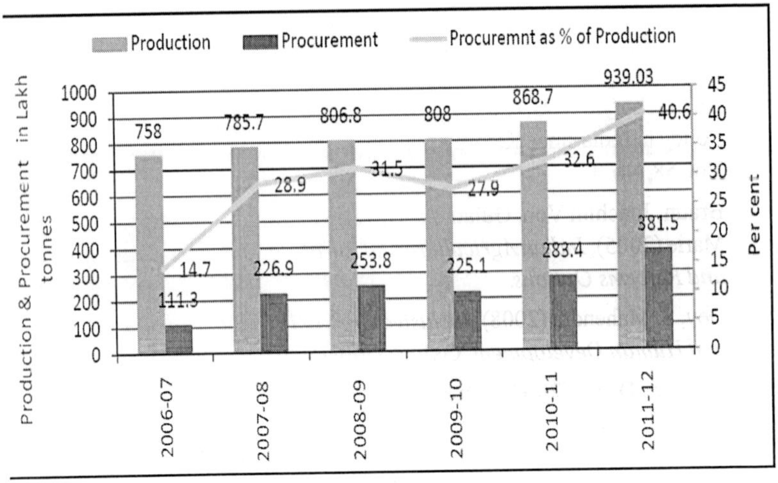

Fig. 1 (a): Production, Procurement and Procurement as per cent of Production of Wheat

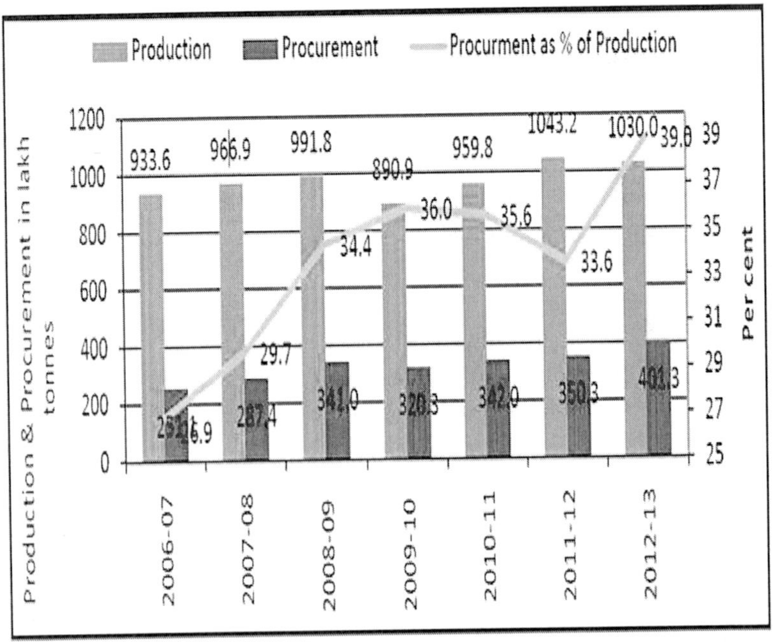

Fig. 1(b): Production, Procurement and Procurement as per cent of Production of Rice

References

- Amitha, D., (2010), 'Promoting Sustainable Agriculture in India'.
- Bhattacharya, B. B. (2003). Trade Liberalisation and Agricultural Price Policy in India since Reforms, *Indian Journal of Agricultural Economics,* Vol. 58, No. 3.
- Braun, Joachim Von, Gulati, A., Hazel, P., Mark W. Rosegrant and Ruel, Marie (2005), *Indian Agriculture and Rural Development-Strategic Issues and Reforms Options.*
- Dev, S. Mahendra (2008), *Inclusive Growth in India, Agriculture, Poverty and Human Development,* Oxford University Press, New Delhi
- Dlotter, D.W. (2003), Organic Agriculture, Journal of Sustainable Agriculture: Our Path Forward, Department Publication Services, Agriculture and Agri-Food Canada Ottawa, Ontario, Canada.
- Evenson, R. E., Pray, C and Rosegrant, M.W. (1999), Agricultural Research and Productivity Growth in India, Research Report No.109, International Food Policy Research Institute, Washington, DC.
- GOI (2007 a) *'Agricultural Strategy for the Eleventh Plan: Concerns and Way ahead,* Yojana Bhavan, New Delhi.
- GOI (2007) *''Report of the Steering Committee on Agriculture for 11th Five Year Plan,* Yojana Bhavan, New Delhi.
- Gulati, Ashok (2009), *''Emerging Trends in Indian Agriculture: What can we learn from these?''* Professooh. Dayanath Jha Memorial Lecture, National Centre for Agricultural Economic and Policy Research, New Delhi.
- Gulati, Ashok, Meinzen-Dick, Ruth and Raju, K.V. (2005), Institutional Reforms in India, Irrigation, Sage Publication.
- International Journal of Management Research and Technology 'Productivity and Sustainability in Agriculture: An Application of LPP Model', Vol. 2 No.2 July-Dec 2008.
- Kumar, Praduman and Mittal, Surabhi (2006), "Agricultural Productivity Tends in India: Sustainability Issues". *Agricultural Economic Research Review*, Volume 19, pp.71-88.
- Kushwara Niru (2003), Environment, Sustainable Development and Rural Poverty in India, Ph.D Thesis, M. J. P. Rohilkhand University, Bareilly Ch. 4.
- Mishra, S. K. and Puri V. K. (2010) , *"Indian Economy",* Himalaya Publishing House, Twenty Eighth Revised and Updated Editions.

- Mishra, V. N. and Rao, Govinda (2003), "Trade Policy, Agricultural Growth and Rural Poor: Indian Experience, 1978-79 to 1999-00", *Economic and Political Weekly*, October 25, 2003.
- Mittal Surabhi (2008 a), "Past Trends and Projection of Demand and Supply for Major Food Crops in India", Background Paper prepared for Planning Commission, Government of India, June, 2006.
- Promoting Sustainable Agriculture in India, Available at: *http://www.artilebase.com/agriculture-articles/promoting-sustaniable-agriculture-in-india-2132445.html#ixzzFWsPazLc*
- Puttaswamaiah, S (2005), Sustainable Agriculture and Exploratory Analysis of the Approcahes in India, Report under the Shastri Applied Research Programme by Indo-Shastri Canadian Institute, New Delhi, at the Gujarat Institute of Development Research, Ahmedabad.
- Rao, Hanumantha, C.H.(2003), "Reform Agenda for Agriculture", Economic and Political Weekly, Feb 15, 2003.
- State of Indian Agriculture (2012-13), Government of India, Ministry of Agriculture, Department of Agriculture and Cooperation Directorate of Economics and Statistics , New Delhi.
- Singh, Punjab (2002), Agricultural Policy-Vision 2020, Planning Commission, Available at *<http://planningcommission.nic.in/reports/genrep/bkpap2020/24_bg2020.pdf>*
- Virmani, Arvind (2004), Accelerating Growth and Poverty Reduction: A Policy Framework for India's Development, Academic Foundation, and New Delhi.
- Vyas, V.S. (2003), India's Agrarian Structure, Economic Policies and Sustainable Development, Academic Foundations Publishers, New Delhi.

5

Agricultural Credit and Agricultural Development in India

Kaberi Sarkar and **Sebak Kumar Jana**

1. Introduction

A large proportion of the population in India is rural based and depends on agriculture for a living. The agricultural sector is important as it plays a vital role in generating purchasing power among the rural population by creating on-farm and off-farm employment opportunities. The main cause of an Indian farmer for his indebtedness is his poverty. He has to borrow for various purposes as he has no past savings. Poverty forces him to borrow and remain indebted as he has very less to pay off his debt. Sometimes crops fail due to flood or drought, and therefore they require funds to support their families. With savings being negligible among the small farmers, agricultural credit appears to be an essential input along with modern technology for higher productivity. An important aspect that has emerged in the last three decades is that the credit is not only obtained by the small and marginal farmers for survival but also by the large farmers for enhancing their income. Hence, since independence, credit has been occupying an important place in the strategy for development of agriculture. The financial requirements of farmers are many, based on which they take short, medium or long-term loans. The short-term loan is for the purpose of cultivation, such as, to buy seeds, fertiliser or fodder for cattle or for household purposes, which is usually taken for less than 15 months. Hence the short term credit is mainly taken for financing crop production programmes. The form of mediumt-erm and long-term credit is for financing capital investment in agriculture and allied activities like land development including purchase of land, minor irrigation, farm mechanisation, dairy development, poultry, animal husbandry, fisheries, plantation, and horticulture. Loans are also available for storage, processing and marketing of agricultural produce. The medium term loan is for a period of 15 months to less than five years, which is taken to make land improvements, buy cattle or agricultural implements. The longterm loans are basically taken to make permanent improvements on land or to purchase additional land or to buy costly agricultural machinery or to repay old debts. This loan is usually for a period of more than five years. All the forms of credit which help the farmers in their agricultural operations are credit for production purpose. The rest which are taken for consumption for household purposes or for celebrations like marriages etc., are unproductive loans.

The sources of agricultural credit can be divided in two basic categories, formal and informal. The informal sources are the moneylenders, landlords and traders; from whom loans can be obtained easily and quickly, but the rates are usurious and their recovery rate is very high and these loans lead to poverty of Indian farmers. The small and marginal farmers often mortgage and ultimately lose their land to money lenders. The pre-dominance of moneylending has reduced a lot due to the multi-agency approach of the institutional sources, like the commercial banks, co-operatives banks and regional rural banks.

Agricultural credit has played a vital role in supporting farm production in India. Though the outreach and amount of agricultural credit have increased over the years, several weaknesses have crept in which have affected the viability and sustainability of these institutions. Agricultural credit is disbursed through a multiagency network consisting of Commercial Banks (CBs), Regional Rural Banks (RRBs) and Cooperatives. Facilitating credit through these institutional sources is vertically integrated with the farmers for providing them critical inputs or processing their produce, which increases the credit flow to agriculture significantly. But still the credit delivery to the agriculture sector continues to be inadequate. It appears that the banking system is still hesitant on various grounds to purvey credit to small and marginal farmers in fear of non-recovery.

The main factors behind financial unsustainability of the rural credit institutions are their overwhelming overdues or non-performing assets, high transaction cost, low financial margins and regulated interest rates. The cooperatives are heading towards a state of financial unsustainability. It appears that the banks, with the sole objective of eliminating in formal finance, have always been allowing leniency in their financial policies and still face high rate of default. They have failed to accumulate enough resource base. Therefore, it is recommended that they should be strengthened to accelerate the flow of credit to meet the credit demands of the agricultural sector and bring overall development in the rural economy.

In this study we aim to analyse the overall effect of institutional credit on agricultural growth of the country. Credit, as one of the critical non-land inputs, has two dimensions from the viewpoint of its contribution to the augmentation of agricultural growth viz., availability of credit or its amount and the distribution of credit. In the following section we would analyse the institutional arrangements of credit for agriculture.

The policy of agricultural credit is guided mainly by the considerations of ensuring adequate and timely availability of credit at reasonable rates. The demand for agricultural credit arises due to: (i) the time lag and risk factor working between the realisation of income and the act of expenditure; (ii) lumpiness of investment in fixed capital formation; and (iii) sudden increases in capital needs that accompany technological innovations.

2. Institutional Arrangements for Agricultural Credit

Before the First Plan began in 1951, almost all the financial needs of rural sector as well as the agricultural sector were provided by the moneylenders. A shortage of supply of rural credit was prevalent in India. At that time, the Reserve Bank was very active in pursuing cooperative movements through a variety of initiatives. Despite all those efforts, about four per cent of the total outstanding debt as at end-June 1951. Only 3.3 per cent of the cultivators had access to credit from cooperatives, and 0.9 per cent from commercial banks. Furthermore, the funds supplied by the moneylenders were subject to high interest rates and other usurious practices. This finding of the Report of the All India Rural Credit Survey (RBI, 1954), AIRCS henceforth, laid the foundation stone for furthering the role of institutional credit to rural sector through formal channel of cooperatives and commercial banks.

Institutional involvement in the sphere of agricultural credit could be traced back to the enactment of the Cooperative Societies Act in 1904.To meet the demand for short and long-term rural credit the Co-operative Credit Structure (CCS) was set up.There are approximately 100,000 village-level Primary Agricultural Credit Societies (PACS), 368 District Central Cooperative Banks (DCCBs) with 12,858 branches and 30 State Cooperative Banks (SCBs) with 953 branches providing primarily short and medium-term agricultural credit in India. The long-term cooperative structure consists of 19 State Cooperative Agricultural and Rural Development Banks (SCARDBs), with 2609 operational units as on 31st March 2005 comprising 788 branches and 772 Primary Agricultural and Rural Development Banks (PA&RDBs) with 1049 branches. Over time the public sector banks have made commendable progress in terms of putting in place a wide banking network, particularly in the aftermath of nationalisation of banks in 1969. The number of offices of public sector banks increased rapidly from 8,262 in June 1969 to 68,355 by March 2005.

The multi-agency approach: At present agricultural credit is disbursed through a multiagency network consisting of Commercial Banks (CBs), Regional Rural Banks (RRBs) and Cooperatives. The evolution of institutional credit to agriculture could be broadly classified into four distinct phases - 1904-1969 (predominance of co-operatives and setting up of RBI), 1969-1975 [nationalisation of commercial banks to the setting up of Regional Rural Banks (RRBs)], 1975-1990 (setting up of NABARD in 1982) and from 1991 onwards (financial sector reforms).

The inadequacy of rural credit continued to engage the attention of the Reserve Bank and the Government throughout the 1950s and 1960s. The

Agricultural Refinance Corporation (ARC) was set up by the Reserve Bank in 1963 to provide funds by way of refinance, but credit cooperatives still did not function too well. Consequently, the All India Rural Credit Review Committee chaired by Shri B. Venkatappiah, was setup in July 1966 to, review the supply of rural credit in the context of the Fourth Five Year Plan in general, and the requirements of the intensive programmes of agricultural production in different parts of the country, and to make recommendations for improving the flow of agricultural credit. After a comprehensive review, the Committee recommended that the commercial banks should play a complementary role, along with co-operatives, in extending rural credit. The setting up of Regional Rural Banks in 1975, and formation of National Bank for Agriculture and Rural Development (NABARD) in 1982 - all these efforts by the Reserve Bank were to institutionalise the credit channel for rural sector. The outreach of banks was enlarged considerably within a relatively short period of time. The concept of priority sector was introduced in 1969 to underscore the imperative of financing certain neglected sectors like agriculture. The channelising of credit to the priority sectors was sought to be achieved through the stipulation that a certain proportion of the total net bank credit be deployed in these sectors by specific target dates. In the 1990s and 2000s, the concept of micro-credit along with micro finance institutions and self help group (SHG)-Bank linkage models evolved with the institutional support of the Reserve Bank and NABARD in order to help the poor in providing credit without collaterals.

Decentralised credit planning through the Lead Bank Scheme was also introduced under which each district was placed with one of the commercial banks (called the district Lead Bank) to spearhead the creditallocation for agricultural lending. In order to emphasise the developmental and promotional role assigned to the ARC in addition to refinancing, the Corporation was renamed as the Agricultural Refinance and Development Corporation (ARDC) by an amendment to the Act in 1975. The Green Revolution then followed in the late 1960s and 1970. snecessitating adequate availability of credit that could enable the purchase of inputs such as fertiliser, high yielding varieties of seeds, pump sets for irrigation, etc. Despite all these efforts, the flow of credit to the agricultural sector failed to exhibit any appreciable improvement due to the fact that commercial banks were not tuned to the needs and requirements of the small and marginal farmers, while the co-operatives, on the other hand, lacked resources to meet the expected demand. NABARD is the Apex institution which has been entrusted with a pivotal role in the sphere of policy planning and providing refinance facilities to rural financial institutions to augment their resource base. Since its inception, the NABARD has played a central role in providing financial assistance, facilitating institutional development and encouraging promotional efforts in the area of rural credit. NABARD also administers the Rural Infrastructure Development Fund (RIDF), which was set up in 1995-96; the corpus of RIDF is contributed by scheduled commercial banks to the extent of their short fall in agricultural lending under the priority sector targets. NABARD has been playing a catalytic role in micro-credit through the Self-Help Groups (SHGs).

Though the geographical spread, functional reach and consequent decline in the influence of informal sources of credit were impressive, still rural financial institutions were characterised by several weaknesses, viz., decline in productivity and efficiency; erosion of repayment ethics and profitability. On the eve of the 1991 reforms, the rural credit delivery system was again found to be in a poor condition. The Report of the Committee on the Financial Sector chaired by Shri M. Narasimham, 1991, provided the blue print for carrying out overall financial sector reforms during the 1990s. Furthermore, weaknesses in the performance of rural financial institutions since 1991 resulted in setting up of various committees/working groups/task forces to look into their operations such as: "The High-level Committee on Agricultural Credit through Commercial Banks" (R. V. Gupta, 1998), "Task Force to Study the Functions of Cooperative Credit System and to Suggest Measures for its Strengthening" (Jagdish Capoor, 1999), "Expert Committee on Rural Credit" (V.S. Vyas, 2001). At present, scheduled commercial banks (excluding RRBs), are expected to ensure that the priority sector advances constitute 40 per cent of net bank credit and within the overall lending target of 40 per cent, 18 per cent of net bank credit goes to agricultural sector. To ensure that the focus of banks on direct category of agricultural advances does not get diluted, lendings under indirect category should not exceed one-fourth of the agricultural sub-target of 18 per cent, i.e., 4.5 per cent of net bank credit.

3. Flow of Agricultural Credit

Credit, as one of the critical non-land inputs, has two-ways of its contribution to the augmentation of agricultural growth viz., availability of amount of credit and the distribution of credit. The foundation for building a broader credit infrastructure for rural credit was laid by the Report of the All India Rural Credit Survey (1954). The Committee that conducted this survey observed that agricultural credit fell short of the right quantity, was not of the right type, did not serve the right purpose and often failed to go to the right people. The Committee also observed that the performance of co-operatives in the sphere of agricultural credit was deficient in more than one way, but at the same time, co-operatives had a vital role in channelising credit to the farmers and therefore summed up that, "Cooperation has failed, but Co-operation must succeed". The Committee, apart from visualising co-operatives as an exclusive agency for providing credit to agriculture, urged a well defined role for commercial banks in delivering credit for agriculture in specialised areas, such as marketing, processing, storage and warehousing. Towards this end, it recommended establishment of the State Bank of India and through it, extension of commercial banking facilities to rural and semi-urban areas. Augmenting credit flow at the ground level through credit planning, adoption of region-specific strategies, rationalisation of lending policies and procedures for bringing down the cost of borrowing were the main issues to be sorted out.

In order to improve the flow of credit to the agricultural sector, the Reserve Bank had advised public sector banks to prepare Special Agricultural Credit Plans (SACP) in 1994-95. Under the SACP, the banks are required to fix self-set targets for achievement during the year (April- March). The targets are generally fixed by the banks about 20 to 25 per cent higher over the disbursements made in the previous year. With the introduction of SACP, the flow of credit to agricultural sector has increased significantly from Rs 8,255 crore in 1994-95 to Rs 1,22,443 crore in 2006-07 which were higher than the projection of Rs 1,18,160 crore. As against the target of Rs 1,52,133 crore for the financial year 2007-08, disbursements to agriculture by public sector banks under the plan were Rs 1,11,543 crore. As recommended by the Advisory Committee on Flow of Credit to Agriculture and Related Activities from the Banking System (Chairman: Shri V. S. Vyas), the Mid-Term Review of Annual Policy of RBI for 2004-05 made the SACP mechanism applicable to private sector banks from the year 2005-06. Disbursements to agriculture by private sector banks under SACP during 2006-07 aggregated to Rs 44, 093 crore against the target of Rs 40,656 crore. As against the target of Rs 41,427 crore for the financial year 2007-08, disbursements to agriculture by private sector banks aggregated to Rs 45,905 crore.

From the Government side, with a view to doubling credit flow to agriculture within a period of three years and to provide some relief to farmers affected by natural calamities within the limits of financial prudence, the Union Finance Minister announced several measures on June 18, 2004. Accordingly, the Reserve Bank and NABARD issued necessary operational guidelines to banks. From the very beginning, the actual disbursements exceeded the targets for each of the last four years. As against the target of Rs 2,25,000 crore for 2007-08, all banks disbursed Rs 2,25,348 crore. During 2007-08, 7.29 million new farmers were financed by commercial banks and RRBs as against the target of Five million farmers fixed by the Union Finance Minister for the year. The Finance Minister, in his Budget Speech for the year 2008-09, urged the banks to increase the level of credit to Rs 2,80,000 crore during the year 2008-09.

A comprehensive credit policy was announced by the Government of India on 18 June, 2004. The share of institutional credit, which was little over saven per cent in 1951, increased manifold to over 68 per cent in 2010, reflecting a remarkable decline in the share of non institutional credit from around 93 per cent to about 30 per cent during the same period. However, the latest NSSO Survey reveals that the share of non-institutional credit has taken a reverse swing which is a cause of concern (Table 1).

Table 1

Relative Share of Borrowing of Cultivator Households from Different Sources (per cent)

Sources	*1951*	*1961*	*1971*	*1981*	*1991*	*2002*	*2010*
1	2	3	4	5	6	7	8
Non-Institutional	92.7	91.3	68.3	36.8	30.6	38.9	29.7
Money Lenders	69.7	49.2	36.1	16.1	17.5	26.8	21.9
Institutional	7.3	18.7	31.7	63.2	66.3	61.3	68.8
Cooperative							
Societies/Banks	3.3	2.6	22	29.8	23.6	30.2	24.9
Commercial Banks	0.9	0.6	2.4	28.8	35.2	26.3	25.1
Unspecified	0	0	0	0	3.1	0	1.5
Total	**100**	**100**	**100**	**100**	**100**	**100**	**100**

Source : All India Debt and Investment Survey and NSSO.

It can be seen from the above data that the role of moneylenders which was very dominant (almost 70 per cent) in 1951 has fallen considerably to 22 per cent in 2010, but this should be totally removed. The rising trend of the institutional sources suddenly came to a decline from 1991-92 to 2001-2002, which was mainly due to a decline in commercial banks' contribution to the institutional sources. Both cooperative credit and commercial bank credit fell considerably in 2010. Commercial bank credit was 35 per cent in 1991 which fell to 25 per cent in 2010. Cooperative credit was 30 per cent in 2002 which showed a fall in 2010 to 25 per cent.

The contribution of cooperative societies, commercial banks and regional rural banks (RRBs) to institutional credit for agriculture can be studied from the following table (Table 2).

Table 2

Institutional Credit to Agriculture (in Rs crore)

Year	*Co-operative Banks*	*Share (%)*	*RRBs*	*Share*	*Commercial Banks*	*Total*	*Per cent (%)*	*Increase*
1	2	3	4	5	6	7	8	9
1985-86	3,874	55	–	–	3,131	45	7,005	–
1986-87	4,207	52	–	–	3,809	48	8,016	14
1987-88	4,420	52	–	–	4,009	48	8,429	5
1988-89	4,851	53	–	–	4,233	47	9,084	8
1989-90	5,082	52	–	–	4,719	48	9,801	8
1990-91	3,408	39	–	–	5,438	61	8,846	-10
1991-92	5,800	52	596	5	4,806	43	11,202	27
1992-93	9,378	62	831	5	4,960	33	15,169	35
1993-94	10,117	61	977	6	5,400	33	16,494	9
1994-95	9,406	50	1,083	6	8,255	44	18,744	14
1995-96	10,479	48	1,381	6	10,172	46	22,032	18
1996-97	11,944	45	1,684	6	12,783	48	26,411	20
1997-98	14,085	44	2,040	6	15,831	50	31,956	21
1998-99	15,916	43	2,538	7	18,443	50	36,897	15
1999-00	18,363	40	3,172	7	24,733	53	46,268	25
2000-01	20,801	39	4,219	8	27,807	53	52,827	14
2001-02	23,604	38	4,854	8	33,587	54	62,045	17
2002-03	23,716	34	6,070	9	39,774	57	69,560	12
2003-04	26,959	31	7,581	9	52,441	60	86,981	25
2004-05	31,424	25	12,404	10	81,481	65	125309	44
2005-06	39,404	22	15,223	8	125,859	70	180486	44
2006-07	33,174	22	15,170	10	100999	68	150156	49
2007-08	35,875	20	17,987	10	128876	70	182738	51
2008-09	36,165	19	19,325	10	132761	71	188251	53
2009-10	32,871	18	23,984	13	121879	69	178734	–

Note: Commercial Banks and RRBs were clubbed together up to 1990-91.

Source: Economic Survey and NABARD various issues.

As can be seen from the data, co-operative banks have lost their dominant position in relation to commercial banks from 55 per cent in 1985-86 to18 in 2009-10. The share of commercial banks including RRBs during the above period increased from 45 per cent in 1985-86 to almost 82 per cent in 2009-10 The efforts to increase the flow of credit to agriculture seems to have yielded better results in the recent period as the total institutional credit to agriculture recorded a growth of around 23 per cent during the period 1995-96 to 2008-09. In terms of total credit to agriculture, the commercial banks recorded a considerable growth (from around 43 per cent to about 69 per cent), while cooperative banks registered a fall (52 per cent to 18 per cent) during the above period. There is a considerable increase in the contribution of RRBs from five per cent in 1985-86 to 13 per cent in 2009-10 (Table 2).

4. Sectoral Deployment of Gross Bank Credit

The growth of direct finance to agriculture and allied activities witnessed a decline in the 1990s (12 per cent) as compared to the 1980s (14 per cent) and 1970s (around 16 per cent). From 1996-97 to 2009-10 only a marginal increase of 2 per cent was observed in the growth of direct institutional finance to agriculture. A comparative analysis of direct credit to agriculture and allied activities during 1980s and 1990s reveals the fact that the average share of long-term credit in the total direct finance has not only been much lower but has also decelerated (from over 38 per cent to around 36 per cent), which had a dampening effect on the agricultural investment for future growth process.

The sectoral deployment of gross bank credit is displayed in Table 3 for the period 1990-91 to 2001-02, the latest year for which the data are available.

Table 3 Sectoral Deployment of Gross Bank Credit

Year	*Gross Bank Credit*	*Priority Sector*	*Agriculture*	*Share of*	*SSIs Agri in Total*	*Other*	*Industry Priority Sector*	*Share of Industry In Total*
1	2	3	4	5	6	7	8	9
1996-97	258991	84880	31442	12.14	35944	17494	102604	39.62
1997-98	300283	99507	34869	11.61	43508	21130	117350	39.08
1998-99	342012	114611	39643	11.59	48483	26494	130516	38.16
1999-00	400818	131827	44381	11.07	52841	34362	147319	36.75
2000-01	469153	154414	51922	11.07	56002	46490	162837	34.71
2001-02	536727	175259	60761	11.32	57119	57299	172324	32.11
2002-03	669534	211609	73518	10.98	60394	77697	235168	35.12
2003-04	764383	263834	90541	11.84	65855	107438	247210	32.34
2004-05	1040909	381476	125250	12.03	74588	181638	352304	33.85
2005-06	1445837	509910	172279	11.92	90239	247379	458808	31.75
2009-10	2045897	876459	267840	13.09	209679	379430	698560	32.75

Source : Report on Trend and Progress of Banking in India, Various issues.

State-wise Distribution of Institutional Credit

There are wide variations in the availability of institutional credit per hectare of gross cropped area in different States. It was as high as Rs 9,403 in Tamil Nadu, Rs 7, 666 in Kerala, Rs 5,352 in Punjab and Rs 4,604 in Andhra Pradesh, while it was as low as Rs 311 in Assam, Rs 667 in Rajasthan and Rs 698 in Madhya Pradesh during 2001-02 (Table 4).

Table 4: Distribution of Flow of Institutional Agricultural Credit in Different States of India (in Rs crore)

	1990-91		*2001-02*				*Rs/hectare GCA*		
Region State		*% to All India*		*% to All India*	*Annual Increase (%)*	*% of GCA (1998-99)*	*1991*	*2001*	*Annual Increase (%)*
1	2	3	4	5	6	7	8	9	10
Northern	1314	12.9	8236	19.9	43.9	20.25	377	2132	38.9
Punjab	642	6.3	4304	10.4	47.5	4.22	856	5352	43.8
Haryana	285	2.8	1821	4.4	44.5	3.22	482	2964	42.9
Rajasthan	326	3.2	1490	3.6	29.7	11.7	168	667	24.7
Himachal Pradesh	20	0.2	248	0.6	93.2	0.51	207	2555	94.5
Jammu Kashmir	20	0.2	83	0.2	25.5	0.57	191	764	25
North-Eastern	41	0.4	207	0.5	34	2.9	96	374	31.4
Assam	20	0.2	124	0.3	42.4	2.09	54	311	39.9
Eastern	846	8.3	3062	7.4	21.8	14.71	463	1092	22.8
Orissa	306	3	414	1	3	4.53	319	479	4.2
West Bengal	285	2.8	1573	3.8	37.6	4.83	329	1708	34.9
Bihar (including Jharkhand)	245	2.4	1076	2.6	28.3	5.25	233	1075	30.1
Central	1722	16.9	5835	14.1	19.9	27.57	349	1110	18.2
Madhya Pradesh (including Chhatt.,)	746	7.5	1821	4.4	11.5	13.67	320	698	9.9
Uttar Pradesh (Including Uttarn.,)	958	9.4	4056	9.8	27	13.9	376	1529	25.6
Western	1386	13.6	5959	14.4	27.5	7.06	430	1831	27.4
Gujarat	520	5.1	2980	7.2	19.5	5.56	501	2809	38.3
Maharashtra	846	8.3	2938	7.1	20.6	11.4	387	1353	20.8
Southern	4880	47.9	18127	43.8	22.6	17.51	1410	5426	23.8
Andhra Pradesh	1477	14.5	5587	13.5	23.2	6.63	1120	4604	25.9
Karnataka	642	6.3	4041	9.7	43.8	6.13	546	3432	44.1
Kerala	835	8.2	2276	5.5	14.4	1.56	2766	7666	14.8
Tamil Nadu	1895	18.6	6166	14.9	18.8	3.44	2857	9403	19.1
All-India	10188	100	41385	100	25.5	100	549	2169	24.6

GCA refers to gross cropped area.

Source : Report of the Advisory Committee on Flow of Credit to Agriculture and Related Activities from the Banking System, RBI, Mumbai, 2004.

The accessibility to institutional credit was higher in the Southern region where the level of agricultural development is also higher. It is a kind of vicious cycle operating in less developed States. Less availability of credit influences adversely the adoption of modern technology and private capital investments, which in turn lowers the productive capacity of the agricultural sector and results in lower productivity and production, and also pushes the farmers to borrow from non-institutional sources. Consequently, the demand for agricultural credit for short and long-term purposes is dampened.

5. Recent Policy Developments

Rural Infrastructure Development Fund (RIDF) was set up under the initiative of the Government of India in 1995-96 by NABARD with an initial corpus of Rs 2,000 crore to provide loans to State Governments for financing rural infrastructure projects and since then, 11 tranches of allocations have been made towards the Fund. Commercial banks make contributions towards the fund on account of the shortfalls in their priority/agriculture sector lending. The scope of RIDF has been widened to enable utilisation of loan by Panchayati Raj Institutions (PRIs), Self-Help Groups (SHGs), Non-Government Organisations (NGOs), etc., since 1999-2000. Many rural infrastructure projects have been started but are lying incomplete for want of resources which represents a major loss of potential income and employment to rural population. The Fund has continued with additional corpus being announced every year in the Union Budget.

Table 5 : RIDF : Tranche-wise Size of Corpus (Rs. crore)

RIDF Tranche	*Year*	*Corpus*
RIDF I	1995-96	**2000**
RIDF II	1996-97	**2500**
RIDF III	1997-98	**2500**
RIDF IV	1998-99	**3000**
RIDF V	1999-2000	**3500**
RIDF VI	2000-2001	**4500**
RIDF VII	2001-2002	**5000**
RIDF VIII	2002-2003	**5500**
RIDF IX	2003-2004	**5500**
RIDF X	2004-2005	**8000**
RIDF XI	2005-2006	**8000**
RIDF XII	2006-2007	**9000**
RIDF XIII	2007-2008	**9500**
RIDF XIV	2008-2009	**9800**
Total		**78300**

Source: 1. NABARD Annual Report.

2. RBI Bulletin

In addressing the distributional aspects of credit in the recent years two innovations, viz., micro-finance and Kisan Credit Card Scheme (KCCS) have emerged as the major policy developments. The KCCS has emerged as the most effective mode of credit delivery to agriculture in terms of the timeliness, hassle-free operations as also adequacy of credit with minimum transaction costs and documentation. Around 59.09 million KCCs were issued till end-March 2006. The cooperative banks (51.5 per cent) had a major share followed by commercial banks (36.9 per cent) and RRBs (11.6 per cent) (Table 6).

Table 6: Agency-wise and Year-wise KCC (Number in Millions)

Year	*Cooperative Bank*	*RRBs*	*Commercial Bank*	*Total*
1	2	3	4	5
1998-99	0.16	0.01	0.62	0.78
1999-00	3.6	0.17	1.37	5.13
2000-01	5.61	0.56	2.39	8.65
2001-02	5.44	0.83	3.07	9.34
2002-03	4.58	0.96	2.7	8.24
2003-04	4.88	1.27	3.09	9.25
2004-05	3.56	1.73	4.4	9.68
2005-06	2.6	1.25	4.17	8.01
2006-07	3.8	1.76	4.54	9.54
2007-08	3.96	1.95	4.21	10.45
2008-09	4.65	1.99	4.64	10.98
Total	**42.82**	**12.58**	**35.19**	**90.59**
Share in Total (Per cent)	**47.28**	**13.87**	**38.85**	**100**

Source : Report on Trend and Progress of Banking in India, RBI.

Micro finance is an approach which ensures banking with the poor with lower transaction cost and high repayment. The micro credit programme, which was introduced in 1992 with a pilot project of linking around 500 SHGs has made rapid progress in India exhibit in gconsiderable democratic functioning and group dynamism. The programme has now assumed the form of a micro finance movement in many parts of the country. There was a massive expansion during 2004-05 with the banking system establishing credit linkage with

539 thousands new SHGs, taking the cumulative number of such SHGs to 4.8 million at end March 2009. Banks extended loans aggregating Rs 22456 crore at end-March 2009 registering a growth of 58.3 per cent over the previous year.

Table 7: SHG-Bank Linkage Programme

	Total SHGs Financed by Banks in '000		*Banks Loans (Rs Crores)*		*Refinance (Rs Crores)*	
Year	*During the year*	*Cumulative*	*During the year*	*Cumulative*	*During the year*	Cumulative
1	2	3	4	5	6	7
1999-00	81.78	114.78	136	193	98	150
	147.9	247.9	138.6	238.6	88.5	188.5
2000-01	149.05	263.83	288	481	251	401
	82.3	129.9	111.8	149.2	156.1	167.3
2001-02	197.65	461.48	546	1026	396	797
	32.6	74.9	89.6	113.3	57.8	98.8
2002-03	255.88	717.36	1022	2049	622	1419
	29.5	55.4	87.2	99.7	57.1	78
2003-04	361.73	1079.09	1856	3904	705	2125
	41.4	50	81.6	90.5	13.3	49.7
2004-05	539.39	1618.48	2994	6899	968	3092
	49.1	50	61.4	76.7	37.3	45.5
2005-06	620	2239	4449	11398	1068	4160
	15	38.3	50.3	65.2	10.3	34.5
2006-07	686	2924	6643	18041	1299	5459
	11	30.6	47.6	58.3	21.6	31.2
2007-08	798	3456	7829	20342	1467	6098
	13.4	45.3	51.4	61.6	26.1	36.2
2008-09	824	4812	8735	22456	1642	7541
	14.3	37.5	61.5	56.4	23.5	34.7

Notes :

1. Figures in parentheses indicate percentage variations over the previous year.
2. Data for 2008-09 are provisional.

Source: Report on Trend and Progress of Banking in India, various issues.

The major thrust of micro finance is through the SHGs, Non-Governmental Organisations (NGOs), Credit Unions and the NABARD is trying to actively promote these institutions through refinance and training, but still the institutional credit delivery system is suffering from poor recovery rate which has a negative effect on sanctions of fresh credit. Several Committees were set up from time to time to look into the various issues relating to credit delivery for agriculture, the recent one being Advisory Committee on Flow of Credit to Agriculture and Related Activities from the Banking System chaired by Professooh. V.S. Vyas, June, 2004.The Government has since approved rehabilitation package for some districts in the States of Andhra Pradesh, Karnataka, Kerala, and Maharashtra. Altogether, the rehabilitation package for the four States involves a total amount of Rs 16,978 crore consisting of Rs 10,579 crore as subsidy/grants and Rs 6,399 crore as loan. In order to give further fillip to micro-finance movement, the RBI has enabled Non-Governmental Organisations (NGOs) engaged in micro-finance activities to access external commercial borrowings (ECBs) up to US $ 5 million during a financial year for permitted end-use, under automatic route, as an additional channel. As a follow-up of the Union Budget proposals, modalities for allowing banks to adopt the agency model for providing credit support to rural and farm sectors and appointment of micro-finance institutions (MFIs) as banking correspondents have also been worked out.

Despite the rapid spread of micro-finance programme, the distribution of SHGs is skewed across the States. More than 50 per cent of the total SHG credit linkages in the country are concentrated in the Southern States. In the States, which have a larger share of the poor, the coverage is comparatively low. The tragic incidents of farmers' suicides in some of the States have been a matter of serious concern. The causes behind are crop losses, consecutive failure of monsoon, recurrent droughts, mounting debts, mono-cropping, land tenancy which led many distressed farmers to commit suicide. They were dependent on rain-fed agriculture and were small and marginal farmers. They had borrowed from non-institutional sources and the interest rates charged on such debts ranged very high. Several measures to tackle the situation can be suggested which include improvement of irrigation coverage; crop diversification; promotion of animal husbandry as an alternate source of income; better accessibility to institutional credit and overall improvement of the marketing infrastructure.

With regard to KCCS, there is a need to upscale its outreach to cover all the eligible farmers by creating greater awareness and giving greater publicity to the scheme. Updation of land records and sensitisation of bank staff through training programmes will further add to the spread of the scheme. The exercise of preparing special agricultural credit plans with higher component of direct finance with a special thrust on small and marginal farmers should also receive high priority.The success of KCC scheme depends on less stipulated norms. High value agriculture needs higher working capital and also entails higher risks. Facilitating credit through processors, input dealers, NGOs, that are vertically integrated with the farmers, through contract farming, for providing them critical inputs or processing their produce, could increase the credit flow to agriculture significantly.

Assessment of Progress in Agricultural Production in India

Since the mid-1990s, the growth of the agricultural sector has been low as well as volatile; the growth decelerated from an annual average of 4.7 per cent per annum during 1980s to 3.1 per cent during the 1990s and further to 2.2 per cent during the 10 Plan period. Growth in agricultural production has decelerated during 2006-07 with the agriculture sector characterised by stagnation in output of major foodgrains. Per capita availability of foodgrains has, thus, fallen close to the levels prevailing during the 1970s.

Volatility in agricultural production has not only affected overall growth but also exerted persistent pressure on maintaining low and stable inflation. Demand-supply gaps were reflected in higher domestic food prices in recent years. All these evidences apparently point to the fact that higher credit to agriculture is not translated into commensurate increase in agricultural output.

In India, the share of agriculture in the gross domestic product has registered a steady decline from 36.4 per cent in 1982-83 to 18.5 per cent in 2006-07. Agriculture growth has remained lower than the growth rates witnessed in the industrial and services sectors. The gap between the growth of agriculture and non-agriculture sector began to widen since 1981-82, and more particularly since 1996-97, because of acceleration in the growth of industry and services sectors (Table 8). Even though the share of agriculture in GDP has declined over the years, the number of people dependent on agriculture for their food and livelihood has remained unchanged. Therefore, a number of measures were taken by the Reserve Bank and the Government of India for facilitating increased credit flows to the agriculture sector. With a view to doubling credit flow to agriculture within a period of three years, several measures have been announced.

Table 8: Average GDP growth rates of agriculture and other sectors at 1999-2000 prices per cent

Period		*Total Economic*	*Agriculture and Allied*	*Crops live stock*	*Non-agriculture*
1	2	3	4	5	6
Pre-Green Revolution	1951-52 to 1967-68	3.7	2.5	2.7	4.9
Green Revolution period	1968-69 to 1980-81	3.5	2.4	2.7	4.4
Wider technology dissemination period	1981-82 to 1990-91	5.4	3.5	3.7	6.4
Early Reform Period	1991-92 to 1996-97	5.7	3.7	3.7	6.6
Ninth and Tenth Plan	1997-98 to 2006-07	6.6	2.5	2.5	7.9
	2005-06 to 2006-07	9.5	4.8	5	10.7

Source: Economic Survey (2007-08).

The increased credit flow to agriculture has not resulted in commensurate increase in production. The average rate of growth of foodgrains production decelerated to 1.2 per cent during 1990-2007, lower than annual rate of growth of population, averaging 1.9 per cent. The per capita availability of cereals and pulses has witnessed a decline during this period. The consumption of cereals declined from a peak of 468 grams per capita per day in 1990-91 to 412 grams per capita per day in 2005-06, indicating a decline of 13 per cent during this period. The consumption of pulses declined from 42 grams per capita per day (72 grams in 1956-57) to 33 grams per capita per day during the same period. The overall production of foodgrains was estimated at 217.3 million tonnes in 2006-07, an increase of 4.2 per cent over 2005-06. Compared to the target set for 2006-07, it was, however, lower by 2.7 million tonnes (1.2 per cent). Over a medium-term, there has generally been a shortfall in the achievement of target of foodgrains, pulses and oilseeds during 2000-01 to 2006-07. The actual production of foodgrains on an average was 93 per cent of the target (Table 10). Actual production, however, was only 87.7 per cent of target for pulses and 85.3 per cent of target for oil seeds. From the very beginning, the actual disbursements exceeded the targets for each of the last four years

(Table 9).

Table 9: Targets and actual disbursement to agriculture by banks (Rs crore)

Agency	*Tar*	*Disbu*	*Tar*	*Disbur*	*Tar*	*Disbur*	*Target*	*Disbur*
1	2	3	4	5	6	7	8	9
Comm	57,000	81,481	87,200	1,25,477	1,19,000	16,64,486	1,50,000	1,56,850
Coop	39,000	31,231	38,600	39,786	41,000	42,480	52,000	43,684
RRBs	8,500	12,404	15,200	15,223	15,000	20,435	23,000	24,814
Other Agencies		193						
Total	**1,05,000**	**1,25,309**	**1,41,000**	**1,80,486**	**1,75,000**	**2,29,401**	**2,25,000**	**2,25,348**

Source: NABARD; *: Provisional; RRBs: Regional Rural Banks.

The production of agriculture crops, besides the weather-induced fluctuations, significantly depends on the availability of inputs like fertilisers, irrigation, certified seeds, credit support and appropriate price signals. Minimum support prices indicated upfront and before the sowing seasons act as effective incentives for acreage response of the agricultural crops. Deviations in foodgrains and agricultural output from their long-term trends are determined, among other factors, by variations in monsoon around its long-term trend and the area under irrigation.

Table 10 : Actual production relative to targets (Per cent)

Crop	*2001 -02*	*2002 -03*	*2003 -04*	*2004 -05*	*2005 -06*	*2006 -07*	*Average (2001-07)*
1	2	3	4	5	6	7	8
Rice	101.5	77.2	95.2	88.9	104.5	100.6	94.7
Wheat	93.3	84.3	92.5	86.3	91.8	100.4	91.4
Coarse cereals	101.1	79	110.6	90.9	93.3	92.9	94.6
Pulses	89.1	69.6	99.4	85.8	88.4	93.7	87.7
Food grains	97.6	79.4	96.9	88.1	97	98.8	93
Oilseeds	37.8	55	102	93	105.2	82.6	85.3
Sugarcane	91.4	89.8	73.1	87.8	118.4	131.7	98.7
Cotton	68.9	57.5	91.5	109.5	112.1	122.3	93.7
Jute and Mesta	106.2	94	93.1	87.1	96.1	99.9	96.1

Source: Economic Survey (2007-08).

The rate of growth of rice and wheat was vey insignificant during the period 2002-03 to 2005-06 in relation to that of pulses. The rate of growth of total foodgrains production was only 1.6 per cent during this period. The rate of growth of cotton production was as high as 20 per cent and that of oilseeds was nine per cent whereas sugarcane showed a declining trend. The rate of growth of production for major crops is shown in Table-11 below.

Table 11: Rate of growth of production for major crops (Per cent)

Year	*Rice*	*Wheat*	*Pulses*	*Food grains*	*Cotton*	*Oilseeds*	*Sugarcane*
1	2	3	4	5	6	7	8
1989-90 to 2006-07	1.17	1.9	-0.03	1.18	2.04	1.25	1.13
1992-93 to 1996-97	1.73	3.6	0.66	1.88	4.88	3.57	3.74
1997-98 to 2001-02	1.13	1.26	-2.52	0.67	5.79	-4.68	1.23
2002-03 to 2005-06	1.75	0.42	3.27	1.61	20.22	9.81	-1.23

Source: Economic Survey (2007-08).

On the productivity front, India is not only low relative to other countries in crop production, there are considerable inter-state variations. The productivity of wheat in 2005-06 varied from a low of 1,393 kg per ha in Maharashtra to a high of 4,179 kg in Punjab. The Steering Committee on Agriculture for the 11th Five Year Plan has observed that not only the yields differed across the States, there was a significant gap between the performance and potential as revealed by actual yield and yield with improved practices adopted by farmers (Table 12).

Table 12: Interstate Variation in Actual Yield and yield with improved practices

State	*Improved practice(I)*	*Farmer practice(F)*	*Actual yield 2003-04(A)*	*Gap (per cent)*	
				I and F	*I and A*
1	2	3	4	5	6
Wheat (Yield : Kg/ha – 2002-03 to 2004-05)					
Bihar	3651	2905	1783	25.7	104.8
Madhya Pradesh	3297	2472	1789	33.4	84.3
Uttar Pradesh	4206	3324	2794	26.5	50.5
Rice (irrigated) (Yield : Kg/ha - 2003-04 to 2004-05)					
Uttar Pradesh	7050	5200	2187	35.6	222.4
Bihar	4883	4158	1516	17.4	222.1
Chhattisgarh	3919	3137	1455	24.9	169.4
Sugarcane					
Maharashtra	127440	99520	51297	28.1	148.4
Karnataka	147390	128000	66667	15.1	121.2
Bihar	74420	49440	40990	50.5	81.6

Source: Economic Survey (2007-08).

Indian agriculture still suffers from: (i) poor productivity, (ii) falling water levels, (iii) expensive credit, (iv) distorted market, (v) many intermediaries who increase cost but do not add much value, (vi) laws that stifle private investment,

(vii) controlled prices, (viii) poor infrastructure, and (ix) in appropriate research. Thus, the supply leading approach with mere emphasis on credit in isolation from the above factors will not help agriculture to attain the desired growth levels. Furthermore, States are required to play a more pro-active role in agriculture development by putting in place adequate infrastructure through means such as RIDF. As noted above, the share of marginal and small farmers in the total credit (both disbursed and outstanding) has been shrinking. The need to augment the credit flow to the lower strata of the farming community, which has more share in the total operational land holdings becomes more important.

The scope for supplementing the land inputs of marginal and small farmers with the non-land inputs such as credit with a view to enhancing the productivity and there by the production performance of Indian agriculture, lies in linking credit supply to input use. There is also a need for exploring new innovations in product design and methods of delivery, through better use of technology and related processes. It needs to be seen whether credit going to farmers especially small and marginal is in sufficient quantity and if so whether it will have any meaningful effect in the absence of other supportive measures for ensuring their economic viability. In this context, creation of production and employment opportunities in the rural sector through public investment assumes critical importance. The SHG-Bank Linkage model is an outstanding example of an innovation leveraging on community-based structures and existing banking institutions. In future, concerted efforts have to be made for enhancing the flow of credit to critical infrastructure areas such as irrigation, marketing and storage, etc., and also to areas such as water she dwaste land development, wind energy, allied a ctivities such as poultry, horticulture, dairying, etc.

6. Long Run Relationship between Agricultural GDP and Agricultural Credit

Step –I: Ordinary least square method:

Primarily, we have studied the effect of agricultural credit on agricultural GDP by a simple regression equation:

$$\text{Ln}\,\psi = \beta_0 + \beta_1 \ln X + \varepsilon \text{——(1)}$$

Y = agricultural GDP in India in constant Prices

X = agricultural credit in India in constant Prices

Step II: The Stationarity Test (Unit Root Test)

It is suggested that when dealing with time series data, a number of econometric issues can influence the estimation of parameters using OLS.

Regressing a time series variable on another time series variable using the Ordinary Least Squares (OLS) estimation can obtain a very high R^2, although there is no meaningful relationship between the variables. This situation reflects the problem of spurious regression between totally unrelated variables generated by a non-stationary process.Therefore, prior to testing Cointegration and implementing the Granger Causality test, econometric methodology needs to examine the stationarity; for each individual time series, most macro economic data are non-stationary, i.e. they tend to exhibit a deterministic and/or stochastic trend. Therefore, it is recommended that a stationarity (unit root) test be carried out to test for the order of integration. A series is said to be stationary if the mean and variance are time – invariant. Several tests of non-stationarity called unit root tests have been developed in the time series econometrics literature. In most of these tests the null hypothesis is that there is a unit root, and it is rejected only when there is strong evidence against it.

Table 13: Stationary Test for ln x

ADF Test Statistic	1.349121	1% Critical Value*		-3.6171
		5% Critical Value		-2.9422
		10% Critical Value		-2.6092
*MacKinnon critical values for rejection of hypothesis of a unit root.				
Augmented Dickey-Fuller Test Equation				
Dependent Variable: D(LNX)				
Method: Least Squares				
Included observations: 37 after adjusting endpoints				
Variable	Coefficient	Std. Error	t-Statistic	Prob.
LNX(-1)	0.013386	0.009922	1.349121	0.1862
D(LNX(-1))	-0.164002	0.171478	-0.956406	0.3456
C	0.051506	0.091121	0.565250	0.5756
R-squared	0.061975	Mean dependent var		0.152153
Adjusted R-squared	0.006797	S.D. dependent var		0.088489
S.E. of regression	0.088188	Akaike info criterion		-1.941097
Sum squared resid	0.264420	Schwarz criterion		-1.810482
Log likelihood	38.91029	F-statistic		1.123178

6

Demand for Agricultural Credit: A Financial Inclusion Perspective

S. M. Jawed Akhtar and **Saba Parveen**

"Financial inclusion is no longer something that is "nice to do" but is now an essential part of the global economic development agenda. It is a public policy issue that we regulators cannot shy away from"-Njuguna Ndung'U, Governor, Central Bank of Kenya.

1. Introduction

Development of rural areas continues to remain a matter of serious global concern. Addressing the need and aspiration of millions of downtrodden of the world community, particularly, that concentrated in the villages of developing nations, probably has been the most challenging task (Khankhoje, D. P. 2003). Poverty reduction has been one of the major goals of the development planning since independence and the planning process has been sensitive to the needs of the poor. Accordingly, the development efforts have been directed on creating adequate livelihoods and provision of services for a better quality life of the poor. However, the poverty as per methodology suggested by Tendulkar Committee put 41.8 per cent of the rural population as BPL, which indicates that concerted efforts are needed to alleviate poverty in the rural areas (Planning Commission, 2011).

Despite an average 7.9 per cent growth in gross domestic product (GDP) during the 11th Plan Period, sometimes peaking at 9 per cent, the performance of India in terms of the Human Development Index (indicative of inclusive growth and the extent of the population benefiting from development) saw a downward slide from 128th and 127th positions in 2000 and 2005 respectively to the 134th position in 2009 and 2011. While a handful are reaping benefits and have entered the billionaires club, millions are being forced into deprivation and disempowerment (Hussain, M, 2012). The emphasis of the 12th Five Year Plan (2012-17) is on inclusive growth which focuses on agriculture and other crucial sector and strengthening of institution and delivery mechanism. The agricultural sector is the only basis of rural people's sustenance and livelihood. The four per cent target for growth in the agricultural sector, which was missed in the 11th Plan, must be achieved in the 12th Plan as this is critical for sustainable development and inclusiveness. Indian agriculture has been facing a dual crisis of low productivity and increasing marginalisation of land holdings.

With the limitations on the expansion of farm area, growth in the agricultural sector depends heavily on the growth of productivity.

India's rural poor are overwhelmingly dependent on agriculture as their primary source of income; the majorities are marginal or small farmers and the poorest households are landless (Bassu, P, 2006). To increase the viability and sustainability of these tiny landholdings is a difficult responsibility behind small and marginal farmers because they are resource lacked and poverty stricken depended on subsistence agriculture with very limited market opportunities. As these tiny operational holdings are uneconomic in nature which requires an innovative and efficient measure to expand their credit base and hence can able to increase agricultural productivity. However, achieving this increase in productivity requires a big push on several fronts and change in perception, both in institutional and governance framework with respect to the changing needs of farmer with the changing economic scenario of India. Rationality emphasises the link between improving access to finance and reducing poverty.

The financial needs of India's rural poor reflect the volatile, uncertain, and irregular income streams and expenditure patterns of these households. The poor need a wide range of financial services from small advances to tide over consumption needs to loans for investment purposes to long-term savings that help them manage life-cycle needs. India has a range of rural financial service providers, including formal-sector financial institutions at one end of the spectrum, informal providers (mostly moneylenders) at the other end, and between these two extremes a number of semi-formal/microfinance providers. Shortly after independence in 1947, the first survey of rural indebtedness (All India Rural Credit Survey) prepared by the RBI documented that moneylenders and other informal lenders met more than 90 per cent of rural credit needs (*ibid*). Hence, at that time, almost all the financial needs of rural as well as agricultural sector were provided by the moneylenders but they are very explosive in nature, charging exorbitant rates of interest along with many unethical practices.

One of the avowed purposes of the institutionalisation of the agricultural credit system was to release the farmers from the clutches of the usurious moneylender by providing cheaper and timely credit. Implicit in this objective was the intension to bring all the farmers in need of credit under the orbit of institutional credit. Commercial banks were nationalised, cooperatives were strengthened, Regional rural banks were established and a whole lot of agricultural policies, credit programmes/policies were initiated and refined over time, the main strategy being the directed lending through priority sector lending targets. In spite of all these measures for strengthening the institutional rural credit network, the original objective of total inclusion remained elusive though with hardly 27 per cent of the farmer households having been covered by institutional credit sources (Thorat, 2007).

The role of credit to agriculture cannot be viewed just as a support to food-producing activity, but it should focus on the *"needs to improve the overall income and economic well being of the farmers"* as agriculture has been the basic requisite for national sovereignty. (Patel, Amrit, 2013). The Indian Government has a long history of expanding financial institutions and sevices, but the level of financial inclusion is less than desirable. As financial inclusion is a process of making formal financial services accessible and affordable to all at a lower transaction cost, but still the vast majority of rural poor doesn't have access to formal finance and the India's vast financial network is still unable to replace moneylenders. Almost, half of the country is unbanked or financially excluded. Financial exclusion is a lack of access to credit from the financial institutional sources which is very high for small and marginal farmers in general and women farmers in particular. They get easily trapped in debt circle due to their heavy dependence on informal sources of credit. Access to credit is the main problem faced by farmers, especially in a situation of massive requirements as created by the changing agricultural scenario. In this context, this paper overview the changing credits needs, changing rural finance scenario and the need of financial inclusion in India.

2. Review of Literature

Patel, Amrit (2013) in his study emphasised that policy should be addressed to create an enabling environment that can significantly enhance the absorption capacity of the geographical areas and farmers in each village and the rural credit policy should needs to focus on farm and non-farm sector development to alleviate rural poverty, deprivation and suffering. Tripathy, K. K. (2013) has focused that despite of the increase in the flow of institutional credit to agriculture and allied activities; the objective of easy accessibility to rural finance has not been fulfilled to the desired extent even after six decades of conscious effort for the institutionalisation of the rural credit. Kumar and Mukhopadhyay (2013) have emphasised that the financial needs and practices of the poor vary widely across different contexts that needs an in-depth understanding of the financial behaviour of the rural poor, as it is essential for designing a right product mix that would addresses their needs. Basu, Priya (2006) has examined that over the years, Indian banking has become more inclusive, but majority of the rural population still does not appear to have access to finance from a formal source, and the poor, particularly small and marginal farmer faces greater problem in getting finance. She also emphasised that the strategies that were designed to increase access to finance for the poor have not delivered their intended outcomes which needs to be reviewed to improve the efficiency of the rural financial institutions. Kochhar, Chanda, D (2009) pointed out emphasissed that banks should adopt two prolonged approach, first is to create a network of community- based financial institutions and other local partners whose proximity to and knowledge of the customer would complement the bank's financial resources and leverage technology to enhance efficiency of credit delivery operations and reduce the cost of finance. Raju, B. Yerram (2013) in his study emphasised that the availability of adequate and timely credit can play an important role in widening the option faced by the farmers and improving their ability to tackle all the changes that are underway in the agricultural sector but this requires a creating of a knowledge base for estimating the farmer's need and priority at every stage of agricultural activity. Awasthi, *et al,*(2012) has focused on the importance of financial inclusion and highlighted various initiatives that can enable poor to come out of abject poverty conditions.

3. Objectives

The study entitled "Demand for Agricultural Credit: A Financial Inclusion Perspective" has following objectives:

(a) To overview the changing credit needs of rural farmers with the changing Indian agricultural scenario.

(b) To analyse the success of the financial inclusion process in India; and

(c) To focus on some of the initiatives and efforts to ensure financial inclusion.

4. Changing Needs of Rural Farmers

Imagine a life without access to finance or financial services; no doubt it would become an incredible and stressful path as most of the dreams would remain unfulfilled. This might be an imagination of an urban people with a clear view of their life and their involvement with the high living status, but can we ever imagine, how would be the life of a rural poor with a hazy view of life based on a value system of exploring more opportunities and success to make their socio economic status to an ever higher aspirations, but for whom success is only livelihood. They still live without finance in spite of a large and ever increasing financial channels on the one hand and their increased needs on the other hand and hence, where sustaining one's life is full of terrible game. Before institutionalisation of rural finance, almost all financial needs of the rural and agricultural sector, which were based on traditional methods of cultivation, culture, social customs and beliefs at that time, were provided by the moneylenders.

Taking into account their seasonal inflows of income from agricultural operations, migration from one place to another, seasonal and irregular work availability and income, the existing financial system need to be designed to suit their requirements, security and safety of deposits, low transaction cost, convenient operating time, minimum paper work, frequent deposits, quick and easy access, product suitable for income and consumption. (Awasthi, N. 2013). It is important to analyse the credit needs of farmers from their capability and deprive situations and increasing diversity in their needs with the changing scenario. So, an in-depth understanding of financial behavi our of rural poor is essential to serve them better. Financial need differs from state to state; cropping patterns and farmer size groups as there is a substantial variation in the state-wise, sector-wise and size group wise etc. needs of farmer. So, it is important to focus on the heterogeneity in the needs of farmer vis-à-vis different states, sector and size group with an overall motive of financial inclusion by offering them customised products and service.

Demand for credit originates from the need of inputs and services as required for various farm operations, and credit can enable farmers to go for short-term credit for purchase of inputs and other services and the long-term credit for investment purposes. Hence, they can take investment decisions for creating asset through adoption of new technology and input which can further initiates them toward commercialised operations and guarantees a higher productivity and income. Hence, credit can play an important role by facilitating technological upgradation and commercialisation of agriculture.

The success of Green Revolution in Indian agriculture to a large extent was based on institutional credit support to agriculture in terms of expansion in inputs like fertiliser, irrigation, private sector capital formation, etc. which further caused the deepening of credit after nationalisation of banks. In the present post-liberalisation context, farmers face challenges on several front. He needs more credit for a diversified range of crop production and investment and also due to the relative change in prices of inputs over time.

With progressive changes in technology in agriculture and the gradual exposure of agriculture to the international markets, the steps being taken for the promotion of agricultural exports, the role of horticulture crops, floriculture and agro-processing, storage and marketing, growing value addition in agriculture, demand for agricultural credit may increase manifold in the future. The agriculture in the near future may become more capital intensive. This would require a more objective assessment of demand for credit needs. (Singh & Sagar, 2004). With the advent of commercialisation in Indian agriculture, changes in the cropping pattern and crop and an increase in prices of input and decrease in price of world output, there is a pressing need to reshape the agricultural policies incompatible with the new demand side perspective of a fast changing economic environment. Declining public investments in agriculture and increasing input prices restrict the capabilities of the farmer to exploit the advantage of open market opportunities and hence, unfortunately diverted them to informal sources, when the option and credit borrowing limit through formal sources ended, which causes a growing number of suicide by farmers in different parts of the country in recent years.

The growing commercialisation of Indian agriculture has encouraged the rise of trader-moneylender, as the formal sector finance is inadequate to meet the growing credit requirements of agriculture (Pradhan, N.C. ,2013). A crop-specific and region-specific like in arid areas, crop production is not viable and more credit is needed for diversification activities, credit policy initiatives are needed. The economic liberalisation offers tremendous opportunities of value addition, through agro-industries, from production and marketing of agricultural produce to the retail levels with an extensive line of post-harvesting technology and marketing intervention etc. which have the ability to increase export potential, farmer's income and rural industrialisation.

But, still there are several inadequacies and weaknesses exist in the current framework of rural credit. The policies designed to correct all these inadequacies must take into consideration that, more than 80 per cent of farmers are small and marginal, who faces great difficulty in accessing credit and remunerative prices. The concept of financial inclusion emerges from the growing poverty and existing exclusion of rural people from the financial services as provided by the various strata's of financial institutions. So, the government must review and analyse the credit policies with the changing credit needs.

An ideal system of agricultural credit would balance policy objectives with the farmer's needs and the lending institution's feasibility within an overall framework of scarce resources (Raju, Y. 2013).

5. Rural Banking and Level of Financial Inclusion

Unrestricted access to public goods and services is a feature of an open and efficient society. It is argued that as banking services are in a nature of the public good, it is essential that availability of banking and payment services to the entire population without discrimination is the prime objective of public policy (Awasthi, N. ,2013). In the pre-independent India, the cooperative credit societies Act were enacted in 1904 to combat rural indebtedness and to provide a formal and legalised institutional status to credit societies (Tripathy, K.K, 2013). Though Cooperative Act came in 1904, till 1950s the progress in terms of outreach by cooperatives was limited. This led to the nationalisation of commercial banks in 1969 and again in 1980, to step up credit supply to the rural people. Then, came Regional Rural Banks (RRBs) in mid-1970s. Thus, the credit architecture consisted basically of cooperatives, commercial banks and regional rural banks. In terms of an agency wise share in rural credit, the progress of institutionalisation was impressive. The share of institutional agencies in the borrowings of cultivator households increased from mere 7.3 per cent in 1951 to 66.3 per cent in 1991 (Satyasai, K.K.,2008). The 1990s saw the partial deregulation of interest rates, increased competition in the banking sector, and new microfinance approaches that combine the safety and reliability of formal finance with the convenience and flexibility of informal finance. But the vast majority of India's rural poor still do not have access to either formal finance or microfinance. Informal-sector lenders thus retain a strong presence in rural India (Basu, P. 2006). Cooperatives at the grass root level i.e. Primary Agricultural Societies (PACs) which have spread far and wide, have proved to be far too inadequate to the task of fulfilling the rural credit need as due to the political interferences, managerial inadequacies and bottlenecks. The performance of RRBs had not been very impressive all along.

Recognisedly, an outstanding aspect of banking development after the nationalisation of banks in July 1969 had been the rapid growth and territorial spread of branch network all over the country, particularly in rural and semi-urban areas as well as in underdeveloped regions (EPW, 2007-08). There were 31,796 commercial bank branches (as on 30th June 2009) in rural areas spread across six lakh villages. While the total number of commercial bank offices has been on the increase since 1969, the number of rural offices, which reached its peak in 1990, has been on the decline since then. The population covered per bank office has virtually remained stagnant since 1985 (Sarangi, U.C. 2010).

The share of non-institutional sources, in particular, moneylenders, declined substantially from 71 per cent in 1971 to 36 per cent in 1991 but increased to 42.9 per cent in 2002. The share of institutional debt has declined from 64 per cent in 1991 to 57 per cent in 2002, with a concurrent increase in non-institutional sources. Thus, it reveals that though there was an increase in the share of institutional debt over the last few decades, the share of non-institutional sources was, nevertheless, not insignificant. (Various publications of RBI & NSSO). Hence, nearly more than 60 years of independence and subsequent institutionalisation of rural finance, we are still facing the problem of financial exclusion.

Financial inclusion can be defined as delivery of banking services at an affordable cost to the vast section of disadvantaged and low-income groups. Though financial inclusion covers a wide array of services by the banking sector, one crucial area relates to borrowings from banks by the lower strata of the unorganised segments of the economy, which per force has to depend upon non-institutional sources when the avenues from formal sources are not forthcoming. Cost and easy availability of credit are the two primary factors to be reckoned with, though there are interlinkages among labour, land and credit markets in agrarian economies with an immeasurable concealed interest cost. Financial inclusion was envisaged and embedded in credit policies in the earlier decades also, though in a disguised form and without the same nomenclature. The role of the banking sector in financing rural households was envisioned in the 1950s, in pursuance of the recommendations of the RBI survey, viz, All-India Rural Credit Survey (Rao, K G K Subba, 2007).

According to CRISIL's (Credit Rating Information Services of India Limited) Financial Inclusion Index, which is a benchmark index developed to measure the extent of financial inclusion in India, financial inclusion depends upon three critical parameter of basis banking services which are branch penetration, deposit penetration and credit penetration.

Table 1 Distribution of Population and Bank Offices in India (1971-2012)

Year	*% of Rural Population to Total Population*	*Bank Offices*		*% of Rural banks to Total Banks*
		Rural	*Total*	
1971	75.1	4,817	13,622	35.4
1981	69.6	17,657	35,707	49.4
1991	65.4	35,206	60,220	58.5
2001	72.2	32,562	65,919	49.4
2003	71.8	32,303	66,535	48.6
2005	71.3	32,082	68,355	46.9
2007	70.9	30,585	72,165	42.4
2009	70.4	31,829	80,514	39.5
2011	70.2	33,779	90,775	37.2
2012	71.0	36,334	98,536	36.9

Sources: Reserve Bank of India; Census Statistics 1971- 2011; Economic Survey, 2012-13.

Table 1 shows that there were drastic increase in bank branches from 4,817 catering demand of the 75 per cent of the population in 1971 to 36,334 in 2012 but catering to only 71 per cent of the population. While the percentage of rural bank offices were highest i.e. 58.5 per cent in 1991, it gradually reduced to 36.9 per cent during 2012. Hence, there is decline in banks penetration in rural areas.

Table 2 : Agency-wise Disbursement of Agricultural Credit during 1970-2011(Rs. Crores)

Period	*Commercial bank*	*Cooperatives*	*Regional Rural Banks*	*Total*
1970-71 to	2442705	1677888	336814	4457407
2012-2013	[54.8]	[37.6]	[07.6]	[100]
1970-71 to	100634	1055874	20529	1177,037
2000-2001	[08.6][04.1]*	[89.7] [62.9]*	[01.7] [06.1]*	[100][26.4]*
2001-2002 to	23,42,071	622014	316285	3280370
2012-2013	[71.4] [95.8*]	[19.7] [37.1]*	[09.6] [93.1]*	[100][73.6]*

Source: Patel, Amrit (figures in parentheses indicate Per cent share in the total credit by all agencies and with * indicate per cent share in 1970-71 to 2012-13).

Table 2 shows that commercial banks emerged as predominant agency among three financial institutions whereas cooperatives shows a declining share from 89.7 per cent in the total credit by the all agencies during 1970-2001 to 19 per cent during 2001-13, in spite of the fact that cooperatives have a great potential in not only facilitating credit needs but also in distributing agricultural inputs and essential items at the grassroots level.

In spite of the revival of credit in the 2000s, as the flow of agricultural credit since 2004-05 has consistently exceeded the target, there still existed a large credit gaps, i.e. gaps between demand for credit and supply of credit, the government wouldn't able to augment that the major beneficiaries of it have been the small and marginal farmers who were the historically neglected section of the rural India and who genuinely needs credit or financial capital to survive them. But the quantity and quality of land owned by these socially deprived groups affected their access to credit as they suffer from discrimination in the delivery of credit services. They typically do not have collaterals; they have no fixed collateral or only have small acres of land that most often cannot be mortgaged. Identification of alternative collaterals is ought to be very costly and cumbersome. Large farmers mostly benefitted from financial institutions apart from their own large saved capital due to rights to large amounts of land areas. The Report of the 'Task Force on Credit Related Issues of Farmers' GOI, 2010, stated that *"In recent years, policy interventions have led to doubling of agricultural credit, but the limited access of small and marginal farmers to institutional credit continues to be a matter of concern. What is worrying is that the proportion of such farmers is increasing and they form more than four-fifths of the operational holdings".*

Table 3 : Regional Differences in Financial Services

Region	*Share in all India GDP (per cent)*	*Share in population (per cent)*	*Regional per capital GDP/National per capita GDP*	*Share in all India credit (per cent)*	*Share in all India deposit (per cent)*	*Share in all India Bank branches (per cent)*
Northern	18	13.8	1.28	21.5	22.9	16.1
North-eastern	3	3.7	0.76	1.5	1.6	2.5
Eastern	14	23.6	0.58	9.2	12.9	17.7
Central	17	26.6	0.64	8.9	13.6	20.3
Western	22	15.5	1.39	32.2	26.4	15.6
Southern	28	16.9	1.63	26.6	22.6	27.4
Total	**100**	**100**	**1.00**	**100**	**100**	**100**

Sources: RBI, Basic Statistical Returns 2002; Hand book of Statistics 2003; Census 2001.

Large regional differences exist in the distribution of financial services, both in terms of the volume of transactions and branch density, with clients in India's economically weaker regions having a disproportionately lower level of financial access. The spread of branches appears to be closely associated with regional shares in population: the eastern and central regions have larger shares in population and therefore, despite their low share in income, occupy the second and third position in terms of share in branches (Basu, P.). Table 3 shows that India's lesser developed and low-income eastern, central, and north-eastern regions account for 54 per cent of the population and 40.5 per cent of total bank branches but only 20 per cent of outstanding credit and 29 per cent of deposits. The following data shows that the rural credit situations looks very slow in spite of many measures and constitution of several committees and task forces.

6. Need of Financial Inclusion

Indeed, finance can act as an effective tool in spreading economic opportunity and fighting poverty. It is being increasingly envisaged that addressing financial inclusion requires a holistic approach addressing both supply and demand side aspects. Although there has been significant expansion in banking in the last few decades, there are still, many supply and demand side bottlenecks persists in the rural financial institution. Lack of financial literacy causes a gap of financial understanding between financial institutions and rural people, gender discriminations as women are more likely to be excluded in spite of their larger contribution in the agricultural sector, low income and seasonal fluctuations in income flow, problems of collateral, information asymmetry and high transaction costs are some of the demand side constraints.

Lack of suitable financial products, as the quality and choice of product and service provided by rural branches are lower than their urban counterpart, inefficient credit delivery methods, low profitability, higher risk, high transaction costs as the cost of dealing with poor people is very high because they have to maintain a high number of accounts with a low volume of financial transaction, spatial divergences, recent financial crisis and unviable policies of government etc. are some of the supply side constraints. The role and function of Rural Financial Institutions are very crucial for the overall development of the rural India. Their ability to serve these rural communities, to a large extent, depends on their efficacy, efficiency and effectiveness. According to Khankhoje, the efficiency relates to the internal functioning of RFIs with a constant eye on their financial viability and sustainability.

Rural households lack access to reliable and affordable credit for agriculture and other livelihood priorities. There is a need to explore innovative approaches to rural and agricultural finance incompatible with the growing and diversified needs of credit in the current scenario of increasing commercialisation and modernisation. As still large gaps existed in the access to finance, there is growing expectation for removing those gaps through a change in perception towards the overall process of credit delivery system by increasing innovative mechanisms which would serve them with a financial product-mix incompatible with the needs. Innovative tools for effectively managing the risks faced by the rural poor can narrow the gaps in flow of finance. It needs world class collaborations to share their expertise, perspective and experiences. The IFPRI's (International Food Policy Research Institutes) Vision Initiate approached the team of World Bank to conceptualise their collection of briefs which points out "the importance of business realities faced by small farmers, including low education levels, the dominance of subsistence farming, and the lack of access to modern financial instruments. These conditions mean that new and innovative institutions are required to reach small farmers. Emerging communication technologies provide new opportunities for rural banking by reducing business costs and alleviating information asymmetries. New financial instruments, such as weather index-based insurance and micro insurance, also have great potential for managing the risks faced by small farmers. In addition, bundling financial services with non-financial services like marketing and extension services offers new opportunities for small farmers to increase their productivity and incomes. Finally, an enabling policy environment and legal framework, enforcement of rules and regulations, and a supportive rural infrastructure all contribute immensely to making sustainable access to finance a reality" (Todd & Sharma, 2010). One such initiative is taken by Barclays (a global financial service provider) in collaboration with CARE and Plan entitled "Banking on Change" as implemented in 11 countries, including India, which represents financial exclusion and challenges the traditional banking practices based on their financial expertise and understanding of rural communities. Their primary effort is expanding access to services to mobilise savings rather than credit and to begin by building their financial assets and skills through savings, rather than debt. Banking on Change works through local organisations and members of the community to engage and train poor people. It relies on the tried and tested methodology of Village Savings and Loan Association (VSLAs). VSLAs have a unique ability to support both the social needs of communities and provide a valuable source for investment in their businesses. Banking on Change has taken a gradual approach to supporting people to move up the financial ladder and has emphasised scaling up access to basic community-managed saving groups as a springboard to accessing formal financial products and services. Barclays employees directly engage with saving groups to understand their financial requirements.

Group members welcome the fact that they can keep their funds in a safe place and that they are treated as equals by the bank. The trust that is being built between the groups and the bank also enables members to demand further services, particularly access to credit as they wish to obtain larger amounts of money, and products which are more flexible (i.e., Ones that allow them to have a longer term repayment facility) (Barclays, 2013).

Any attempt to expand financial inclusion is essentially a small step in a long journey. Thus, financial inclusion is by nature incremental. This means that expanding financial inclusion requires, among other things, a paradigm shift that goes beyond opening bank accounts and facilitating direct cash transfers to the financially excluded.(Ananth & Sabri, 2013). There is an urgent need on the part of government to improve access to finance for India's rural poor, to meet their diverse financial needs through holistic credit policies.

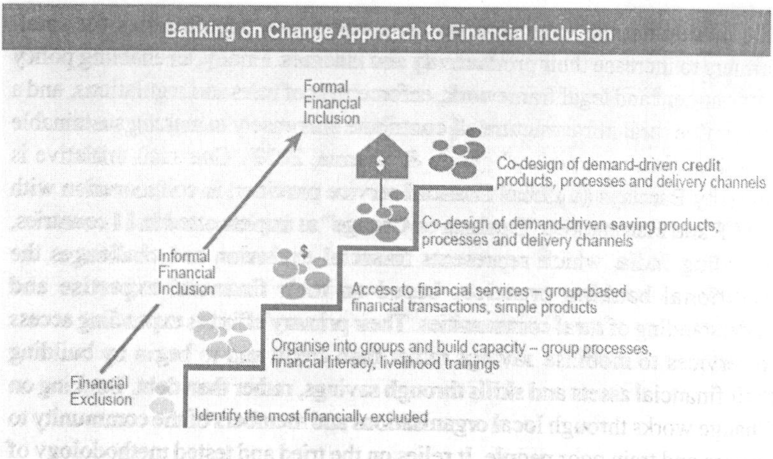

Fig. 1

Source: Barclays, http://www.care.org/sites/default/files/documents/Banking_on_Change_Breaking_Barriers__April2013.pdf

Like Barclays, there are many financial inclusion initiatives taken by various NGO's, Corporations, International Agencies and so on. One of the major challenges for the banks in the country is to include the 50 per cent of the excluded population. Reserve Bank of India has made sustained efforts to enhance the penetration of formal financial institutions in the unbanked areas and flow of credit to financially excluded households. The Reserve Bank of India has adopted a bank-led model for financial inclusion based on technology or Information and communication technology and on new delivery models so that to attain greater reach and penetration along with minimised cost of providing financial services in far areas of the country.

Considering that financial literacy is an important adjunct for promoting financial inclusion, consumer protection and ultimately financial stability, RBI has adopted an integrated approach wherein efforts towards Financial Inclusion would go hand in hand (R. Rajan, 2014). The RBI has permitted banks to engage Business Facilitators (BFs) and Business Correspondents (BCs) as intermediaries for providing financial and banking services. The BC Model allows banks to provide door step delivery of services specially to do 'cash in-cash out' transactions, thus addressing the 'last mile' problem.

The RBI has used the FIPs (Financial Inclusion Plans) to gauge the performance of banks under their financial inclusion initiatives (*ibid*) by maintaining a structured and comprehensive monitoring mechanism for evaluating banks performance vis-à-vis their targets. The RBI has enabled various initiatives under the theme of financial inclusion like relaxation of know your customer (KYC) norms, branch licensing norms and opening of branches in unbanked rural centres etc., and on the success which expectation of all depends.

7. Conclusion and Suggestions

When poor people have limited saving or borrowing options, their investment plans are stifled and it becomes harder for them to break out of poverty. If households have no access to insurance and are unable to accumulate small savings that enable them to pay for household and business expenses, especially during lean seasons, they are forced to limit their exposure to risk, even if high returns are expected, once again making the pathway out of poverty more arduous than necessary. Inadequate access to financial services is thus part of what is often called the "poverty trap". Credit needs of small and marginal farmers are not only growing but are getting diversified due to increasing commercialisation and modernisation of agriculture. Simultaneously, for a variety of other needs, farmers incur considerable expenditure, resulting in increased borrowings. But the financial institutions have demonstrated a lack of interest in agriculture finance and poorer households face difficulties in obtaining basic banking services. There is an immediate need of changing perception towards financial inclusion into a reality rather than famous policy propaganda. Our suggestions are:

1. To integrate technology with banking channels as advances in communication technology affect rural banking in many ways and develop innovative techniques and mechanisms of credit delivery.
2. In-depth study is needed through financial researches in different regions and strata of farmers, to know why farmers still depends on informal sources.
3. Need of greater flexibility in the policies of rural financial institutions with the changes in the policies of forward and backward parameters of agricultural and rural sector, region specific, sector specific needs, based on short and long run changing needs of farming communities and emergencies.
4. Need of government's efforts towards decentralisation of professionals at the grassroots level and support toward innovative initiatives of world's helping organisations and communities.
5. Restructuring of institutions of rural finances and facilitating efficiency in them through enhanced regulatory supervisions and so on.
6. Since, financial inclusion cannot be addressed by a single product or technological innovation, but needs a set of solutions best fitting to

their national contexts in pursuit of increased financial access for poorer populations. At last, it can only be achieved by an active participation of all the stakeholders and without financial inclusion; we can't be able to perceive the fulfillment of the objective of inclusive growth.

References

1. Ananth and Sabri (2013), "Challenges to Financial Inclusion in India", *Economic and Political Weekly,* Vol. XLVIII, No.7, February 16, pp.77-83.
2. Awasthi, *et al* (2012), "Demand Elasticity: A Hurdle for Financial Inclusion in India, *VSRD-IJBMR,* Vol. 2 (2), 2012, pp. 54-64.
3. Basu, Priya (2006), *Improving Access to Finance for India's Rural Poor, The World Bank*, Washington, D.C, ISBN-10: 0-8213-6146-5.
4. Hussain, M (2012), "Twelth Five Year Plan: Taking "Inclusive Development" from Myth to Reality" *Economic and Political Weekly,* Vol. XLVII No. 52, December.
5. http://www.care.org/sites/default/files/documents/Banking on Change_Breaking_Barriers__April2013.pdf
6. http://pib.nic.in/archieve/eec/2011/Planning2011.pdf
7. Khankhoje, D.P. (2003), " Some Dimensions of the Efficacy of Rural Financial Institutions", edited by Pal Suresh *et al*, *Institutional Change in Indian Agriculture,* NCAEPR, New Delhi, p. 301.
8. Kochhar, Chanda. D (2009), "Reaching Out to Rural India: The ICICI Bank Eeperience", *CAB CALLING,* Vol. 33, No. 4, Oct-Dec, p.1-5.
9. Kumar and Mukhopadhyay (2013), "Patterns of Financial Behavior among Rural and Urban Clients: Some Evidence from Tamil Nadu, India", *IMTFI,* Working Paper, pp.1-22.
10. Patel, Amrit (2013), "Agricultural Credit by Banks" *Kurukshetra,* Vol. 62, No. 2, December, pp.10-14.
11. Pradhan, N C (2013), Persistence of Informal Credit in Rural India: Evidence from "All-India Debt and Investment Survey' and Beyond", *RBI Working Paper Series*, pp.1-23.
12. Raju, B.Yerram (2013), "*Agricultural Banking: Getting the Perspective Right",* Konark Publishers Pvt Ltd, New Delhi, ISBN 978-93-220-0832-1.
13. Rao, K.G.K. Subba (2007), "Financial Inclusion: An Introspection", *Economic and Political Weekly*, February.3, pp. 355-360.

14. Satyasai, K.J.S. (2008), "Rural Credit Delivery in India: Structural Constraints and Some Corrective Measures", *Agricultural Economics Research Review,* Vol. 21, Conference Number, pp. 387-394.

15. Sarangi, U.C. (2010), "Report of the Task Force on Credit Related Issues of Farmers", *Ministry of Agriculture, Government of India.*

16. Singh & Sagar (2004), *State of the Indian Farmer, Government of India,* Academic Foundation, New Delhi, ISBN 81-7188-370-2.

17. Todd and Sharma (2010), "Innovations in Rural and Agriculture Finance", *IFPRI & The World Bank Vision 2020,* pp.1-34.

18. Tripathy, K.K. (2013), "Status of Rural and Agricultural Finance in India", *Kurukshetra,* Vol. 6 No. 2, December, pp. 3-8.

19. Financial Inclusion- Indian Experience, Text of speech by Smt. Usha Thorat, Deputy Governor, Reserve Bank of India at the HMT-DFID Financial Inclusion Conference 2007, Whitehall Place, London, UK on June 19, 2007. *RBI Monthly Bulletin July 2007,* pp.1165-1172.

20. http://www.iibf.org.in/documents/reseach-report/Report-16.pdf.

21. *Government of India (2010),* Report of the Task Force on Credit Related Issues of Farmers (Chairman: U. C. Sarangi), Submitted to the Ministry of Agriculture, GOI, June.

7

Demographic Dividend in India: Addressing Education and Skill Development

Anup K. Mishra and **Santosh K. Singh**

1. Introduction

Globalisation, over the years, is transforming the lives of the people. Not only the national economies but also the national cultures are globalising. Today, globalisation means much more than mere opening up of economies and competition. In fact, globalisation has acquired much wider concept. It is now more understood as 'Functioning on a Planetary Scale on Real Time', meaning that 'information is exchanged or communicated as it is produced'.

There are wide diversity of factors and forces that are attributing to the after-effects of globalisation. In essence, it is how economic growth potentials, work force requirements, and the work-market that are getting reoriented, as ultimately they not only create conditions but also determines the state of socio-economic development.

Under the new global economic climate, the ability to create such conditions will depend increasingly on the way the government culture the education system. It is so because, knowledge is the most highly valued commodity in the global economy, and the nations have little choice but to increase their investment in education. The call of the day is not merely quantity but the quality of education. This is more so because the problem today is not merely of employment but more of employability.

Over the past few years, we have repeatedly placed excessive faith in India's demographic dividend. Some even take it too far, and predict how this will lead us to economic superdom. We, thus, are bandying our only card—labour—as our trump card. We are also being told that all our problems will be solved, if we fix the problem of skilling the teeming millions of young people. These precepts need closer examination. Currently, less than 20 per cent of our workforce is formally or non-formally skilled; the rest is unskilled. While a majority of the unskilled population is counted as employed, the reality is more than half of them are falsely counted as employed in agriculture.

Hence, the moot question arises that

- Is lack of skills hampering job creation, or is inadequate job creation a disincentive for investments in formal skilling?

There are some challenges related to those seemingly favourable demographics, however. The first is in finding jobs for all these people. Second, and more importantly, India's young people will need to develop the right skills for the modern job market.

The present study has been divided in to eight parts viz. A-H. Section A to C depicts the introductory part and D to G sketched the analytical part of the study and the last part G is the concluding part of the study.

2. Conceptual Background

Acceptance of the concept of globalisation in conjunction with Information Technology, one then can visualise changing format of national economy and social culture, as there is vast change in the knowledge, attitude and work culture of the fellow citizens. No society or population can remain immune to the effects of such change. It will perhaps be more correct to state that it is changing the very basics and essentials of human relations and social life.

Transmission of Knowledge

In the present day, movement of capital depends upon information, communication and transmission of knowledge in the global market. As knowledge is easily transmittable, it has become fundamentally supporting to globalisation.

Now the question is can we really draw the clear line of cut-off between the above prepositions, is not, is such impact on transitional stage? Inclusion of such event brings three propositions, namely.

- Globalisation is having a profound impact on Education at national, regional and even local levels, reintegrating the individuals into the new society based on information and knowledge.
- As the opposite case, Globalisation is having a little impact on Education at national, regional and even local levels.
- Globalisation is having an increasing impact on Education at national level; yet, the regional and even local levels are still far away from its vaccination.

3. The Problem

The matrix of the problem could be seen as follows:

- **Work Flexibility in the Labour Markets and Education Systems**

Work in the labour market is becoming more flexible. Increasingly, worker now have more options to change their kinds of jobs and their jobs now tend to be more multitasked.

Such flexibility in the job market demands pressure to increase not only the average level of education and higher education, but also for technical education for higher skills.

- **Rising Pay-off to Higher and Technical Education**

The pay-off to levels of higher education along with technical education is fast increasing. Worldwide, there is a clear shift towards Skill-Intensive Products and Knowledge-Oriented Markets.

Rising relative incomes for higher educated and skill oriented labour, in turn, increases the demand for university education as well as of technical education.

- **Pressure to Increase Spending on Higher and Technical Education**

Along with the increases in the demand for university and technical education, there is now the pressure to increase spending on Higher and Technical Education to generate a more educated labour force.

However, in most of the developing countries, guaranteeing of the demand for additional resources for higher and technical universities is coupled with the role of both government and private sector.

- **The Consequential Decentralisation and Privatisation of Education System**

In order to meet the initial increasing pressure to increase spending on Higher and Technical Education to generate a more educated labour force, decentralisation and privatisation of education system seems to be the immediate alternative with the governments.

In this regard, it is argued that decentralisation and privatisation of education system is the most effective strategy for ensuring quality and flexibility in the supply of a more educated labour force in a globalised economy. In other words, the pressure to supply more educated and more technical labour force appear to have a private-sector bias.

- **The Quality of National Education**

The ultimate goal to invest more and more in human resources and in quality education and technical training at all levels is translated with increased privatisation and marketisation of education financing and management.

Consequently, there lies the wider implication of testing of education quality and the real effect of technological change.

- **Information Technology and The Quality of Education**

The planetary role of Information Technology to extend Quality education at lower cost is vital to the development of globalised labour market. However, the extent of its effectiveness differs from country to country.

The capacity of globalisation to have profound impact on the transmission of knowledge on the local and regional levels is often hurdled by age long rigid and deep-rooted culture-influenced knowledge. Beyond occasionally, using computers in classrooms, the teaching methods and national curricula remains largely unchanged.

However, there seems to be a common agreement to the need that the fundamental role of educational institutions should not only be to transmit skills needed in the global economy, but also to effect the future of the individuals at the local, regional and national level.

- **Cultural Transformation Through New Meaning and Value of Knowledge**

As and when individuals are exposed to and adopt higher global knowledge to enable them to be a stronger force in the labour market, there is inculcation of new meaning and value of life. Such cultural transformation seems to be inevitable.

However, with such globalisation, there lies the danger of many groups to be marginalised by the market values of this culture. Such groups tussle against globalised market forces that tend to threaten their traditional culture, and thus are anti-market. This there from, amount to an intellectual struggle (towards inclusive growth) over the globalised meaning and value of knowledge.

4. Comparative Evaluation of the Present Status of Level of Education

- In the present paper the study is comparative in nature and tries to evaluate the status of level of education at all-India level. The following two tables (1and 2) are based on the 66th round of NSSO (2009-10) depicting. (1) levels of education at different MPCE levels and (2) levels of vocational training at different age groups. For the comparative study we have taken the analysed results from our earlier study (Mishra, Anup K., *et.al*, 2011).

Table 1: Number of non-literates and number of educated persons per 1000 persons of age 15 years and above for monthly per capita consumer expenditure (MPCE) class during 2009-10 (all-India)

MPCE Classes	*Male*		*Female*		*Person*	
	Not literate	*Educa-ted*	*Not literate*	*Educa-ted*	*Not literate*	*Educa-ted*
			Rural			
0-10	413	144	653	63	535	103
10-20	361	163	633	59	497	111
20-30	330	183	581	87	455	135
30-40	302	198	579	84	440	142
40-50	286	227	531	116	406	173
50-60	272	240	501	126	385	184
60-70	233	297	463	152	347	225
70-80	207	328	434	170	318	251
80-90	181	378	407	215	292	298
90-100	121	518	303	335	208	430
All	260	282	498	148	378	216
			Urban			
0-10	297	195	515	137	406	165
10-20	221	280	430	190	325	235
20-30	178	337	374	242	276	290
30-40	141	384	311	289	224	337
40-50	101	485	252	358	175	423
50-60	69	588	209	423	136	510
60-70	55	636	146	504	99	572
70-80	41	704	114	577	76	643
80-90	29	816	77	712	51	768
90-100	6	918	43	805	23	866
All	104	561	236	439	167	503

Source: NSSO 66th Round, *Status of Education and Vocational Training in India, Report No. 515, pp. 24.*

Table 2 : Per 1000 distribution of persons of age 15 – 29 years by vocational training received / being received for each age group (all-India) 2009-10

Age group (years)	*Vocational training*	*No vocational training*	*Total (incl. n.r.)*	*% With no vocational training*
Rural male				
15-19	95	891	1000	89.0
20-24	63	926	1000	93.0
15-24	97	897	1000	90.0
25-29	73	918	1000	92.0
All (15-29)	79	917	1000	92.0
Rural female				
15-19	27	967	1000	97.0
20-24	43	950	1000	95.0
15-24	35	958	1000	96.0
25-29	45	951	1000	95.0
All (15-29)	38	956	1000	96.0
Rural person				
15-19	35	958	1000	96.0
20-24	68	921	1000	92.0
15-24	50	941	1000	94.0
25-29	70	925	1000	93.0
All (15-29)	56	936	1000	94.0
Urban male				
15-19	38	944	1000	94.0
20-24	149	828	1000	83.0
15-24	91	889	1000	89.0
25-29	188	801	1000	80.0
All (15-29)	121	862	1000	86.0
Urban female				
15-19	38	946	1000	95.0
20-24	86	894	1000	89.0
15-24	62	920	1000	92.0
25-29	77	913	1000	91.0
All (15-29)	67	918	1000	92.0
Urban person				
15-19	38	945	1000	95.0
20-24	119	860	1000	86.0
15-24	78	903	1000	90.0
25-29	134	856	1000	86.0
All (15-29)	95	888	1000	89.0

Source: NSSO 66th Round, *Status of Education and Vocational Training in India, Report No. 515, pp. 24.*

Based on the data of these two tables (1 and 2), some correlations and Time trends are drawn and the results are presented over the tables 3 to 5.

Table 3 : Correlation Coefficients Between monthly percapita consumer expenditure (MPCE) class and Levels of Education

Area	*Sex*	*Education*	*2004-05[1]*	*2009-10[2]*
Rural	Male	Not Literate	- 0.933	-0.914
		Literate	0.998	0.983
	Female	Not Literate	-0.982	-0.943
		Literate	0.995	0.992
	Person	Not Literate	-0.963	-0.933
		Literate	0.998	0.988
Urban	Male	Not Literate	- 0.794	-0.739
		Literate	0.950	0.880
	Female	Not Literate	- 0.866	-0.797
		Literate	0.972	0.905
	Person	Not Literate	-0.837	-0.776
		Literate	0.960	0.893

1-For data and value calculations see the research article in Mishra, Anup K., *et.al.*, 2011, *12-The value have been calculated from the data of Table-1.*

Table 4: Trend Values of Literates and Not literates for 2004-05[1] and 2009-10[2]

Sex	*Rural not literate*		*Urban not literate*
Female	2004-05	y = -35.424x + 703.33	y = -51.861x + 532.33
		R^2 = 0.9646	R^2 = 0.9844
	2009-10	y = - 45.59 x + 892.03	y = - 56x + 664
		R^2 = 0.95	R^2 = 0.9869
Male	2004-05	y = -28.63x + 428.07	y = -29.927x + 278.4
		R^2 = 0.9791	R^2 = 0.9276
	2009-10	y = - 38.98 x + 595.42	y = - 33.028x + 357.52
		R^2 = 0.99	R^2 = 0.9339
Person	2004-05	y = -32.503x + 567.07	y = -41.085x + 405.07
		R^2 = 0.977	R^2 = 0.9679
	2009-10	y = - 43.18 x + 750.02	y = - 44.846x + 511.17
		R^2 = 0.77	R^2 = 0.9699
		Rural literate	Urban literate
Female	2004-05	y = 25.689x - 62.061	y = 69.283x - 99.424
		R^2 = 0.768	R^2 = 0.9506
	2009-10	y = 25.267x + 1.7333	y = 73.036x + 22
		R^2 = 0.8243	R^2 = 0.9763
Male	2004-05	y = 38.346x - 45.167	y = 73.052x - 13.924
		R^2 = 0.8629	R^2 = 0.9811
	2009-10	y = 27.5x + 103.91	y = 78.503x + 102.53
		R^2 = 0.692	R^2 = 0.9923
Person	2004-05	y = 32.36x - 55.424	y = 71.594x - 57.364
		R^2 = 0.8264	R^2 = 0.9698
	2009-10	y = 30.861x + 35.467	y = 76.345x + 61
		R^2=0.86	R^2=0.9876

1-For data and value calculations see the research article in Mishra, Anup K., *et.al.*, 2011, *2-The value have been calculated from the data of Table-1.*

Table 5 : Trend Values of Vocational and No Vocational Trainings

		2004-05[1]	2009-10[2]
Rural male	Vocational	y = 17.3 x + 77 R^2 = 0.4908	y = 12.6x + 50.5 R^2 = 0.3361
	No Vocational	y = - 16.8 x + 913 R^2 = 0.4917	y = 5.2x + 895 R^2 = 0.1621
Rural female	Vocational	y = 4.1x + 68.5 R^2 = 0.5102	y = 2.1x + 35.7 R^2 = 0.21
	No Vocational	y = - 6.3x + 926.5 R^2 = 0.6873	y = -2.1x + 962.7 R^2 = 0.2381
Rural person	Vocational	y = 10.4x + 73.5 R^2 = 0.5116	y = 7.8x + 42.5 R^2 = 0.3433
	No Vocational	y = -11.1x + 918.5 R^2 = 0.5607	y = -7.9x + 956 R^2 = 0.3651
Urban male	Vocational	y = 29.3x + 102.5 R^2 = 0.4932	y = 19.1x + 77.1 R^2 = 0.298
	No Vocational	y = -29.4x + 893 R^2 = 0.5057	y = -36.8x + 957.5 R^2 = 0.5514
Urban female	Vocational	y = 10.4x + 86.5 R^2 = 0.2614	y = 7.1x + 63.5 R^2 = 0.1894
	No Vocational	y = -10.6x + 908 R^2 = 0.2931	y = -7.3x + 936.5 R^2 = 0.1919
Urban person	Vocational	y = 20x + 96 R^2 = 0.4225	y = 22.3x + 52.5 R^2 = 0.4684
	No Vocational	y = -20.4x + 899.5 R^2 = 0.4441	y = -11.8x + 925.8 R^2 = 0.2651

1-For data and value calculations see the research article in Mishra, Anup K., *et.la.*, 2011-*12The value have been calculated from the data of Table-2*

- Based on the Result of correlation for 2004-05 and 2009-10 (Table-1), clearly we find that with the rise in monthly per capita consumer expenditure (MPCE) class, there have been corresponding fall in illiteracy levels (both rural and urban). As a corollary, with rise in MPCE, the level of literacy is very high. This confirms that with the dynamic income, the consumer expenditure as an important factor towards the level of literacy in the country. This is also validated by the NSS data, where the highest frequencies of 'not literate' are in the lowest MPCE slab, and the highest frequencies of 'literate' are in the highest MPCE slab.
- In as much as the trends of 'not literates' are concerned, all are marked with falling trends. That is, the levels of illiterates (both female and male

in both rural and urban) are reducing ***(in 61st and 66th round, Table 4)***. It is quite appealing to mark the fall in the female illiteracy levels (both rural and urban) are greater than the fall in male.

- Observing the trend of MPCE and literacy we find that with the increase in the level of MPCE the trend of increasing in literacy is low in 2009-10 in comparison of 2014-05 data but in contrast it has been high in the urban area. It seems that in rural area the increasing trends in literacy is not merely from MPCE but in addition there may be some other factors which affects the literacy rate.

  With the rising 'age-groups', the trends of 'vocational' and 'no vocational' training are presented in the **Result Table 5.** The markable features are.

- Fall in 'no vocational training' are greater for male than female in both rural and urban sectors in 2004-05 and 2009-10.
- The surprising fact is that in 2009-10 the number of 'no vocational' training persons has increased in comparison with 2004-05.This shows that government has failed to provide opportunities for vocational training for the working age group.
- Fall in 'no vocational training' of urban person is almost double than rural person in 2004-05 and two third in 2009-10. This indicates that the maximum percentage of working age groups is working without any vocational trainings or skills.
- Clearly, thus, there lies the need to work more towards higher 'vocational training' not only for female but also specially for both male and female in the rural sector.

5. Comparative trends of VT vs. WPR

Observing the comparative trends of vocational training (VT) Vs Work population ratio (Wpr) we see that vocational training and work population ratio of age 15-19 had declined from 2004–05 to 2009–10 (Graph 1a and 1b). In the age group of 20–24 and 25–29 the decline trend of VT is less from 2004-05 to 2009-10 but reverse in the case of Wpr in the same age group (Graph1c and e and 1d and f)). Overall in the age of 15–29 we observe that the person with vocational training are getting less participation in work in 2009–10 with respect to the period 2004–05(Graph 1g and 1h). Hence, we may say that due to decline trends in VT the Wpr is declining more steeply in the graph. This seems that lack of VT is decreasing the employability in India.

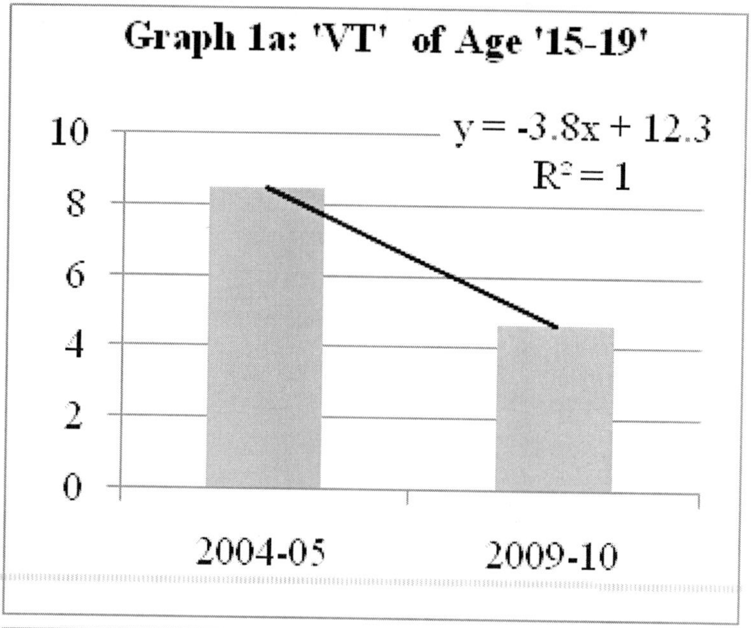
Graph 1a: 'VT' of Age '15-19'
y = -3.8x + 12.3
$R^2 = 1$
10
8
6
4
2
0
2004-05
2009-10

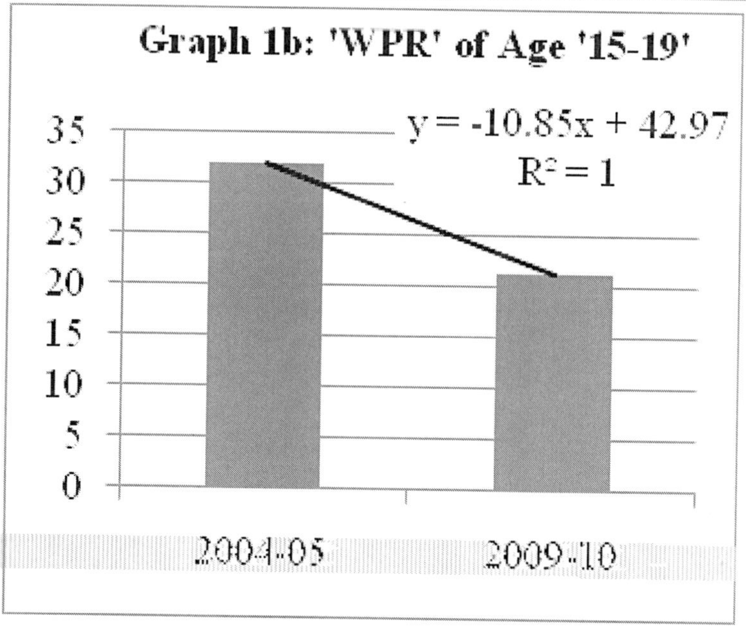
Graph 1b: 'WPR' of Age '15-19'
y = -10.85x + 42.97
$R^2 = 1$
35
30
25
20
15
10
5
0
2004-05
2009-10

Graph 1c: 'VT' of Age '20-24'

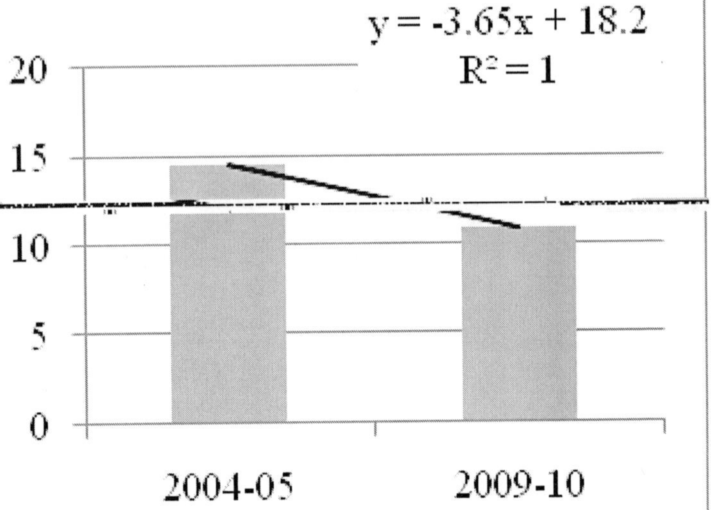

Graph 1d: 'WPR' of Age '20-24'

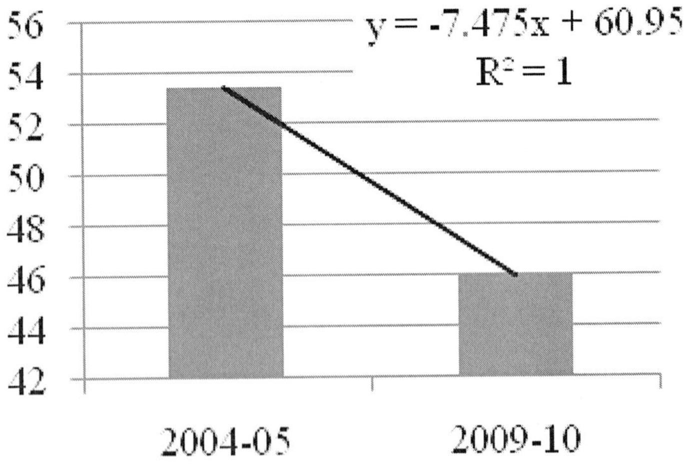

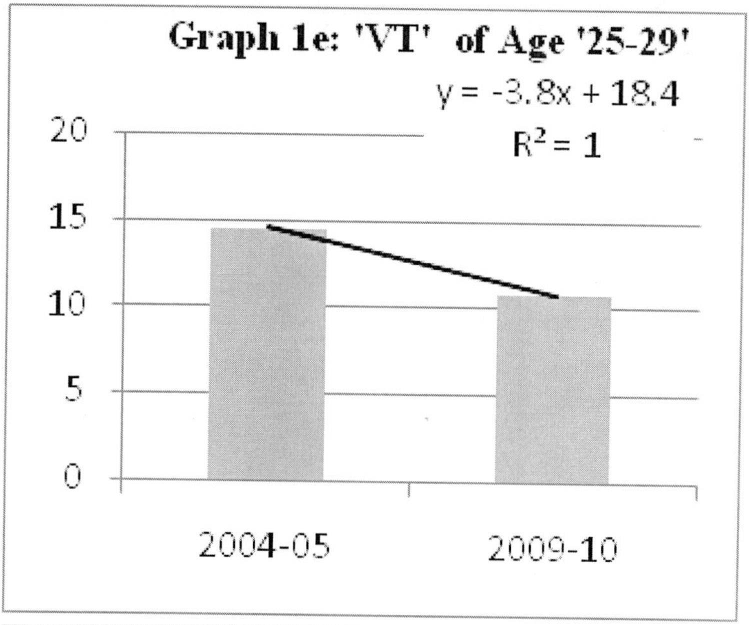
Graph 1e: 'VT' of Age '25-29'
y = -3.8x + 18.4
R² = 1
20
15
10
5
0
2004-05
2009-10

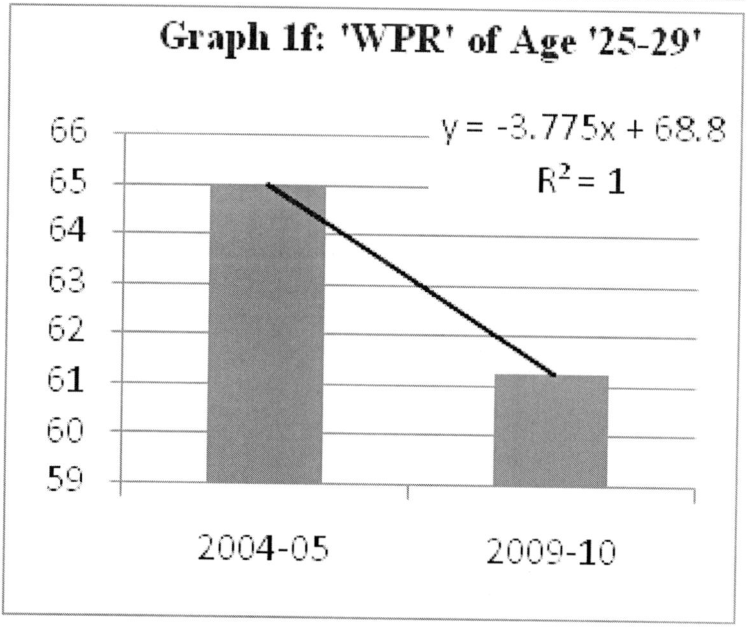
Graph 1f: 'WPR' of Age '25-29'
y = -3.775x + 68.8
R² = 1
66
65
64
63
62
61
60
59
2004-05
2009-10

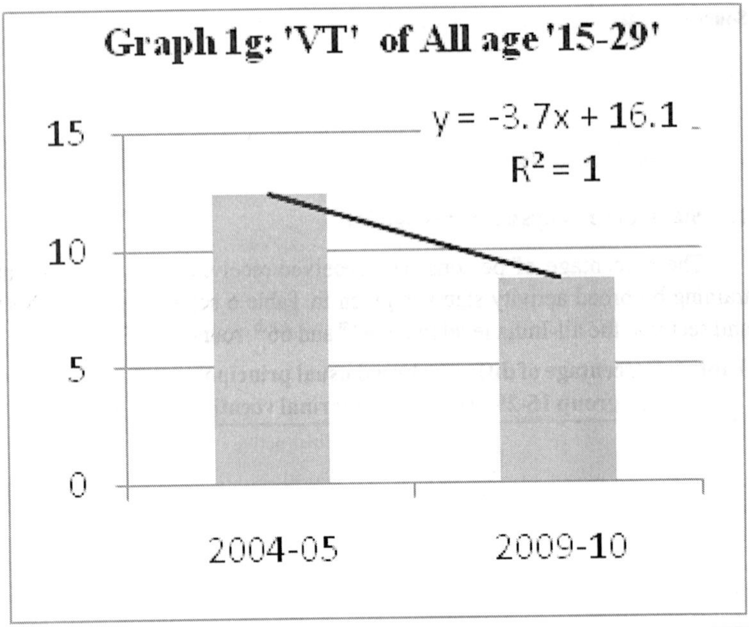
Graph 1g: 'VT' of All age '15-29'
y = -3.7x + 16.1
R² = 1
15
10
5
0
2004-05
2009-10

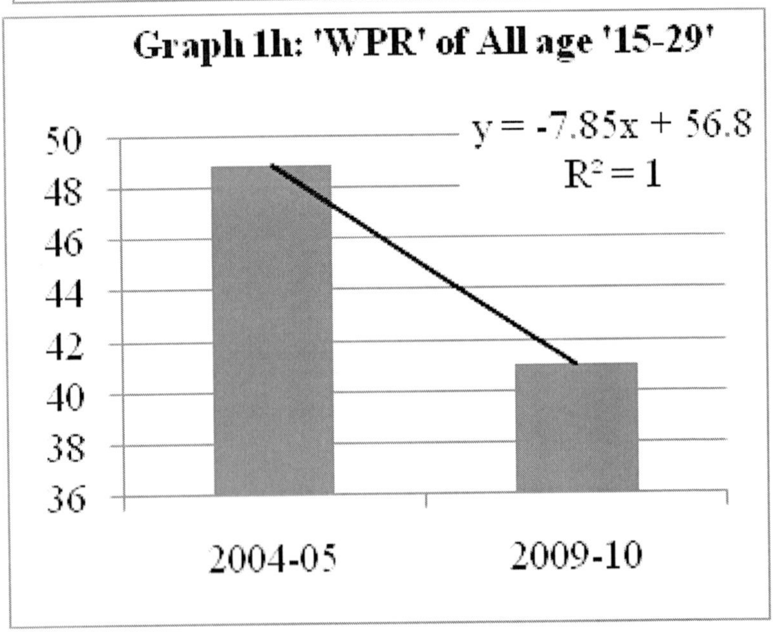
Graph 1h: 'WPR' of All age '15-29'
y = -7.85x + 56.8
R² = 1
50
48
46
44
42
40
38
36
2004-05
2009-10

Source: **1**-Data for the Graph 1a,1c,1e,1g have been extracted from NSSO (Status of Education and Vocational Training in India), Report no. 517 (pp. 42) and 551 (pp. 39)

2-Data for the Graph 1b,1d,1f,1h, have been extracted from NSSO (Employment and Unemployment Situation in India, 2009-10), Report no. 537, pp. 79

1. Status of Employability through VT

The percentage of persons who received/receiving formal vocational training by broad activity status is given in Table 6 separately for each sex and sector at the all-India level in the 61st and 66th round of NSSO.

Table 6: Percentage of different broad usual principal activity status in the age group 15-29 who received formal vocational training

Category of persons	Usual principal activity status							
	Employed		*Unemployed*		*Not in labour force*		*All*	
	2004-05	*2009-10*	*2004-05*	*2009-10*	*2004-05*	*2009-10*	*2004-05*	*2009-10*
Rural								
Male	1.4	1.2	6.9	8.2	0.9	2.5	1.5	1.5
Female	1.5	0.9	12.4	16.6	0.8	0.7	1.3	0.9
Person	1.4	1.1	8.8	10.9	0.8	1.1	1.4	1.2
Urban								
Male	5.4	5.4	12.1	12.7	3.3	4.4	5.2	5.4
Female	8.9	6.9	17.4	19.1	3.2	2.3	4.5	3.4
Person	6	5.6	13.8	14.8	3.2	2.8	4.9	4.4
Rural + Urban								
Male	2.4	2.4	9.1	9.9	1.7	3.2	2.6	2.7
Female	2.6	2	14.3	17.6	1.5	1.2	2.1	1.6
Person	2.5	2.3	10.8	12.4	1.6	1.6	2.4	2.2

Source: Status of Education and Vocational Training in India, NSSO 61st (pp. 43) and 66th (pp. 40).

It is observed that the proportion of persons who received vocational training, is the highest among the unemployed and that too, among the females in both the round. Among unemployed females, the proportion was as high as 12 per cent in the rural areas and 17 per cent in the urban areas in the year 2004–05 which increases to 17 per cent in the rural areas and 19 per cent in the urban areas in the year 2009-10. Among the unemployed males, the proportion was 7 per cent and 12 per cent in the rural and urban areas, respectively in the year 2004–05, which slightly increases to eigth per cent and 13 per cent in the rural and urban areas in 2009-10 respectively. The proportion was around two per cent for persons not in the labour force and two to three per cent for the employed in 2004-05 and the proportion was one per cent in rural areas and Three percent in urban areas in 2009-10 and for employed persons, the proportion was one per cent in the rural areas and six per cent in the urban areas.

2. Helpfulness of Vocational Training in Employment

Table 7 presents the percentage of persons of age 15 - 59 years who received formal vocational training by the helpfulness of vocational training has been presented for each category of persons at the all-India level.In 66th round, for persons who received formal vocational training, information was collected regarding the helpfulness in getting a job.

Table 7: Percentage of age 15 – 59 years who received formal vocational training by the helpfulness of vocational training for each category of persons

Category of person	Helpfulness of the formal vocational training received				
	Helpful in taking up self employmen activity	*Helpful in taking up wage/salaried activity*	*Not helpful*	*Not appli cable*	*All (incl. N.r.)*
		Rural			
Male	21.0	37.6	29.2	8.0	100
Female	14.7	21.7	47.2	15.4	100
Person	18.6	31.5	36.1	10.9	100
		Urban			
Male	13.8	60.3	19.1	6.3	100
Female	13.3	35.2	32.4	18.6	100
Person	13.6	51.4	23.9	10.7	100
		Rural+Urban			
Male	16.5	51.8	22.9	6.9	100
Female	13.8	29.8	38.4	17.3	100
Person	15.5	43.7	28.6	10.7	100

Source: Status of Education and Vocational Training in India, NSSO 66th Round, pp. 43.

The table shows that at the all-India level 59 per cent of those received formal vocational training reported the training as helpful in getting a job (self-employment activity or wage/salaried employment), 16 per cent reported the training as helpful in taking up self-employment activity and 44 per cent reported the training as helpful in taking up wage/salaried employment. In the rural area, nearly 19 per cent reported the training as helpful in taking up self employment activity compared to 14 per cent in urban areas and in rural areas 32 per cent reported the training as helpful in taking up wage/salaried employment compared to 51 per cent in urban areas. *It is noticed that nearly 36 per cent in rural areas and 24 per cent in urban areas reported that the training was not helpful in getting a job.*

3. Conclusions

While concluding the contents of the present study in context of 61st and 66th round of the NSSO data we find that as a corollary, with rise in MPCE, the level of literacy is very high. This confirms that with the dynamic income, the consumer expenditure as an important factor towards the level of literacy in the country.The surprising fact is that in 2009-10 the number of 'no vocational' training persons has increased in comparison with 2004-05.This shows that government has failed to provide opportunities for vocational training for the working age group.Clearly, thus, there lies the need to work more towards higher 'vocational training' not only for female but also specially for both male and female in the rural sector.

Overall in the age of 15–29 we observe that the person with vocational training are getting less participation in work in 2009-10 with respect to the period 2004-05(Graph 1g and 1h). Hence, we may say that due to decline trends in VT the Wpr is declining more steeply over the period. This seems that lack of VT is decreasing the employability in India.

It is also observed that the proportion of persons, who received vocational training, is the highest among the unemployed and that too, among the females in both the round. The most concerning fact of the study is that nearly 36 per cent in rural areas and 24 per cent in urban areas reported that the vocational training was not helpful in getting a job in 2009-10.

Thus, interdependence and segmentation of labour market has meaningful bearing for national educational planners, especially in terms of technical education and Vocational trainings. This shows the need of readdressing the contents of globalisation under which, there should be the Planetary Role of Information Technology. With the use of Information and Communication Technology, it may not only change the dynamics of technical education and vocational training but also may remove the age long barriers which had been causing the under growth in the field of education and employable vocational training.

References

Bloom, D. E., Canning, D. and Sevilla, J., 2003. *The Demographic Dividend; A New Perspective on the Economic Consequences of Population Change.* Santa Monica: RAND.

Goel, V. P., n.d.*http://www.unevoc.unesco.org/.* [Online] Available at: http://www.unevoc.unesco.org/up/India_Country_Paper.pdf[Accessed 01 January 2014].

Mishra, Anup K., P.K. Sen and Rajkishore Pandey, 2011.*Globalisation and Quality Education:* How Can this Be Ensured, Published in the Edited Book entitled 'Teaching and Research in Economics' by Anil k. Thakur and S.S. Somra, 80-96, Deep and Deep Publications, New Delhi, ISBN 978-81-8450-361-6.

NSSO, 2006. *Employment and Unemployment Situation in India, 2004-05,* Part – I, 61st Round, Report No. 515, New Delhi.

NSSO, 2006. *Status of Education and Vocational Training in India 2009-10,* 61th Round, Report No. 517, New Delhi.

NSSO, 2011. *Employment and Unemployment Situation in India 2009-10,* 66th Round, Report No. 537, New Delhi.

NSSO, 2013. *Status of Education and Vocational Training in India 2009-10,* 66th Round, Report No. 551, New Delhi.

Parihar, S. S. 2014, Indian Demographic Dividend, Prospects and Challenges In The Changing Global Economic Scenario. *International Journal of Advance Research.*

Subrahmanya, M. H. B., 2010. Auto SMEs in Bangalore: Does Innovation Promote Employment and Labour Productivity?.*Economic & Political Weekly,* 13 March, xlv(11), pp. 59-66.

Swaminathan, P., 2007. The Interface between Employment and Education in India: The Need for a Discourse. In: K. Kumar and J. Oesterheld, eds. *Education and Social Change in South Asia* .s.l.:Orient Longman Limited, pp. 325-358.

8

Inclusive Growth of Self-Help Groups in India

Jasmin Treesa T.J. and **JasminTreesa T.J.**

1. Introduction

A self-help group may be registered or unregistered. It typically comprises a group of micro entrepreneurs having homogeneous social and economic back-grounds; all voluntarily coming together to save regular small sums of money, mutually agreeing to contribute to a common fund and to meet their emergency needs on the basis of mutual help. They pool their resources to become financially stable, taking loans from the money collected by that group and by making everybody in that group self-employed.The inclusive growth approach takes a longer-term perspective, as the focus is on productive employment as a means of increasing the incomes of poor and excluded groups and raising their standards of living. Financial inclusion is integral to the inclusive growth process and sustainable development of the country. It is a policy of involving a wider section of population deposit mobilis sation and credit intermediation. Financial Inclusion may be defined as the "process of ensuring access to appropriate financial products and services needed by all sections of the society in general and vulnerable groups such as weaker sections and low income groups in particular, at an affordable cost in a fair and transparent manner by regulated, mainstream institutional players". Thus, on the whole, Financial Inclusion has the potential to bring in the unbanked masses into the formal banking system, channelize their savings, stoke their entrepreneurial ambitions by making available credit and thus give a fillip to the economy. Micro Finance has emerged as an important engine for financial Inclusion in India. Micro Finance is banking the un-bankables, bringing credit, savings and other essential financial services within the reach of millions of poor people. It is based on the premise that the poor have skills which remain unutilised or underutilised. By extending services to socially and economically disadvantaged segments of the society, micro finance can become a powerful tool for financial inclusion which then leads to the sustainable growth in the economy (Jones, 2006).

In India, being a developing country there are many people to be embodied under the umbrella of Financial Inclusion. In India, out of 19.9 crore households, only 6.82 crore households, have access to banking services (Economic Review, 2012). Micro Finance is emerging as a powerful instrument for promoting Financial Inclusion in India. Today, micro finance scene is dominated by Self-Help Groups (SHGs) with a bank linkage programme aimed at providing a cost effective mechanism for providing financial services to the unreached poor. Micro Finance through SHGs is an innovative approach for financial inclusion of the poor. Credit facility through SHGs helps the poor in the acquisition of income generating asset and create self employment opportunities and thereby alleviating poverty. Women's access to savings and credit gives them greater economic role in decision-making through their decisions regarding savings and credit. When women control decisions regarding credit and savings, they optimise their own and the household's welfare. At the present juncture, it is important to examine the promise of SHGs in strengthening financial inclusion and inclusion of marginanlised and vulnerable rural,who has been excluded from the formal credit markets for a long period of time.The major objectives of this paper are as follows:

(a) To understand the working and progress of SHGs in India;
(b) To examine the role of Self-Help Groups in helping the rural population to be on the path of financial inclusion.

For analysing such facts, data for the study has been gathered from secondary sources including report of RBI, NABARD, NSSO, Financial Access Survey of World Bank, books on financial inclusion and SHGs and other articles written by eminent authors.

2. Results

For channelising institutional credit to the poor for agriculture and rural development activities a formal system was necessitated. The possibility of collaboration between banks and SHGs for mobilisation of rural savings and delivery of credit to the poor was recognised by the national bank. The need for combining the formal banking sector with the informal system of SHGs thus materialised with the pilot project on 'Linking SHGs with Banks' was launched by NABARD in February 1992. The linking of SHGs with banks primarily aims at integrating informal savings and credit groups with mainstream banking by providing them to enhance their resource base. The linking process, emphasised by NABARD since 1992, has worked around the following broad concepts:

(a) Saving first, no credit without savings;
(b) Savings as partial collateral;
(c) Bank Loan to SHG for on-lending to members;
(d) Income generation programmes to be popularised along with the SHG concept;
(e) Credit decisions for on lending to be the authority of SHG members;
(f) Interest rates and other terms and conditions of loans to be decided by SHG members;

(g) Joint liability of members as a substitute for physical collateral;

(h) Ratio between savings and credit contingent upon credit worthiness and could increase over a period on good repayment record;

(i) Small loans at first and gradual increase to higher credit amounts based on repayment performance and needs.

Table 1: Highlights of the SHG-Bank Linkage Programme 2011-12

Sr. No.	*Particulars*	*Achievements*	
		Physical (No. in lakh)	*Financial (in crore)*
1	**Total number of SHGs saving linked with banks**	**79.60**	6551.41
(i)	Out of total (ofwhich) exclusive Women SHGs	62.99	5104.33
(ii)	Out of total (of which) SGSY SHGs	21.23	1395.24
2	**Total number of SHGs credit linked during 2011-12**	**11.48**	**16534.77**
(i)	Out of total (of which) exclusive Women SHGs	9.23	14132.02
(ii)	Out of total (of which) SGSY SHGs1	2.10	2643.56
3	**Total number of SHGs having loans outstanding as on 31 March 2012**	**43.54**	**36340.00**
(i)	Out of total (of which) exclusive Women SHGs	36.49	30465.28
(ii)	Out of total (of which) SGSY SHGs	12.16	8054.83
4	Average loan amount outstanding/SHG as on March 2012 (in Rs)		83455.01
5	Average loan amount disbursed/SHG during 2011-12 (in ')*		144046.41
6	Estimated number of families covered upto 31 March 2012	103 million	
7	No. of Banks and Financial Institutions submitted MIS (in number)	433	
8	**Data on Joint Liability Groups**		
(i)	Joint Liability Group promoted during the year 2011-12 (lakh)	1.92	
(ii)	Loan disbursed to Joint Liability Groups (JLGs) during the year 2011-12		1700.39
(iii)	Cumulative Joint Liability Groups promoted as on 31 March 2012 (lakh)	3.32	

(iv)	Cumulative loan disbursed to JLGs as on 31 March 2012		2845.68
9	**Support from NABARD**		
(i)	**Capacity building for partner institutions**		
	Number of Programmes conducted during 2011-12	5048	10.26
	Number of participants covered during 2011-12	186952	
	Cumulative number of participants trained upto March 2012	2847770	
(ii)	**Refinance Support**		
	Refinance to banks during 2011-12		3072.59
	Cumulative refinance released upto 31 March 2012		18479.60
(iii)	**Revolving Fund Assistance (RFA and Capital Support) to MFIs**		
	RFA and refinance outstanding as on 31 March 2012		52.02
	Capital support outstanding as on 31 March 2012		20.89
(iv)	**Grant assistance to SHPIs for promotion of SHGs**		
	Grant assistance sanctioned during 2011-12 Cumulative sanctioned upto 31 March 2012		37.95 184.17
(v)	Grant assistance to JLPIs for promotion of JLGs		
	Cumulative sanctioned upto 31 March 2012		36.68

Source: Status of Micro Finance in India, 2011-12.

Table 1 highlights the SHG-Bank Linkage Programme 2011-12. During the year 2011-2012, 11.48 lakh SHGs were saving linked with banks amounting to Rs 16543.77 crore

Table 2 : SHG Bank Linkage in India-Cumulative Progress (1992-2010)

Year	*Number of SHGs Financed*	*Bank Loan (Rs in crore)*
1992-93	255	0.29
1993-94	620	0.65
1994-95	2122	2.44
1995-96	4757	6.06
1996-97	18598	11.84
1997-98	14,317	23.76
1998-99	32,995	57.07
1999-00	94,645	192.98
2000-01	1,14,775	193.00
2001-02	2,63,825	480.90
2002-03	4,63,478	1026.30
2003-04	7,17,360	2048.70
2004-05	1,079,991	3904.20
2005-06	1,618,476	6898.00
2006-07	2,238,565	11398.00
2007-08	2,924,973	18041.00
2008-09	3477965	26816.72
2009-10	4559443	39070.23

Source: NABARD, 2010.

Table 2 shows the cumulative progress of SHG Bank Linkage in India. There has been tremendous increase in the number of SHGs financed and bank loan. The number of SHGs financed has increased from 255 in 1992-1993 to 4559443 in 2009-10. Moreover the amount of bank loan has also increased from Rs 0.29 crore in 1992-1993 to Rs 39070-23 crore in 2009-10.

Table 3 : Overall Progress under SHG-Bank Linkage for last 3 years (crore/ lakh)

Particulars		*2009-10*		*2010-11*		*2011-12*	
		No. of SHGs	*Amount*	*No. of SHGs*	*Amount*	*No. of SHGs*	*Amount*
SHG Saving with Bank as on 31st March	Total SHGs	69.53	6198.7	74.62	7016.30	79.60	6551.41
	All women SHGs	53.10	4498.66	60.98	5298.65	62.99	5104.33
	% of women groups	76.4	72.6	81.7	75.5	79.1	77.9
Loans disburrsed to the year	Total SHGs	15.87	14453.3	11.96	14547.73	11.48	16534.77
	All women	12.94	12429.37	10.17	126322.3	2.10	2643.56
	% of women groups	81.6	86	85	86.8	80.4	85.5
Loans Outstanding Against SHGs as on	Total SHGs	48.51	28038.28	47.87	31221.17	43.54	36340.00
	All women SHGs	38.98	23030.36	39.84	26123.75	36.49	30465.28
	% of women groups	80.3	82.1	83.2	83.7	83.8	83.8

Source: Status of Micro Finance in India, 2011-12.

Table-3 gives the growth of SHGs – saving as well as credit linked–for the last 3 years. Under the SHG-Bank linkage programme, over 103 million rural households have now access to regular savings through 7.96 million SHGs linked to banks. Increasing awareness at the SHG level about the advantage of using the savings for internal loaning is also partly responsible for the decline in saving balance with banks.

3. Conclusion

The SHG-Bank Linkage Programme has emerged as a dominant, relevant and effective programme in terms of borrowers and loans outstanding in India. It is flexible, independence creating, and imparts freedom of savings and borrowing according to the heterogeneous needs and requirements of the group members. The SHG-Bank Linkage Programme has dominant share in promoting Financial Inclusion in India.

Reference

1. Anand, Jaya, (2000), 'Micro Finance in Kerala', *Kurukshetra*, 48 No.11, August 13, pp.16.0
2. Andreas Berkhof, Malcolm Harper (2005), 'SHG-Bank Linkage', *Economic* and Political Weekly, Vol. XL, No. 17, April 23.
3. Basu, Priya and Pradeep Srivastava (2005) 'Exploring Possibilities, Microfinance and Rural Credit Access for the Poor in India', *Economic and Political Weekly*,Vol. XL, No.17, April 23-29, pp.1747-1756.
4. *Economic Review* (2012).
5. Jones, D. Conroy (2008), Financial Inclusion: A new micro finance initiative for APEC', *The Hindu*, June 13.

9

Factors Affecting Child Health: A Study of Respondent Mothers and their Children's Health in Rural West Bengal

Paramita Roy and **Arunangshu Mondal**

1. Introduction

Children are the future of our nation. India's commitment for her nation's children is evident in the Parts III and IV of the Indian Constitution. But for a country with 158.8 million children in the age group of 0-6 years, the task of reaching out to them is quite difficult. The children are the most vulnerable section in society. The age group upto six years and below is also most important because most of the physical, mental, social and cultural development of a child takes place during this period. To combat the various problems of the children, the Government of India has taken various measures viz. welfare programmes, policies, and legislations. One of such successful initiatives is the Integrated Child Development Services (ICDS) launched by the Indian Government in 1975 which provides an integrated package of health care service delivery for children and mothers.

The most common problems that the children in India face are pneumonia, diarrhoea, malnutrition, acute respiratory tract infection, polio, measles, diphtheria, anaemia, poor hygiene, unsafe drinking water, etc. Though there is a decreasing trend still the infant and child mortality is a cause for concern in India. The NFHS-3 (2005-06) shows that in India the IMR is 57 deaths per 1,000 live births compared to the NFHS-2 (1998-99) estimate of 68 deaths per 1,000 live births.

According to the West Bengal Census 2011, West Bengal is the fourth most populous state in India. In fact, it is considered the ninth most populated state in the world. Of the total population of West Bengal state, around 68.11 per cent live in the villages of rural areas among which 12.11 per cent are children below six years. Of the total population of Birbhum district, around 87.20 per cent live in the villages of rural areas of which 12.72 per cent are children below six years. The Government of India is also bound by the declarations of the Millennium Development Summit in September 2000 where representatives from 189 countries committed their nations to a new global partnership to reduce extreme poverty and set out a series of time-bound targets for 2015 that have become famously known as the Millennium

Developmental Goals (MDGs). One of the eight goals (specifically the fourth goal) is dedicated to reduce child mortality to two-thirds the mortality rate among children under five between 1990 and 2015. As a member signatory India is also committed to achieve this goal. It was seen that in 1990, the under-five mortality rate was 116 per 1000 live births in India. As per the MDG target the under-five mortality goal for 2015 for India is 38 per 1000 live births (UNICEF, 2010). Accordingly the Government of India has initiated various policies and programmes viz. National Health Policy, National Population Policy, National Rural Health Mission etc. where the goal of the Millennium Summit has been clearly reflected with regard to the reduction of the below-five IMR.

The good intention of the government was evident in the Five Year Plans in India. The First Five Year Plan (1951-56) to the Fifth Five Year Plan (1974-79) was based on the recommendations of the Bhore committee (1946), Mudaliar committee (1961) etc.The life expectancy at birth increased from about 32 years as per 1951 census to about 52 years during 1976-81.The IMR rate came down from 146 during the fifties to 110 in 1981. About 50,000 PHCs including 340 upgraded PHCs with 30 bedded hospitals, 106 medical colleges with admission capacity of 11,000 per annum and five lakh hospital beds were established. The main focus of the health planning during the period between the Sixth Plan (1980-1985) and the Eleventh Plan (2007-12) was at improving the availability of "Health Human Resources", building rural health infrastructure, improving the availability of medicines etc. During Eleventh Plan period, the Government took time bound goals towards reducing IMR to 28 per 1000 live births, reducing TFR to 2.1, reducing MMR to 1 per 1000 live birth, providing clean drinking water for all by 2009 and ensuring no slip-back, reducing malnutrition among children below three years to half its present level and reducing anaemia among women and girls by 50 per cent. The 12th Five year Plan aim at locating a health sub-centre in every panchayat and anganwadi centre in every habitation, their formal inter-linkage being a must for integrating the delivery of health, nutrition and pre-school education services. The 12th plan aims to increase total health expenditure as percentage of GDP to 2.5 per cent by the end of the Plan Period.

2. Rationale of the Study

The health of a nation is an essential component of development and it plays a significant role for nation's progress. Health is an important indicator of wellbeing. In short, health is wealth. Children are the future of our nation. They can positively contribute to the socio-economic development of the country. It has been well documented that the children across caste, class and religion face various problems related to their quality of life particularly health. It is of great significance to study the factors affecting child health so that the areas of intervention can necessarily be identified. Contributing to policy making in the form of important feedback from grassroots village level studies is the need of the day as a generic approach to policy design fails to internalise the specificities of the issue. The particular research setting is chosen keeping in mind the socio-economic levels and religion followed so as to see whether these factors do have an effect on child health. Further the researcher's familiarity with the field as part of his fieldwork practicum was an added rationale for choosing the particular villages.

The study aims to have a direct contribution to both micro and macro level field and policy level interventions. In the field level, the understanding of the factors affecting child health will help awareness generation about the basic requirements for rearing a child regarding nutrition, hygiene, immunisation etc. The study will also contribute to an understanding of the working of the ICDS programmes at the village level. Further the research will identify whether child healthcare is dependent only on the immediate care-giving or whether it is holistically linked to the heath care system, environmental factors and background of the families.

3. Objectives of the Study

(1) To study the policies and programmes on child health in India.

(2) To analyse the factors that correlate strongly with child health in the context of the selected villages in Birbhum.

4. Policies and Programmes on Child Health in India

Periodically the Government of India has launched various policies and programmes on child health to improve the health status of the children of the country. It was in August 22, 1974 that the then department of Social Welfare of the Indian Government of India considered the formulation of a National Policy for Children. The just finished National Policy on Education and the U.N. Declaration of the Rights of the Child primarily guided it. It was decided that the resources would primarily be tapped from our country itself. The major areas of focus were the nutritional requirement of the children but also of the expectant mothers. Free and compulsory education up to fourteen years was also mentioned in this policy and also the emphasis on physical education and sports at school and community levels.

1970s
- National Policy for Children, 1974.
- Integrated Child Development Services, 1975.

1980s
- National Health Policy, 1983.
- National Control of Diarrhoeal Diseases Programme, 1984.
- Early Childhood Care and Education for 3-6 Years Age Group
- Children Under the Programme of Universialisation of
- Elementary Education, 1986.
- Acute Respiratory Infection Control Programme, 1987.

1990s
- National Nutrition Policy, 1993.
- Integrated Programme For Street Children, 1993.
- National Creche Fund Scheme, 1994.
- Pulse Polio Immunisation Programme, 1995.
- Mid Day Meal Scheme, 1995.
- Reproductive and Child Health Programme, 1997.
- Childline Services, 1998-99

2000
- National Population Policy, 2000.
- National Commission for Children Bill, 2001.
- National Health Policy, 2002.
- National Charter for Children, 2003.
- Integrated Management of Neonatal And Childhood Illness, 2003.
- National Guidelines on Infants and Young Child Feeding, 2004.

The policy also focused on prevention of child labour and the differently abled children. Another point of emphasis was the location of the children in the family and priority of the child's interest in settling litigation. The need for constituting a National Board was felt. Partnerships with the NGOs, charities and trusts were sought to enhance people's participation. Another interesting mention was that of the socially handicapped children who were forced to adapt the harsh realities of life.

- The National Plan of Action for Children, 2005.
- National Rural Health Mission, 2005.
- Reproductive and Child Health Programme Phase -2, 2005.
- National Urban Health Mission, 2006.

- Rajib Gandhi National Creche Scheme for the Children of Working Mother, 2006
- Policy on Micro Nutrient- Vitamin-A, 2006.
- 2005 — National Rehabilitation Centre, 2008-09.
- Navajat Sishu Surakha Karyakaram, 2009.
- Facility Based Integrated Management of Neonatal And Childhood Illness, 2009.
- Facility Based New Born Care, 2011.
- Home Based New Born Care, 2011.
- National Early Childhood Care and Education Policy, 2012.

Note: The black sentences denote the policies and the brown sentences represent the programmes initiated by the government of India.

The ICDS launched in 1975 upheld the national policy for children in that it focused on pre-school children and the effects of malnutrition, morbidity, reduced learning and mortality. The ICDS also focused on enhancing the capability of the mother to look after the health needs of the children. It also serves as a platform for referral services. In 1993, the National Nutrition Policy stresses on shortterm and long-term changes in the system to provide essential foods to expecting mothers and children by popularising low-cost nutritious food and controlling deficiencies of micronutrients among vulnerable groups.

In the policy scenario, another major landmark was the launching of the National Commission for Children Bill in 2001. Though late, this move carried on the essence of the National Policy for Children of 1974. The Commission oversees the implementation of the existing laws for children, conducts research and undertakes appropriate measures for awareness generation of children's issues. Close to its heels came the National Charter for Children in 2003. The Right to Health of the Child for survival, life and liberty and the right to play and leisure and the duties of both the parents in rearing the children form the highlights of the charter. In 2005, the National Plan of Action for Children provided specific target oriented goals that reminded the planners the extent of improvement required in areas of child health, nutrition, child and environment and child development. Thus, it was a measure to pull up the strings towards making efforts at child welfare more vibrant and effective.

As per the policies, there were a myriad of programmes that had very specific objectives like reducing infant deaths due to diarrhea, pneumonia, TB, polio and respiratory infections and were introduced by the government to improve the quality of life of the children. Apart from that various other initiatives that had indirect implications for child health had been introduced by the government. These include the mid-day meal scheme, universalisation of education programme, rural and urban health missions, crèche schemes etc.

5. Review on Factors Affecting Child Health

Som S. *et al.* have emphasised the fact that immunisation coverage is influenced by socio-economic variables. The study was based on a sample of 1279 children aged between 12 and 35 months. Data was obtained from the DLHS and RCH-2 surveys that were conducted from 2002 to 2004. Approximately 54 per cent of children in Wests, Bengal were covered for immunisation. The results for receiving full immunisation varied greatly between the various districts, ranging from 23.3 per cent in Murshidabad to 72.2 per cent in Hugli. Low rates of coverage were found among the groups of poor minorities, especially in rural areas. The educational level of the parents was found to have a significant influence on child immunisation coverage. Thus, the study concluded that in order to improve upon the rates of child immunisation coverage, efforts should be concentrated on the poor children from minority groups and those living in rural areas.

In a concurrent study by Sengupta Paramita *et al.* (2004) the risk factors for low birth weight of children was analysed in Ludhiana, Punjab. The fact that half of all prenatal and one-third of all infant deaths were directly or indirectly related to low birth weight, made an important target for public health interventions, which required a clear understanding of the multi-factorial origin of low birth weight. The study was conducted with 50 cases (low birth weight newborns) and 100 (normal birth weight newborns) in Christian Medical College Hospital, Ludhiana, Punjab. The study found that pre-maturity, ante-natal complications and maternal weight gain (<10 kg) during the pregnancy were found to be significant risk factors for low birth weight. The study also identified maternal height less than 155 cms as a significant risk factor for low birth weight. Thus, the study concluded that the need for improving maternal nutritional is necessary for providing better ante-natal care.

A study on nutritional status of children in India through a household socio-economic survey as the contextual determinant was made by Barun Kanjilal and others. The data was collected from the NFHS-3 (2005-06) survey. According to this study, across the states, a disproportionate burden of stunting is observed among children from poor socio-economic status, more so in urban areas. The states having lower prevalence of chronic childhood malnutrition shows much higher burden among the poor. Children from highest socio-economic status quintile posses better nutritional status than those from the poorest quintile. Thus, the study concluded that, in spite of the declining trend of chronic childhood malnutrition in India, the concerns remain for its disproportionate burden on the poor. The socio-economic gradient of long-term nutritional status among children needs special focus, more so in the states where chronic malnutrition among children apparently demonstrates a lower prevalence. The paper calls for state specific policies which are designed and implemented on a priority basis, keeping in view the nature of inequality in childhood malnutrition on the country and its differential characteristics across the states.

Ajay Kumar *et al.* launched a field study on women and child health in Uttar Pradesh. The data collected from NFHS-3(2005-06) showed that, every sixth malnourished child in India lived in UP which ranked second with respect to prevalence of malnutrition amongst children under three years of age in India. About 56 per cent children born to illiterate mothers were underweight. 57 per cent of children born to malnourished mothers were underweight. One in every twenty new born was put to the breast within the first hour of birth. Only 1 in 16 children receive one dose of vitamin A supplement. By the age of 6-9 months, only 1 in 5 children receive both breast milk and solid foods. By the age of 12-23 months, only one in five children were fully vaccinated.

The prevalence of high mortality of children under five years of age urban areas was the issue under study by Wadgave Hanmanta *et al.* The sample size for this study was 420. According to this study out of 420 children, 298 were males and 182 were females. 75 per cent of female children were found to be more at risk as compared to male children. Delayed weaning (70.47 per cent), low weight (70 per cent), repeated attacks of diarrhoea and respiratory infections (54.28 per cent) were most common risk factors found in the present study. High risk children were more in the age group of 13-48 months. Prevalence of high risk children was more in lower socio-economic group.

A study on an awareness, satisfaction and utilisation of Integrated Child Development Services by mothers in rural Orissa was initiated by Das Bandana *et al.* (2008). A study was conducted in five villages of Orissa that were under ICDS scheme for at least last 20 years. 200 mothers of children aged one to six years were interviewed. In rural Orissa ICDS is well accepted as a welfare programme by the community programme by the community majority of mothers were aware about and also were utilising most of the six packages of services provided by ICDS.The most acceptable services were immunisation and pre-school education with awareness/ satisfaction more than 95 per cent. The services that were less popular were referral services, health check up of children and supplementary nutrition. Misconceptions about the purpose of pre-school education and supplementary nutrition were also common. Thus the study concluded that an effectiveness of ICDS can be advanced by increasing awareness about some of its services and especially by improving the quality/quantity of supplementary diets.

Tanu Midha *et al.* carried out a study on breast feeding practices in rural Kanpur (2008).The study conducted at the primary health centre at block Patara in Kanpur district on mothers of children in 6 to 24 months of age. The study concluded that about 22 per cent infants were initiated on breast feeding within one hour of birth. Mothers of 51per cent of infants exclusively breast fed their babies for six months. Approximate 72.7 per cent infants were given pre-lacteals. Birth interval more than or equal to three; male child and institutional deliveries were factors leading to early initiation of breast feeding.

The causes and contributory factors of infant deaths was the subject of study of Sanat Rathod *et al.* in the Corporation area of Bhavnagar; Gujarat (2009). According to this study, information on all infant deaths registered from 1st January 2009 to 31st December 2009 was obtained from Bhavnagar municipal corporation office. The study concluded that 76 per cent of infant deaths were in neo-natal period, of which 53 deaths were in first 24 hours of life and 7 in day 1-7 (62.5 per cent in early neo-natal period). Male: female ratio in infant deaths was 57.3 per cent and 42.7per cent In 12.5 per cent cases, it was home deliveries conducted by untrained dais. Only 48 per cent had ever started breastfeeding started within half an hour and 20 per cent gave colostrums, 20.8 per cent also gave prelacteal. In 57.3 per cent cases, maternal health problems was reported during pregnancy/delivery, out of which most common was anemia (52.7 per cent). In immediate causes of infant deaths most common was severe birth asphyxia (27 per cent).

Katara PS *et al.* (2009) conducted a study on feeding practices among infants aged up to six months in urban slums of Vododara. Number of participants for this study was 192 infants up to six months of age. The study shows that, early initiation of breastfeeding was seen in 75 per cent of infants, pre-lacteal feed was given in 36 per cent of infants and colostrums was given in 87 per cent of infants.15.5 per cent infants received exclusive breast feeding while majority(76.8 per cent) were given water with breast feeding. Thus, the study concluded that still early initiation of breast feeding and exclusive breast feeding is not participated at a desired level.

Ram Rama *et al.* carried out a study on bio-social determinants of low-birth weight- in a hospital-based study in Bihar (2009). 81 live births were the participants for this study. The study shows that 33 per cent of newborn babies were found to be of low birth weight. Statistically significant association was observed between low birth weight and mother's age, religion, occupation of mothers and mothers consuming extra meals together with iron and folic acid during pregnancy. No significance was found between the occurrence of low birth weight and literacy status of mothers and type of family.

6. Methodology

- The researcher is following descriptive research design. The main feature of descriptive research design is that the researchers have prior knowledge about the problem to be studied. Here the researcher's have knowledge about the problems of child health and the various factors that affects the child health.
- To conduct the study the researcher used both qualitative data and quantitative data.
- The 1st and 2nd objectives of the study include secondary sources. Data pertaining to the 3rd objective will involve primary data collected from the field.
- Interview schedule including open-ended questions for the mothers, ICDS workers have been developed as tools of data collection.
- Here the universe is the total number of children in two villages namely, Mahidapur and Surul i.e., 570 according to Anganwadi centers reports in these two villages.
- Total sample size is 100 out of 570.
- To conduct this research the researcher used proportionate random sampling technique. For village Surul, the numbers were randomly selected from the range 1 to 212. For Mahidapur village numbers were randomly selected from the range 1 to 358. On the basis of this, the researcher took 40 samples from Surul village and 60 samples from Mahidapur village.
- The process of data collection is carried in two stages: A pilot study was undertaken to understand the factors that are affecting child health. Then in depth interview was carried on with each of the mother using the structured questionnaire.

(Random Number Generator StatTrek. Available from: http://stattrek.com/statistics/random-number-generator.aspx).

DATA ANALYSIS

Table 1. : Cross Table of factors related to child health

Indicators	*Under weight at birth*	*Malnourished*	*Immunized*	
			Yes	*No*
Mother's age at child birth:<18 yrs	6	13	24	2
Mother's age at child birth:>18 yrs	12	19	73	1
	Total=18	Total=32	Total=97	Total=3
Mother's education: Primary\<	8	22	46	3
Mother's education Secondary>	10	10	51	0
	Total=18	Total=32	Total=97	Total=3
Family Income: Rs 1000 -2500	12	25	66	2
Family Income: Rs 2500-5000	6	7	31	1
	Total=18	Total=32	Total=97	Total=3
Caste: General	5	14	97	3
Reserved	13	18	0	0
	Total=18	Total=32	Total=97	Total=3
Religion: Hindu	6	9	38	2
Muslim	12	23	59	1
	Total=18	Total=32	Total=97	Total=3
Family Size: 3-6 members	12	25	80	3
Family Size: 7-10 members	6	7	17	0
	Total=18	Total=32	Total=97	Total=3
Father's Occupation Farming	11	3	12	0
Daily Labour	4	22	53	3
Self Employment	3	7	32	0
	Total=18	Total=32	Total=97	Total=3
Mother's Income Self – Employed	6	15	36	2
No Income	12	17	61	1
	Total=18	**Total=32**	**Total=97**	**Total=3**

Source : Fieldwork (2012).

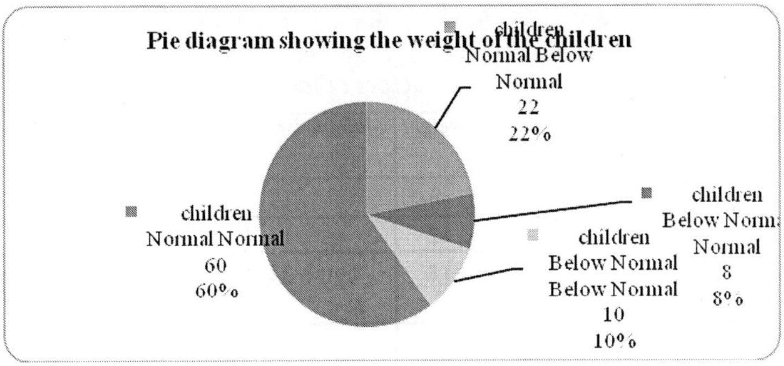

It is seen that 22 per cent of the children have become below normal in weight from a normal birth weight. This is a significant observation as it requires further probe on the factors which can be responsible for such a weight loss. Moreover 18 per cent of the children were below normal at birth and only eigth per cent of them have become normal whereas the rest have remained below normal.

The table was an exercise to gain an overall idea regarding the factors that can be associated with child health. This attempt was to acquire learning on our third objective. From a closer look it can be identified that probably mother's education and income, religion, family size and father's occupation are certain possible variables significant in the health of children.

7. Analysis of Qualitative Data

The researcher took the following data for qualitative analysis. These are – household assets, number of days in a week visit the ICDS centre, immunisation date (without looking at card), breast feeding practices, health problem of the child and diet of the child (morning, afternoon and night).

The researcher observed that the household assets of these respondents are mobile, cycle, TV etc are common. Only three respondents family have motor cycle. The researcher did not find any four wheelers among these families.

In the case of frequency of visiting the ICDS in a week, the researcher found that almost all mothers visited the ICDS centers regularly along with their child/children. They also said that even if they were busy with their work then their family members visited the ICDS centers along with the child/children. So, it might be said that all child/children regularly visited the ICDS centers whether it was with their mothers or their other family members.

When the researcher asked about the next immunisation date (without looking at card) to the mothers, it was found that majority of the mothers informed that they were unable to give this answer without looking at the card. They informed that they were not educated enough to remember such things. They also informed that the ICDS worker informed them about the next immunisation date and on that day they immunised their child/ children.

In the case of breast feeding practices among the mothers, it has been seen that all mothers breastfed their child. They informed that they were continuing the breastfeeding up to *annaprasan* (the first rice feeding ceremony of the child which will take place roughly at the age of six months) and after that they will give the complementary feeding along with the breastfeeding. Some mothers informed them they will continue the breast feeding up to one year while some informed that if possible they might continue the practice for more than one year. They were unsure about the guidelines that the Government made i.e., National Guidelines on Infant and Young Child Feeding, 2004. So it can be said that they follow the traditional culture regarding the breastfeeding practice as well as the guidance that they get from the ICDS worker.

The researcher found that the common problem that their children faced is that of fever. Beside this the researcher also found that some children were weak among those that were malnourished. Only two children suffered major diseases since from birth that is ARI and asthma.

The researcher observed the dietary pattern of the child. It was noticed that at morning the children were sent to the ICDS centre where they ate whatever the ICDS worker cooked. Beside this at home they also ate biscuits, tea etc. In the afternoon, most of the children took lunch with their parents i.e. rice. At night some children ate rice or roti etc whatever their family members or parents prepared for their dinner. Children who were below six months were exclusively breastfed.

8. Testing of Hypothesis

Table 2 : Significant factors affecting weight of child at birth

Indicators	*Chi-square value*	*Degrees of freedom*	*p-value*	*Significance*
Mother's age at child birth	0.46	01	p=0.50	Not signi ficant
Mother's edu cation	11.92	01	p<0.001	Significant
Family Income	2.71	01	p=0.10	Not signif icant
Caste	13.63	01	p<0.001	NotSign ificant
Religion	1.06	01	p=0.30	Not sign ificant
Family Size	14.22	01	p<0.001	Significant
Father's Occu- pation	15.09	02	p<0.001	Significant
Mother's Income	9.79	01	p<0.001	Significant

Source: Authors' calculations based on field data (2012).

Mother's education and income are significant factors affecting the weight of the child at birth. Another factor which comes out important is the size of the family. Whereas the awareness and knowledge level of mothers do affect pre-birth care-taking of pregnant mothers, the size of the family indicates how this care has the possibility of getting too diluted with a larger family size. Even the mothers have expressed preference for smaller families where they can make people understand the level of care that should be taken before a child is born of the mother. Thus, there is a need for continuing the effort of supportive nutritious food services for the women of the weaker sections for a proper birth weight of their babies. The mother's income helps the family to spare some extra care for the pregnant mothers. However, most mothers also feel that working also enhances the importance of the women in the family and their effort to command some care for themselves in the family. Father's income too has expectedly come out as a significant variable as the income from the prime income earners does determine the distributional effects of care in the family.

Table 3: Significant factors affecting nutritional status of child

Indicators	*Chi-square value*	*Degrees of freedom*	*p-value*	*Significance*
Mother's age at child birth	1.10	01	p=0.30	Not signi-ficant
Mother's ed-ucation	10.76	01	p<0.001	Significant
Family Income	11.38	01	p<0.001	Significant
Caste	15.02	01	p<0.001	Not Signi ficant
Religion	0.58	01	p=0.50	Not sign ificant
Family Size	10.83	01	p=0.001	Significant
Father's Occu pation	15.09	02	p=0.20	Not signi ficant
Mother's Income	14.77	01	p<0.001	Significant

Source: Authors' calculations based on field data (2012).

The education and the income of the mothers were again significant in determining the nutritional status of the children after birth till the time of the survey. Family size, too, was significant in determining the same. But income of the family which did not prove to be significant in determining the weight of the child at birth was significant in determining the nutritional status of the child after birth. This was perhaps because most of the families were quite aware about the growing demands of supportive nutrition on the one hand which the families had to provide in addition to the daily food received in the ICDS centre. Some families also pointed out the growing prices of consumption items in general which made the family income a crucial variable in determining the health of the children. This was also because in most homes the food cooked for the children was the same as the food for the entire family. The occupation of the father, however was not a significant variable in determining the nutritional statues of the child after birth.

9. Summary and Conclusion

This sample of a hundred mothers with children going to ICDS presents the picture of rural mothers in the present day.

- Most of the mothers (97per cent) were between eighteen and twenty-five years when interviewed and they reported that majority of them (64 per cent) were minors when they were married and still a majority of them were minors or just about eighteen when they had given birth to their first child.

- However the sizes of the families were mostly reasonably small with 83 per cent of the families having a maximum of six members.
- Almost two-thirds of the fathers and half of the mothers had a minimum of secondary education.
- Most of the families had a BPL card with a monthly income of the fathers below Rs 5000 and those of the earning mothers around Rs 2500 per month. Majority of the fathers were daily labourers and the mothers had home-based employment.
- Household assets like mobiles, cycles and television sets were common.
- One-third of the children were malnourished.
- Another area of concern was that only 18 per cent of the families had sanitation facility at home.
- However, around eighty per cent of the households had pucca houses, 88 per cent had bank accounts and 99 per cent had ration cards.
- Factors like caste, religion, father's occupation and family size were probable factors in the determination of child malnutrition.
- Education of the mother might have an association with child malnutrition.
- Almost all the children were immunised and the mothers had full trust on ICDS and did not make any own effort to learn about the immunisation schedules or types of immunisation.
- The children below six months were exclusively breast fed and those above six months were fed the same diet as that of other family members.
- The education of the mothers and the income earning status of the mothers were significant factors in determining the health status of the child.
- The occupation of the father was a significant variable in determining the nutritional status of the child after birth.
- Family size proved to be a significant variable in determining the health of the child before and after the birth of the child.
- Caste and religion did not play a significant role as a determining factor in the health of the children.

The research brings out certain encouraging observations in the issues related to the rural awareness about opening and maintaining bank accounts and ration cards. Most of the people have also managed to build pucca houses. This shows an improvement in the basic living patterns of these people. Most of the girls are still marrying at a young age though most of them have become fortunate to study till primary and some of them till the higher secondary level. This perhaps shows that education has helped to improve their economic quality of life, not the social quality of life. The ICDS as a welfare scheme have had a tremendous effect on the immunisation and nutritional status of rural children. The rural mothers were very confident on the ICDS. Income proved to be very significant in determining the health of the child and so it was clear that providing for income earning opportunities for the women particularly, prove useful in improving the child's health. The education level of the mothers need to be raised as it had a positive chain effect in raising the age at marriage, taking pre-natal care of oneself, and maintaining the health of the child after birth.

10. Policy Concerns

One area of serious concern that still looms large is that many girls are getting married at a very young age and automatically they are becoming mothers at a very young age. Probably this is due to the dowry problem that is still troubling the rural society. Awareness and a stricter enforcement of laws is a necessity to help the rural women.

The existence of malnutrition demonstrates the need for intensification of the ICDS programme primarily because it has become a household name to the rural mothers. Since most of the mothers are educated the ICDS workers should encourage the mothers to know more about the details of the immunisation schedules, the common diseases of children and the basic information on hygiene. There is a need for qualitative thinking put into the working of the ICDS.

The respondents mostly had mobiles and televisions and these could be used for awareness generation and sending alert messages for childcare guidelines and immunisation dates.

The education of women must be designed so as to make it flexible giving a chance for rural women to continue learning even after marriage. There should also be flexible home-based jobs as education and income of the mothers proved to be very important in determining the health of the child.

There is a need to revise the concept of malnutrition as followed by the ICDS workers beyond the consideration of just the present weight of the child. Existence of recurring illnesses, disorders of the skin, eyes etc., can be some other variables which can be included after consultation with the pediatricians. Thus, there is a need of inter-collaborative research.

The study points out that the core factors like education and income have positive trickling effects on a child's health. Thus, there should be concerted efforts at improving the fundamental factors of the economy which would perhaps take care of the secondary factors like family size, age at marriage and health of children. Gradually self-sufficiency would set in and excessive dependence of the people on the state would be removed.

References

1. Das, B. *et al.* (2012), Awareness, Satisfaction and Utilization of Integrated Child Development Services by mothers in rural Orissa, *Indian Journal of Maternal and Child Health,* Apr-Jun, Vol. 14(2).
2. Kanjilal, B. *et al.* (2010), Nutritional Status of children in India: household socio-economic condition as the contextual determinant, *International Journal for Equity in Health.*
3. Kumar, A. *et al.* (2005-06), Field Study on Women and Child Health Profiles in Uttar Pradesh, *Kurukshetra,* February-2010, Vol. 54:24-26.
4. Katara, P.S. *et al.* (2009), A study on Feeding Practices among Infants aged up to 6 months in urban slums of Vododara, *Indian Journal of Maternal and Child Health,* 2011, Vol. 13(2).
5. Midha, T. *et al.* (2010), Breast Feeding Practices in Rural Kanpur - A Cross-sectional Study, *Indian Journal of Maternal and Child Health,* Volume-14 (1).
6. Rathod, S .et al. (2009), Analysis of causes of Infant Mortality by Autopsy Method in corporation Area of Bhavangar; Gujrat. *Indian Journal of Maternal & Child Health,* 2012, Vol14(2).
7. Rama, R . *et al.* (2011), Bio-Social Determinants of Low-Birth Weight- A Hospital Based Study in Bihar, *Indian Journal of Maternal and Child Health,* Vol. 13 (4).
8. Som, S. *et al.* (2010), Socio- economic Impact on Child Immunization in the District of Wests Bengal, *India, Singapore Medical Journal,* Vol. 51 (5) pp. 406-412.
9. Sengupta, P. *et al.* (2009), Risk Factors for Low Birth Weight, Ludhiana, Punjab, *Indian Journal of Maternal and Child Health,* Jan-Dec, Volume-11.
10. Wadgave, H. *et al.* (2012), Prevalence of High Risk under five mortality in Urban Areas, *Indian Journal of Maternal and Child Health,* Apr-Jun, Volume-14(2).
11. http://www.health.gov.bt/doph/cdd/ariCdd.pdf for Acute Respiratory Infection Programme (1987).
12. http://www.wcd.nic.in/childlineservice.htm for Childline Services (1998-99).
13. http://mohfw.nic.in/NRHM/Documents/CH/F_IMNCI_Modules/Facility_based_care_facilitator_Guide.pdf for Facility Based Integrated Management of Neonatal and Childhood Illness.
14. http://www.mohfw.nic.in/NRHM/Documents/Brief_Note_on_CH_Nov_2011.pdf for Facility Based Newborn Care Services (2011).

15. http://www.mohfw.nic.in/NRHM/Documents/Brief_Note_on_CH_Nov_2011.pdf for Home Based Newborn Care (2011).
16. http://www.census2011.co.in.
17. Integrated Child Development Services (ICDS) Scheme (1975) http://www.wcd.nic.in.
18. Integrated programme for Street children (1993) http://wcd.nic.in/streetchildscheme.htm.
19. Integrated Management of Neonatal and childhood Illness (IMNCI-2003) http://www.mohfw.nic.in/NRHM/Documents/Brief_Note_on_CH_Nov_2011.pdf
20. http://www.mdm.nic.in for Mid Day Meal scheme (1995)
21. http://www.wcd.nic.in/national_policy_for_children_1974.pdf National Policy for Children (1974).
22. www.health.gov.bt/doph/cdd/ariCdd.pdf for National Control of Diarrheal Diseases Programme (1984)
23. http://www.wcd.nic.in/nnpfor National Nutrition Policy (1993)
24. www.mohfw.nic.in/NRHM/.../National_Health_policy_2002.pdf for National Health Policy (NHP-1983).
25. http://www.wcdhry.gov.in/NCFS.htm for National creche fund scheme (1994).
26. National Population Policy (NPP-2000 http://india.unfpa.org/drive/NationalPopulation-Policy2000.pdf
27. http://www.wcd.nic.in/ncchildren.htm
28. http://www.mohfw.nic.in/NRHM/National_Health_policy_2002.pdf for National Health Policy (NHP-2002).
29. http://www.wcd.nic.in/nationalcharter2003.htm for National charter for Children (2003).
30. http://wcd.nic.in/nationalguidelines.pdfm for National Guidelines on Infants and Young Child Feeding (2004).
31. http://www.nrhmorissa.gov.in/pdf/Nutritional_Rehabilitation_Center.pdf) for Nutritional Rehabilitation Centers (2008-09).
32. http://www.mohfw.nic.in/NRHM/Documents/Brief_Note_on_CH_Nov_2011.pdf
33. http://www.wcd.nic.in/.../National%20ECCE%20Policy%20draft%20(1)National Early Childhood Care and Education (ECCE) Policy (2012).

34. http://www.nihfw.org/NDC/DocumentationServices/NationalHealthProgramme/REPRODUCTIVEANDCHILDHEALTHReproductive and Child Health Programme (RCH-1997).

35. http://www.mohfw.nic.in/NRHM/RCH/guidelines/NPIP_Rev_III.pdf for Reproductive and Child Health Programme-Phase-2 (2005).

36. http://www.iccw.in/creche_scheme for Rajiv Gandhi National Creche Scheme for the Children of Working Mothers (2006).

a. **Note:** All the websites were visited during May 2011 to Apr 2012.

10

Role of Credit and Banking of Rural Development in Agriculture Sector

Ms. Sony S. Hiremath

1. Introduction

Reserve Bank of India (RBI) had a mandate to promote rural credit and banking by virtue of the provisions of Section 54 of the RBI Act. Through the State Bank of India (SBI) Act in 1955, the SBI was made an important organisation for extending rural credit to supplement the efforts of cooperative institutions. These cooperative institutions, better known as primary agricultural credit societies (PACS)[1]. also provide other agricultural inputs to the farmers. The next step to supplement the efforts of cooperatives and commercial banks was the establishment of regional rural banks in 1975 in different states with equity participation from commercial banks, central and state governments. In 1982, to consolidate the various arrangements made by the RBI to promote/supervise institutions and channel credit to rural areas, the National Bank for Agricultural and Rural Development (NABARD) was established [2].

2. Economic Development - Role of Rural India

India is known as country of villages and the agriculture and allied activities are the backbone for the economic development of the country. Agriculture Sector assumes vital importance since it provides livelihood to three and four of the country's population besides becoming significant source for raw material for many industries. Thus, agriculture is an important engine for economic growth of the country.

Agriculture is a tradition which has shaped the culture and economic life of the people and therefore will continue to be central to all strategies on planned socio-economic development of the country. Rapid growth of agriculture is essential not only to achieve self-reliance but also to bring about equity in distribution of income and wealth resulting in reduction of poverty levels. In this context, it is worth to recapitulate the thoughts of first Prime Minister of India Sri. Pandit Jawaharlal Nehru *"If Agriculture does not go right, nothing else will"* which speaks the importance attached to the agriculture in those years.

Table 1 : Rural and Urban Banking at Glance

Group	*Population*	*Branches (Crore)*	*Per Branch (in '000)*	*Share of population*	*Share of Deposit Advances*
Rural	83 (68)	34 (37)	24	9	8
Urban	38 (32)	59 (63)	6	91	92
Total	**121**	**93**	**13**	**100**	**100**
Source: Census 2011 and RBI Banking Statistics – Handout Dec'11				*() denotes per cent*	

3. **The important functions of NABARD are as follows:**

   (a) Providing finance and also refinance for production and marketing in the rural areas.

   (b) Coordinating and advising the operations of institutions engaged in rural credit.

   (c) Promoting research in agriculture and rural development.

4. **Objectives of the Study**

   (a) To explore the current scenario of agricultural credit.

   (b) To identify the factors responsible for growth of agricultural credit.

   (c) To know whether agricultural credit is effective to promote the economic standard in future.

Regional Rural Banks plays a key role as an important vehicle of credit delivery in rural areas with the objective of credit dispersal to small, marginal farmers and socio-economically weaker section, of population for the development of agriculture, trade and industry .But still its commercial viability has been questioned due to its limited business flexibility, smaller size of loan and high risk in loan and advances. Rural banks need to remove lack of transparency in their operation which leads to unequal relationship between banker and customer.

5. **Conclusion**

Concerted efforts have been initiated by the Government of India through several plans and measures to alleviate poverty in rural India, there still remains much more to be done to bring prosperity in the lives of the people in rural areas. At present, technology dissemination is uneven and slow in the rural areas. Good efforts of organisations developing technologies, devices and products for rural areas could not yield high success. Experiences of many countries suggest that technological development fuelled by demand has a higher dissemination rate. However, in India, technology developers for rural areas have been catering to needs (with small improvement), rather than creating demand. Besides, there is also an imbalance between strategies and effective management programmes. Propagation of technology/schemes for rural development is slow and there is a lacking in wider participation of different stakeholders. An ideal approach may therefore, include the government, panchayats, village personals, researchers, industries, NGOs and private companies to not only help in reducing this imbalance, but also to have a multiplier effect on the overall economy.

References

1. Ministry of Rural Development, Govt. of India, Chapter VII- *Rural Development*, pp. 88-99.
2. Article of Dr. C Rangarajan, Chairman, Prime Minister's Economic Advisory Council titled *"Financial Inclusion – Not an Option but a Compulsion"* published in September 2010 issue of "The Banking & Financial World".
3. Paper presented by Dr. K. G Karmakar, Managing Director, NABARD on *"Financial Inclusion* – Branchless Banking and Beyond".

11
Rural Credit Market and Village Economies

H. R. Prajapati

1. Introduction

The rural economy is regulated via agriculture and related activity, which provide livelihood for rural people. According to NSSO Report 2011, agriculture sector employs 52.9 per cent of the total workforce, which constitute 46 per cent of the total geographical area of the country. The rural economy can played a vital role in achieving the goal of inclusive and sustainable growth of the Indian economy. The fact shows that 33.8 per cent of the rural population lived below the poverty line in 2009-10, which emphasise the need for high and sustainable growth in the agriculture sector. The major source of income, employment and livelihood of rural people face a lot of distress due to low growth in agriculture sector in the last decade, which had created attention and concern for policy makers. To add to this concern, the NSS 59th round, 2006 report, stated that around 27 per cent of the farmers were not interested in farming as it was not profitable and 40 per cent of all the farmers wanted to quit the farming profession if they had other choice. The secondary sector of rural economy also facing problem and small and medium scale industries viz. handloom, textile, carpet, lather, etc. are collapsed due to lack of credit, infrastructure, market and high cost. The service sector of rural economy has not, capacity to provide employment and livelihood for the rural people. Thus, for the sustainable development of rural economy need to diversify the primary and secondary sector along with the support of treasury sector.

In most of the states, agriculture sector is not diversified and farmers depend only on one type farming system such as Wheat-Paddy, Paddy-Paddy, Paddy-Groundnut, Paddy-Mustard, Paddy-Pulses, Pearl millet-Mustard, Pearl millet-Wheat, Maize-Wheat, Sorghum-Wheat, Cotton-Wheat, Sugarcane-Wheat, Soybean-Wheat etc. (Das, 2002). They had not classified their land into different types of farming, for instance horticulture, vegetables, livestock, wadi, cash crop and cereals. If they diversified then their income comes form many sources and one crop not get sufficient return other will compensate and here credit, technology and information play major role. The state like Gujarat which conveys farmers to diversify their agriculture farming achieved two digit highest growth rates the previous decade. The above diversification requires more credit and technological innovations of farmers that push agriculture towards commercialisation. These village economies have a large proportion of cultivators, particularly small and marginal farmers,who are not able to make additional investments in agriculture farming diversification to reap the benefits of market demand. The diversification of agriculture farming further accentuated the need for the rapid development of rural infrastructure and larger flow of credit to farming community (Shivamaggi, 2000).

Most of the theoretical and empirical studies of rural credit markets characterised as high lending costs and high demand, resulting in high interest rates being charged to the borrowers. These studies also assumed that all households have a positive demand for formal credit, which is bound by the government regulations to lend at a subsidised fixed interest rate, is the cheapest source of credit. These simplicity assumptions usually suggest a large scale credit rationing to the formal rural sector in economic modelling. However, this might not always be true that the degree of effective credit rationing might not be as high as it is generally assumed in literature and farm households may have a low demand for credit (Swain, 2002).

In village economies credit delivery system has two broad sources, formal and informal, the entire rural finance not only encompasses credit to farming community but also the development of various farming and non-farming sectors of the rural economy. In India, credit cooperatives society, commercial banks (CBs) and Regional Rural Banks (RRBs) are the major financial institutions of formal rural credit that provide to the agricultural sector and other rural business activities at the village level. Along with above major institution, Land Development Banks (LDBs) constitute the rural financial institutions (RFIs) for rural economy credit requirement on the basis of land holding.

2. Economists Thought on Rural Credit Market

The early economists have two views on rural credit markets, monopoly or perfect in nature, each market comprise a different explanation for the usually high interest rates in the informal sector. Both views fail to deal the rural credit market problem and then another imperfect information paradigm, induction mechanism and screening mechanisms are tried to search the cause of existence rural informal credit sector in developing economies, like India, Pakistan, Thailand etc.

Monopoly Market

First view of rural credit market stated that in the village economy, moneylender performs as a monopolist, without any competition, he is free to charge a "usurious" interest rate. This traditional view is detained by studies of the rural credit system in the early 1950s in India; agricultural credit presented a "two-fold problem of inadequacy and unsuitability" (RBI 1954). Introduction of government lending agencies and promotion of rural cooperatives were needed to "provide a positive institutional alternative to the money-lender himself, something which will compete with him, remove him from the forefront and put him in his place" (RBI, 1954 and Hoff and Stiglitz, 1990). On other hand the perspective of policy research, that official view overstates the problems of rural capital markets because it ignores the thriving informal credit markets that often exist. It seems to assume that there is no competition among moneylenders, a mode for understates the problems. The past 65 years experience of government intervention in India, Pakistan, Thailand, and other developing countries shows that the creation of a positive institutional alternative-rural banks and credit cooperatives has failed to drive the traditional moneylender out of the market ("to put him in his place").

Perfect Markets

The second view of rural credit markets is associated with George Stigler of the Chicago school, is that imperfections in credit markets are not likely to be important. In the "perfect markets" thought, it assumed that credit markets are approximately Pareto-efficient. In general, high interest rates reflect not monopoly power but high default rates and high information costs. Moreover, Stigler argued in his 1967 paper on credit markets that "there is no 'imperfection' in a market possessing incomplete knowledge if it would not be (privately) remunerative to acquire (produce) completes knowledge." But this statement is true only if private and social benefits from increasing information are the same. In general they are not the same, either for information about technology (Hirschliefer, 1971), or for information in labour markets (Spence 1974 and Stiglitz 1975), or for information in credit markets. The only ground for government intervention in credit markets is to redistribute income to the poor (at some cost in efficiency). This view also fails to take into consideration the fact that imperfect information may limit the effective degree of competition within a market, a point to which need to concern (Hoff and Stiglitz, 1990).

From above review it is clear that both views are inadequate to tackle the problem of rural credit markets, neither the traditional "monopoly" nor the "perfect markets" thought are able to explain other features of rural credit markets that are at least as important in solving the puzzle of high interest rates charge by informal sector in rural credit market. The Hoff and Stiglitz (1990) pointed out some features of rural credit market as; The formal and informal sectors coexist, despite the fact that formal interest rates are substantially below those charged in the informal sector; Interest rates may not equilibrate by credit supply and demand: there may be credit rationing, and in periods of bad harvests lending may be unavailable at any price; Credit markets are segmented. Interest rates of lenders in different areas vary by more than can plausibly be accounted for by differences in the likelihood of default. Local events—a failure of a harvest in one area seem to have significant impacts on the availability of credit in local markets. There are a limited number of commercial lenders in the informalsector, despite the high rates charged; In the informal sector, inter-linkages between credit transactions and transactions in other markets are common; Formal lenders tend to specialise in areas where farmers have land titles.

Both monopoly and the perfect markets thought are not accounted these features and not consider in the rural market analysis as a whole. So an alternative approach is needed to understand the functioning of rural credit markets, which can help in appropriate policy formation.

The "Imperfect Information" Paradigm

In the 1980s major advances have been made in theoretical understanding of the mechanism of credit markets. As Hoff and Stiglitz (1990) illustrated that these advances have developed a paradigm that emphasises the problems of imperfect information and imperfect enforcement. Lenders exchange money today for a promise of money in the future and take actions to make it more likely that those promises are fulfilled. Lending activity thus entails : (i) the exchange of consumption today for consumption in a later period, (ii) insurance againstdefault risk, (iii) information acquisition regarding the characteristics of loan applicants (screening problem), (iv) measures to ensure that borrowers take those actions that make repayment most likely (incentives problem); and (v) enforcement actions to increase the likelihood of repayment by borrowers who are able to do so. It is this broadening of the perspective of what is entailed by lending activity that provides the background for the new theories of rural credit markets.

They have distinguished two types of mechanisms for resolving the problems of screening, incentives, and enforcement. Indirect mechanisms depend on the propose of contracts by lenders such that, when a borrower responds to these contracts in his own best interests, the lender obtains information about the riskiness of the borrower, and induces him to take actions to reduce the chance of default and to repay the loan whenever he has the resources to do so. These mechanisms may be in the credit market itself (in loan terms such as the interest rate and loan size), or they may rely on contracts in related markets (in rental agreements, for example) that willinfluence a borrower's behaviour in credit markets. In the first case, the interest rate serves the dual function of a price and an indirect screening or incentive mechanism. As Hoff and Stiglitz (1990) discuss again, this means that the equilibrium interest rate need not clear the market-there may be credit rationing. Notice, however, that these indirect mechanisms are equally applicable whether there is competition or monopoly in the market.

Direct mechanisms entail lenders'. (a) expending resources in actively screening applicants and enforcing loans and (b) limiting the range of their lending activity to members of a particular kinship group, residents of a given region, or individuals with whom they trade. These direct mechanisms (through personal relationship, trade-credit linkages, usufruct loans, and other means) tend to lead to a monopolistically competitive structure with interest rate spreads between different segments of the rural credit markets. Hoff and Stiglitz (1990) argued that the entry of institutional credit into a rural credit market is unlikely to break the power of moneylenders unless the new institutions themselves find substitutes for the direct mechanisms used by moneylenders to overcome the problems of screening, incentives, and enforcement.

3. Brief History of Formal Rural Credit System

In India the progress of formal credit to rural economy could be broadly classified into four distinct phases; first was (1904-1969) predominance of co-operatives and setting up of RBI, second was (1969-1975) nationalisation of commercial banks and setting up of Regional Rural Banks (RRBs), third was (1975-1990) setting up of NABARD and fourth from (1991 onwards) financial sector reforms. In fact, genesis of institutional involvement in the sphere of agricultural credit could be traced back to the enactment of the Co-operative Societies Act in 1904. As we known, establishment of the RBI in 1935 reinforced the process of institutional development for agricultural credit and it was first central bank in the world to have taken interest in the matters related to agriculture and agricultural credit, and continue to do so.

The RRBs were established after the recommendation of Narasimham Working Group (1975) under the provisions of an Ordinance promulgated on the 26th September 1975 and the RRB Act, 1976 with an objective is to ensure sufficient institutional credit for agriculture and other rural sectors. This institution mobilise financial resources from rural / semi-urban areas and grant loans and advances mostly to small and marginal farmers, agricultural labourers and rural artists and also it was created to meet the excess demand for institutional credit in the rural areas, particularly for economically, socially backward marginal and small farmers as well as weaker sections of the society. Although the commercial banks and the cooperative banks had reasonable records in terms of geographical coverage and disbursement of credit, in terms of population groups the cooperative banks were dominated by the rural rich, while the commercial banks had mostly provide services for urban needs.

The RRB present minimal risk because of their small size, but the risk of contagion always remains. In case of RRBs, assets quality raises some cause for concerns, with 5.9 per cent of their assets being classified a non-performing at end March 2008, along with a stagnant recovery performance. The ratio of recovery to demand has been however around 80 per cent over the last few years. Profitability remains low with eigth (out of 91) being loss making banks at end of March 2008. Annual policy statement by the RBI in 2004 had indicate that sponsor banks in consolation with state government (base capital is held by the central government, stare government and sponsor banks in the ratio of 58: 15: 35 in that order) would initiate steps for the amalgamation of RRBs sponsored by them (RBI, 2009).

The process of amalgamation began in September 2005 as a result, the number of RRBs has declined to 86 including 41 stand alone RRBs of which one RRB is newly incorporated by Dec. 2008. The SARFAEST act has been extended to loans advanced by RRBs and only eligible RRBs are permitted to accept foreign currency (NRE/FCNR) deposit. In the mean time several measures has been undertaken to enlarge their scope of operations and improve profitability. Sponsor banks have been advised to provide lines of credit at reasonable rates to arrangement their resource base. They have been also allowed to access inter RRBs term money/borrowing and also to the repo/ CBLO market. They have been permitted to setup off site ATMs, issue credit/ debit cards and handle pension/ government business.

Currently RRBs are not required to be Basel I, II, and III compliant and there is no stipulation for risk-based capital adequacy norms for these entitles. Through all principles as delineated in BCPs area applicable to RRBs given their importance in rural credit delivery and financial inclusion, an assessment of Basel core principles related to RRBs, was taken up by the Advisory panel on financial regulation and supervision. This panel feels that giving the varying status of RRBs as regards their financial health, computerisation quality of Governance etc. These banks could be appropriately categorised and roadmap could be prescribed for operationalisation of Basel norms. (RBI, 2009)

However, within a very short time, most banks were making loss. Credit as one of the critical non-land inputs, has two-dimensions from the viewpoint of its contribution to the augmentation of agricultural growth viz., availability of credit (the quantum), the distribution of credit and proper accessibility. The demand for agricultural credit arises due to lack of simultaneity between the realisation of income and act of expenditure; lumpiness of investment in fixed capital formation; and stochastic surges in capital needs and saving that accompany technological innovations. Flow of institutional credit in agriculture and allied activities was increased from Rs 2,29, 400 to Rs 4,46,779 during the period 2006-07 to 2010-11 and the share of RRBs was increased from Rs 20,435 to Rs 43,968 at the same period but the share of RRBs in percentage remain constant and varies between 9 to 10 per cent of total credit (NBARD, 2010).

4. Literature on Rural Formal Credit System

The theoretical model of rural credit in developing economies developed by Eswaran and kotwal, Braverman and Stilitz, (1989) which was based on the assumption that there is an excess demand for bank credit at prevailing interest rates also underline the oft-repeated objective of the government of increasing credit disbursements in order to simulate agricultural investment. Binswanger *et al.*, (1985), Binswanger and Rosenzweig, (1986), Siamwalla *at al.* (1985) Sated that if some household do not demand or credit informal credit is less costly than formal credit for a significant percentage of household, credit market out-comes, will typically reflect the demand for credit as well as costs of both formal and informal credit.

Kochar (1991) reveals that the household's land holding is the only household level variable which has a significant effect on formal sector interest rates. Yaron, *et.al* (1997) Furthermore, in the context of "accessibility", the issue of outreach (i.e., in terms of both breadth and depth) and sustainability of financial institutions are often debated. Rhyne (1998), the possible trade-offs between sustainability and the depth of outreach has been, therefore, the subject of an ongoing discussion in the rural credit markets.

All India Rural Credit Review Committee (1969) fined that commercial banks have generally been more successful than co-operative banks in mobilising deposits in the semi-urban areas. This may be partly on account of superior customer services and partly because of a more sustained drive for deposits. The committee also point out that an important implication of the challenge which awaits banks generally and co-operative banks in particular is that they can win the confidence and support of the prospective depositor, urban or rural.

The Banking Commission (1972) viewed that proximity of institutions to the depositor and availability of varying schemes tailored to suit the liquidity and other considerations, which weigh with the depositors, the return on deposits appeared to be of some significance. The Commission also stated that efficient service and personalised attention have been found to be among the most important considerations in depositor's choice of a bank. It recommended waiting time of customers at the cash counters be reduced by procedural adjustments and introduction of teller system. Raju, *et.al* (1972) in their study on impact of Dena Bank's direct finance in Raipur district of M.P. found that the bank borrowing has a positive and significant impact on the total farm returns. They also found that the borrowing increase the productivity of other inputs used in farming.

Working Group on Customer Service (1977) noted that there was considerable ignorance about the facilities and services offered by banks and the roles they were required to play. Most bank customers are not aware of various schemes and services offered by banks. The group recommended educational campaign to be carried out by banks illustratively and every customer of bank should be provided a booklet containing the range of services offered by banks. The survey conducted by the group and pointed out that by and large less educated people and females are away from banks. The Productivity, Efficiency and Profitability (PEP) Committee (1977) opined that the rationale behind the need for a business plan or performance budget is that banking operations should be re-oriented to provide better service and to obtain the maximum business growth by adopting a market approach.

Bell, (1990) and Sarap (1991) the inequalities in the banking system across the regions and social classes persisted. This was because of the insistence on collateral which could not be provided by the poor, complicated administration procedures, long distances from the villages to the branches, the cultural gap between bank officials and the poor, political interference, inflexible lending policies and procedures, lack of provision for consumption credit and a widespread belief that the poor were non-bankable. Singh (1991) Rajasekhar and Vyasulu (1991) all the studies culminated in an alarming growth in overdue payments. This, in turn, adversely affected the recycling of credit, and led to lower profit margins. Many Commercial Banks (CBs), Regional Rural Banks (RRBs) and co-operatives were consequently incurring losses.

Vyasulu and Rajasekhar (1993) the formal banking system began to face problems of higher transaction costs due to lending small amounts to large numbers of borrowers and recurring losses in the late 1980s. The managerial inadequacies within the banking system also caused problems. Shivamaggi, (2000) the rural banking system in India made tremendous quantitative achievement by neglecting the qualitative aspects of the credit delivery system and the Indian policy-makers were unable to arrive at a banking structure and operational system, which was suitable for the credit needs of the agriculturists. Sheokand (2000) discussed the evolution of Indian banking and its failure to provide credit facilities to poor people. NABARD started Self-Help Group – Bank Linkage Programme in 1992, which was considered as a landmark development in banking with the poor. This programme was observed that Regional Rural Banks' security-oriented individual banking system was replaced by the delivery of credit to focused groups. According to him the government sponsored programmes had occupied much of the economic space but did not achieve the objective of alleviating poverty.

Yunus (2006) in a study explained the differences between Grameen Bank and conventional banks. He explained that the Grameen Bank methodology was almost the reverse of the conventional banking methodology. Conventional banking was based on the principle that the more you have, the more you get. As a result, more than half of the population of the world was deprived of financial services of the conventional banks as conventional banking was based on collateral, focused on men, located in urban centres and owned by rich with the objective of profit maximisation. On the contrary, the Grameen Bank started with the belief that credit should be accepted as a human right, where one who did not possess anything to get the highest priority in getting a loan. Grameen Bank methodology was not based on the material possession but on the potential of a person. He also described poor people as a 'human bonsai'. They were poor because society had denied them the real social and economic base to grow on. Grameen Bank's effort was to move them from the flowerpot to the real soil of the society.

5. Progress of Rural Banking

The progress of rural baking system is judged by the various parameters such as number of branch offices in rural area, credit advances and deposit in rural areas and credit deposit ratio of rural, banks and their percentage with total banking system in all the areas.Table 1 shows the growth of bank offices, deposits and credit deposit ratio in rural areas along with the percentage share of rural areas with all the areas during the period of 1969 to 2012, for all SCBs. The Indian banking system is categorised areas into four categories; rural areas, semi-urban areas, urban areas and metropolitan areas. The impact of bank nationalisation on the growth of scheduled commercial banks in rural areas is clear: the share of rural bank offices in total bank offices jumped from 17.6 per cent in 1969 to 35.5 per cent in 1975 and further increased steadily thereafter, and attained a peak of 58.2 per cent in 1990. After that 1990 onwards, there was a gradual decline in the share of rural bank offices, and the share fell below 50 per cent in 1998 and thereafter. In fact, the absolute number of bank offices closed in the 1990s because 2,706 rural bank offices were closed between March 1994 and March 2000, most in 1995 and 1996 (Ramachandran and Swaminathan, 2001).

An expansion of formal credit to rural areas had been seen after nationalisation of banks. The proportion of credit disbursed to rural areas increases three times in the 1970s, and continued to rise in the 1980s. At the end of 1980s, however, the share of total bank credit that went to rural areas declined, from 15.3 per cent in 1987 and 1988 to 10.6 per cent in March 2000, then further decline reached 7.4 per cent in 2010 and then again marginal increase shown in March 2014 recorded 8.3 per cent. Rural deposits also grew rapidly after nationalisation; their share of aggregate deposits doubled in the 1970s, from 6.3 per cent in 1969 to 12.6 per cent in 1980 and continued to grow, although at a slower pace, in the 1980s. Once again, the peak was reached in 1990, when rural deposits accounted for 15.5 per cent of aggregate deposits, then further decline and recorded lowest 9.2 per cent in March 2010 then further marginal increased and reached 9.8 per cent in March 2014. The pace of deposit mobilisation in rural areas fell in the 1990s.

Table 1 : Growth of Rural Banking and Rural Credit of SCBs in India, 1969 to 2014 (Rs crores)

Year	*RBank*	*% of*	*RCredit*	*% of*	*Rural*	*% of*	*R C-D*	*% of total*
1969	1443	17.6	115	3.3	306	6.3	37.6	71.9
1975	7122	35.5	608	6.0	1171	8.5	51.9	73.5
1980	16111	46.9	2643	10.7	4644	12.6	56.9	66.9
1985	29408	54.6	7489	14.1	11722	13.6	63.9	61.9
1990	34867	58.2	17352	14.2	28609	15.5	60.7	66.0
1995	35008	56.2	28183	12.7	57399	15.3	49.1	59.2
2000	32673	48.7	48753	10.6	120539	14.7	40.0	56.0
2005	32082	46.9	109976	9.5	213104	12.2	51.6	64.9
2010	32289	38.4	2498043	7.4	4235021	9.2	59.0	72.7
2014	43641	37.7	5202778	8.3	7904652	9.8	65.8	78.0

Source: Shetty (1997) for 1969 to 1995 and Banking Statistics: Basic Statistical Returns, for 1997 to 2014, at March.

Given the pattern of growth of gross bank credit and aggregate deposits, it is not surprising that the credit-deposit ratio in rural areas rose after 1969. The ratio peaked at 68.6 per cent in 1984 and remained above 60 per cent until 1990. From 1985 to 1988, the share of the rural sector in gross bank credit was higher than its share of total deposits, and in these years, the rural credit-deposit ratio exceeded the all-India credit-deposit ratio. In the 1990s, the credit-deposit ratio fell sharply, coming down almost to the level of 1969. Credit deposit ratio of rural areas again stated to increases after 2000s and reached 65.8 per cent in March in 2014, which is good sign for the growth of rural banking and help in the policy of financial inclusion.

Growth of Formal Credit and Rural Economy

The existing Agricultural Credit System is geared to the needs of food-grains production: with the share of foodgrains production falling as a proportion of total agricultural production. It is a matter of credit that agriculture credit has not fallen as a proportion of agricultural GDP. With the share of agriculture in GDP falling continuously, from 36 per cent in 1981 to 29 per cent in 1991 and 22 per cent in 2001 to 14 per cent in 2011, it is expected that the share of agricultural credit would also fall as a proportion of total credit, unless this trend is corrected by increasing commercialisation of agriculture.

Long back Indian Credit Market System was dominated by the moneylenders and other informal sources who have been charging unexpected higher interest rates, as a result of which exploitation occurred. Significant changes have been brought about during the last 50 years as a result of the serious attention paid by RBI since 1930s, policy-maker and government. In 1951 the share of non-institutional credit to cultivator household was 92.7 per cent, out of which 69.7 per cent was contributed by moneylenders. Later it came down 81.3 per cent in 1961, out of which moneylenders had 49.2 percent share *(Rakesh Mohan, 2004)*. But after 1970s a tremendous change occurred in the Indian rural credit market as it reached at 36.3 per cent which is shown in Table1. In the 1980s it reached the lowest at 16.1 per cent, followed by a minor increase in 1990s and then reached at 17.5 per cent, but in 2002 it was 26.8 the highest then again fall 18.2 in 2010.

Table 2 Relative Share of Cultivator Borrowing from Different Sources in India

Sources of credit	*1951*	*1961*	*1971*	*1981*	*1991*	*2002*
***Non-institutional credit** which of*	***92.7***	***85.2***	***68.3***	***36.8***	***30.6***	***38.9***
Money lender	69.7	60.8	36.3	16.1	17.5	26.8
***Institutional credit** which of*	***7.3***	***14.8***	***31.7***	***63.2***	***66.3***	***61.1***
Cooperative societies/ banks	3.3	9.1	22.0	29.8	23.6	30.2
Commercial banks	0.9	0.4	2.4	28.8	35.2	26.8
Unspecified	3.1	5.3	-	-	3.1	-
Total	**100**	**100**	**100**	**100**	**100**	**100**

Source: Various round All India Rural Credit Survey & all India Debt and Investment Survey.

In Table 2 decadal Scenario of institutional credit to household's shows that in first two decade the shares of institutional credit was very low and in 1970s it shows to increase after nationalisation of banks. The share of Commercial Banks were increased rapidly, from 2.4 per cent to 28.8 per cent during 1971 to 1981 and again increased 28.8 per cent to 35.2 per cent during 1981 to 1991, then fall at 26.8 during 1991 to 2002. The share of Cooperative Societies and Regional Rural Banks grew at a slow rate and varied between 22 to 30 per cent of total agriculture credit. In 1991, the share of non-institutional credit was lowest. It was possible due to expansion of rural credit by commercial banks and RRBs with cooperative societies. Then again increase in the share of non institutional credit was observed due to demand supply gap of rural credit. The share of moneylender was high in the 2002; it was due to existence of commission activates in the banking system. Moneylenders are of two types- agriculturist moneylenders who combine their moneylending job with farming and professional moneylenders whose sole job is moneylending.

Within the formal credit disbursement the lower size holding receives lesser credit by banks which are presented in Table 3. In the last decade the share of short run and long run direct institutional credit outstanding to small and marginal land holding (<2.5 acres) increases from 22.91 per cent to 31.79 per cent during 2000 to 2012 and the medium size land holding (2.5-5 acres) increased from 23.21 perc ent to 32.29 per cent and for the large farmers (> 5 acres) reduced from 58.87 per cent to 35.93 per cent during the same period.

Table 3 : Pattern of Direct Formal Credit to Farmers by SCBs According to Land Holding

Year	*< 2.5 Acres (per cent)*	*2.5 -5 Acres (per cent)*	*> 5 Acres (per cent)*	*Total (Rs Billion)*
2000-01	22.91	23.21	53.87	314.86
2001-02	23.34	25.81	50.85	375.29
2002-03	21.83	25.17	53.00	449.61
2003-04	25.72	24.28	50.01	575.65
2004-05	26.12	26.45	47.43	784.76
2005-06	26.60	26.18	47.22	1117.43
2006-07	26.68	27.02	46.31	1399.61
2007-08	26.69	26.79	46.51	1740.44
2008-09	27.45	27.26	45.29	2193.40
2009-10	28.83	26.97	44.20	2703.68
2010-11	28.68	30.75	40.56	3092.92
2011-12	31.79	32.29	35.92	3913.89

Source: Calculated by Author, RBI HSB data Table, No. 60, 2014.

The progress of banking system and its expansion of rural credit is shows in Table 4 for the period of 1970 to 2010. Commercial Banks, along with RRBs, are showing rising share and on the other hand the share of cooperatives falls in every decade. This is reflected in the increasing concern in recent years over the effectiveness, governance and financial health of rural cooperative banks. The education played important role in understanding the banking system structure; because the illiterate people hesitate to access the banking services. The young farmers also take more attention on the banking services and access credit from banks than aged farmers.

Table 4 : Decadal Average Share Direct Formal Agricultural Credit Disbursement (per cent)

Decade	*Cooperative*	*State Govt*	*SCBs[1]*	*RRBs[*]*	*Total[2]*
1970-80	(70.48)	(6.11)	(22.43)	(0.96)	16869.9
1980-90	(52.8)	(3.72)	(38.45)	(5.01)	67579.2
1990-00	(49.47)	(2.26)	(41.66)	(6.59)	215402.1
2000-10	(41.60)	(0.08)	(54.38)	(13.61)	1130715

Source: Computed by author from data; Handbook of Indian Economy 2007-08, 2011-12.

These cooperative banks provide 41 per cent of total rural credit continues to be extended by them and hence, it is essential that they be revitalised and put on a sound business footing. Schedule Commercial Banks (SCBs) accounted for around 54 per cent of the total credit, followed by co-operatives with share of around 42 per cent and lastly, Regional Rural Banks (RRBs) which accounted for around 14 per cent, the govt. financing is negligible in 2010.

Figure 1 Direct Institutional Credit to Agricultutre & Allied Activites (S+L)

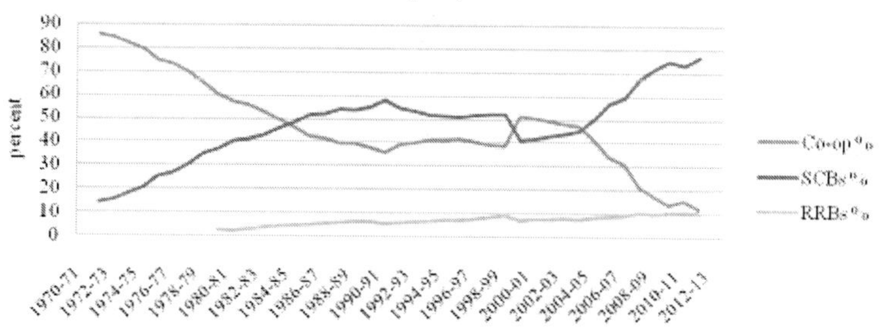

Source: Handbook of Statistics on Indian Economy, RBI (2013-14).

Figure 1 shows the growth of institutional credit to agriculture and allied activities by different agencies after the green revolution the share of commercial banks and regional rural banks continuously increasing but on the other hand the share of co-operative societies continuously falls, it red occurly due to structural change of Indian rural credit system, changes of govt. policies and changes of consumers preferences.

Rural Credit Policy

Rural credit markets were at the center of policy planners in India over the past 65 years. All the governments were promoted to banking institution and aid agencies for supplying cheap credit to farmers in a numerous types of institutional settings. The results of many of these efforts were not feed the demand supply gap of rural credit. Despite high levels of subsidy to rural credit in India, many farmers especially small farmers still depend for credit on moneylenders and relatives whose interest rates remain extremely high. The reason of failure of formal credit institutions not to drive out rural borrwers from the trap of the traditional moneylender because the public policies were based on an inadequate understanding of the workings of rural credit markets. Generally, rural credit market has dual in nature in developing countries like India. One is formal and other is informal, in the formal credit market, institutions/ banks or the government facilitate intermediation between depositors and lenders and charge relatively low rates of interest that usually are government-subsidised. On the other hand in informal credit markets, money is lent by private individuals—professional moneylenders, traders, commission agents, landlords, friends, and relatives–generally out of their own equity, which is generally charges higher rate of interest than formal market (Hoff and Stiglitz, 1990).

The aims of India's rural credit policy is to facilitate affordable and cheap farmer credit to the people who have either been the part of farm credit system or have been ignored by the mainstream formal financial institutions. The Reserve Bank of India (RBI) and the Government of India (GOI) have emphasised the significance of rural finance and attempted to create an enabling environment for rural banking towards hassle-free credit inflows to the farm and non-farm sectors in rural areas. The institutional capital formation in the agricultural sector is on the decline and the traditional concern about accessibility of agricultural credit to the needy rural inhabitants is still alive even after increasing bank branch network, channelling credit through rural credit co-operatives, evolving specialised rural banking institutions (*i.e.*, Regional Rural Banks, cooperative society, and commercial banks) and the setting up of apex rural financial agencies like the National Bank for Agriculture and Rural Development (NABARD). The aim of recent financial inclusion policy is to educated, (financial literacy), facilitates credit and motivate for banking transaction habit to poor and rural consumer in the village economics.

6. Conclusion

Theoretical works referred to simply as "imperfect credit markets" and assess the nature and sources of those imperfections, which have a framework for assessing the consequences of alternative government policies. While the findings of rural credit market studies generalise to other developing countries, exploring the effectiveness of the institutions and mechanisms for screening and monitoring loan applicants which are more complicated in country like India. For evaluating a variety of government schemes and policy interventions in credit markets, taking into account the information asymmetries and enforcement problems are common in developing countries.

References

1. Basu, P. and Srivastava, P. (2005), 'Scaling-up *Microfinance for India's Rural Poor',* World Bank Policy, Research Working Paper, No. 3646, World Bank, Washington DC.

2. Bell and Clive (1990), 'Interactions between Institutional and Informal Credit Agencies in Rural India', *The World Bank Economic Review*, Vol. 4 (3), pp. 297-327.

3. Binswanger, H.P, et al (1985), 'Credit in rural South India theoretical Issues and empirical analysis, Word Bank, *Agriculture and rural development department,* Washington D.C. report No. ARU 59.

4. Sarangi, U.C. (2010), 'Report of the Task Force on Credit Related Issues of Farmers", Task Force_ Report final loaded on website_new.pdf Sumatra PDF.

5. Das, P. (2002), 'Cropping Pattern (Agricultural and Horticultural) in Different Zones, their Average Yields in Comparison to National Average/ Critical Gaps/Reasons Identified and Yield Potential', Indian Council of Agriculture Research, New Delhi.

6. GoI (1991). 'Report of the Committee on the Financial System', chairman M Narasimham, Ministry of Finance, Government of India, New Delhi.

7. Hoff, K and Stiglitz, J.E. (1990), "The Economics of Rural Organisation Theory, Practice, and Policy", in chapter 2, *Imperfect Information and Rural Credit Markets: Puzzles and Policy Perspectives*', (ed) Hoff, K., Braverman, A., and Stiglitz, J. E., Oxford University Press.

8. Imperfect Information and Rural Credit Markets: Puzzles and Policy Perspective.

9. Kochar, A. (1991), 'An Empirical Analysis of Rationing Constraints in Rural Credit Market in India,' PhD. Diss., University of Chicago.

10. Kursho, A.M. (1989), 'A Review of the Agricultural Credit Systems in India, Reserve Bank of India, Bombay.

11. Mishra and Puri (2008), *"Indian economy"*, Himalaya Publication House, Mumbai.

12. Mohan. R. (2006), 'Agricultural Credit in India Status, Issues and Future Agenda' *Economic and Political Weekly*, March 18, 2006.

13. Mohan, R. (2009), *Monetary Policy in Globalized Economy*, Oxford University Press, New Delhi.

14. NABARD (2001), Report of the Expert Committee on Rural Credit, chairman V S Vyas, National Bank for Agriculture and Rural Development.

15. Rajasekhar, D. and Vyasulu V. (1991), 'The Half-Life of Credit: Stimulating Fund Flows in the Priority Sector', *Economic and Political Weekly*, Vol. 36 (39), pp.
16. Ramachandran, V. K. and Swaminathan, M. (2001), "Does Informal Credit Provide Security? Rural Banking Policy in India", International Labour Office, Geneva, Switzerland.
17. RBI (1954), 'All-India Rural Credit Survey', Vol. 1, the Survey Report, vol. 2, the General Report, Vol. 3, the Technical Report, Bombay.
18. RBI (1954), 'Report of the All India Rural Credit Survey Committee (1951-54)', Reserve Bank of India, Bombay.
19. RBI (2009), "India's Financial Sector an Assessment", Vol. 3, Cambridge University press, New Delhi, p p. 329.
20. Report of the All India Rural Credit Review Committee (1969), Government of India, pp. 331-674.
21. Report of the Productivity, Efficiency and Profitability Committee on Banking (1977), Reserve Bank of India, Bombay.
22. Rutherford, S. (2000), *The Poor and Their Money*, Oxford University Press, Delhi.
23. Sahoo, B. B (2011), 'Value Chain System Agriculture Financing', *Yojana*, Vol. 55.
24. Sahu, B.G. and Rajasekhar D. (2005), 'Banking Sector Reform and Credit Flow to Indian Agriculture' *Economic and Political Weekly*, December 31, 2005.
25. Saraiya R.G. (1972), Report of the Banking Commission, Govt. of India, pp 89, 97.
26. Sarap, K. (1990), 'Factors Affecting Small Farmers' Access to Institutional Credit in Rural Orissa, India', *Development and Change*, Vol. 21, No. 2, pp. 281-307.
27. Satish P. (2006), 'Institutional Credit; Indebtedness and Suicides in Punjab', *Economic and Political Weekly*, June 30, 2006.
28. Satish, P. (2007), 'Agricultural Credit in the Post-Reform Era; A Target of Systematic Policy Coarctation' *Economic and Political Weekly*, June 30, 2007.
29. Shivamaggi, H.V. (2000), 'Reforms in Rural Banking: Need for Bolder Approach', *Economic and Political Weekly*, Vol. 35 (20), pp. 1714-8.
30. Spence, M. (1974), 'Job Market Signaling', *Quarterly Journal of Economics*, Vol. 87, pp. 355-74

31. Stigler, G. E. (1967), 'Imperfections in the Capital Market', *Journal of Political Economy*, Vol. 75 (3), pp. 287-92.
32. Stiglitz, J. E. (1975), 'The Theory of Screening, Education, and the Distribution of Income' *American Economic Review*, Vol. 65, pp. 283-300.
33. Subrata, R. K. (2010), "Agriculture Growth in India", Serial Publication, New Delhi.
34. Talwar, R. K. (1977), Working Group on customer service in Ranks, Reserve Bank of India, Bombay, pp. 42-112.
35. Vyasulu, V. and Rajasekhar, D. (1993), 'Credit for Rural Development: Managerial Reforms in Indian Banks, *Development Policy Review*, Vol.11 (4), pp. 393-412.
36. Kishore, K. N. T. (2012), 'Agriculture Credit in India: An Integrated Rural Credit Approach', *International Journal of Scientific and Research Publications*, Vol. 2(3) pp. 1-5.

12

A Review of Financial Inclusion Initiatives for Rural Development : Issues, Challenges and Recommendations

Sonam Agrawal

"The test of our progress is not whether we add more to the abundance of those who have much; it is whether we provide enough for those who have too little." **–Franklin D. Roosevelt**

There is a long history of financial inclusion in India. It has traditionally been understood to mean opening new bank branches in rural and unbanked areas. Nowadays, however, financial inclusion is seen to be something more than opening bank branches in unbanked areas to take formal financial services across the length and breadth of the country. In the context of the various shortcomings in delivering subsidies, direct transfers using technology have been thought of. The beneficiary needs to have at least one bank account. Since in a logistics point of view it is impossible to open that many physical branches — the brick and mortar type — the accent will be on opening electronic accounts. Technology adaptation would be a key feature in this scheme for financial inclusion.The RBI has, in the recent past, taken several steps to further inclusion. Very recently, it circulated for public comment two sets of draft guidelines for issuing licences to payment banks and small banks.These niche banks with lower entry-level norms than for normal commercial banks are meant to further inclusion. While it will take a while for these banks to come up, it is obvious that the RBI is betting on them to provide banking services to those who remain outside the purview of formal banking.

1. Understanding Financial Inclusion

1.1 Definitions

Financial inclusion may be defined as the process of ensuring access to financial services and timely and adequate credit where needed by vulnerable groups such as weaker sections and low income groups at an affordable cost.

(The Committee on Financial Inclusion, Chairman: Dr C. Rangarajan).

Financial Inclusion, broadly defined, refers to universal access to a wide range of financial services at a reasonable cost. These include not only banking products but also other financial services such as insurance and equity products.

(The Committee on Financial Sector Reforms, Chairman: Dr Raghuram G. Rajan).

Recently, the RBI Governor Raghuram Rajan outlined, in conceptual terms, what inclusion should be, “Simplicity and reliability in financial inclusion in India, though not a cure all, can be a way of liberating the poor from dependence on indifferently delivered public services and from venal politicians,” he said. Further, “in order to draw in the poor, the products should address their needs — a safe place to save, a reliable way to send and receive money, a quick way to borrow in times of need or to escape the clutches of the money-lender, easy to understand life and health insurance and an avenue to engage in savings for the old age.”

1.2 Steps Taken by the Government and Reserve Bank for Rural Areas

Pradhan Mantri Jan Dhan Yojan (PMJDY) -has been the latest scheme announced by PM Narendra Modi. According to this scheme, each family can have a bank account opened easily, free of cost and with zero balance and no subsequent requirement of a minimum balance.With each account, the family will get a RuPay debit card which can be used to withdraw money. The account holder will get a life cover and accidental cover of Rs 30,000 and Rs 100, 000 each. An overdraft limit of Rs 5000 will also be provided if a person saves money in the account.

Compulsory Requirement of Opening Branches in Un-banked Villages- Banks are directed to allocate at least 25 per cent of the total number of branches to be opened during the year in un-banked (Tier 5 and Tier 6) rural centres.

Financial Literacy Centres (FLCs)-718 FLCs have been set up as at end of March 2013 and all the rural branches of scheduled commercial banks are advised to scale up financial literacy efforts through conduct of outdoor Financial Literacy Camps at least once a month, to facilitate financial inclusion through provision of two essentials i.e. ‘Financial Literacy’ and easy ‘Financial Access’. A total of 2.2 million people have been educated through awareness camps / choupals, seminars and lectures during April 2012 to March 2013.

Basic Saving Bank Deposit (BSBD)- All banks are advised to open accounts with minimum common facilities such as no minimum balance, deposit and withdrawal of cash at bank branch and ATMs, receipt/ credit of money through electronic payment channels, facility of providing ATM card.

Relaxed and simplified KYC norms- They have been introduced to facilitate easy opening of bank accounts, especially for small accounts with balances not exceeding Rs 50,000 and aggregate credits in the accounts not exceeding Rs One lakh a year. Further, banks are advised not to insist on introduction for opening bank accounts of customers. In addition, banks are allowed to use Aadhar Card as a proof of both identity and address.

ICT Based Accounts -In order to provide efficient and cost-effective banking services in the un-banked and remote corners of the country, RBI directed commercial banks to provide ICT based banking services – through Business Eorrespondents (BCs). These ICT enabled banking services have CBS connectivity to provide all banking services including deposit and withdrawal of money in the financially excluded regions. The number of ICT-based transactions through BCs increased from 26.52 million in March 2010 to 250. 46 million in March 2013, while transactions amount increased steadily from Rs.6.92 billion to Rs 233.88 billion during the same period.

Financial Inclusion Initiatives by Private Corporate- A few large private corporate have undertaken projects such as E-Choupal/ E- Sagar (ITC), Haryali Kisan Bazaar (DCM), Project Shakti (HUL), and so on. These pioneering projects have brought about vast improvement in the lives of the participants and set the tone for economic development in their command areas; which is a pre-requisite for Financial Inclusion efforts to be undertaken by the banking system.

1.3 Successful Implementation of Policies by Select Banks of India

State Bank of India- During the Financial Year 2013-14 the State Bank has successfully implemented a range of Financial Inclusion policies. The Bank has set up 45,487 BC Customer Service Points (CSPs) through alliances both at National and Regional level. It is offering various technological enabled products through Business Correspondent (BC) channel, such as, Savings Bank, flexi RD, STDR, Remittance and SB-OD facilities. During FY 14, the Bank has opened 1.50 crore small accounts with simplified KYC. It has also issued 24 Lakh FI RuPay ATM Debit Cards to FI customers. With a view to facilitate transactions through alternate channels, Linking of villages to branches through CSPs in a Hub and Spoke model has been launched. SBI is the sole Sponsoring Bank for DBT for LPG transactions which are processed centrally for all the three Oil Marketing Companies. As per RBI guidelines, the Bank has set up Financial Literacy Centres (FLCs) with the objectives of facilitating financial inclusion through provision of two essentials i.e. Literacy and easy access, inculcating saving habits, educating about financial products like insurance, borrowing and so on. Apart from providing financial literacy at the centre itself, the FLCs are conducting Camps in villages, Seminars and workshops to create awareness among the people.

Canara Bank- It has successfully covered all the allotted 1624 villages (spread over 24 states) with population above 2000 for providing banking facilities and has engaged the same number of BCAs. The bank has also opened 542 ultra small branches, one of which has already been upgraded as regular branch. It has also opened 17.31 lack Basic saving bank deposit accounts (BSBDA). A micro insurance campaign was conducted at Harmaghatta village, Shimoga Distt. During the year 2012-13, farmers club was formed, the strength of which has increased to over 1500 in different parts of the country.

As per the guidelines of the Ministry of Finance, the bank has signed MoUs with Shree Kshetra Dharamshala Rural Development Programme (SKDRDP) in Chitradurga Distt., Wayanad Social Service Society Manantwadi in Wayanad distt., and People Service Society and Hope Foundation in Palakkad distt., in Kerala state for the implementation of the scheme. 'One Family One Account scheme' has already been successfully campaigned as a precursor to Direct Benefit Transfer programme implementation. 29 Biometric ATMs have also been installed to help rural illiterate farmers to access accounts and withdraw money. Canara Gramin Vikas Vahini vehicles have also been provided to help spread Financial literacy among the rural households in 37 dists across the country. A host of other facilities like Kisan Credit Cards (KCC), General Credit Card (GCC), Self help groups (SHGs), micro credit groups (MCGs), differential rate of interest scheme (DRI), micro pension and micro insurance under Canara Nayee Disha scheme are also running.

ICICI Bank-Joining Prime Minister Narendra Modi's 'Digital India' programme, ICICI Bank has developed Akodara in Sabarkantha district of Gujarat into a 'Digital Village'. It has digitised all its offerings- from opening an account to sale of goods to purchase of products, including milk from the vendor or kirana stores. At the same time it has digitised the school records, the Gujarat syllabus and even teaching methods and tools.

Allahabad Bank- Has prepared an action plan under Pradhan Mantri Jan–dhan Yojana (PMJDY) which is under implementation in mission mode. The facility of e-KYC has been made available at all branches and KIOSK locations of BCA.

Kotak Mahindra bank- Has covered 49 villages through its own rural bank branch network and 693 villages by engaging Business Correspondents. The number of RuPay debit cards issued and AADHAR seeded accounts has improved.

UCO Bank- UCO Mobile Bank is an infrastructure that provides banking services at the doorstep of customers in unbanked areas by linking to a base branch. The "Bank on Wheel" model of implementation of Mobile Van of UCO Bank is extended in 24 locations at present covering 228 numbers of villages and 1,39,625 households. The van also contains a biometric ATM inside it. Its other initiatives include 'UCO Mitra Shakha' i.e., ultra small branches, 'UCO Sathi' CSP deployment, and financial literacy centres across various districts.

Bank of India- The Bank of India provides a range of financial products and services at an affordable cost. It provides a SMART CARD known as STAR ABHILASHA CARD, which has photo identification. Money can be remitted without any charges. It is virtually brings banking at your doorstep whereby Business Correspondents/ Facilitators and their Branch officials call on the customers for all their banking and credit requirements. Other products/ services offered include Credit up to Rs. 25000 under Samanya Credit Card for consumption purpose and Pension Payments.

2. Some Vital Statistics- Good and Bad

NSSO 59 th Round Survey Results shows that 51.4 per cent of farmer households are financially excluded from both formal/ informal sources. Of the total farmer households, only 27 per cent access formal sources of credit; one-third of this group also borrowed from non-formal sources. Overall, 73 per cent of farmer households have no access to formal sources of credit. Across regions, financial exclusion is more acute in Central, Eastern and North-Eastern regions.

CRISIL Financial Inclusion Index (Inclusix) for constructing the index, CRISIL identified three critical parameters of basic banking services namely, branch penetration, deposit penetration and credit penetration. The CRISIL Inclusix indicates that there is an overall improvement in the financial inclusion in India. On a scale of 100, it increased from 35.4 in March 2009 to 37.6 in March 2010 and to 40.1 in March 2011.

RBI Working Paper Study Sadhan Kumar (2011) worked out an Index on financial inclusion (IFI) based on three variables namely, penetration (number of adults having bank account), availability of banking services (number of bank branches per 1000 population) and usage (measured as outstanding credit and deposit). The results indicate that Kerala, Maharashtra and Karnataka has achieved high financial inclusion (IFI >0.5), while Tamil Nadu, Punjab, A,P,H,P, Sikkim, and Haryana identified as a group of medium financial inclusion (0.3 <IFI<0.5) and the remaining states have very low financial inclusion.

World Bank 'Financial Access Survey' observed that in our country, financial exclusion measured in terms of bank branch density, ATM density, bank credit to GDP and bank deposits to GDP is quite low as compared with most of developing countries in the world.

Banking Outlets-The number of banking outlets in villages with population more than 2000 as well as less than 2000 increased consistently since March 2010.

Jan DhanYojana- the Union Territory of Puducherri and Himachal Pradesh are claiming to have achieved 100 per cent financial inclusion. Speaking at a

FICCI-IBA conference on the paradigm shift in global banking, Reserve Bank of India (RBI) executive director VS Das said that each household in Puducherri and Himachal Pradesh has, at least, one bank account. States such as Gujarat, Karnataka and Kerala will also achieve a 100 per cent penetration in coming months. However, a lot needs to be done in Bihar, Uttaranchal, Chhattisgarh and the North-East.

Kerala has crossed the milestone of 100 per cent coverage of households with bank accounts under the Pradhan Mantri Jan Dhan Yojana. Only 48 per cent of Indian adults have bank accounts and nearly half of them lie dormant, says a report. According to a nation-wide survey on financial behaviour, India has the highest account dormancy rate even more than countries like Kenya, Tanzania, Uganda, Nigeria, Pakistan and Bangladesh.

Borrowing-The survey compiled by the Financial Inclusion Insights programme, operated by global strategic research consultancy Inter Media and supported by the Bill & Melinda Gates Foundation noted the majority of Indians borrow money from family and friends and not from financial institutions.

3. Issues and Challenges in Financial Inclusion for the Rural Sector

The three big challenges are high cost, lack of robust technology, and lack of awareness. Other 'barriers' in the way of larger financial inclusion include response of the banks and lack of reliable data.There is a need for greater stakeholder coordination, greater consumer understanding, trust and protection.The key is to work on innovative business strategies and delivery models revolving around appropriate product design, technology, and minimal use of manpower to make financial inclusion more profitable.To encourage corporate to take part, there is a need for the government to incentivise financial inclusion through fiscal initiatives.

Product design is the most critical component of a viable financial inclusion strategy, for this banks and other financial service providers will have to develop a better understanding of the potential customers.

Business correspondents- BCs are not making enough income due to catering of services to low-income customers with low volume transactions.

Political tussle- Financial inclusion, long considered a tool to touch the lives of the unbankable, has taken a strange political turn. One example of this was seen in Rajasthan. The Rajasthan government and the country's third-largest lender, Punjab National Bank (PNB), are locked in a tussle over the fate of 26 lakh bank accounts. Last year, the Vasundhara Raje government had promised to credit Rs 1,500 for every woman, provided she opened an account with PNB. The government had agreed to park the sum with PNB and issue biometric cards for customers to access this money. However, after the BJP lost the state elections in November 2008, the new government — led by chief minister Ashok Gehlot — has placed the scheme 'under review' and has stopped issuing biometric cards.

Red Tapism and Corruption- the successful implementation of any government policy or programme depends upon its institutions and bureaucracy. Needless to say, both have failed miserably.

Financial literacy- a very large chunk of the rural population is not even aware of the incentives, leave alone exercising that option. They don't know how to write cheques and how to open bank accounts.

Lack of ATMs- a survey on financial access in 2011 revealed that India had 10.6 branches and 8.9 automated teller machine (ATMs) per 0.1 million population. Compared to this, China had 23.8 branches and 49.6 ATMs, while Brazil had 46.2 branches and 119.6 ATMs per 0.1 million people.

The limited number of financial services players also impedes the progress of financial inclusion.

4. Recommendations

Following are the recommendations pertaining to specific stakeholders:

Business correspondents-For optimum usage of BCs in reaching the poor villagers, BCs have to be adequately compensated so that they are sufficiently incentivised to promote financial inclusion as a viable business opportunity. Banks should initiate suitable training and skill development programmes for effective functioning of BCs.

ATM network-Banks should enhance their ATM network in rural and un-banked areas to serve poor villagers. ATMs will only help the cause of inclusion.

RuPay network-To reduce the overall transaction costs associated with small ticket transactions in rural areas, domestic RuPay cards should be utilised.

KCCs/GCCs-To enable farmers to withdraw cash from ATMs anywhere in the country, banks need to convert KCCs/GCCs to electronic credit card. Further, banks may explore the possibility of issuing multipurpose cards which could function as debit cards, KCC and GCC as per the requirements in rural areas.

Priority lending-To achieve meaningful financial inclusion, banks should give priority for small farmers as compared to large farmers while sanctioning credit. Simplifying mortgage requirements and exemption from stamp duty for loans to small and marginal farmers should be done. Some states have waived stamp duty on loans to farmers. Various limits have been put in place, for example, for loans up to Rs 1 lakh, no stamp duty is imposed on loans with property as underlying assets in a few states. While stamp duty is a state subject, the ministry of agriculture can ask state governments to exempt farmer loans from the levy.

Extra incentives to lend in rural area- The RBI should mandate that commercial banks have a certain per cent of their portfolio in small loans. In addition, important social considerations should be factored into loan decisions. The children have to be attending a school before they are eligible for a loan. Similar conditions should be imposed for eligibility of loans in India. The government could also add extra incentives to lend in rural areas.

Use of Vernaculars-A large section of people in the country did not know English and thus it is necessary to make use of Hindi or other regional languages to address their needs. As part of Financial Literacy initiatives, if banks were to undertake pro-active steps in helping the common public to get over their English phobia, it is felt that the number of complaints would increase manifold.

Mobile and internet banking -Mobile banking can prove to be the solution for India in those areas where banking through PCs cannot be solely relied upon. Usage of Internet, on the other hand, would facilitate transparency in product pricing and characteristic and it would also enable product segmentation to suit the distinct group of customers apart from reducing the distribution costs.

Post office banks-sSetting up Post Banks can act as a "game changer", (according to industry body Assocham), besides raising rural savings and investment levels. Just Rs 100 per household saved every month could bring over Rs 12,000 crore from 45 per cent of unbanked households in rural areas.The Department of Posts (DoP) has applied for a banking licence. The Reserve Bank of India is expected to issue licences to shortlisted entities in January 2014.

Linking of Mahatma Gandhi, National Rural Employment Guarantee (MGNREG) and other government payments in rural areas through the India Post Bank, besides handling five million self-help group units, can be very helpful. Moreover, establishing linkages between Post Bank and the proposed Women's Bank, with at least one woman employee in each post office bank branch; apart from utilising PSU banks' training facilities and bringing Post Bank under some PSU bank for operational oversight can be equally beneficial.

India Post has already been handling several financial schemes in villages like National Small Savings, Recurring Deposits, Public Provident Fund, Postal Insurance, and so on.

Rural insurance-Over 70 per cent of total population resides in the rural areas of the country. However, insurance reaches less than three per cent of the total population. Due to high competition and relatively high market saturation in the urban areas, rural areas provide ample business opportunities for insurance firms –both life and non-life.

Further research-In financial inclusion, there are a few potentially interesting areas for future research –viz., (a) the most appropriate delivery model for different geographical regions given their unique characteristics, (b) The unbanked segments- not only the rural, but also urban or metropolitan areas are largely served by the unorganised sector even today. Research into the products, practices and procedures of this unorganised sectors an absolute imperative to identify and understand the same which the bottom of the pyramid populace finds so convenient and comfortable to deal with. This could throw up valuable leads for the organised sector – banks and financial institutions to follow and (c) Further, in order to measure the intensity of moneylenders especially in rural areas, research agencies should, inter alia, conduct a census of moneylenders in rural India.

5. Conclusion

The Government of India, alongwith the Reserve Bank has taken several steps since long for financial inclusion which specifically targets the rural sector because it has been the neglected and less developed sector. Various initiatives were taken in the past that aimed at bringing the villages of India and its people in the mainstream. Attempts have been made to facilitate access to banking, insurance and credit facilities to the poor and illiterate population, the latest one being the PMJDY.

Not only the banks and financial institutions but also private corporate are engaging in fulfilling this long cherished dream. The results have been both encouraging and discouraging. Various policy loopholes, inefficiency and unwillingness on the part of implementing authorities, lack of incentives, bureaucratic hurdles have been responsible for the failure of the schemes in promoting rural development and slow growth of the rural areas.

Nevertheless, there is always scope for improvement. The dark areas can be spotted and corrective measures can be taken. Use of technology, incentives, better infrastructure, and targeted implementation, deploying the available resources in a better manner and future research and development can definitely bring about better growth and development opportunities for the rural sector.

References

Publications

1. Garg, Bhoomika, (2014), *Financial inclusion and rural development, researchjournali's journal of commerce*, Vol. 2, No.1 February 2014.

2. Canara bank's initiatives under financial inclusion, financial inclusion division, PC & FI wing, Canara Bank, Bangalore.

3. "Financial Inclusion in India- an assessment", speech delivered by Shri P Vijaya Bhaskar, executive director, Reserve Bank of India, at the MFIN access-assist summit organised in New Delhi on December 10, 2013.

4. Verma, Dr Priyanka, and Singh, Anupam. (2014), Financial Inclusion in India: Panacea or Mirage to Rural Economic Development , SSRN, May 2014.

5. Singh, B. Anurag, and Tandon, Priyanka., *Financial Inclusion* in India: an analysis, IJOMFSMR, Vol.1, No. 6, June.

6. Reserve Bank of India, "Report on Financial Inclusion".

Websites

7. http://www.thehindu.com/opinion/columns/C_R_L__Narasimhan/the-challenge-of-financial-inclusion/article6345276.ece

8. http://articles.economictimes.indiatimes.com

9. http://www.kotak.com/personal-banking/financial-inclusion.html

10. https://www.allahabadbank.in/english/Financial_Inclusion.aspx

11. https://www.sbi.co.in/portal/web/agriculture-banking/financial-inclusion

12. http://www.bankofindia.co.in/FI-BOI/FI.html\

13. https://www.ucobank.com/rural-banking/financial-inclusion.aspx

13
Interest Free Micro Finance for Financial Inclusion and Rural Development

Manzoor. K

1. Introduction

India is still a rural country. Three-fourth of its population resides in rural areas with diversified, social, economic and cultural differences. Many of them are very poor. If the economic conditions of these people are to improve, rural development is necessary. Making financial services accessible to the poor and bringing them to the mainstream of the financial sector has been recognised as one of the most effective ways of poverty alleviation.

The modern commercial banking system revolves around the basic principles of capital certainty for deposition and certainty as to the rate of return on deposits. The concept of Islamic Banking is evolved on two basic principles; Sharing of profit and loss and significantly, the prohibition of the collection and payment of interest. In support of this thought, a number of Islamic banks have been established in the recent years not only in Islamic countries but also in European, African and Asian countries to cater to the growing demand, driven by globalisation and the vast wealth of some Muslim countries in the Middle East and Southeast Asia.

Micro Finance Institutions played a great role in delivering financial services to the poor people. They provide a variety of financial services to the poor rural households who have been ignored by the mainstream financial institutions because of their inability to provide collaterals as security. Micro entrepreneurs play significant roles in India's economic growth. But the exorbitant rates of interest charged by the Micro Finance Institutions pauses a challenge to the very existence of these enterprises. Here comes the role of Interest Free Micro Finance.

2. The Concept of Micro Finance

Micro Finance is a term having a broad meaning and it covers all type of micro products and micro services targeted at the poor population of any country or region, state, province or society. It refers to loans, savings, insurance, transfer services and other financial products targeted at low income clients. Among all these financial services, Micro Credit is more popularly used in different parts of the world as an intervention strategy of poverty eradication, employment generation and small enterprise creation.

Micro credit gives more emphasis on loans, while micro finance includes support services where channels for thrift, market assistance, technical assistance, capacity building, insurance, social and cultural programmes are opened. Thus, where micro finance is "credit plus", Micro credit is "only credit". (Ghroude, 2009)

3. Importance of Micro Finance

The role of micro credit in eradication of poverty was stressed by the United Nations in its Economic and Social Council meet on July 25, 1997, in which the council called for strengthening the micro credit institutions.The United Nations Economic and Social Council proclaimed the year 2005 as the International Year of Micro Credit to call for building inclusive financial sectors and strengthening the powerful, but often untapped entrepreneurial spirit existing in communities around the world. There are five goals associated with "The International Year of Micro Credit" which are:

1. Assess and promote the contribution of microfinance and microcredit to the MDGs.*
2. Increase public awareness and understanding of microfinance and microcredit as vital parts of the development equation.
3. Promote inclusive financial sectors.
4. Support sustainable access to financial services, and
5. Encourage innovation and new partnerships by promoting and supporting strategic partnerships to build and expand the outreach and success of microcredit and microfinance. (www.yearofmicrocredit,2005).

Since the 1980s Micro Finance has grown and spread to become a major tool in fighting poverty across the globe. Grameen Bank**, a community development bank established by Micro finance god father and Nobel Prize winner, Muhammed Yunus in 1983 has loaned money to over seven million women in Bangladesh.

---

* The **Millennium Development Goals** (**MDGs**) are eight international development goals that were established following the Millennium Summit of the United Nations in 2000, following the adoption of the United Nations Millennium Declartion
All 189 United Nations member states at the time (there are 193 currently), and at least 23 international organisations, committed to help achieve the Millennium Development Goals by 2015: (www.wikepedia, accessed on 24-01-2015).

** The **Grameen Bank** is a Nobel Peace Prize-winning microfinance organisation and community development bank founded in Bangladesh. It makes small loans (known as microcredit or "grameen credit")[to the impoverished without requiring collateral. The name Grameen is derived from the word *gram* which means "rural" or "village" in the Sanskrit language. (www.wikwpdedia,accessed on 24-01-2015).

4. Financial Inclusion

Indian economy in general and banking services in particular have made rapid development in the recent past. However, a sizable section of the population, particularly the vulnerable groups, such as weaker sections and low income groups, continue to remain excluded from even the most basic opportunities and services provided by the financial sector. In order to address the issues of financial inclusion, the Government of India constituted a "Committee on Financial Inclusion" under the Chairmanship of Dr C. Rangarajan. The Committee submitted its final report to Union Finance Minister on 04 January 2008. The Committee on Financial Inclusion has defined Financial Inclusion as *"the process of ensuring access to financial services and timely and adequate credit where needed by vulnerable groups such as weaker sections and low income groups at an affordable cost".*

The committee strongly recommends for linkning micro-credit with micro insurance and says that the Country has moved on to a higher growth trajectory. To sustain and accelerate the growth momentum, we have to ensure increased participation of the economically weak segment of the population in the process of economic growth. Financial inclusion of hitherto excluded segments of population is a critical part of this process of inclusion". (Rangarajan, 2008).

59th Survey result of NSSO gives us the extent of financial exclusion in India.

51.4 per cent of farmer households are financially excluded from both formal/ informal sources.

- Of the total farmer households, only 27 per cent access formal sources of credit; one third of this group also borrowed from non-formal sources.
- Overall, 73 per cent of farmer households have no access to formal sources of credit.
- Across regions, financial exclusion is more acute in Central, Eastern and North-Eastern regions. All three regions together accounted for 64 per cent of all financially excluded farmer households in the country. Overall indebtedness to formal sources of finance of these three regions accounted for only 19.66 per cent. (www.rbi.org.in,2015).

The Government of India and the Reserve Bank of India have been making concerted efforts to promote financial inclusion as one of the important national objectives of the country. Some of the major efforts made in the last five decades include - nationalisation of banks, building up of robust branch network of scheduled commercial banks, co-operatives and regional rural banks, introduction of mandated priority sector lending targets, lead bank scheme, formation of self-help groups, permitting BCs/BFs to be appointed by banks to provide doorstep delivery of banking services, zero balance Basic Savings Bank Account, etc. The fundamental objective of all these initiatives is to reach the large sections of the hitherto financially excluded Indian population.

RBI has taken some important measures for achieving financial inclusion at quicker pace. Measures include creation of Local Area Banks, (LABs), Introduction of Kisan Credit Cards Schemes* and establishment of special agricultural branches of PSBs. More importance on improved Micro-credit system and SHG-Bank linkage programme. Role of NGOs, SHGs, MFIs, Post Offices as effective intermediaries is not worthy in the process of better inclusion.

5. Problems with the Interestbased Micro Finance

The advent of MFIs in the Microfinance sector appears to have resulted in a significant increase in reach and the credit made available to the sector. Between 31st March 2007 and 31st March 2010, the number of outstanding loan accounts serviced by MFIs is reported to have increased from 10.04 million to 26.7 million and outstanding loans from about 3800 crores to 18344 crores. While this growth is impressive, number of studies both in India and abroad have questioned whether growth alone is effective in addressing poverty and what the adverse consequences of a too rapid growth might be. In particular, in the Indian context, specific areas of concern have been identified: These are

(a) Unjustified high rates of interest

(b) Lack of transparency in interest rates and other charges.

(c) Multiple lending

(d) Upfront collection of security deposits

(e) Over-borrowing

(f) Ghost borrowers

(g) Coercive methods of recovery

Lending was meant to the poorest of the poor in Microfinance sector, but mow the sector is much concerned about "profit from the poor" than poverty alleviation, focusing on capital cycling quickly through loaning only to the commercial clients which generates more cash for the lender. (Tameemuddhin, 2011).

---

* A **Kisan Credit Card** is a credit card to provide affordable credit for farmers in India. It was started by the Government of India, Reserve Bank of India (RBI), and National Bank for Agriculture and Rural Development (NABARD) in 1998-99 to help farmers access timely and adequate credit.

The Andhra Pradesh issue has brought forward a lot of problems and loopholes in the functioning of Indian MFIs. The chain of suicides committed by the clients of certain MFIs point the finger towards the inhuman methods adopted by many MFIs for the collection of loan installments. Due to the over debt burden, delinquency rate started increasing considerably and the frustrated MFIs resorted to harassing their customers for the repayment of the loan. The government intervention in the form of Andhra Pradesh Microfinance Institution (Regulation of Money Lending) Ordinance, in 2010 and Malegam Committee Recommendations of RBI are indeed a real need of the hour.

Contrary to public posturing that the MFIs are saviors of the poor and charge reasonable interest rates, several big MFIs in Andhra Pradesh have been charging very high interest rates, closer to the ones charged by traditional moneylenders. Under the new regulations, several commercial MFIs have disclosed to the authorities that their effective rate of annualised interest goes up to 60.5 per cent.

The Bhartiya Samrudhi Finance Ltd. of Basix[*], charges interest rates up to 60.5 per cent. In the case of SKS Micro Finance[*], Trident share and other MFIs , the effective maximum interest rates are upwards of 30 per cent. This is despite the fact that these MFI is borrow money from state-owned and private banks at concessional rates, usually in the range of 11 to 13 per cent, under the priority sector lending and other facilities.

The Suicides by over 60 poor borrowers in the state of Andhra Pradesh have brought the operation of the Micro Finance Institutions (MFIs) under public scrutiny. These debt driven suicides were due to the coercive methods of loan recovery used by the commercial MFIs. The majority of suicides took place in the Warangal district of Andhra Pradesh and as many as 17 borrowers of SKS Micro Finance were among those who reportedly committed suicide. The Commercial MFIs operate as profit making non-banking Financial corporation's (NBFCs) in India. In August 2010, SKS Micro Finance raised nearly $380 million in an Initial Public Offering (IPO). Promoters and private

---

* The Holding Company of the BASIX Group is called Bhartiya Samruddhi Investments and Consulting Services Limited (BASICS Ltd.), which started operations in 1996 as India's first "new generation livelihood promotion institution". It set up two fund based companies - Bhartiya Samruddhi Finance Ltd, a micro-finance NBFC in 1997 and Krishna Bhima Samruddhi Local Area Bank Ltd in 2001.(wikepedia.org,2015).

** **SKS Microfinance Limited** (SKS) is a non-banking finance company (NBFC), regulated by the Reserve Bank of India. The company operates across 19 of 28 Indian states.According to a CRISIL Report on Top 50 Indian Microfinance Institutions (MFIs), SKS Microfinance is the largest MFI in India with more borrowers, more branches and more loans as of 30 September 2008. (enwikepeida.org/wiki/sks/on,2015).

equity investors of SKS Micro finance became instant millionaires while their borrowers remain desperately poor. MFIs were dumping money on borrowers who were finding it difficult to repay and having to borrow from moneylenders at a higher cost in order to stay in good standing with the MFIs. Basically there are three areas of Micro Finance sector in India which are being questioned – Rate of interest, lending practices and coercive recovery methods. (Kavalit Singh, 2011).

6. The Relevance of Interest Free Micro Finance

As a way of escape from the above issues of traditional interest based MFIs, a handful of Interest free MFIs have come forward to provide interest-free financial services. Many of the countries of the world studied the evils of interest and introduced interest free banks and microfinance institutions. Asian Development Bank* in its 2006 report points out that "the special characteristics of interest free finance can provide alternative means to reach undeserved group in small rural areas and agriculture producers". In India main factors which inhibit these institutions to enter in to real banking business is the prohibition from the Reserve Bank of India. But Non- Banking. Financial Companies and Interest free Micro Finance Institutions are doing Interest Free Banking activities so as to benefit thousands of people of the country.

Report of the Committee on Financial Sector Reforms (CFSR) under the chairmanship of Dr. Reghuram Rajan submitted its final report in September 2008 to Prime Minister with specific recommendation of interest free banking in India as a remedy of financial exclusion. In his words, "Another area that falls broadly in the ambit of financial infrastructure for inclusion is the provision of interest free banking. Certain faiths prohibit the use of financial instruments that pay interest. The non-availability of interest free-banking products results in some Indians, including those in the economically disadvantaged strata of society, not being able to access banking products and services due to reasons of faith. This non-availability also denies India access to substantial sources of savings from other countries in the region." *(Reghuram Rajan, 2008).*

While interest-free banking is provided in a limited manner through NBFCs and co-operatives, the Committee recommends that measures be taken to permit the delivery of interest-free on a larger scale, including through the banking system. This is in consonance with the objectives of inclusion and growth through innovation. The implementation of Islamic MFI can accelerate the growth of financial inclusion. It is estimated that over 400 interest free

---

* The **Asian Development Bank (ADB)** is a regional development bank established on 22 August 1966 which is headquartered in Metro Manila, Philippines to facilitate economic development of countries in Asia.

financial institutions, registered and unregistered, are operating in different states of the country in different forms.

In 2005, Government of India asked Reserve Bank of India to examine Islamic Banking instruments and constituted a Working Group headed by M. Anand Sinha, Chief Manager, Department of Banking, Operation and Development along with senior Bankers from SBI, ICICI and Oman International Bank that came up with its report in 2006 which said in the current statutory and regulatory framework it would not be possible for banks in India to undertake Islamic Banking activities and concluded that if the banks are allowed to do Islamic Banking appropriate amendments are required in Banking Regulation Act, 1949. (Muhamad Yahya, 2014).

India's central bank has allowed a firm in the southern state of Kerala to operate as a non-banking financial company that follows Islamic principles. A small step towards developing syariah-compliant* finance in the country. Cheraman Financial Services said it had obtained approval to operate from the Reserve Bank of India (RBI) and would follow the Islamic ban on interest. RBI governor Duvvuri Subbarao has said Islamic banking was not possible in the country but syariah-compliant products could be delivered through alternative means. (www.islamicfinance.2015) Interest Free Micro Finance is working by following the principles of Islamic Finance.

7. The Principles of Islamic Finance

The most important principles on which the modern Islamic Finance frame works rest on:-

1. *Prohibition of the payment or receipt of interest:*

   Money itself is considered to have no intrinsic value. It is merely a store of wealth and medium of exchange.

2. *Prohibition of uncertainty or speculation:*

   Everybody participating in a financial transaction must be adequately informed and not cheated or misled.

3. *Prohibition of financing certain economic sectors:*

   Investment is forbidden in what are considered to be socially detrimental activities like gambling, pornography, alcohol, armaments, etc.

---

* **Islamic banking** : Banking activity that is consistent with the principles of sharia and its practical application through the development of Islamic economics. As such, a more correct term for 'Islamic banking' is 'Sharia compliant finance'. Sharia prohibits acceptance of specific interest or fees for loans of money (known as *riba*, or usury), whether the payment is fixed or floating. Investment in businesses that provide goods or services considered contrary to Islamic principles (e.g. pork or alcohol) is also *haraam* ("sinful and prohibited").

4. *Importance of profit and loss sharing.*

   The investors and investee must share the risk of all financial transaction:

5. *Asset-backing principle.*

   Financial transactions should be unpinned by identifiable and tangible underlying asset. (Shaikh, 2009).

8. Instruments Used in Interest Free Institutions:

The literature separates Interest free finance into three main activities: Concessional financing, Trade financing and participatory mechanisms. I would like to go through main instruments of financing that are in use in Interest free banks and Micro Finance Institutions.

(a) Partnership contracts (*Mudaraba*): Trustee partnership is a mode of financing through which the investor or institution provides capital finance for a specific venture indicated by the customer. The investor institution is the owner of the capital and the customer-entrepreneur is responsible for the management of the business and provides professional, managerial and technical expertise for initiating and operating the business enterprise or project. Profit is shared according to a pre-agreed ratio. Losses if any are entirely absorbed by the capital provider. In cases of proven negligence or mismanagement by tentrepreneurrs, however, they may be held responsible for the financial losses.

(b) Joint Venture (*Musharaka*) Facility: A joint venture involves a partnership in which both the bank and its customer-client contribute to entrepreneurship and capita. It is an agreement whereby the customer and the bank agree to combine financial resources to undertake any type of business venture, and agree to manage the same according to the terms of the agreement. Profits are shared between the bank and the customer in the pre-agreed ratio. Losses are shared strictly in proportion to their respective capital contributions.

(c) Cost-Plus Sale (*Murabaha*): Cost plus implies a sale on a cost-plus basis. The mechanism may be described as follows. Individual A is in need of commodity X on debt. He approaches Bank B. Now, B buys X from the vendor/ supplier at price P. This price is also known to A. Next, B sells X to A at a marked-up price, say P+M, where M is the agreed profit or mark-up taken by B. The payment of price P+M is now deferred to a future date and is made in full or I parts. In a *Murabaha*, both parties of the transaction must know the cost and the profoit or mark-up.

(d) Leasing (*Ijara*) Facility: In simple terms, it means leasing or hiring of a physical asset. It is a popular debt-based product in which the Interest Free Bank assumes the role of a lesser and allows its client to use a particular asset that it owns. The client or lessee is in need of the asset. Through leasing, it receives the benefits associated with ownership of the asset against payment of predetermined rentals.

(e) Deferred Delivery Sale *(Salam)* Facility: It is essentially a forward agreement where delivery occurs at a future date in exchange for spot payment of price. Unlike earlier mechanisms *salam* was originally designed as a financing mechanism for small farmer and traders. Under a *salam* agreement , a trader in need of short term funds sells merchandise to the bank on a deferred delivery basis. It receives full price of the merchandise on the spot that serves its financing need at present. At a pre agreed future date, it delivers the merchandize to the bank. The bank sells the merchandise in the market at the prevailing price. Since the spot price that the bank pays is pegged lower than the expected future price, the transaction should result in a profit for the bank.

(f) Manufacture –Sale (*Istisna*) Facility: An *Istisna* is a contract of manufacture. A seller under this agreement undertakes to develop or manufacture a commodity with clear specifications for an agreed price and deliver after an agreed period of time. The unique feature of manufacturing contract is that nothing is exchanged on spot or at the time of contracting, It is a pure and perhaps the only forward contract where the obligations of both parties relate to the future. The buyer makes payment of price in parts over the agreed time period or in full at the end of the time period.

(g) Benevolent Loan (*Qard hasan*) : This is the simplest of all financing scheme. Under this scheme, a borrower in need of specific amount of funds borrows the same from a lender as *quar hasn* with or without a clear stipulation regarding the maturity date. The loan is repaid on maturity without an increment or interest. When no maturity is stipulated, the loan is repaid when asked by the lender, again without any increment. The lender is allowed to ask for an asset as collateral. This is the simplest of all financing schemes. Under this scheme, a borrower in need of a lender is allowed to charge the borrower actual administrative expenses incurred in operation of the mechanism .(Muhammed, 2010).

Interest Free Micro Finance models in India

Hundreds of Interest Free Micro Finance Institutions are working in India. These institutions are known as *muslim* funds or *bilasudi* funds in north India and interest free Nidhis or societies in Kerala. The highest number of such institutions is in Kerala, followed by Uttar Pradesh, Andhra Pradesh, Maharastra and Karnataka. Co-operative option has been widely explored and practiced to interest free microfinance and other non-microfinance activities, given the banking and financial constraints. (Rahmathullah, 1999).

Example from working models Al-Khair Cooperative Society Ltd, Patna is taken up for detailed illustration.

9. Al–Khair Co-operative Credit Society Limited.

The term Al-Khair is an Arabic word which means "boon" and true to its name, it has become now a boon to every poor irrespective of caste, creed or religion. It is registered under Multi-state Cooperative Society Act. 2002 and added interest free products to its repertoire with permission to operate in four states–Bihar, Jharkhand, U.P. and Delhi. (Tameemuddin, 2011).

Objectives

The main objective is to fight poverty through co-operation.To defeat the business of interest based cruel system of money-lending which is eroding the productive capacity of micro entrepreneurs. To finance such enterprises that creates self-sustainable economic system and helps in reducing poverty.To provide all kind of social benefits to its members in order to enhance the lives of their members.

Management

The society is managed by the Board consisting 21 members. The term of the Board is Five years. The Board is elected by the general body in Annual General Meeting.The Board appoints Chief Executive of the Society. There is other staff like Accountants and Daily deposit collectors. All of them play their respective role in the development of society.The Board has a Chairperson and a Vice-chairperson. The chief executive is the ex-official member.

Share/Membership

Each member has to purchase shares in the Society. Each share is of Rs 10 and minimum ten shares are required to be purchased initially by a member. An admission fee of Rs 25 and a donation of Rs 15 are also mandatory for the person to become member of our Society. The number of members as well as the share at ACCSL has seen a rising trend during the period 2005-2010 (Table, 1). The total number of members increased from 1448 in 2005-06 to 3178 in 2009-10. The value of members' share also increased significantly in the five year period from Rs 4.54 Lakhs to Rs 14.36 Lakhs. (www.alkairsocierty.org,2015).

Table 1 : Al-Khair Progress Details 2005-2010 (Last Five Years)

Share			
Year	*Amount (Rs)*	*Actual Increase(Rs)*	*Increase (per cent)*
2005-2006	454,090.00	121,700.00	36.61
2006-2007	556,190.00	102,100.00	22.48
2007-2008	805,890.00	249,700.00	44.89
2008-2009	1,112,540.00	306,650.00	38.05
2009-2010	1,436,330.00	323,790.00	29.10
Membership			
	Numbers	*Actual Increase*	*Increase (per cemt)*
2005-2006	1448	361	33.21
2006-2007	1750	302	20.86
2007-2008	2244	494	28.23
2008-2009	2974	730	32.53
2009-2010	3178	204	6.86

www.alkairsociety.org/reports.

Deposits

On the deposit side, ACCSL has been consistently showing positive growth. The deposit balance has risen remarkably from Rs 22.50 Lakhs to Rs 1.20 crores during 2005-10. (Table 2)

Table 2

Deposit Balance			
Year	*Amount (Rs.)*	*Actual Increase (Rs.)*	*Increase (%)*
2005-2006	2,250,964.00	476,717.00	26.87
2006-2007	2,460,218.00	209,230,056.50	53.00
2009-2010	12,053,371.00	5,615,896.50	87.24

www.alkairsociety.org/reports

Loan

There are three popular loan products Demand Loan, *Morabaha* Loan and Short Term Business Loan (STBL) whose minimum and maximum limits are Rs, 1000 to 20,000, Rs 1000 to 40,000 and Rs 1000 to 20,000 respectively. To its sustenance Al-Khair involves itself in income generating products. Under the *Morabaha* loan, Al-Khair buys goods from a dealer and sells on installments to the clients at a fixed mark-up 8-15 per cent. There is also an investment product. Growth Fund, based on the principle of sharing the profits at the ratio of 70:30. 70 per cent Al-Khair gives to the investor. In 2010, there was 24 per cent return on the investment. In STBL the profit is shared on a pre-determined basis i.e., 70:30 ratio. 70 per cent of the profit goes to the businessman and 30 per cent to Al-Khair. The most attractive feature of loaning of Al-Khair is that the loss arises from the business is borne entirely by the society. Percentage of defaulters on account of timely repayment is low. Cases of non-refund of loan are rare arising either due to death or failure of business. (Ramzan, 2012). The amount of loan outstanding increased by almost 50 per cent in 2009-10. It was Rs 53.18 Lakhs in 2005-06 and it increased to Rs 98.90 Lakhs. During the five year period total loan amount was Rs, 2.52 crores which is clear from the Table 3.

Table 3 : Loan Amount

Year	*Amount (Rs.)*	*Actual Increase (Rs)*	*Increase (Per cent)*
2005-2006	5,318,994.00	2,568,788.00	93.40
2006-2007	7,783,507.00	2,464,513.00	46.33
2007-2008	5,528,353.00	-2,255,154.00-	28.97
2008-2009	6,600,033.00	1,071,680.00	19.39
2009-2010	9,890,180.00	3,290,147.00	49.85
Total	**25,230,887.00**		

FREwww.alkairsociety.org/reports

Loan sanction and disbursal process :

A committee named as Loan and Admittance of Members Committee (LAMC), consisting of the members of society, process, and sanction and monitors the loan. Every branch has its own LAMC. In its weekly meetings, the committee examines all the loan applications, the records of disbursement and recovery of loans in that week, tries to resolve the issues related to bad debts, and finds ways and means to spread the loaning in a socially just manner. It is based on the loanable fund availability that the committee sanctions different types of loans. The credit process ranges from the preloan screening, analysis, approval to post disbursement management such as collection, delinquency follow-up, and qualification for additional loans. Eligibility for loan is decided on the basis of deposit profile of the person and credit limit is equal to ten times of his share value. Loanable worth is decided on the basis of his deposit behaviour. Loan may be granted up to 100 times of his daily deposit with credit limit. LAMC processes the loan applications and approve the loan amount. The loan able fund is presently 69 per cent of the deposit balance. (Najmul Hoda, 2010). Details of Income and expenditure Both the income and expenditure has shown a rising trend over a period of five years. A marked improvement has been seen in the net profit for ACCSL.

Table 4 : Profit and Loss Statement (all figures in rupees)

Year	*Income*	*Expenditure*	*Profit and Loss*
2005-06	378,193.00	351,209.00	26984
2006-07	423,463.00	448,576.00	-25113
2007-08	609,623.00	592,501.00	17122
2008-09	721,167.00	941,570.00	-220403
2009-10	1,357,076.00	1,344,090.50	12985.5

www.alkairsociety.org/reports

Through its products Al-Khair society has been helping in financial inclusion of the excluded lot in India with interest free products since the year 2002. It is a pioneer in interest free microfinance services in India. Though the society has been working for the last eigth years, the figures are very humble. But the environment and interest free practices without seeking capital support from Commercial Banks or any other Government financial institution makes Al-Khair a unique financial institution in India. The Zakat share of the Company's earnings and the funds collected through other possible means are being utilised to offer benign loans and financial aid for such charitable purposes as medical treatment, education, self employment schemes, house repair etc.

10. Conclusion

Evils of interest based system have become so obvious that men are in search of an alternative and Islamic economics, banking and finance have accepted to be the much needed panacea. In India we have a network of interest free Micro Finance in the informal sector. Each institution adopts a distinct style based on the economic and social conditions of each locality. Thus, the Islamic banking and microcredit programmes may complement each other in both ideological and practical terms. Interest free financial system based on Islamic principles is wide spread now, aimed at the implementation of financial system devoid of interest. It helps to avoid the menaces caused out of interest and acts as viable alternative for rural credit expansions as to achieve poverty alleviation and economic well being of the common man.

References

1. Arshad, Ajmal. (2010), 'Interest Free Micro Finance in India: Exploring the Cooperative Model' International seminar on Islamic Finance in India. October 4-6, Kochi, Kerala.
2. Ghorude, K.N. (2009), 'Micro Finance for Financial inclusion and sustainable Rural development' , *Southern Economist*,Vol. 48, May 1.
3. Huda, Najmul and SL Gupta. (2010), "Faith based Model of Micro Finance A case study of Al-Khair Cooperative credit society", Proceedings of the seminar on Islamic Finance in India on October 4-6. at Kochi,India.
4. Hulme. D and T. Arun. (2011), " What is Wrong and Right with Micro Finance," *Economic and Political Weekly*, XLVI(48) ; pp. 23-26.
5. Kavaljit Singh.(2011), "Taming the 'wild west' of Micro Finance ', *Main stream*, April 1-7.
6. Malyadri, P.(2011), Micro Finance crisis in Andhra Pradesh: Some issues", *Kurukshetra* Vol. 59. No. 3 January.

7. Malegam,Y.H. (2011), *Report of the sub-committee of Central Board of Directors to study issues and concerns in the MFI*, Reserve Bank of India.
8. Mahmud, Ahamad Saikh. (2009), *Towards Interest-Free Banking,*Kitab Bhavan, New Delhi.
9. Mundra, S.S. (2014), " Banking: Inclusion Innovation and Implementation" *Southern Economist.* Vol. 53, No.13 November.
10. Mufti Muhammed Yaha Qasmi.(2014), 'RBI Governor, Dr Raghuram Rajan and Islamic Banking', *Islamic Tijara*-Islamic Finance Magazine from Mumbai, April-June.
11. Nair, T.S. (2011), "Micro Finance : Lessons from a crisis", *Economic and Political Weekly* . XLVI (6) pp. 23-26.
12. Najatulla Siddiqi, Muhammed.(2010), *Banking without interest* Markazi Maktab Islamic Publishers, New Delhi.
13. Ramzan Shaheed,c.p.(2012), "Role of Participatory Micro Finance for Financial inclusion", proceedings of the seminar on interest free Micro Finance, Kochin University of Science and Technology ,17. March.
14. Rahmathullah. (1999) ,"Problems, of interest Free-Banking in India in the Muslim and Arab Perspective" , *International Islamic Magazine* , Vol. 4,7-12.New Delhi, The Insititute of Islamic and Arab Studies.
15. Reguram Rajan.(2008), chapter 3 "Broadening access to finance", Report of the Committee on Financial Sector Reforms' September, 12.
16. Rao Srinivasa, K.(2011), "What is wrong with Micro Finance ?", *Kurukshetra*, Vol. 59.N0. 3 pp. 26-29.
17. Rangarajan, C. (2008), *Report of the committee on Financial Inclusion*, Govt. of India, 8 Janavary.
18. Tameemudheen, Humble . (2011) , " Ahair-An Interest Free Micro Finance experiment in India", *Indian Micro Finance Business News*, January 7.
19. Uzair Muhammed .(2000), *Interest Free Banking*, Kitab Bhavan , New Delhi.
20. Yunus Muhammed with Alan Jolis.(1998), *Banker to the poor,* The Autobiography of Muhammed Yunus, London, Arun Press.**Web sites utilized:**
21. www.alkairsociety.org/report.
22. www.rbi.org.in.
23. http://www.yearmicrocredit.org..
24. www.wikipedia.org
25. www.islamicfinance.org

14

A Peep into Past Rural Self-Employment Programmes Initiated by the Government of India

Dr Shankar Chatterjee

1. Introduction

The unemployment is a major issue in every country as wage employment cannot be provided to all. Even developed countries cannot provide job to all those who seek it, so the alternative is self-employment. As per available data, in USAthe unemployment rate rose from 5.0 per cent in December 2007 to 10.0 per cent in October 2009, and subsequently scaled down to 6.1 per cent inJune 2014 (http:Unemployment_in_United_States). In India, more than 20 per cent in age bracket of 15-24 years were jobless albeit, they have been seeking job but unable to ge tit, Census of 2011 (The Times of India, 2 July 2014). In absolute term the figure reached to 4.7 crore of which 2.6 crore were male and 2.1 crore female (*ibid*). According to NSSO (66th round) Report of the Government of India published in 2013, Kerala has the highest unemployment rate and Rajasthan and Gujarat have the least unemployment rate among the major States of India (http: Unemployment_in_India). However to create income generation opportunities for the unemployed youths, self-employment is the best alternative as wage-employment cannot be provided to all vis-à-vis unemployment allowance etc., are not sustainable way out. Muhammad Yunus, the Nobel laureate, in his book Banker to the Poor has highlighted some advantages of self-employment over wage employment.

(a) The hours are flexible and can adapt to fit any family situation. It allows people to choose between running a business full-time or part-time when they need to meet crises, or to put their business on hold and work full-time for a salary.

(b) Self-employment is tailor-made for anyone who is street-smart and has many acquired from books and technical schools. This means the illiterate and the poor can exploit their strengths, rather than be held back by their weaknesses.

(c) It allows a person to turn hobbies they enjoy into gainful employment.

(d) It allows individuals who cannot work well in a rigid hierarchy to run their own show.

(e) It offers a way out of welfare dependency, not just to become wage slaves, but to open a store or start a manufacturing business.

(f) It can help those who have found a job and are still nonetheless poor.

(g) It gives those who have just been fired from a job moral support to start a business before they become depressed and isolated.

(h) It gives the victims of prejudice who would not be hired because of their colour or national origin a chance to earn a living.

(i) The average cost of creating a self-employment job is ten, twenty or hundred times cheaper than creating an employment job.

(j) It helps isolated poor person gain self-confidence, step by step.

Before carrying out the discussion further, the definitions of self and wage employment programmes as defined by NSSO 55th Round are presented.

Self-employed: Persons who operate their own farm or non-farm enterprises or engaged independently in a profession or trade on own account or with one or a few partners are deemed to be self-employed in household enterprises. The essential feature of the self-employed is that they have autonomy (i.e, how, where and when to produce) and economic independence (i.e., market, scale of operation and money) for carrying out their operation. The fee or remuneration received by them comprises two parts – share of their labour and profit of the enterprise. In other words, their remuneration is determined wholly or mainly by sales or profits of the goods or services which were produced. Self-employed persons can be further categorised as own – account workers, employers or helpers in household enterprises.

Regular salaried/ wage employee: These are persons who work in others' farm or non-farm enterprises (both household and non household) and, in return, receive salary or wages on a regular basis (i.e. not on the basis of daily or periodic renewal of work contract). This category includes not only persons getting time wage but also persons receiving piece wage or salary and paid apprentices, both full time and part-time.

2. Major Rural Self-employment Programmes in India:

After independence many self-employment programmes for rural youths were launched by the Ministry of Rural Development, Government of India time to time which are discussed at length here. One massive self-employment programme recently wrapped up was Swarnajayanti Gram SwarojgarYojana (SGSY) which was restructured under the banner of National Rural Livelihoods Mission (NRLM) that is "*Aajeevika*", and formally launched on 3rd June, 2011. In fact, based on the Report of Professor. R. *Radhakrishna* Committee on 'Credit Related Issues related to SGSY', set up by the Ministry of Rural

Development in April, 2008, SGSY has been restructured as National Rural Livelihoods Mission (NRLM). Prior to that, SGSY was initiated from 1st April 1999 by merging six then self-employment programmes viz. Integrated Rural Development Programme (IRDP), Development of Women and Children in Rural Areas (DWCRA), Training of Rural Youth for Self Employment (TRYSEM), Supply of Improved Toolkits for Rural Artisans (SITRA), Million Wells Scheme (MWS) and *Ganga Kalyan*Yojana (GKY). Salient features of these six programmes are mentioned below for the benefit of readers, scholars, researchers and others.

IRDP: Integrated Rural Development Programme (IRDP) was initially taken up in 1977-78 in 2300 selected blocks of the country and extended to all the blocks from 2nd October, 1980. The main objective of IRDP was to endow with rural youths living below poverty line forincome generating assets and self-employment opportunities. Assistance under IRDP was given to a target group of rural poor belonging to families Below Poverty Line (BPL), in the form of subsidy by the Government and term credit by the financial institutions.

Target Group: The target group consisted of families of small and marginal farmers, agricultural labourers and rural artisans etc, whose per capita monthly expenditure did not exceed the poverty line. Within the target group, special safeguards were provided by reservation that is, (i) 50 per cent benefits for SCs/STs, (ii) 40 per cent for women and (iii) 3 per centfor physically handicapped persons. In addition, priority was also given to women headed households, assignees of surplus land, freed bonded labourers and acceptors of small family norm.

Pattern of Subsidy: The ceiling on subsidy in respect of individuals was Rs, 4000 in normal areas; Rs 5000 in DPAP / DDP areas; Rs 6000 for SCs / STs families and physically handicapped persons; Rs, 7500 or 50 per cent of the project cost, whichever was less for unemployed educated youth; and for activities involving at least five persons, the ceiling was fixed at Rs 1.25 lakh or 50 per cent of the project cost, whichever was less.

Funding Pattern and Release of Funds: IRDP was financed on 50:50 cost-sharing basis by the Centre and the States. The funds were released directly to the DRDAs.Under IRDP from 1980-81 to 1998-99, an amount of Rs 11267.00 crore was disbursed as subsidy against bank credit of Rs 21344.00 crore. In spite of this huge investment, less than 20 per cent beneficiaries could cross poverty line as shown by various Concurrent Evaluation studies on IRDP carried out by the Government of India – First Round was in 1985 (Oct.) – 1986 (Sept.); Second Round (1987); Third Round (1989); Fourth Round 1992 (Sept.) – 1993 (Aug.) and Fifth Round (July 95- June, 96). The progress of IRDP since its inception may be seen from the Table-1.

Table 1 : Performance of IRDP during 6th, 7th, 8th and 9th Plans

Plan	*No.of families assisted (Lakh)*	*Subsidy disbursed (Rs crore)*	*Credit mobili sation (Rs crore)*	*Total inves tment (credit+ subsidy) (Rs crore)*	*Subsidy credit ratio*	*Per inves tment (Rs)*
6th Plan	150	1661	3102	4763	1:1.87	2491
7th plan	200	1359	4000	6359	1:1.70	3180
8th Plan	*Year – wise*					
1992 -93	20.69	679.68	1036.80	1616.48	1:1.79	7889
1993 -94	25.39	800.82	1408.44	22.9.26	1:1.76	8746
1994 -95	22.15	818.30	1450.58	2268.88	1:1.77	10313
1995 -96	20.89	870.20	1701.33	2571.53	1:1.96	12310
1996 -97	19.24	905.94	1969.16	2874.10	1:2.17	14943
Ninth Plan	*Year – wise*					
1997 -98	17.07	863.11	1996.64	2859.75	1:2.31	16753
1998 -99*	7.82	407.98	980.72	1389.69	1:2.40	17771

Source: Compiled from Self Employment Programmes IRDP, TRYSEM and DWCRA, Ministry of Rural Development, Govt. of India in Annual Report 1998-99, Ministry of Rural Development, Government of India.

Although the above table is self-explanatory but few important points as observed from the table are:

(a) Around five Crore rural households were benefitted under IRDP.

(b) Investment on each family over a period of time scaled up.

(c) Subsidy credit ratio went up comparatively at higher rate in later years.

Few Salient Features from Concurrent Evaluation of IRDP: For the benefit of researchers few findings from Concurrent Evaluation of IRDP collected from Main Findings of the Survey carried out during September 1992 to August 1993, by the Government of India, Ministry of Rural Areas and Employment, published in October, 1996 are presented below.

Positive Points

1. In case of selection of beneficiaries, data revealed that 52.60 per cent of the families were selected by the *Gram Sabha*, 41.66 per cent by local officials and around 6 per cent by public representatives and other agencies.
2. Around 95 per cent of the beneficiaries felt that type of assets provided to them was according to their choice and 69.76 per cent had the opinion that assets were of good quality.
3. With regard to overdue/recoveries from the beneficiaries, the survey divulged that in 59 per cent cases there was no overdue and only in 41 per cent cases little overdue was reported.
4. A large percentage (94 per cent) of beneficiaries did not borrow any money from private sources to fund/supplement their income generation projects.
5. The evaluation revealed that 15.96 per cent of the old beneficiary families could cross the revised poverty line of Rs 11000 while 54.4 per cent of families were able to cross the old poverty line of Rs 6400.

Areas of Concern

1. The important point of concern is that only 3.62 per cent of total old beneficiaries were given a second dose.
2. Around 57 per cent beneficiaries were not aware about Group Life Insurance.
3. Only 31 per cent beneficiaries were provided with *Vikas Patrika, i.e.* monitoring card.
4. Linkage between IRDP and TRYSEM/DWCRA was found to be at low ebb as only 2.09 per cent beneficiaries reported one of their family members assisted under DWCRA, whereas 3.02 per cent received training under TRYSEM.

2. Development of Women and Children in Rural Areas (DWCRA): Development of Women and Children in Rural Areas (DWCRA) was launched as a sub-scheme of IRDP in the year 1982-83 in 50 districts. It subsequently was extended in all the districts of the country by 1994-95. While IRDP was in implementation, it was observed that the fruits of benefit did not percolate to poor women as expected, in view of this, Development of Women and Children in Rural Areas (DWCRA) was launched.

The basic unit under DWCRA was a group of 10-15 poor women who came together to help each other in order to use their collective strength to break social bonds that have denied them income generating and self-fulfilling opportunities. The group size may be smaller in difficult terrain and far flung areas. One woman amongst the members functioned as the group organiser who facilitated inselection of activity, procurement of raw-materials, and marketing of products.

Each DWCRA group was extended with a sum of Rs 25, 000 as Revolving Fund (RF) to meet capital expenditure requirement of economic activities. Progress of DWCRA, over a period of time showed that since its inception to 1998-99, against the target of forming 239785 number of groups, 245463 groups were formed benefitting 3803576 women indicating achievement exceeded the target. The progress of DWCRA during each plan period is shown as below:

Table: 2 Coverage achieved during each plan

Plan	*Target (No. of groups)*	*Achievement (No. of groups)*	*Women benefitted*
Sixth plan	6035	3308	52170
Seventh Plan	35000	28031	469707
Annual plan 1990-91	7500	7139	109557
Annual Plan 1991-1992	7500	9378	208012
Eighth Plan	91900	141514	2268327
Ninth Plan			
1997-98	30000	36436	460409
1998-98	61850*	19657*	235394*
TOTAL	91850	56093	695803
Grand Total	**239785**	**245463**	**3803576**

(*) – As on 21.1.1999

Source: **Compiled from:** Self Employment Programmes IRDP, TRYSEM and DWCRA, Ministry of Rural Development, Govt. of India and Annual Report 1998-99, Ministry of Rural Development, Government of India.

3. Training of rural Youth for Self-employment: (TRYSEM): Training of Rural Youth for Self-employment (TRYSEM) was launched on 15th August 1979 aimed to provide entrepreneurial skills to enable rural youths to take up self-employment. Later on (1983), wage employment was also encouraged for the youths. The youths in the age group of 18-35 years from the BPL families were entitled for training. There was no age limit for rural artisans. For the safe guard of the marginalised sections of the society, guidelines emphasised 50 per cent of selected youths should be from SC and ST communities, 40 per cent women and 3 per cent physically handicapped persons. There were no educational qualifications for selection of trainees and while in training they were provided with stipend in between Rs 200 and Rs 500 per month. For enabling the trainees to start individual activity, there was provision of Rs 800 as an allowance for purchase of toolkits by the trainees.

From inception of the programme to 1997-98, number of youths trained was 4148425. Of the total youths, 1755359 were self-employed and 2332374 were provided with wage employment. Again the number of SC/ST and women trained was 1774395 and 1912514 respectively during the period.

4. Supply of Improved Toolkits to Rural Artisans (SITRA): The programme was launched as sub-scheme of IRDP in 1992 with the objective of earning income through self-employment. The average cost of tool kit was Rs. 2000 and in case of power driven tools the average cost was Rs 4500. Out of the total cost, 90 per cent was borne by the Government of India and 10 per cent was the share of beneficiary. Out of the total beneficiaries 50 per cent was reserved for SC and ST communities. There were no provisions of reservation for women and physically handicapped persons. During Eighth Plan, an amount of Rs 149 crorewas released to 8.32 lakh beneficiaries.

5. Million Wells Scheme (MWS): Million Wells Scheme (MWS) was launched as a sub-scheme of National Rural Employment Programme (NREP) and Rural Landless Employment Guarantee Programme (RLEGP) during 1988-89. It continued as a sub-scheme of *JawaharRozgar*Yojana from April 1989 to December 1995. From 1st January 1996, MWS was initiated as an independent scheme. The objective of the scheme was to provide open irrigation wells free of cost to poor, small and marginal farmers, freed bonded labourers, provided they were below the poverty line. Although up to 1992-93, the target group for MWS was small and marginal farmers belonging to SCs/STs and freed bonded labourers but from 1993-94 onward, MWS was extended to include poor small and marginal farmers belonging to non-SC/ST category as well. From inception to November 1998, a sum of Rs 6168 crore was allocated, of which 4728 crore was spent to construct 1263090 wells.

6. *Ganga Kalyan*Yojana (GKY): Launched in 1996-97 as a sub scheme of IRDP, GKY continued up to1st February 1997. Later on from 1st April 1997, it was made an independent programme. The objective of GKY was to provide irrigation through exploitation of ground water (bore-wells and tube-wells) to individual and group of beneficiaries belonging to marginal and small farmers identified as BPL families. Financial assistance was extended through subsidy and credit by financial institutions. The monetary limit of subsidy per group (5 to 15 members) was Rs 40, 000 and for individual the minimum subsidy was Rs 5000 per acre of land subject to Rs. 12500. During 1997-98, Central allocation was Rs, 200 crore for the Yojana which was later on reduced to Rs 100 crore in view of the lack of gearing up the same. Physical achievement showed that during 1997-98, 1674 individual projects and 92 group projects were completed.

7. Swarnajayanti Gram SwarojgarYojana (SGSY): SGSY as massive self-employment programme continued for more than a decade. As mentioned already, it was initiated by amalgamating then six self-employment programmes viz. Integrated Rural Development Programme (IRDP), Development of Women and Children in Rural Areas (DWCRA), Training of Rural Youths for Self-Employment (TRYSEM), Supply of Improved Toolkits for Rural Artisans (SITRA), Million Wells Scheme (MWS) and *Ganga Kalyan* Yojana (GKY). The objective of the Swarnajayanti Gram SwarojgarYojana (SGSY) was to bring the assisted poor families (Swarojgaris) above the Poverty Line by ensuring appreciable sustained level of income over a period of time. This objective was to be achieved inter alia, by organising the rural poor into Self Help Groups (SHGs) through the process of social mobilisation, their training and capacity building and provision of income generating assets. SGSY laid stress on the cluster approach. Under SGSY, generally a self-help group consisted of 10 to 20 persons. However, in difficult areas like deserts, hills and areas with scattered and sparse population and in case of minor irrigation and disabled persons, this number may be from 5-20. SGSY has been restructured as National Rural Livelihoods Mission (NRLM), subsequently renamed as "*Aajeevika*", to implement it in a mission mode across the country and formally launched on 3rd June, 2011. However, the progress of SGSY may be seen from the following table.

Table 3: Financial and Physical Progress under SGSY: 1999-2000 to 2012-13

(Rs. in Crore)

Sl. No.	*Items*	*1999-2000*	*2000-01*	*2001-02*	*2002-03*	*2003-04*	*2004-05*	*2005-06*	*2006-07*
A	**Financial Progress**								
1.	Total Allocation	1472.33	1332.50	774.50	756.37	1065.83	1332.67	1332.67	1466.00
2.	Budget Allocation / Revised Allocation	950.00	620.00	550.00	710.00	800.00	1000.00	1000.00	1200.00
3.	Central Allocation	1105.00	1000.00	581.50	567.90	800.00	1000.00	1000.00	1100.00
4.	State Allocation	367.34	332.50	193.00	188.47	265.83	332.67	332.67	366.00
5.	Central Releases	946.76	544.94	536.27	706.04	797.55	996.59	1029.56	1188.35
	Percentage of Central Releases	99.66	87.89	97.50	99.44	99.69	99.66	102.96	99.03
6.	Central Releases (Subsidy to DRDA)	869.55	462.11	401.10	504.64	645.20	900.10	910.27	1040.16

Sl.No. Items	1999-2000	2000-01	2001-02	2002-03	2003-04	2004-05	2005-06	2006-07
Per cent age of Central Releases (Subsidy to DRDAs)	78.69	46.21	68.98	88.86	80.65	90.01	91.03	94.56
7. State Releases	261.47	200.76	156.07	181.14	192.64	261.81	315.67	338.91
Per cent age of State Releases	71.18	60.38	80.87	96.11	72.47	78.70	94.89	92.60
8. Opening Balance as on 1st April	776.66	854.74	661.58	415.77	287.38	249.01	241.83	262.97
9. Misc. Receipt	54.33	90.57	80.80	76.66	89.66	100.28	90.76	82.51
10. Total Funds Available	**1962.01**	**1608.18**	**1299.55**	**1178.22**	**1214.88**	**1511.20**	**1558.5**	**1724.55**
11. Total Funds Utilised	**959.86**	**1117.94**	**970.32**	**921.11**	**1043.43**	**1290.83**	**1338.78**	**1424.20**
Per cent of Utilisation of Funds Available	48.92	69.52	74.67	78.18	85.89	85.42	85.90	82.58
Per cent of Utilisation to Allocation	65.19	83.90	125.28	121.78	97.90	96.86	100.46	97.15
Per cent of Utilisationo f Subsidy	36.79	52.67	86.16	65.78	68.37	66.52	67.59	68.18
Per cent of Utilisation on Revolving Fund	5.06	6.73	8.79	12.58	15.14	10.79	11.08	9.86
Per cent of Utilisation on Infrastructure Development	22.16	24.45	15.79	14.79	14.47	14.10	13.30	12.99
Per cent of Utilisationo n Training / Skill Development	4.65	4.32	4.97	4.47	4.91	5.90	6.31	7.26
Per cent of Utilisation on Others	0.79	0.82	1.05	1.76	2.34	2.06	2.16	2.15
10. Total Credit Target	3205.00	3205.00	3200.87	2525.21	2129.33	2507.67	2515.65	2869.12
11. Total Credit Mobilised	**1056.46**	**1459.44**	**1329.68**	**1184.30**	**1302.10**	**1658.18**	**1823.16**	**2291.21**
Per cent age of Credit Mobilised	32.96	45.54	41.54	46.90	**61.15**	**66.12**	**72.47**	**79.86**
12. Credit Disbursed to SHGs	187.30	256.64	318.34	459.08	707.82	1027.66	1275.41	1803.34
13 Credit Disbursed to Individual Swarojgaris	869.16	1202.80	1011.34	725.21	594.28	630.52	547.75	487.87
14. Total Subsidy Disbursed	**541.69**	**701.85**	**665.62**	**605.89**	**713.38**	**858.81**	**904.83**	**971.05**
15. Subsidy Disbursed to SHGs	124.58	167.93	209.94	282.53	**444.36**	**586.08**	**671.22**	**771.46**
16. Subsidy Disbursed to Individual Swarojgaris	417.11	533.92	455.68	323.35	269.01	272.73	233.61	199.59
Ratio of Investment on SHGs vs. Individuals	0.24	0.24	0.36	0.71	1.33	1.79	2.49	3.75
17. Total Investment	**1598.15**	**2161.29**	**1995.30**	**1790.18**	**2015.48**	**2516.99**	**2727.99**	**3262.27**
18. Per Capita Investment (In Rupees)	17113	21481	21284	21666	22472	22555	23699	19281
19. Credit Subsidy Ratio	1.95	2.08	2.00	1.95	1.83	1.93	2.01	2.36
B. Physical Progress (No.)								
1. Self-Help Groups (SHGs) formed	292426	223265	434387	398873	392136	266230	276414	246309
2. Women SHGs formed	176263	153284	296175	221085	233136	191666	213213	176712
3. Per cent age of Women SHGs	60.28	68.66	68.18	55.43	59.45	71.99	77.14	71.74
4. No. of SHGs passed Grade-I	125402	214011	176002	189634	204987	219604	210639	222029
5. No. of SHGs passed Grade-II	74234	101291	54040	94754	90673	105839	91920	156353

Sl.No.	*Items*	*1999-2000*	*2000-01*	*2001-02*	*2002-03*	*2003-04*	*2004-05*	*2005-06*	*2006-07*
6.	SHGs taken up Economic Activities-Target							52876	77018
7.	SHGs taken up Economic Activities-Achievement	29017	26317	30576	35525	50717	68102	80130	137931
8.	Per cent **age of SHGs Taken up Eco. Activity to Grade-II**	**39.09**	**25.98**	**56.58**	**37.49**	**55.93**	**64.34**	**87.17**	**88.22**
9.	SHGs Swarojgaris Assisted-Target							528757	770175
10.	SHGs Swarojgaris Assisted - Achievement	347912	318803	364676	414419	577532	788573	873485	1472066
11.	Individual Swarojgaris Assisted-Target							330473	320906
12.	Individual Swarojgaris Assisted-Achievement	585956	687349	572792	411848	319363	327355	277631	219860
13.	**Swarojgaris Assisted – Special Projects**								
14.	**Total Swarojgaris Assisted-Achievement**	**933868**	**1006152**	**937468**	**826267**	**896895**	**1115928**	**1151116**	**1691926**
15.	Per cent **age of SHGs Swarojgaris Assisted**	**37.25**	**31.69**	**38.90**					
16.	SC Swarojgaris Assisted	278938	310886	284040	246556	274893	352864	383124	600364
17.	ST Swarojgaris Assisted	134944	137850	143619	130260	138909	149115	165407	241291
18.	**Total SC/ST Swarojgaris Assisted**	**413882**	**448736**	**427659**	**379816**	**413802**	**501979**	**548531**	**841655**
19.	Minorities (Swarojgaris) Assisted								
20.	Women Swarojgaris Assisted	416690	409842	385891	382613	470740	606141	662764	1247132
21.	Disabled Swarojgaris Assisted	8529	6737	6059	6118	8504	12680	14793	31864
22.	Per cent age of SC/STs Assisted	44.32	44.60	45.62	45.97	46.14	44.98	47.65	49.75
23.	Per cent age of Minorities assisted								3.58
24.	Per cent age of Women Assisted	44.62	40.73	41.16	46.31	52.49	54.32	57.58	73.71
25.	Per cent age of Disabled Assisted	0.91	0.67	0.65	0.74	0.95	1.14	1.29	1.88

Source: **GOI, Ministry of Rural Development, Annual Report 2012-13.**

A	**Financial Progress**							
1.	Total Allocation	2268.82	2643.44	2688.66	3116.46	2865.66	2877.69	25993.61
2.	Budget Allocation / Revised Allocation	1697.70	2350.00	2350.00	2984.00	2681.29	2681.29	21574.28
3.	Central Allocation	1702.24	2020.00	2051.54	2380.00	2191.00	2196.72	19695.90
4.	State Allocation	566.58	623.44	637.12	736.46	674.66	680.97	6297.72
5.	Central Releases	1697.70	2337.89	2230.00	2665.18	2394.89	1774.78	19846.49
	Per cent age of Central Releases	100.00	99.48	94.89	89.32	89.32	66.19	91.99
6.	Central Releases (Subsidy to DRDA)	1540.28	1989.60	1974.96	2230.67	1834.46	1328.22	16631.31
	Per cent age of Central Releases (Subsidy to DRDAs)	90.49	98.49	96.27	93.73	83.73	60.46	84.44

Sl.No.	Items	1999-2000	2000-01	2001-02	2002-03	2003-04	2004-05	2005-06	2006-07
7.	State Releases	475.69	542.57	608.31	551.08	500.30	122.30	4708.74	
	Per cent age of State Releases	83.96	87.03	95.48	74.83	74.16	17.96	74.77	
8.	Opening Balance as on 1st April	302.58	438.80	857.17	905.55	820.83	330.56	528.96	
9.	Misc. Receipt	75.62	32.08	55.20	64.90	46.79	20.05	68.59	
10.	**Total Funds Available**	**2394.17**	**3003.05**	**3495.65**	**3752.21**	**3202.39**	**1801.14**	**29705.72**	
11.	**Total Funds Utilised**	**1965.97**	**2285.40**	**2779.19**	**2804.04**	**2318.17**	**413.15**	**21632.38**	
	Per cent of Utilisation of Funds Available	82.12	76.10	79.50	74.73	72.39	22.94	72.82	
	Per cent of Utilisation to Allocation	86.65	86.46	103.37	89.98	80.89	14.36	89.30	
	Per cent of Utilisation o f Subsidy	65.57	76.23	70.56	64.68	72.25	61.77	65.94	
	Per cent of Utilisation on Revolving Fund	9.52	10.83	12.04	10.42	9.22	10.74	10.20	
	Per cent of Utilisation on Infrastructure Development	15.98	15.78	16.30	15.14	14.35	14.64	16.02	
	Per cent of Utilisationo n Training / Skill Development	9.76	9.42	9.52	9.33	8.25	10.20	7.09	
	Per cent of Utilisation on Others	5.48	1.93	0.17	0.17	0.17	0.27	1.52	
10.	Total Credit Target	3743.55	3929.80	4443.91	5210.63	6020.00	0.00	45505.76	
11.	**Total Credit Mobilised**	**2760.31**	**3530.07**	**4447.03**	**4585.98**	**4399.00**	**1673.54**	**33500.46**	
	Per cent age of Credit Mobilised	73.73	89.83	100.07	88.01	**73.07**	**0.00**	**62.23**	
12.	Credit Disbursed to SHGs	2090.70	2513.38	3475.21	3753.02	3568.07	1283.94	22719.92	
13	Credit Disbursed to Individual Swarojgaris	669.60	1016.69	971.82	832.95	830.93	389.61	10780.54	
14.	**Total Subsidy Disbursed**	**1289.10**	**1742.27**	**1962.13**	**1814.11**	**1675.90**	**254.53**	**14701.16**	
15.	Subsidy Disbursed to SHGs	990.97	1150.94	1477.21	1499.17	**1310.81**	**219.94**	**9907.15**	
16.	Subsidy Disbursed to Individual Swarojgaris	298.14	591.33	484.92	314.94	365.09	34.59	4794.01	
	Ratio of Investment on SHGs vs. Individuals	3.18	2.28	3.40	4.58	4.08	3.55	2.09	
17.	**Total Investment**	**4049.41**	**5272.34**	**6409.16**	**6400.09**	**6074.90**	**1928.07**	**48201.62**	
18.	Per Capita Investment (In Rupees)	28765	29932	31817	31375	36222	44010		
19.	Credit Subsidy Ratio	2.14	2.03	2.27	2.53	2.62	6.58	2.45	
B.	**Physical Progress (No.)**								
1.	Self-Help Groups (SHGs) formed	306688	563530	389259	311314	233713	61924	4396468	
2.	Women SHGs formed	231670	404972	292788	207280	153558	40949	2992752	
3.	Per cent age of Women SHGs	75.54	71.86	75.22	66.58	65.70	66.13	68.07	
4.	No. of SHGs passed Grade-I	251163	322322	439275	280575	181070	73217	3109930	
5.	No. of SHGs passed Grade-II	116878	138641	161496	171657	148138	48387	1554301	
6.	SHGs taken up Economic Activities-Target	106036	138169	155288	185525	187821	178937	1081670	

Sl.No.	Items	1999-2000	2000-01	2001-02	2002-03	2003-04	2004-05	2005-06	2006-07
7.	SHGs taken up Economic Activities-Achievement	181386	114452	136411	312288	242948	85087	1530887	
8.	Per cent **age of SHGs Taken up Eco. Activity to Grade-II**	**155.19**	**82.55**	**84.47**	**181.93**	**164.00**	**175.85**	**98.49**	
9.	SHGs Swarojgaris Assisted-Target	1060365	1381689	1552884	1855250	1878210	178937010816700		
10.	SHGs Swarojgaris Assisted - Achievement	1154269	1470032	1736214	1743726	1468796	40749213137995		
11.	Individual Swarojgaris Assisted-Target	292380	380981	269598	322093	102972	98101	2117504	
12.	Individual Swarojgaris Assisted-Achievement	253503	291392	278136	296113	208321	30607	4760226	
13.	**Swarojgaris Assisted–Special Projects**	**291523**	**100451**	**70827**	**70147**	**0**	**0**	**532948**	
14.	**Total Swarojgaris Assisted-Target**	**1352745**	**1762670**	**1822482**	**2177343**	**1981182**	**188747112934204**		
15.	**Total Swarojgaris Assisted -Achievement**	**1699295**	**1861875**	**2085177**	**2109986**	**1677117**	**43809918431169**		
16.	**Per cent age of SHGs Swarojgaris Assisted**	125.62	**105.63**	**114.41**	**96.91**	**84.65**	**23.21**		
17.	SC Swarojgaris Assisted	561052	601299	753640	734775	537667	127097	6050195	
18.	ST Swarojgaris Assisted	**251783**	274530	322142	361891	251337	45202	2748280	
19.	**Total SC/ST Swarojgaris Assisted**	**812835**	**875829107578210966667890041722998798475**						
20.	Minorities (Swarojgaris) Assisted	142399	**275121**	241866	244225	273355	39212	1276672	
21.	Women Swarojgaris Assisted	1083905	1206513	1502285	1424059	1103553	34932211251450		
22.	Disabled Swarojgaris Assisted	36113	42315	45869	40838	24505	4506	289430	
23.	Per cent age of SC/STs Assisted	47.83	47.04	51.59	51.98	47.05	39.33	46.70	
24.	Per cent age of Minorities assisted	8.38	14.78	11.63	11.57	16.30	8.95	11.04	
25.	Per cent age of Women Assisted	63.79	64.80	72.05	67.49	65.80	79.74	61.05	
26.	Per cent age of Disabled Assisted	2.13	2.27	2.20	1.94	1.46	1.03	1.57	

Source: GOI, Ministry of Rural Development, Annual Report 2012-13. *As on November, 2012.

The Table, 3 depicting point by point data and that too year wise have been included keeping in mind of the students, researchers, scholars and others so that these data collected from most authenticated source can be used in future for academic use. Although Table 3 is self-explanatory but few important observations are presented below:

(a) Total allocation over a period of time has escalated but utilisation of funds never touched 100 per cent indicating available fund was never utilised. Even in many years utilisation was less than 80 per cent. Thus it is evident that many Below Poverty Line Families were deprived of financial assistance. Hope such anomaly will not be crop up in NRLM.

(b) In the initial phase per capita investment had fluctuating trend meaning sometimes declined or remained stagnant but later years the same increased. Keeping in mind inflationary factor, the per capita investment should always be increased in each and every year.

(c) In addition to swarojgaris assisted under group, individual swarojgaris were also assisted under SGSY in a huge number.

(d) It is heartening to note that women preferred to take up self-employment overwhelmingly and thus almost all the years women swarojgaris assisted were more than 50 per cent.

(e) Minorities and disabled persons were also assisted under SGSY but disabled target of 3 per cent was never achieved. And for minority's target of 15 percent could be achieved only in 2011-12.

National Rural Livelihoods Mission (NRLM): Performance of SGSY was assessed through various studies and reports including those conducted by NIRD&PR, Hyderabad; BIRD, Lucknow; Centre for Management Development,Thiruvananthapuram; Reports of theSteering Committee constituted by the Planning Commissi on for the 11th Planand the Professor. *Radhakrishna* Committee on Credit Related Issues related to SGSY,set up by the Ministry of Rural Development in April, 2008. Based on all these SGSY has been restructured as NationalRural Livelihoods Mission (NRLM), subsequently renamed as "*Aajeevika*", to implement it in a mission mode across the country. The programme was formally launched on 3rd June, 2011. *Aajeevika* is a Centrally Sponsored Scheme and the financing of the programme would be shared between the Centre and the States in the ratio of 75:25 (90:10 in case of North Eastern States including Sikkim and completely from the Centre in case of UTs). The Central allocation earmarked for the States would broadly be distributed in relation to the incidence of poverty in the States.

NRLM Approach: Towards building, supporting and sustaining livelihoods of the poor, NRLM harnesses the innatecapabilities of the poor, complements them with capacities (information, knowledge, skills, tools,finance and collectivis Sation) to deal with the rapidly changing external world. Dedicated support structures build and strengthen the institutional platforms of the poor.These platforms, with the support of their human and social capital, offer a variety of livelihoods services to their members. These services include financial and capital services, production and productivity enhancement services that include technology, knowledge, skills and inputs, market linkages etc. Being conscious of the livelihoods activities being varied, NRLM works on three pillars- enhancing and expanding existing livelihoods options of the poor; building skills for the jobmarket outside; and nurturing self-employedand entrepreneurs. The interested rural BPL youths are offered skill development after counseling and matching the aptitude with the job requirements, and placed in jobs that are remunerative. Self-employed and entrepreneurially oriented poor are provided skills and financial linkages and nurtured to establish and grow with micro-enterprises for products and services indemand.These platforms also offer space for convergence and partnerships with a variety of stakeholders, by building an enabling environment for poor to access their rights and entitlements, public services and innovations. The aggregation of the poor, through their institutions, reduces transaction costs to the individual members, makes their livelihoods more viable and accelerates their journey out of poverty.

Framework for Implementation for *Aajeevika*: Keeping with the flexible nature of the programme, the Ministry has prepared a 'Framework for Implementation of *Aajeevika'* The 'Framework' has been developed after extensive consultations with various stake holders including the State Governments, Civil Society Organisations, Bankers and academicians.

Universal Financial Inclusion: *Aajeevika* works on both demand and supply side of financial inclusion. On the demand side, it will promote financial literacy among the poor and will provide catalytic capital to the SHGs and their federations. On the supply side, it will coordinate with the financial sector and encourage use of Information, Communication and Technology (ICT) based financial technologies, business correspondents and community facilitators like 'Bank *Mitras'*. It works towards universal coverage of rural poor against loss of life, health and assets. Further, it will work on remittances, especially in areas where migration is endemic.

Provision of Interest Subsidy: To ensure affordable credit for the rural poor, *Aajeevika* has made a provision for subsidy on interest rate above 7 per cent per annum for all eligible SHGs, who have availed loans from mainstream financial institutions, based on prompt loan repayment (This would not be applicable when a SHG avails capital subsidy. Interest subsidy would be provided to this SHG, when they avail a fresh loan after repaying the capital subsidy linked loan). This subsidy would be available to SHGs, where at least 70 per cent of the members are from BPL households, till a member accesses credit, through repeat cumulative loaning, up to Rs 1.00 lakh per household. NRLM works on three pillars - enhancing and expanding existing livelihoods options of the poor; building skills for the job market outside; and nurturing self-employed and entrepreneurs. The interested rural BPL youth would be offered skill development after counseling and matching the aptitude with the job requirements, and placed in jobs that are remunerative. Self-employed and entrepreneurially oriented poor will be provided skills and financial linkages and nurtured to establish and grow with micro-enterprises for products and services in demand. These platforms also offer space for convergence and partnerships with a variety of stakeholders, by building an enabling environment for poor to access their rights and entitlements, public services and innovations (Annual Report, 12-13). However with the passing of time and after carrying out of the impact study ultimate objective of NRLM will be assessed.

Conclusion

In this article different self-employment programmes which were initiated by the Government of India time to time have been analysed so that those who are interested can make use of it. And to collect and collate the information I had to devote much time in the libraries. The sources are most authenticated so without any issue data can be used. To tackle, social unrest one of the major objectives is to address unemployment issue for which self-employment is the best alternative. And Noble Laureate like Muhammad Yunus has favoured self-employment among rural women belonging to poor echelons of the society for income generation as well as for eradication of poverty.

Reference

1. Ministry of Rural Development, Government of India, "Annual Report, 2012-13" New Delhi.
2. http://en.wikipedia.org/wiki/Unemployment_in_India.
3. http://en.wikipedia.org/wiki/Unemployment_in_the_United_States.
4. Yunus Muhammad "Banker to the poor"; the story of the Grameen Bank", (2007) Published by Penguin Books.

15

Employment Structure in Kerala with a Special Preference to Palakkad District

Sasi, C

1. Introduction

Kerala is basically an agrarian state having majority of the people engaged in agriculture. The development experience felt by Kerala is highly a contradictory in nature, because it is a state with high social development along with poor economic development. The term employment structure of a country means the distribution of work force in various occupations of the country. All occupations of the country are broadly divided into three; Primary or agricultural sector, Secondary or industrial sector, and Tertiary or Service sector. Primary sector include agriculture and allied activities including fishery, forestry, animal husbandry and mining. In the secondary sector large scale and small scale industries are included. The service sector includes trade, transport, communication and banking.

2. Posing the problem

Palakkad is basically an agrarian district. In such terms the employment structure implies the proportions of employment covered by all the three sectors, which is primary, secondary and tertiary sector respectively. Since Palakkad is an agrarian we might think the proportion of people engaged in agriculture should be greater. But it was not so, because the people were not prefers to work under agriculture due to the higher cost of production and low return. If it continues, the development is unattainable.

Importance of the Study. The employment structure of any country is important because it contributes to the national income. This is one of the important indicators of economic development. So their change affects the development of that place.

3. Methodology

The study analyses the employment structure in Palakkad district. Only secondary data are taken into account to study it. Secondary data are collected from the publication of the department of econonmics and statistics, Goverment of Kerala and State Planning Board and also from Books, Journals, Periodicals, Economic Survey of the State Planning Board. Agricultural Statistics published by the Department of Economics and Statistics and from various websites of different departments of Kerala Goverment.

Objective

- To study the employment structure of Palakkad district.

4. Review of literature

(a) **Agrawal, A.N. (2009 ISBN: 978-81-224-2697-7)** in his book Indian Economy Problems of Development and Planning PN 126-132 says employment structure implies the distribution of population in various sectors. That is the population distributed in various occupations categorised into three sectors namely Primary sector, Secondary Sector and finally Tertiary sector.

(b) **S.K. Misra and V.K. Puri (2011 ISBN: 978-93-5051-074-2).** In his book Indian Economy he says the employment structure of our economy is showing a change. That is a shift away from agriculture is clearly a recent phenomenon. And he says if it continues the employment structure would undergo a significant change.

(c) **Competition Success Review General Studies Indian Economy (Special issue 2013 RNI No.10485/64 PR Nos. DL(C)-01/1071/ 2012-14).** By explaining the concept and of National Income the article shows the trends in employment structure in PN 37-39. It says the share of primary sector shows a substantial decrease over the last six decades. The share of secondary sector has gone up, while the share of service sector increased from 28 per cent to 58 per cent in 2012 from 1950.

5. Features of Employment Structure in India

(a) Predominance of agriculture.

(b) Little change in employment structure.

Over the 90 years since 1901, the Indian employment structure has remained almost static: there has been no significant change in it. There is of course, a slight decline in the proportion engaged in agriculture, and a very small rise in that engaged in industries and services. But the pace of this change is undoubtedly very slow. The progress in industrial and service sector is not big enough to produce any significant impression on the agricultural sector. Nor is agricultural progress adequate to make available the required resources for the developing industries and services.

Although there is no significant change in the overall picture of occupational pattern, yet one can discern some significant developments in some parts of the sectors, and in some regions of the country besides a slow declining trend in the proportion of labour force in agricultural sector. This declined from nearly 72 per cent in 1971 to nearly 67 per cent in 1991. It is reported to be further lower to nearly 58 per cent in 2001. Moreover, the number of workers in modern industries is on the increase. This is indicative of the fact that the country is producing new products and using new and modern techniques. Furthermore, there is an impressive expansion of job opportunities in services like education, health, science, railways, communication, etc. These changes are indicative of the fact that the process of modernisation of the economy is underway. But these changes, important though they are not quantitatively so large as to produce a noticeable change in the overall occupational pattern. However, since the figures relating to occupational distribution of working population at the All-India level have not yet become available, it is difficult to establish low far these trends have framed up.

However, of particular importance are the changes that have taken place in the 1981-91 decade. Alongside, and perhaps reflecting the modest rise in per capita income, the shift away from agriculture is somewhat significant in 1991 compared to 1981 or even earlier. Equally significant is the fact that this shift can perhaps be related to the rise in service sector. It is so in the sense that just as there is a fall in the share of agriculture, there is an almost equal rise in the services sector. Or in other words the fall in the agricultural sector has been largely made up by a rise in the service sector. The manufacturing sector has shown a marginal fall of no significance. This means that the change in the occupational structure in 1981-91 decades signifies rising work in the services sector, rather than in the commodity sector. This perhaps points to the emergence of positive growth forces in the economy.

Table 1 : Occupational Distribution of Working Population (percentage)

Sector and industrial categories	*1901*	*1911*	*1921*	*1931*	*1941*	*1951*	*1961*	*1971*	*1981*
Agricultural sector	71.7	74.9	75.0	74.8	72.1	71.8	72.1	68.8	66.7
Cultivators	50.6	49.8	54.4	54.1	50.0	52.1	43.4	41.5	38.4
Agricultural labourers,	16.9	20.6	17.4	24.8	16.7	16.7	26.3	25.2	26.4
Livestocck, forestry fishing...etc	4.2	4.5	4.2	4.9	2.6	2.3	2.4	2.2	1.9
Industrial Sector	12.6	11.1	0.5	10.2	10.7	12.2	11.2	12.9	12.7
Mining and qua rrying	0.1	0.2	0.3	0.3	0.6	0.5	0.5	0.5	0.6
Large and Small scale industries	11.7	9.0	9.3	8.9	9.0	10.6	9.5	10.9	10.2
Service sector	15.7	14.0	13.5	15.0	17.2	16.0	16.7	16.5	20.5
Trade and com- merce	6.1	5.5	5.7	5.6	5.2	4.0	5.6	5.9	7.5
Transport, storage and communi- cation	1.1	1.1	0.9	1.0	1.5	1.6	2.4	2.5	2.8
Other services	8.5	7.4	6.9	8.4	10.5	10.4	8.7	8.1	10.2
Total	**100**	**100**	**100**	**100**	**100**	**100**	**100**	**100**	**100**

Source: Census Report.

6. Working Population of the District

Work force has a key role in the economy of the region. Population, work force and employment are closely interrelated. A change in the size of labor force, level of employment and job opportunities will affect components of population change particularly fertility and migration. As per census 2001, the work participation rate of Palakkad District is 36.2 per cent, where as that of the state in 32 per cent. Out of the total population of 26.17 lakhs, 9.45 lakhs are workers. The total workers are further divided into main and marginal workers. Main workers constitute 29 per cent of the total population and marginal workers constitute 7 per cent of the total population (figs. 4.1 and 4.2). Whereas in Census 1991, the work participation rate of Palakkad District was 35.3 per cent. Out of the total population of 23.82 lakh, 8.45 lakh populations were workers. Main workers constituted 33 per cent of the total population and marginal workers constituted only two per cent of the total population. Palakkad occupies the 1st position among the districts in the percentage of Agricultural Labourers (33.6 per cent) and has 6th position in the percentage of main workers (81.3 per cent). The District holds 9th rank in Work participation rate of Marginal Workers (18.7 per cent). The district recorded 3rd rank in total female work participation rate (36.11 and 21.2 per cent) and the 5th in male work participation rate (51.99 per cent). In Urban and Rural work participation rate (34 per cent and 36.5 per cent) the district occupies the 4th place.

The change in the number of total workers and the main workers over a period of time is shown in the follwing table. It is evident from the table that amajor change happened in the occupational structure of Palakkad District in the last decade. The main workers content decreased from 33 per cent to 29 per cent and the 0

marginal workers increased from two per cent to seven per cent. Ie.12 per cent decrease in the main workers content and 35 per cent in creasein the marginal workers content.

Table : Decadal variation of workers –Palakkad District

Year	*1981*	*1991*	*2001*
Total Workers	723348	845141	945052
Total Main Workers	667618	786363	768620

Source : Planning board.

The total workers are gradually increasing overthe last three decades (from 1981 to 2001), the number of main workers shows decreasing trend between 1991and 2001 indicating a dim picture about the current economic base of the District. The number of the total workers of the district show increase in figures during 1991-2001,the growth rate of the workers during this period (growth rate is 11.82 per cent) is greater than the growth rate of the total population (Growth rate of total population is 9.87per cent) of the same period. This indicates that the opportunity of working is increasing in proportion to the growth of population. It is to be noted that the main workers have decreased by 2.25 per centand the marginal workers haveincreased by 30 per cent with an increase of 9.87 per cent in the total population. This indicates a reduction in work opportunities in primary sector. More and more workers are getting marginal employment.

7. Occupational Structure

The main workers are classified in to four categories viz. cultivators, agricultural labourers, household industrial workers and other workers as per the Census 2001. The other workers category includes the primary sector workers like fishermen, workers engaged in mining and plantation workers also. Occupational Structure of Palakkad District as per 1991 and 2001 Census is shown in the table.

Table 3 : Workers Classification- Palakkad District

Category	*1991*	*2001*
Cultivators	96958	85638
Agricultural labors	347299	317192
MSPH	21904	32832
Other workers	378649	509390
Total workers	**845141**	**945052**

Source: Department of town and country planning Kerala.

8. Occupational Structure – Variation in Urban and Rural Areas

The share of cultivators and agricultural labourers in the total workers are 11 Per cent and 43 per cent in urban area and rural areas of the district respectively. This indicates that as far as the workers classification is considered, almost 90 per cent the workers in urban area depends on the tertiary sector for their livelihood. Household industrial sector share in both urban and rural area is a very low at three to four per cent of the total main workers. The following table shows the four-fold category of workers in the urban and rural areas of the District.

Table 4

	Cultivators		*Agricultural labors*		*HH Industrial workers*		*Other*		*Total workers*	
	Persons	*per cent*	*Persons*	*per cent*	*Persons*	*per cent*	*Persons*	*per cent*	*persons*	*per cent*
Rural	71462	11	213690	32	22533	3	855687	54	663372	100
Urban	2483	3	9513	9	4634	4	88618	84	105248	100

9. Occupational Structure – Temporal Variation

The number of various categories of workers from 1981 to 2001 in the district is shown in the table.

Table 5 : Four -fold Workers classification

	Cultivators	*Agricultural labourers*	*HH industrial workers*	*Others*
1981	100000	400000	20000	280000
1991	97289	347299	21904	319871
2001	73945	223203	27167	444305

Source: District Planning Board.

Cultivators and agricultural labourers show drastic decrease in total numbers (a decrease of approximately 33 per cent) during the period from 1981 to 2001, whereas the other workers show an increase of 39 per cent. This is a clear indication of the weakening of the primary sector, mainly the agricultural sector, in the district. The Table 6 shows the variation of the number of different category of workers in the urban areas from 1981 to 2001. There is significant increase in the category of other workers, whereas number of cultivators and agricultural labourers remains without much variation. The number of house hold industrial workers shows an increasing trend. Cultivators and agricultural laborers show drastic decrease in total numbers (a decrease of approximately 33 per cent) during the period from 1981 to 2001, whereas the other workers show an increase of 39 per cent. This is a clear indication of the weakening of the primary sector, mainly the agricultural sector, in the district. The table shows the variation of the number of different category of workers in the urban areas from 1981 to 2001. There is significant increase in the category of other workers, whereas number of cultivators and agricultural labourers remains without much variation. The number of house hold industrial workers shows an increasing trend.

Table 6 : Number of various categories of workers in urban areas

Year	*Cultivators*	*Agricultural labours*	*HH industrial workers*	*Others*
1981	2462	8633	2163	45669
1991	2580	11624	2750	53916

16

MGNREGP: A Programme for Inclusive Growth and Development: An Assessment

Aboobacker Sidheeque, K. P

1. Introduction

Since India became part of the global economy and underwent economic reforms in 1991, it has been growing at a faster rate comparable with growing economies across the world. The economy of India is the 10th largest in the world by nominal GDP and 3rd largest in the world by purchasing power parity[1]. By 2008, India had established itself as the world's second fastest growing economy. The contributions of different sectors to India's GDP changed drastically from the 1950 to 2014. The Agriculture per cent of GDP of India is 17.4 (per cent) with a global rank of 54. The Industry per cent of GDP of India is 25.8 (per cent) with a global rank of 110.The Services per cent of GDP of India is 56.9 (per cent) with a global rank of 12[2].2 In terms of employment levels, Agricultural sector accounts for 53 per cent, Industrial sector accounts for 22 per cent, and Service sector accounts for 25 per cent.

In the last two decades a significant proportion of the population across the country has reaped the benefits of this economic growth. They have become part of global economy and market, and their lives have transformed in to one of global citizen with all comforts and luxury in life. The fruits of economic growth have not benefited every one uniformly. Some are left behind and some others are not touched by the benefits of economic growth. The period of 1999-2000 to 2004-2005 saw rapid economic growth in the country but it has not impacted on the unemployment problem of the country. According to the 2011 census nearly 68.84 per cent of the total population of the country lives in rural India and 31.16 per cent live in urban area. In absolute numbers, the 121 crores Indians, 83.3 crores live in rural areas while 37.7 crores stay in urban areas[3]. Over the last decade, poverty has witnessed a consistent decline with the levels dropping from 37.2 Per cent in 2004-05 to 29.8 per cent in 2009-10. The number of poor is now estimated at 269.3 million, of which 216.5 million reside in rural India[4]. But of course there are criticisms against the methodology of calculation. It is proved globally that the so-called trickle down effect does not work in all the societies and India is no exception to this.

The challenges which stand against the greatest objective of inclusive growth are mainly poverty and unemployment. The rural economy of India is characterised by a persistence of huge volume of surplus labour leading to disguised, under and open unemployment. Most of the rural unemployment is in unorganised sector, predominantly in agriculture. So this unemployment and under employment are the causes of rural poverty, though the poverty ratio in India has declined from 56.5 per cent in 1973-74 to 22 per cent in 2011 – 12. So unemployment and poverty are the crux of the problem in rural India. The number of poor is now estimated at 269.3 million, of which 216.5 million reside in rural India.This needs to be addressed in such a manner which will be instrumental in generating income on long-term basis and in building human resources through skill formation and infrastructural avenues for sustainable and inclusive rural development.

The creation of employment opportunities for the unskilled work force has been a major challenge for development planners and administrators. So since independence rural development in general and poverty alleviation in particular have been the core objectives of the development policy of the country. Since independence the Government has launched a number of wage employments, self employment, and target based programmes to redress rural poverty and unemployment problem of the country.

In the first three Five Year Plans (1951-66) the dominant thinking in policy planning was that, poverty could be effectively tackled through general growth process and benefits of growth would be automatically trickled down to general poor masses. In the first five year plan the emphasis was given to agricultural development which shifted to industrial sector in the next two Five Year Plans. During this period the emphasis however was placed on land reforms, community development, and co-operative movement. No attempt was made to tackle poverty through direct anti-poverty programmes.

But it was in the fith five year plan the focus was shifted from growth oriented strategy to one of directly attacking poverty. The planners recognised that a large section of the rural poverty arose out of non-availability of wage employment and lack of productive assets with the household to engage in gainful self employment. The Government of India had executed many programmes from time to time or plan to plan for redressing the problems of rural economy in general and rural poverty in particular. It was during the tenth five year plan (2002-2007) the idea of inclusive growth came to the centre of discussion among the policy makers.The data of Indian economy show that the problems were existed immediately after the independence still exist even today. By recognising the drawbacks of existing developmental programmes, the policy makers introduced a new programme called MGNREP to meet avowed objectives of inclusive growth and sustainable development of our five year plans.

2. Poverty Alleviation Programmes in India

Poverty alleviation programmes in India can be broadly classified in to the following heads such as Self employment programmes, Wage employment programmes, Food safety programmes, Social security programmes. Under self-employment programmes, Government of India introduced the programmes like, Integrated Rural Development Programme (IRDP) in 1970, *Swarnjayanti Gram SwarozgarYojana* (SGSY) in 1999. Under wage employment programmes the important programmes were, National Rural Employment Programme (NREP) and Rural Landless Employment Guarantee Programmes (RLEGP). These two programmers were later merged in 1989 into more well-known *Jawahar Rozgar Yojana* or JRY. In 1999 this was renamed as *Jawahar Gram Samridhi Yojana* or JGSY. A special wage employment programme in the name of Employment Assurance Scheme or EAS was launched on October 2, 1993 for the drought prone, desert, tribal and hill area blocks in the country. It was further expanded to all the blocks in 1997-1998. The Food for Work Programme was started as part of EAS in eight drought prone States in 2000-2001. Here part of the wage was provided in the form of foodgrains. Though foodgrains were supplied free of cost to these States, the uptake of the foodgrains was very poor. Considering the fragmented efforts of different wage employment programmes in the country, all these programmes were merged into one programme called *Sampoorna Gramin Rozgar Yojana* or SGRY in 2001. As a part of the food security programmes the central government initiated Public Distribution System and in June 1997 introduced a new version called, targeted public distribution system or TPDS. As a part of social security programmes the central government has launched the National Social Assistance Programme or NSAP in August 1995. Under NSAP, there are three schemes, National Old Age Pension Scheme, National Family Benefit Scheme or NFBS, National Maternity Benefit Scheme.

The above mentioned programmes are in one way or in another way failed to meet their goals. So, poverty still exists as a major threat on Indian economy. The Government of India initiated a new movement or programme towards poverty alleviation in 2005. That is called as NREGA.

3. National Rural Employment Guarantee Act, 2005

The National Rural Employment Guarantee Act (NREGA), which came out in 2005 as a part of United Progressive Agenda for Common Minimum Programme (CMP), explicitly recognises the "Right to Employment". It intends to provide for 100 days of unskilled manual work in a year to one adult member of every household in the rural areas whose adult members are volunteer to do such work. This programme eventually replace the existing wage employment generation programmes, such as SGRY and the National Food For Work Programme (NFFWP) to become the sole wage employment programme in the country.

4. Objectives of the Study

(1) To identify the socio-economic background of the sample beneficiaries.

(2) To examine whether the primary objectives of the scheme have been realised in the study area.

The study is based up on a survey carried out in the 'Peruvayal Panchayath' of 'Kozhikode' district, in which there are 75 Panchayaths[5]. The enquiry is actually carried out on 11th ward of the 'Peruvayal Panchayath'. This ward was chosen by considering the researcher's familiarity with the area and on the expectation that relatively reliable data can be collected. In this ward 67 persons had registered and all of them are interviewed. A pretested schedule was used for the purpose of data collection. Using interview method the researcher directly collected the required data from 67 respondents. The data was collected during the March 2014. The objectives of the study are examined by using various statistical tools like simple average, ratios, and percentages.

The National Rural Employment Guarantee Act, which was enacted in 2005 by the Parliament of India, and introduced in 2006 with the objective of providing 100 days of employment in every financial year to adult members of any rural household willing to do unskilled manual work at the wage rate fixed by the act.

The most striking feature of MGNREGA is that it is the first tangible commitment by the government to the poor, in the sense that they can expect to earn a living wage by performing unskilled manual work of minimum 100 days and demand this as right. The act also ensures unemployment allowances if a household is not provided with employment within a specified time period. If effectively implemented, NREGA can not only enhance the income of the rural poor in the short-term but also can create durable assets in the villages and thus generate productive infrastructure in a sustainable manner which is much needed for poverty alleviation in the long run.

5. Indicators of Performance of MGNREGA

Arguably one can assess the performance of MGNREGP not only in terms of its success in achieving the objectives but also in terms of how well the guidelines were followed in the implementation. In view of these guidelines the performance of a Grama Panchayath in implementing MGNREGP can be assessed by looking in to the following indicators.

(a) Average person-days created per house hold who demanded employment.

(b) Types of jobs undertaken under the scheme.

(c) How the total person-days created in Grama Panchayath (during a financial year) are distributed in favour of the vulnerable section of the population. Eg . SC,ST, Women.

(d) To what extent rural people are aware of the different entitlements of MGNREGP.

(e) Whether Gram Panchayath functionaries are cooperative in helping the potential MGNREGP beneficiaries.

(f) Whether the wages are disbursed in stipulated time.

(g) Whether the Gram Panchayath's pay unemployment allowances in case they fail to provide the work demanded within the time period.

Among all these the most important indicators of MGNREGP performance is average – person days created per household which demand employment since employment generation for the rural poor is the fundamental objective of the Act.

6. Overview of the Performance of MGNREGA (National and State)

The performance of the MGNREGA in national and state level could be analysed by looking at various data mainly on the average person-days created per household who demanded employment, different types of jobs undertaken as part of the scheme and how the total person-days created in Grama Panchayath (during a financial year) are distributed in favour of the vulnerable section of the population. Eg. SC, ST,Women. By looking at the national figures (Mahatma Gandhi National Rural Employment Guarantee Act, 2005, Report to the People 2nd February 2014), the total number of job card issued on demand under the scheme during the financial year 2012-13 was 12.79 crores as compared to the 3.78 crores in 2006-07. The employment provided to the household against the total job card issued was only 2.10 crores in 2006-07 and more than doubled the number into 4.98 crores in 2012-13. The number of person days work created was 90.5 Cores in 2006-07 and 229.86 crores in 2012-13. Out of the total person days work created the share of SC population was 25 per cent in 2006-07 and jumped into the psychologically celebrated mark of 50.96 per cent in 2012-13 and the share of ST population was 36 per cent in 2006-07 and reduced to 18 per cent in 2012-13. More importantly the share of women to the total work created was 40 per cent in 2006-07 and rose into the great achievement level of 51per cent in 2012-13 against the mandatory minimum share for women in the programme stipulated under the Act is 33 per cent. By considering the women's share, MGNREGP got a huge success which none of its predecessors could achieve. Another important target of the programme was to provide 100 days of employment to the household. Here the average person days of work per household created was only 43 in 2006-07 and 46 in 2012-13. Creation of the rural assets was also one of the important objectives of the programme. The important works undertaken was water conservation (46 per cent), works on individual lands (11per cent), rural connectivity (12 per cent) and land development (6 per cent) respectively.

The performance of Kerala economy regarding the effective implementation of the programme is also critical in the detail analysis. In Kerala the number of households who demanded employment was 1596790 and the number of households provided employment was 1366447 (Financial year 2013-14, till December, 13). Out of these, the percentage share of the SC population was 15.79 per cent and ST population was 2.90 per cent. The participation of the women to the total work force is 93.45 Per cent in kerala as per the latest estimate during the financial year of 2013-14, till December, 13 against the national average of 51 per cent. The average person days per household are just 40 in Kerala, which is below than the national average of 46. There are only just 2.71per cent of the total household completed the 100 days employment in kerala. The percentage share of total expenditure spent on the wage is 97.65 per cent and the share of expenditure spent on the material is 2.355 respectively (2013-14 financial year, till December 13).

7. Analysis of the Data and Major Findings

For the detailed analysis of the ground level functioning of the MGNREGP, the researcher conducted a primary survey. The important objective of the study was to examine whether the primary objectives of the programme had been achieved in the study area or not. A detailed questionnaire was used for the collection of data and the notable results evolved from the field are explained below.

7.1 Socio Economic Background of the Sample Respondents

One of the main objectives of the study is to understand socio-economic background of the beneficiaries. In the study area, the investigator found the following facts explained in the following tables.

Table 1: Ageand Gender Based Distribution of Sample Respondents

Age of worker	*Numbers*	*Gender*	
		Female	Male
Below 30	0	0	0
30-40	06	06	0
40-50	56	56	0
Above 50	5	01	04

It is found that among the MGNREGP beneficiaries majority are between the age group of 40-50, while the second major group is formed in the age group of 30 to 40. Here one of the important points is that, the worker from the age group of below 40 (their productivity and efficiency to do manual work is higher than the any other age group) is just six. At the same time the participation of workers above the age 50 (their productivity and efficiency is much lower than any other age group) is five.This shows the reluctance of young and male population's participation in this programme and it adversely affected bringing up of works which demand higher physical energy, especially related to community asset creation in rural area. Low participation from the male population is mainly because of the existing wide wage gap between the wage offered in open market and the wage offered by the MGNREGP in Kerala. In addition to that, female population considered her earning from the work as a help to male who is the main bread winner of the family. By looking to the works undertaken by the MGNREGP in the study area justifies the findings. The works undertaken by the MGNREGP are as follows, Cleaning of canals, drainages, and roads. Afforestation programmes mainly under the 'Haritha Keralam'(green Kerala) Programme. Water conservation and water harvesting activities, land development related to agricultural sector. So for these types of work do not demand higher manual power so women can easily undertake such works. But the MGNREGA is insisting to undertake works which will create rural assets and improve rural infrastructure. Without the sufficient participation from the male population MGNREGP can't undertake such works like, construction of ponds or construction of new roads etc.

Table 2 : Sample Respondence from the Vulnerable Sections of the Society

Vulnerable Sections	*Total number*	*In percentage*
Women	63	94
Widow	06	9
SC/ST	05	7.5
Minority	18	27

The above table clearly shows the distribution of the benefit of MGNREGP across various vulnerable sections of the society. The women population gained maximum benefit in the study area since they constitute major chunk of the total beneficiaries. In the case of SC and ST and minority communities, their share to the total beneficiaries is less than proportionate to their share to total population in the study area.

Table 3 : Economic Back Ground of the Sample Respondence

Family category	*Number*	*Percentage*
BPL	55	82
APL	12	18
Total	**67**	**100**

The above table shows the economic background of the sample Respondence. The majority of the sample Respondence coming from the BPL category (55) out of the total 67. The tables 2 and 3 clearly show a favourable distribution of MGNREGP work towards the economically and socially back ward sections of the society. Based on the collected data, the study shows that, one of the major objectives of MGNREGP that is inclusiveness of the downtrodden and backward sections of the society is more or less satisfied.

We also looked in to the economic empowerment standard of the sample beneficiaries. The striking feature arose from the sample respondents is that, all of them are the part of Self-Help Group named 'KUDUMBASHREE'. Everybody have their own bank account in that group. They also have a small amount of saving through KUDUMBA SREE.

Table 4: Education Level of The Job Card Holder.

Level of Education	*In Numbers*	*In percentage*
Illiterate	03	4.5
Primary	20	30
Upper primary	19	28
High School	20	30
Plus Two	03	4.5
Degree	02	03
Total	**67**	**100**

The above table shows the education level of the sample respondents. The data reveal that among the sample respondents 4.5 per cent of total workers got Degree education. The striking feature is that all of them are females. The percent of Illiterates among the sample beneficiaries is also 4.5 per cent.

The mode of payment to the beneficiaries of MGNREGP is through bank account. One of the inventive ideas of the programme is to pay the wages through account in banks. This is because in earlier programmes it was observed that when the payments were made through contractor or any other middlemen, the appropriate amount of wages could not reach the beneficiaries. Again there was discrimination of wage rate by contractor himself. So to stop this practice in this programme wages are paid through account in banks. This practice also enables the people of rural area to have the practice of banking and thereby involve every citizen in the financial system of the country.

In the study area, it was observed that, the all 67 beneficiaries received their wage through account in banks. Here, panchayath direct the beneficiaries to open a zero balance account in the local RRB, namely 'SOUTH MALABAR GRAMIN BANK'.

Table 5 : Number of Person Days of Work.

Person days of work	*Frequency*	*In percentage*
Less than 50	0	0
51-60	10	15
61-70	07	11
71-80	15	22
81-90	0	0
91-100	35	52
Total	**67**	**100**

The above table gives details of the person days of work that have been done by the sample households. One of the important objectives of MGNREGP is that to provide 100 days of employment to every rural household who are willing to do unskilled manual work at the statutory minimum wage rate. In the study area, the average person days of work of sample beneficiaries are 83 days which is higher than the national average of 46.2 days and state average of 40 days. The 52 per cent of the beneficiaries got 100 days of employment and 22 per cent got the days between 70 and 80. None of the sample beneficiaries in the study area had worked less than 50 days of employment. When we compare with the national and state performances the table depicts that, in the matter of employment generation the programme had achieved a higher status. The important reason for the higher employment generation is basically because of the agrarian features of the mainland and less time gap between the identification of the works and execution of the action plan in the study area which have a favourable impact on the success of the programme.

During the data collection the researcher understood that, though the works are being executed at the earliest, the disbursements of wages through bank accounts got delay. The major reason for the delayed payment of wages to beneficiaries is less manpower allotted for the document works of NREGA at the Panchayath level. The local money lenders got a huge setback after the implementation of the scheme in the study area. Earlier the local moneylenders had exploited the poor by charging a higher interest rate, now the poor can easily manage their urgent needs by taking loans from the Local Self Help Groups on the assurance of the repayment of the sum, after getting their MGNREGP wages through bank accounts.

8. Summary and Conclusion

Though Indian economy has been growing at a faster rate in recent times, it has had a little impact on the gravity and magnitude of unemployment problem, especially in the rural areas of the county. According to the 2011 census 269.3 million live in below poverty line, of which 216.5 million reside in rural India. This is a clear indication that the trickle down effect of growth has hardly worked. The major cause of massive poverty in rural area is open and under employment in massive scale. Since independence the Government has launched umpteen target based wage employment and self employment programmes with a view to redressing the problem of rural poverty and unemployment. But none of the programmes, till date, have been successful in achieving their intending goals fully. In this stream, the Government of India's latest initiative is the implantation of MGNREGP, which was enacted in 2005 by the parliament of India and implemented in 2006. The important objective of the programme is to provide 100 days employment in every financial year to adult members of any rural household willing to do unskilled manual work at the wage rate fixed by the act. It is the flagship programme of the Government of India both in political and in economic perspectives. This programme was implemented with the avowed objective of uplifting the poor by providing them gainful employment.

The research question taken up for enquiry in our study included: (1) to analysethe socio economic back ground of the beneficiaries of MGNREGP in the study area. (2) examine whether the primary objectives of the scheme has been realized in the study area. The participation of socially and economically backward communities is very crucial for realising the main objective of the programme, which is uplifting the rural poor and attaining the inclusiveness in the developmental process. In the study area the participation of economically and socially back ward sections of the society in the programme is quite impressive. Out of the total beneficiaries around 84 per cent are from BPL families and 94 per cent of the total beneficiaries are from female population. The participation of SC/ST and minority community in the study area is less than proportionate to their share in the total population. The implementation of the scheme in the study area has more or less succeeded in realising one of the primary objectives of providing 100 days of employment. In the study area the average person days of work accounts 83 days which was far above the national average (46 days) and the state average (40 days). This is mainly because of the agrarian features of the study area and easefulness related to the identification of proper works, less time gap between the drawing up of action plan and its implementation. But the scheme has failed in achieving the important objective of creation of rural infrastructure and community assets. The main works which were carried out in the study area were cleaning of drainages, roads, canals, and land developmental activities they didn't undertake any works like construction of roads, ponds, canals, etc, which are really an asset to the people of rural area. An important finding of the study is that majority of the male population has totally boycotted the programme and the smaller number of male participants belongs to the above 50 age category. The major reason for the state of affairs seems to be the wide wage gap existing between the wage rate as per the scheme and the open market wage rate in Kerala.

Some of the important principles of the programme have been generally violated by the authorities concerned. According to the principles of the MGNREGP anyone who applies for work under the scheme should be provided work with in the 15 days of application. If Panchayath failed to provide employment within this stipulated time, the worker is entitled to unemployment allowances. Another principle of the scheme is that wages should be distributed within 15 days of the completion of respective works. Both the principles scaled above have been violated.

9. Suggestions

The suggestions to take the scheme to greater heights and make it sustainable as recommended by stakeholders at different levels include; (1) 100 days of employment per adult member per household instead of per household, (2) upward revision of wages taking into account the local situation; (3) flexibility in schedule of working hours; (4) region based specific plans instead of adapting blue-print type of guideline; (5) permission to take up work involving material cost; (6) appointment of skilled personnel wherever required and (7) providing better infrastructure like improved tools, vehicles for transportation and human resources at Panchayath level.

References

1. ''India''. International Monetary Fund. Retrieved 2014-04-08.
2. Data source: CIA- The world fact book
3. Employment across various sectors, NSSO 66th Nationwide Survey, Planning Commission, Governement of India (June 3, 2014)
4. (http://data.worldbank.org/indicator/SP.URB.TOTL.IN.ZS)
5. www.kozhikodedistrictpanchayath.in

6. Mahatma Gandhi National Rural Employment Guarantee Act, 2005, Report to the People 2nd February 2014.

7. Gopal K.S. (2009) "NREGA, social audit: Myths and Reality", *Economic Political Weekly,* January 17, 2009.

8. Shah Mihir (2009) "Multiplier accelerator synergy in NREGA", *The Hindu* (http: //www.hindunet.com/2009/04/30 stories/2009 043055630800.htm).

9. Debaprasad Biswal (2010) Determinants of participation and its socio-economic impact in Kishorenagar block of Orissa". A dissertation submitted in Department of Economics *Pondicherry University.*

10. Jha Raghavendra, Bhattacharya Sambit Gaiha Raghav and Shankar Shyalshri (2008), "Capture of anti Poverty Programmes, an analysis of National Rural Employment Guarantee Praogramme in India", ASARC working paper 2008/07.

11. Chakroborty Pinaki (2007), "Implementation of Employment Guarantee Progaremme, a preliminary appraisal", *Economic and Political Weekly,* February 17, 2007.

12. Das Vidya and Pradhan Pramod, (2007), "Illusion of change", *Economic and Political Weekly,* August 11, 2007.

13. Sankar P.S, Rao Raghu, Bannerji Nivedita and Shah Mihir (2006), "Revising the schedule of rates; an imperative for NREGA", *Economic and political weekly,* April 29, 2006.

14. Gaiha Raghav, (2005), "Does the Employment Guarantee scheme benefit the rural poor in India, some recent evidence", *Asian survey,* Vol. 45, No. 6, November- December- 05.

15. Gaiha Raghav, Kulkarni Vanish, Pandey Manoj and Imei Katsushi (2009), " National Rural Employment Guarantee Scheme, Poverty and prices in Rural India", ASARC working paper, 2009/03.

16. Dreze Jean, Khera Reetika, Siddhartha.K (2008), "Myths and Reality", Yojana, 1. Mehrotra Santosh, 2008 "NREGA two years on where do we go from here?", *Economic and political Weekly*, August 2, 2008.

17. Mathur Lalit, (2008) "Fulfilling the promise" *Yojana,* Vol.52, August 2008.

18. Chandrasekhar C. P and Ghosh Jayati (2008), "How feasible is a rural employment guarantee?",*http://www.jstor.org/ stable/.*

19. Gaiha Raghav, Sankar Shylashri and Jha Raghavendra (2008), " Targetting accuracy of NREGA, evidence form Rajasthan Andhra Pradesh and Maharastashtra, ASARC working paper, 2010/03.

20. Ambasta Pramathes, Sankar Vijay P.S. and Shah Mihir (2008), "Two

years of NREGA the road ahead", *Economic and Political Weekly,* February 23, 2008.

21. Rao V.M. (2007), "Making safety nets effective for hardcore poor", *Economic and Political Weekly,* August 18, 2007.
22. Aakel K.V and Kidambi Soumya (2007), "Challenging corruption with social audit", *Economic and Political Weekly*, February 3, 2007. 17. Rao S.K (2008), "Need for Introspection", *Yojana*, August, 2008.
23. Vanik Anish (2008), "A tale of two villages", *Yojana*, August, 2008.
24. Khera Reetika (2008), "Employment Guarantee Act", *Economic and political Weekly*, August 30, 2008.
25. Sainath, P. (2008), "NREGA: A fine balance", http:// www.India together.org/2008/jul/psa-finebal.htm.
26. Banerjee Kaustav, Shah Partha (2010), "The NREGA, the Maoists and the developmental woes of the Indian state", *Economic and political Weekly*, July 2010, Vol.XLV, No.28, pp. 42 47.
27. Datt Ruddar, Sundaram K.P.M. (2009), " Indian Economy", 59 th Edition 2009, S.Chand and Company Ltd.
28. Mishra S.K, Puri V.K (2009), " Indian Economy", 27th Revised and updated Edition 2009, Himalaya Publishing House.
29. C.A.K.Yesudian (2007), "Poverty alleviation programmes in India; A social audit", *Indian J Med Res* 126, October 2007, pp. 364-373.
30. Subrata Mukherjee, Saswata Ghosh (2009), What determincs the success and failure of "100 Days Work" at the Panchayath Level? A study of Birobhum District in West Bengal. Occasional paper, Institute of Development Studies Kolkata.

17

Empowering Women through Education: A Rural Indian Perspective

Ismail Thamarasseri

1. Introduction

"The education and empowerment of women throughout the world cannot fail to result in more caring, tolerant just and peaceful life for all." Aung San SuuKj.

Education is the key factor for women empowerment, prosperity, development and welfare. Discrimination of women from womb to tomb is well known. There is continued inequality and vulnerability of women in all sectors- Economic, Education, Social, Political, Health Care, Nutrition, Right and Legal etc. women oppressed in all spheres of life, they need to be empowered in all walk of life. In order to fight against the socially constructed gender biases, women have to swim against the system that requires more strength. Such strength comes from the process of empowerment and empowerment will come from the education. And rural development will come from women empowerment. modern education and facilities have influenced much in women empowerment. But still rural women in rural India are lagging behind in comparison to women living in urban areas. Moreover, women of SC, ST communities living in village areas are more lagging behind incomparison to general women living in these places. On the other hand, we did not think about the rural development without empowering the women.There is continued in equality and vulnerability of women in all sectors – Economic, Social, Political, Educational, Heal the Care, Nutrition, Right and Legal etc. Education is the key factor for women empowerment and rural development.

Women constitute almost half the human race. Education has been recognised as an essential agent of social change and development in any society of any country. Education is considered as a potent instrument through which processes modernisation and social change come to existence. Education exposes people to new thoughts and ideas and provides necessary skills. Hence, to think harmonious development without educating women is impossibility. Moreover it has been rightly said that to educate a woman is to educate the whole family. Therefore, the emphasis with regard to women education should be to equip her multiple role as citizens, housewives, mother and contributor to family income, builders of new society and builder of the nation. (Sonowal, 2013)

Rural women still remain a disadvantaged segment of Indian society. Statistics show that whereas 86.1 per cent females are engaged in agriculture, the figure of males is 74 per cent. But there are hardly any special programmes for enhancing women's agricultural skills. While 7.1 per cent rural females are engaged in manufacturing, the percentage for rural males is 7 i.e., less than that of females. But most of the training programmes have hardly any female participation.While rural males have opportunities in construction, trade,transport, storage, and services, these are mostly denied to rural females. Obvio usly, opportunities must be created to enable them to acquire the skills necessary for entering these newly emerging occupations.

2. Women's Empowerment in India - An Overview

Women's empowerment in India is heavily dependent on many different variables that include geographical location (urban/rural), educational status, social status (caste and class), and age. Policies on women's empowerment exist at the national, state, and local (*Panchayat*) levels in many sectors, including health, education, economic opportunities, gender-based violence, and political participation. However, there are significant gaps between policy advancements and actual practice at the community level.One key factor for the gap in implementation of laws and policies to address discrimination, economic disadvantages, and violence against women at the community level is the largely patriarchal structure that governs the community and households in much of India. As such,women and girls have restricted mobility, access to education, access to health facilities, and lower decision-making power, and experience higher rates of violence. Political participation is also hindered at the *Panchayat* (local governing bodies) level and at the state and national levels, despite existing reservations for women.

The impact of the patriarchal structure can be seen in rural and urban India, although women's empowerment in rural India is much less visible than in urban areas. This is of particular concern, since much of India is rural despite the high rate of urbanisation and expansion of cities. rural women, as opposed to women in urban settings, face inequality at much higher rates, and in all spheres of life. Urban women and, in particular, urban educated women enjoy relatively higher access to economic opportunities, health and education, and experience less domestic violence. Women (both urban and rural) who have some level of education have higher decision-making power in the household and the community. Furthermore, the level of women's education also has a direct implication on maternal mortality rates, and nutrition and health indicators among children. (Reecha, 2012)

3. ICT and digital divide for Women in India

The concept of gender equality is a common concern all over the World. The same has now acquired new dimensions with the advent of Information and Communication Technology (ICT). The ICT has a potential to bring development for a nation. It can reduce trade distortions, eliminate poverty, empower weaker segments including women, etc. The same is, however, possible only if a nation follows sound ICT strategies and policies. We have to our priorities to those areas where we are lagging far behind. One such area is the unequal access of ICT to women. Traditional technologies continue to be important for large numbers of people around the world, particularly in rural areas. However, new technologies have a vast potential for empowerment which needs to be fully exploited. Over the past decade, there has been a growing understanding that these technologies can be powerful instruments for advancing economic and social development through the creation of new types of economic activity, employment opportunities, improvements in health-care delivery and other services, and the enhancement of networking, participation and advocacy with insociety. ICT also have the potential to improve interaction between Governments and citisens, fostering transparency and accountability in governance.The term "digital divide" refers to the differences in resources and capabilities to access and effectively utilise ICT for development that exist within and between countries, regions, sectors and socio-economic groups. The digital divide is often characterised by low levels of access to technologies. Poverty, illiteracy, lack of computer literacy and language barriers are among the factors impeding access to ICT infrastructure, especially in developing countries. Another hindrance pertains to ICT is lack of its access to women. (Dalal, 2006)

4. Education of the Women and Rural Population

"Women all over the world have a great role to play in bringing peace in the tension-ridden world", (*Speech of Late Prime Minister Rajiv Gandhi, Hindustan Times,* March 25, 1986). That is, women use holding important positions in all walks of life; no high office is barred to them. No development programme can be successful in India unless it is seen from grassroots development perspectives. This is due to the fact that the soul of India lies in villages, as Mahatma Gandhi said during the national movement and this is also true today, when more than two-thirds of the people live in rural areas. Therefore, rural development constitutes an inseparable and necessary component of the national development process. However, no rural development can be conceived of ignoring the development of the women who constitute half of the rural population but enjoy an unequal, differentiated and lower socio-economic status.

5. Problems of Rural Women

The problems of rural women are different from those of male persons. The women's issues, issues in rural areas can be categorised into three main groups, namely, socio-cultural, economic and political. They are as follows;

(a) Socio-Cultural Issues

Socio-culturally, women in rural areas are treated as inferior and subordinate to their male counterparts. The main causes are as follows:

- *Established tradition*: Superstition, worn-out customs, social beliefs, norms and unwritten taboos that have pervaded the Indian rural society for ages.
- *Female illiteracy*: The inferior status of rural women is mostly due to the lack of female literacy in rural areas.
- *Health condition is very poor*: The health condition of rural women is very poor. It has been admitted that, age-old tradition, social taboos, superstition, ignorance and poverty prevent the rural women to avail the medical facilities.
- *Lack of adequate hospital facilities*, lack of medicine, absence of lady doctors in remote areas, and no provision of mobile dispensaries, which are responsible for bad health plight of rural woman.
- *Imparting health education to the rural women is completely absent.*
- In the *economic point of view*, rural women are in a state of poverty. Rural people in general, are poor.
- *Severe malnutritious*: In Social status, the position of women was very low and they were neglected of having nutritional food by the man.
- *High Mortality Rate*: In the early stages, status of women was very low in the society. So they were neglected from health care measures and they were considered as liability rather than asset.
- *Low Social Status*: The status of women was very low as compared to man in rural areas. The soul power to control any family matters are jealously guarded and control by men in the household. In spite of the fact that women are engaged in both productive and reproductive work.
- *Early Marriages*: In the earlier period the marriage age of women was 12 or 13 years. So the girls faced by so many psychological and physical problems.

(b) Economic Issues

In the economic point of view, rural women are in a state of poverty. Rural people, in general, are poor. But rural women are poorer than the rural men. Women have little property rights. For, land and whatever savings the family possess, that belong to the male persons. Even if rural female participation in the economic process is always higher than the total male participation and the urban female participation, their work always remain unpaid or underpaid. They do not earn cash money as they are not engaged in gainful employment in formal sectors.

Lack of Economic Power: Women's are not equal to men in society. In the case of wage, women's average wage was very low as compared to men. So focuses on improving women's control over material resources and strengthening women's economic security. Its strategies are built around strengthening women's positions as workers and income earners by mobilising, organising or unionising and providing access to support services.

(c) Political Issues

Political status of women can be defined as the degree of equality and freedom enjoyed by women in the shaping and sharing of power and in the value given by society to this role of women. The Indian constitution guarantees political equality through the institution of adult franchise and Article 15, which prohibits discrimination interaction on grounds of sex. The participatory institution in the village area is the Panchayats. Realising the low participation of rural women in these local institutions, provision are made for reservation of seats for women in local bodies by 73rdAmendment of the constitution, 1992. This is certainly a significant step in political empowerment of women and consequently, their participation in decision-making bodies of rural areas.

6. Need for Uplift of Women in Rural Areas

According to Gandhiji, the spirit of India lies in the villages. The development of the country such as India is predominately dealt with the progress of the villages. Substantial part of the village population consist women class. So the all-round development of the village can only possible.

- *Mother, is the backbone of the family:* An ignorant mother of family can't lead the family successfully. An educated mother would not like their children to be less educated than themselves.
- *To Eradicate Health Problems:* Careful look at the research priorities reveals that low priority to women's health issues as the establishments predominately manned by the males. In order to

remedy this, it is important that women get a chance to functional all levels of healthcare establishments.

- *To Check Population Explosion:* The enormous population growth leads to increase in shortage of water, environmental pollution and decline in resources. Women should be aware of population problems. A literate mother will be aware of the population problems.
- *To Eradicate Social Evils:* There is urgent need to create awareness among the women to eradicate social evils. No amount of government help can achieve the desired results, unless the women themselves realise the need of such a change. This requires proper education to women about their rights and duties.
- *Upliftment of Society:* Nearly 50 per cent of our population is women. So for the all round development, it is necessary to activate woman in the process of nation making.
- *Progress of Nation:* For the progress of the country the women participation is necessary in each and every development process of the nation.
- *To Provide Economic and Social Security:* One of the biggest problem facing rural women is a sense of insecurity. The economic independence creates confidence and provides social security.
- *Evil of Dowry System:* The voluntary organisations have a very significant role to play both in prevention an cure of this social evil as the judiciary could not do much without clear evidence.

7. Status and Power of Rural Women

In primitive time women would appears to have been fully equal, both mentally and physically to man. Gradually, the man overpowered the women through establishments and laws which were controlled the whole society of the nation. As far as rural woman concerned the status of them are very low than the urban woman. Now a days the state of rural women in the society is far better than that of before. It is the result of the progressive works of various voluntary organisations, women bodies, political parties and governmental bodies. Voluntary organisations can contribute much than government agencies to promote the status of rural woman and the woman themselves should be aware of their rights and duties in the society.The collective strength of rural women can promote much progressive works in the process of development in the states. For example, in Kerala the *Kudumbasree*, i.e., the small organised units of women in village, ward level are contributing their collective women power in the developmental process of Kerala. They started many small scale industries such as soap making, hand weaving, cattle farming and vegetable cultivation etc. Now a days *Kudumbasree* is one of the important organisations which contribute various factors which lead to the development of villages.

8. Women's Education in Rural Areas

The women's education is now considered to be a de sirable among higher income group in rural areas. The female literacy as well as the proportion of school goers among women is indeed very low than men. The two main occupations in rural areas are cultivation of land and labour including agriculture labour. It is formed that female literacy among the labour is very low. Among the cultivators a useful classification is that of the size of landholding. The pace of education is much slower among women than among men. The advanced communities forming a minor fraction of village population have now realised the importance of educating their daughters and this process is gradually persuading the other weaker sections of the rural population.The first step in the education of rural women in dealt with literacy and enrollment in primary schools in the villages. But even in the big villages the schools have just been started. The percentage of school going girls is very low in rural areas.

9. Causes of the Backwardness of Women Education

There is a strong tendency to withdrawn the girls from education when they grow up. At the secondary stage, the parents like to separate the girls from schools. As the schools were none in these villages. But the boys were sent to secondary schools in the neighbouring villages and many of them may stay therefore their study. But very few rural parents are willing to do this.With the advance of women's education in rural areas the number of girls reaching higher stages of education is little increased. The progress of education in rural areas is inevitably changing the patterns of social and cultural life. This not only influences the backward classes of rural communities but also the women folk of these communities. Educated mothers would not like their daughters to be less educated than what they themselves are. It is in this that lays the best guarantee of the progress of women's education in future, in the rural areas.

10. Women Empowerment-Rural Areas

The year 2001 has been declared as the year of women's empowerment for enhancing the states and sustainable achievement in women's empowerment. According to Dr Amertya Sen, there are mainly three problems faced by the women i.e., illiteracy, lack of health and malnutrition. Education is the most significant factor of development and the only tool for realising empowerment.There is a great number of girl students who dropout from school at secondary level and higher secondary level. Especially in the rural areas the preference is given to home related works and not to education. For the empowerment of these rural women, open and distance education can play very important role.

11. Potentialities of Rural Women

Women's potentialities as mothers, as household managers, as income-earners and as protectors of the environment are always undervalued and this has become major factor for male dominance in society. Women not only give birth to children, but they raise them to full citizens who will have an active role in building the nation and the society. Women can perform these functions, only when they are properly educated and they themselves can maintain good health. A woman's education and good health are assets for the society as she is the builders of the future citizens. Women are household managers as they have to manage the domestic activities in an efficient manner. Particularly in rural areas, in many families the male persons migrate to the nearby urban area to earn cash money and they come home occasionally. The burden of household management falls upon the shoulders of women. Therefore, women need education to manage the household affairs. Rural women, in most cases, are income-earners. It is estimated that rural women earn more than the rural male folk.

12. Suggestions for Removal of Backwardness of Rural Women:

In case of the backwardness of rural women, many plans and programmes had already been implemented by the government, but the response of the rural women to these measures very negligible. Hence, following suggestions can be made for development of women from grassroots development perspective.

- The potentialities of rural women should be properly identified and encouraged and not to be ignored.
- Education of rural women should be undertaken on war-footing measures, as immediate and urgent need by opening primary schools in every village and providing sufficient cost-free study materials.
- Monetary incentives should be given to the teachers of the rural primary schools as well as to the parents of girl child for sending their children to school.
- Adequate health facilities including free medicines, vitamins pills, medical education, nurses, and midwife and lady doctors should be provided for women in rural areas.

- Periodic appraisal of the progress of rural women by the governmental agencies as well as by the non-governmental agencies is necessary.

13. Role of New Media in Women Empowerment

Today, Information Technology has changed the communication paradigm, making it no longer difficult to reach a large number of people. It can be seen that new media has played a significant role in the empowerment of women through the help of Information and Communication Technology. Out of the total 150 million Internet users in the India, around 60 million women in India are now online and use the Internet to manage their day-to-day life. With easy access to Internet at homes, cyber cafes, offices and growing adoption of smart phones, the Internet is being nce the late 1980'sand the use of ICT has dramatically expanded since 1990's. The use of internet as a form of new media, the creation of different websites that focus on women empowerment in terms of education, literacy, health , knowledge , lifestyle and many, more areas have been proliferated. Today it is possible, to find anything related to empowerment by typing keyword searches using a reliable internet browser. New Media have a huge potential for the empowerment of women, however the overall use of this media by women is very low. New Media has played an important role in empowering the women. In sum, the way new media has played its part in portraying about the atrocities faced by the women and empowering the women, no other sector has done. (Khan & Moin, 2013)

14. Conclusion

Education is the key factor for women empowerment, prosperity, development and welfare. Discrimination of women from womb to tomb is well known. There is continued inequality and vulnerability of women in all sectors- Economic, Education, Social, Political, Health Care, Nutrition, Right and Legal etc. Women oppressed in all spheres of life, they need to be empowered in all walk of life. In order to fight against the socially constructed gender biases, women have to swim against the system that requires more strength. Such strength comes from the process of empowerment and empowerment will come from the education. And rural development will come from women empower-ment.The rural women are backward in Education, Economic, Social, Decision Making, Judicial, Political aspects, etc. Moreover they are lagging behind in general awareness, communication skills, and health and family welfare aspects. And this backwardness is hampering the rural development. Let's conclude with the words of Swami Vivekananda; "To educate your women first and leave them to themselves, They will tell you what reforms are necessary."

Reference

1. Aggarwal, J.C. (2003). *Development and Planning of Modern Education*. New Delhi: Vikas Publishing House (P) Ltd.
2. Centre for Education and Development of Rural Women. *Innovations for Empowerment of Rural Women*. Pune: Indian Institute of Education.
3. Chandra, S.S. (2003). *Adult and Non-Formal Education*. New Delhi: Surjeet Publishers.
4. Dalal, Praveen. *Use of ICT for Women Empowerment in India.* retrieved from: http://cyberlawindia.blogspot.com/ 08/30/2006.
5. Khan, E., and Moin, A. (2013). Women Empowerment: Role of New Media. *Excellence International Journal of Education and Research, 1*(3). Retrieved December 17, 2014, from http://www.ocwjournalonline.com/
6. Nanda, S.K. (2000). *Indian Education and its Problems Today*. New Delhi: Kalyani Publishers.
7. Pathak, C.K. (2003). *Adult Education- Millennium Challenges*. New Delhi: Rajat Publishers.
8. Reecha., U. (2012). Women's Empowerment in India -An Analytical Overview: The Asia Foundation.
9. Sonowal, M. (2013). Impact of Education in Women Empowerment: A Case Study of SC and ST women of Sonitpur District, Assam. *IJCAES Special issue on Basic, Applied & Social Sciences, 3*(1), 27-27. Retrieved December 17, 2014.
10. Venkataiah, S. (2002). *Vocational Education*. New Delhi: Anmol Publishers (P) Ltd.

18

Kudumbasree-The Self-Help Group Model Poverty Alleviation Programme in Kerala

Dr. K Baby

1. Introduction

State Poverty Eradication Mission, Kudumbasree started its operation on 1st April 1999. It is launched with the active support of Government of India and NABARD for wiping out absolute poverty from the State within a period of 10 years. It is a Society registered under the Travancore Cochin Literary, Scientific and Charitable Societies Registration Act, 1955. This project is implmennted through Local Self Governments formed and empowered by the 73rd and 74th Constitutional Amendments. To fight poverty by Community Action through "Kudumbasree" is a joint programme of the Government of Kerala and NABARD implemented through Community Development Societies (CDSs) of Poor Women, serving as the community wing of Local Governments. To eradicate absolute poverty in ten years through concerted community action under the leadership of Local Governments by facilitating organisation of the poor for combining self-help with demand-led convergence of available services and resources to tackle the multiple dimensions and manifestations of poverty holistically. Kudumbasree is the State Poverty Eradication Mission launched by the Government of Kerala in 1998 for wiping out absolute poverty from the State through concerted community action under the leadership of Local Self Governments, Kudumbasree is today one of the largest women-empowering projects in the country. The programme has 41 lakh members and covers more than 50 per cent of the households in Kerala. Built around three critical components, micro credit, entrepreneurship and empowerment, the Kudumbasree initiative has today succeeded in addressing the basic needs of the less privileged women, thus providing them a more dignified life and a better future. It is the State Poverty Eradication Mission that has been paraphrased as Kudumbasree in local language, meaning 'prosperity of the family', which helps enjoy the economic opportunities by a good number of the poor women folk's in Kerala.

The anti-poverty programme under Kudumbasree has been launched by the State Government of Kerala with the active support of the Central Government of India and the National Bank for Agriculture and Rural Development (NABARD) aiming at removing absolute poverty within ten years with the full co-operation of the Local self governments. Poverty is a multi faceted state of deprivation. Hence a multi- pronged strategy alone can help eradicate poverty. The Mission of the Kudumbasree,therefore, states :" To eradicate absolute poverty in ten years through concerted community action under the leadership of local governments, by facilitating organisation of the poor for combining self-help with demand led convergence of available services and resources to tackle the multiple dimensions and manifestations of poverty. Kudumbasree Project is the inevitable offspring of the collective experience derived from the bleak plight of the anti-poverty programmes of the past. It is a major Government to Public (G2P) initiative in Kerala aiming at women empowerment.

2. Mission Statement

Kudumbasree believes that poverty is a multi-phased phenomenon. Hence, it has adopted a holistic approach to tackle multiple manifestations of poverty and this approach is equivocally stated in the mission statement of the project, which goes like this. "To eradicate absolute poverty in ten years through concerted community action under the leadership of Local Self-Governments, by facilitating organisation of the poor for combining self-help with demand led convergence of available services and resources to tackle the multiple dimensions and manifestations of poverty holistically". Through Kudumbasree the convergence of ideas, resources and material and dovetailing of all antipoverty programmes of various departments of the State as well as Central Government are envisaged. Centrally sponsored Urban Poverty Alleviation Programme (UPA), SJSRY (Swarna Jayanthi Shahari Rozgar Yojana) was implemented in Kerala by Kudumbasree in place of State Urban Development Agency (SUDA) in other States. State level and District level monitoring is done by Kudumbasree and at Urban Local Body level, planning and implementation is done by the UPA Cell under the leadership of Project Officer, Community Organisers and Volunteers.

3. Need for the Formation of Kudumbasree

In spite of the tremendous development Kerala could achieve in several areas like literacy and healthcare, more than 15 lakh families of the State are still in the clutches of poverty. Manifestations of poverty like ill health, mal-nutrition, unemployment, non-existence and non-availability of basic needs and facilities are seen throughout the State in varying intensity. The situation is worse in tribal belts, coastal belts and urban slums. Especially women and children are the prime victims of poverty. Poverty cannot be removed simply by giving doles or by charity. Most of the anti-poverty programmes implemented in the State during the last decades, though seemingly well conceived, have failed due to various reasons. Almost all the programme adopted income criteria for identifying the poor, which lacked people's involvement and was also susceptible to under reporting and manipulations.

The programmes of the past presumed that the poor are totally resource less and therefore did not envisage any involvement and commitment from the poor themselves. The poor were never involved in the identification and assessment of their own problems and needs. The programmes therefore tend to supply the outsiders' perception rather than meeting the felt needs of the poor. The poor remained mere beneficiaries of others' decisions, as they were not involved in the implementation of the programmes. The programmes were also generally individual oriented and did not harness community's group dynamics.

Every programme of the past tried to meet only one of the disadvantages in the lives of the poor and the programmes were implemented by a host of agencies with no coordination with one another. The programmes therefore lost focus and the resources got scattered. Being implemented by different agencies also meant many parallel structures for delivering, resulting in high delivery costs. The programmes were also centrally planned with little flexibility to suit local needs. The target-oriented programmes did not take into account the resource handling capabilities of the poor.

All these experiences emphasised the necessity to adopt a holistic approach to fight poverty, with the active participation of the community. The phenomenal success of the Community Development Society (CDS) systems of Alappuzha Municipality and Malappuram district also encouraged the planners to formulate a participatory community-based programme for fighting poverty. The concept of Kudumbasree thus took definite shape.

As part of SJSRY implementation, some good models of Micro Enterprise are being tried out in Kerala under Development of Women and Children in Urban Area (DWCUA) and Urban Self Employment Programmes (USEPs). Poor women of the community mobilise their resource, pool it and use for taking up various development activities. Spirit of 'Self-Help' is the guiding principle in this process. Kudumbasree also undertakes a series of training programmes as part of capacity build up exercise of poor people.

4. Objectives of Kudumbasree

The State Poverty Eradication Mission (SPEM), known as 'Kudumbasree', has certain stipulated objectives behind its formation.The objectives of Kudumbasree Mission fall into two categories: specific and general.To put in one simple sentence, the specific objective of Kudumbasree is the 'eradication of absolute poverty from the State of Kerala by 2008 A.Ds. Obviously the task ahead is not as simple as the sentence sounds. The means, approach and methods for the realisation of the goal are of paramount importance. To attain the goal, the holistic development of the poor families through self-help, people's participation and group action should be achieved. This is sought to be achieved through the following measures:

- Identification of the poor families through risk indices based surveys, with the active participation of the poor and the communities to which they belong.
- Empowering the poor women to improve the productivity and managerial capacities of the community by organising them into Community Based Organisations (CBOs).
- Encouraging thrift and investment through credit by developing CDSs to work as informal banks of the poor.
- Improving incomes of the poor through improved skills and investment for self-employment.
- Ensuring better health and nutrition for all.
- Ensuring basic amenities like safe drinking water, sanitary latrines, improved shelter and healthy environment.
- Ensuring a minimum of Five years of primary education for all children, belonging to risk families.
- Enabling the poor to participate in the decentralisation process through the CDS, as it is a sub-system of the local body, under which it works.

To achieve the specific objectives of the Mission, several auxiliary objectives have to be pursued methodically. These objectives can be classified as the general objectives of the Mission.

5. General Objectives

The very motto of Kudumbasree Mission is based on women empowerment; 'reach out to the family through women, reach out to the community through family'. Naturally, the empowerment of women through community-based organisations is counted as the first and foremost objective of the mission.

- **Empowerment of Women through Community Baseds Organisations**

Status of women in the society is still secondary and their role in developmental process is deplorably marginal. Apart from social taboos and lack of awareness and exposure, exploitation of women is taking place in different walks of life. The Project proposes to enable and enlighten the women to realise their own latent potentials, and strengthen them to contribute to the development of their families and community. The empowerment of women is sought to be achieved through the CDS strategy, which is an exclusively women-managed programme. Frequent group meetings, sharing of experience and training are expected to broaden their outlook. Improved economic status of the women gained through CDS thrift and self-employment will boost their status in their own families and community. The enlightened, income-generating women will refuse to accept poverty as their destiny. Once they realise their collective strength, they will fight poverty and atrocities against them most valiantly.

Community Based Organisations will be the tools and devices to bring about these changes among women folk of the poor class. One woman from every identified poor family will be made a member of a Neighbourhood Group (NHG). The NHGs will be federated into ward level Area Development Societies (ADS) and ADSs will be federated into town/panchayat level Community Development Societies (CDSs). Thus, this three tier CDS system of poor women will be coming up all over Kerala. These organisations and their activities will empower the poor women of the State to fight against poverty and social evils.

Table 1 : The Three-tiered Structure of Kudumbasree Mission 2013-2014

Serial No.	*Name of Group*	*Number of groups*
1	Number of NHGs	211731
2	Number of ADS	17486
3	Number of CDS	1061
Total		230278

Source: Economic Review 2013.

- **Thrift and Credit Operations and Informal Banking**

The CDS system will promote thrift habit among the poor women and encourage them to use the pooled resources to meet the immediate needs of the members. The CDS will therefore start functioning as informal bank of the poor women. If the resources in any NHG are enough to encourage loan for income generating activities, these loans will be appraised and sanctioned. All operations relating to thrift collection and loan sanctioning will be transparent and take place only in group meeting. Kudumbasree Mission understands and accepts the resourcefulness of the poor in terms of finance, skills, entrepreneurship and overall managerial capabilities. In connection with the thrift and credit operations and informal banking, NHG members will be given ample training in community finance management.

- **Decision Making by the Poor**

Kudumbasree mission believes in encouraging community-based bottom up planning. The ultimate aim is to hand over the decision-making and implementation power to the empowered women. At NHG level, micro-plans are made, based on the analysis of local problems with the aim of removing the risk factors for reducing their impact. NHG plans will be consolidated into ward level plans (mini plans), which will finally be integrated to form 'action plan' of the CDS. CDS will be empowered for bottom up planning, implementation and monitoring and can directly approach and receive funds from the Government, UNICEF, NABARD, banks and other donors. The CDS and ADS will maintain bank accounts and will be directly responsible for implementation of planned activities at panchayat/ward and NHG level. Now, there is the practice of maintaining bank accounts by the NHGs themselves.

- **Convergent Community Action**

Apart from the latent potential and will of the community itself, initiatives, resources, programmes and commitment of various governmental organisations, non-governmental organisations and local governments are expected to converge through the CDS system. The CDS would function as an extended arm of the government and local bodies, for the implementation of various programmes. Social Welfare Programmes directed at poor in the areas of education, literacy, health, human resources development, empowerment of women, skill upgradation, vocational training, eradication of social evils, environmental improvement and such other areas will be implemented through the CDS system.

- **Micro Enterprises and Income Generation Activities**

Income generation is one of the prime responsibilities of every Kudumbasree NHG. In each NHG an Income Generating Volunteer (IGV) is entrusted with this responsibility. It is the duty of IG volunteers to explore the possibilities, which would help and boost the income generating activities of the group. The IG volunteer will identify all potential agencies; departments and organisations engaged in the promotion of self-employment activities. She will also interact with NABARD and commercial banks, in connection with mobilising of finance. Kudumbasree intends to promote and encourage micro-enterprises and micro- entrepreneurship among poor women. The project envisages the forming of at least one flourishing micro-enterprise in every NHG to ensure the sustainable economic development of the individual, group, families, community and the State.

- **Linkage Banking**

Linkage of the NHGs with linkage banking programme of NABARD, providing loans to all houseless families of the State, providing sanitary latrines in every household of the State, and the preparation and implementation of special programme packages for the development of scheduled castes and scheduled tribes are also the objectives of the mission.

6. Participatory Development Approach

Enthused by the phenomenal success of the Alappuzha and Malappuram models of participatory development with the active involvement of the stake holders, the State Government of Kerala resolved to extend the participatory women-based programme to the entire State of Kerala in 1998. The Project has been envisaged as a mission for eradication of poverty, which has been christened as "Kudumbasree" ("Prosperity of the Family") and becomes the Magna Carta of the poor. Kudumbasree, the State Poverty Eradication Mission of Kerala, proved a revolutionary initiative that has changed the lives of thousands of poor people in the state through its various progrmmes since its inception in 1998. The unique experimentation is being implemented through the Community Based Organisations (CBOs) of the poor aiming at a multi-pronged attack on poverty. It is the Community Development Societies that work for the removal of risk factors, which are the basic causes as well as effect of poverty. With this end in view, the NHGs are identifying the most critical needs of the members. The micro plans or the NHG plans thus become the basis of delivery of services and resources through the CDS system. Each group is involved in the process of identifying their needs and problems, and accordingly preparing plans and implementing the programmes.

The Focus

Kudumbasree Mission focuses on:

- **Training for Change**

It is stated that empowerment of women is the prime motto of Kudumbasree. Therefore, the decision-making power must rest solely in the hands of the poor women. In order to exercise this power, they need proper orientation and training. To achieve this objective a number of specially designed training programmes are being conducted with focus on community structures, leadership, roles and responsibilities, thrift and credit operation, community financial management and accounting. These training programmes are organised with the support of UNICEF, NABARD and other institutions. More than one lakh women have been trained so far.

- **Education**

The massive training programmes have helped further strengthen the already existing awareness among women on the need for educating their children and acquiring literary skills for themselves. Resultantly, the apathy in sending the children to schools has disappeared to a greater extent. The poor women are getting realised that their children do need education and that education alone can enhance their status and provide them gainful employment.

- **Share and Care**

The NHGs are encouraged to meet as frequently as possible and most of them do meet once in a week. They are able to discuss every problem in the meeting and suitable solutions are come up. The NHGs provide the poor women to share their grieves and joys.

- **Community Health Care**

The trained women Community Health Volunteers are now able to provide basic medical care to the poor rural and urban women folks. With the emergence of the Community Health Volunteers the health scenario in the less cared groups are undergoing revolutionary changes. The incidence of cholera, malaria, typhoid and diarrhea has come down considerably.

- **Environmental Sanitation**

Environmental sanitation becomes the matter of greater concern of women today. Lack of sanitary latrines and safe drinking water are the twin basic problems faced by the poor people. Concerted efforts are made to address these problems.

- **The Poor Women's Bank**

The Thrift and Credit Societies are formed with the objective of encouraging the poor women to save their meager means to widen the resource base of the NHGs. Women bring their little bit of savings when they come to attend the group meetings. This money is entrusted to the Community Volunteer, who in turn deposits it in the nearest bank. Each member is given an individual pass book. The Thrift and Credit Societies are considered as poor women's bank. The poor women I, who were hitherto dependent on their men folk for every need and did not know the meaning of economic independence, has managed the impossible under Kudumbasree members can avail loans to meet their urgent needs like medical treatment, purchase of school books and uniforms for children, to pay off their old debts, etc. It is interesting to note that more than 90 per cent of the savings in the thrift societies are given away as loans. The selection of beneficiaries, the rate of interest, the quantum of loans and the period of repayment, etc. are all decided and implemented by the women themselves. Since the decisions regarding the repayment of loans with the rate of interest are taken by the NHGs, the monitoring mechanisms are inbuilt and defaulting is rare. For the same reason the NHGs are also very considerate to genuine reasons of non-repayment and extensions are given. It is observed that 100 per cent repayments are ensured which are rare in banking history. The Thrift and Credit Societies becomes the largest informal bank in Asia.

- **Community Financial Management**

Formation of thrift societies and conduct of income generating activities have led to a large financial flow at NHG and ADS levels. This has necessitated proper maintenance of accounts and keeping records in a systematic way. So poor women activists were given proper training in "Community Financial Management".

7. Organisation of Kudumbasree

Organisation of Kudumbasree refers to the organisational structure of Kudumbasree, which shows the various levels of authority of the officials functioning in it. It has five levels. In the upper level there is the Chairman of Kudumbasree, in the upper middle level there is the Vice Chairman and in the upper lower level there is the Executive Director. In the middle level there are four Directors for various regions – South, Central and North - and for the Finance and Administration. In the lower level there are District Mission Coordinators of the fourteen districts and an Administration Officer, an Accounts Officer and four Programme Officers.

8. Action Plan of Kudumbasree

Women empowerment has the central place in the programmes of Kudumbasree. Without women empowerment, poverty eradication is practically impossible. Kudumbasree aims at promotion of income generation activities for poor women, which will help them earn more income that will help achieve economic self-sufficiency. Instead of being passive recipients, women are empowered to become active leaders in this process. The action plan charted by Kudumbasree to achieve this goal is listed below:

- **Formation of Women Collectives**

The women from Below Poverty Line (BPL) families are organised into Neighbourhood Groups (NHGs) representing 15 to 40 families. A five-member woman volunteer team elected from the NHGs will be the nucleus of the programme. NHGs are federated democratically into Area Development Societies (ADS) at the ward level and then into Community Development Societies (CDS) at the local body level. These organisational structures provide opportunities for collective public action. All the volunteers and office bearers are women belonging to BPL families. Weekly meetings of NHGs, sharing of experiences, discussions, organised trainings, etc., provide opportunity to broaden their outlook on public health, hygiene, mother and childcare, nutrition, immunisation, education (pre-primary and primary) and social and economic status.

- **Skill Upgradation Training :**

To facilitate economic empowerment, suitable skill upgradation trainings are also imparted to the members. Some of the areas where skill upgradation is imparted are:

  - Data entry operation and digitization
  - Catering
  - Toy manufacturing
  - Soap manufacturing
  - Paper cover manufacturing
  - Direct marketing
  - Revival of traditional system of health care

- **Thrift-Credit Operations and 24 Hour Informal Banking System**

Enabling women to realise their latent potential and strengthening them through self-help are the main objectives of Kudumbasree. Small savings generated at the families are pooled at various levels as thrift and used to attract credit from banks which will operate as 24 hour Informal Bank for the poor, linking with financial institution. NABARD has introduced a system of linkage-banking in order to extend the facilities of banking to hitherto unreached areas. Through the Thrift and Credit Society financial capability, security and feeling of secured will be imparted to the poor women.

- **Better Living Conditions - Infrastructural Facilities**

The needs identified at NHG level are shaped as 'micro plans' which are integrated into 'mini plans' at ADS level and 'action plan' at CDS level. This will be the anti-poverty sub-plan of the local body and this will facilitate convergent delivery of Government programmes meant for the poor. Rather than the traditional system of heavily subsidised approach, Kudumbasree promote 'self-help' approach for building houses, latrines, access to drinking water, sanitary facilities, etc., availing the minimum support from Government. Common infrastructural facilities in the community strengthen them further.

- **Micro Enterprises for Sustainable Economic Development**

Providing skill upgradation trainings, self-employment opportunities and infrastructural development through wage employment schemes are the preparing grounds for further development of successful micro enterprises. Kudumbasree is given necessary resource support and facilitate forward or backward linkages, etc., to promote micro entrepreneurship among poor women.

- **Power to the People especially the Poor Women**

The skill for identification of needs, fixing priorities, availing resources and bridging gaps between needs and resources in a cost-effective manner are taught to the poor women groups in various phases. In the process of decentralisation of power to the local bodies and common man, Kudumbasree can act as a healthy sub-system facilitating participation of poor women in the planning, implementation and monitoring of the programme.

- **Leadership-Decision Making Power**

Interaction in women collectives will help the members have better knowledge and general awareness which will lead to the emergence of leadership. This will help ensure efficient women leadership to elected bodies in future.

- **Reaching out Families through Women**

'Reaching out families through women, and reaching out the community through families' is the ultimate goal of Kudumbasree for the fulfillment of its dream of a Kerala free of absolute poverty.

The Strategies

Kudumbasree aims at empowerment of women to become the active leaders rather than passive recipients. The strategies thus form of:

- Formation of women collectives
- Information and training
- Skill upgradation
- Thrift-Credit operations
- Infrastructure development
- Micro enterprises development
- Power to the people, and
- Leadership

The ultimate objective, therefore, sets as 'reaching out family through women, and reaching out community through family.'

9. Major Activities

The State Poverty Eradication Mission, Kudumbasree, implements its programmes by organising the poor, by creating community-based structures of women below poverty line with focus on self help and through demand-led convergence of available services and resources under the leadership of the local governments. The major activities carried out are listed below:

- **Microfinance Operations**

Thrift and Credit Societies are set up at Neighbourhood (NHG) level to facilitate the poor and to avail easy credits, which have now grown up to Informal Banks of the poor women at their doorsteps. Now, 10,687 Thrift and

Credit Societies are in operation in the58 urban areas enveloping the major 58 towns. In the rural segment, 1,45,674 Thrift and Credit societies are in operation covering all the 991 Village Panchayats in the State. Most of the Thrift and Credit Societies are capable of providing financial assistance to income generating activities. Through microfinance operations, Rs 651.42 lakhs of thrift are raised and internal lending to the extent of Rs 1473.12 lakhs are provided.The NHGs, which are able to avail loans, are linked with banks under linkage banking programme of NABARD. Till date, 99,356 NHGs were upgraded and 71,702 of NHGs were linked with banks. Rs 258.78 Crore is distributed as loan to NHGs for internal banking and credit of Rs 32281/lakhs flow through linkage banking. Linkage banking programme becomes an effective tool to augment resources of NHGs.

- **Micro Enterprises**

Micro Enterprises foster the economic status of women as an effective means to eradicate poverty. The income generating activities under individual and group initiatives to meet the livelihoods of the poor women are massively promoted. Canteens/ Catering units, IT units , Group farming units, Fruit Processing units, Foot ware units, Condiments units, Umbrella units, Building materials units Horticulture units, Electronics units, Ready made garments units, Soap powder units, Toys units , Grocery shops, are some of the examples of Micro Enterprises that are undertaken by poor women under Kudumbasree. Mission. Women entrepreneurs are given training in entrepreneurship development, skill development, project management, and performance improvement by the Entrepreneurship Development Institute of India, Ahmadabad.

- **Micro Housing or Bhavanashree**

Under this programme poor families, who are in dire need of constructing new houses are able to avail loans from banks and the repayment of which is ensured by tri-party agreement between the beneficiaries, the Community Development Societies and the financial institutions/Banks.19, 922 houses were constructed by using credit amounting to Rs, 6765.91 lakhs.

- **The Destitute Identification, Rehabilitation and Monitoring Programme or Ashraya**

This programme, named as "Ashraya" in local language (meaning 'depending') aims at uplifting the poorest of the poor from their destitution. Poorest of the poor families, which lack adequate food, drinking water, shelter, educational facilities for children, sanitation facilities, employment opportunities, and land for shelter, and worst sufferers of illness and chronic diseases are identified and rehabilitated under various schemes. The programme launched in 391 Village Panchayats and 6 Municipalities.

- **Lease Land Farming or Haritashree**

Lease Land Farming Programme, named 'Haritashree' in local language, lends helping hands to those cultivators who are having no land at all. So Kudumbasree pools uncultivated lands on rent and provide the willing cultivators for agricultural operations. Last year, lease land farming was done in 18,489 hectares benefiting 3,15,613 families hailing from 31,980 NHGs in the state.

- **The S3 Programme**

Kudumbasree addresses the multifaceted deprivations of the poor families, which lack food, health-care, education, basic amenities such as shelter, drinking water, safe latrines and employment. It is felt that poverty reduction would foster economic development if it sustains the secured gains. So, sustainability economic development assumes greater importance in the process of attacking poverty. So much so, Kudumbasree has evolved a project to build a model in select Panchayats on the concept of comprehensive development. The project focuses on self sufficiency, self-reliance and sustainability (**S3**) of the village Panchayats. The project envisages to address the problems of Child Development, Geriatric care, mentally and Physically Challenged, Education, Adolescent care, women Empowerment, Enterprise development, Unemployment of the educated youth, Agriculture/Animal husbandry/Dairy development, Revamping the traditional sectors, Basic minimum Needs and Destitute Identification and Rehabilitation. Initially the programme was piloted in three Panchayats viz.,Venganoor in Trivandrum district, Kodakara in Trissur district and Munniyoor in Malappuram district. Later on, the programme extended to 14 Panchayats and the extension of the programme to another 70 Panchayats is done.

- **Children's Neighborhoods or Balasabha**

The children from poor families are organised to develop their intellectual faculties by performing cultural activities from time to time. Termed as Balasabha in local language it functions as a platform of the children to help develop their overall capabilities that combines education, entertainment and empowerment. Till 2013-14, 27463 Balasabha comprising 504979 children were organised in different places in Kerala.

- **Solid Waste Management or Clean Kerala Business**

Solid waste is serious menace for all the urban and semi urban areas of Kerala Now Kudumbasree mission tries to tackle this problem by setting up 'Clean Kerala Business' units in an organised and planned manner entrusting to women entrepreneur groups to segregate, collect and transport solid waste from the households, commercial establishmentshotels , etc.,75 Clean Kerala Business units are formed in the state so far.

- **Special Employment Programme for Educated Youth**

A special employment programme for the educated youth has been initiated and 50,000 educated youth were assigned with the task of Kudumbasree such as identification process, setting up of innovative micro enterprises, etc., 211 group and 170 individual enterprises have been formed under this programme, thus benefiting 1307 people.

- **Special School for the disabled children or Buds**

Special Schools, called 'Buds', are set up aiming at providing for the developmental, social, and emotional needs of the disabled children. These children are being provided with the necessary medical attention, physical and mental therapy, mobility equipments, hearing aids, and vocational and educational training.

- **Self Employment Programmes under SJSRY**

Swarna Jayanthi Sahari Rozgar Yojana (SJSRY) is an anti poverty programme launched by the Government of India and is meant for the urban areas of the state. It covers the 53 Municipalities and 5 Corporations. Individual enterprises and Group enterprises with a minimum number of 10 persons can be set up. 1365 group and 15382 enterprises were undertaken under this programme.

- **GRQ Project**

The Goat-Rabbit-Quail (GRQ) Project is a unique micro enterprises project for rearing the three species together to earn a steady income to the family entrepreneurs. The predominantly non-vegetarian population of Kerala necessarily ensures the potential market for the produce. The GRQ project aims at utilising the inherent advantage of the homestead farming practiced by number of families. Quail rearing as an activity can ensure a weekly cash flow and that combined with the quarterly and half yearly cash flow of rabbit and goat would ensure a source of steady income to the family.

- **Nutrimix- the Baby Food Products Production Project**

The Nutrimix Baby food Production Project is an ambitious project recently launched by the Kudumbasree mission. The Project envisaged starting 500 baby food production units in different parts of Kerala. 21 Nutrimix production units have already been started. It is estimated that 2500 women can find gainful employment through the programme, which targets the massive baby food market dominated by big brands. The expected turnover is Rs 200 Crore per annum. Some select Kudumbasree Production units and their activities in Kannur and Kasargod.

10. Conclusion

Kudumbasree became the lifeline to many of the poor women in the state of Kerala. It assumed the status of helpline to many. It is a massive anti poverty programme of the Government of Kerala aiming at eradicating poverty and salvages the destitute from the wretches of extreme deprivation. The formation of 1,65,840 NHGs of the women from 33, 45, 509 risk families, covering urban, rural and tribal areas of the state helps develop 2, 42, 489 poor women into vibrant micro entrepreneurs. Resultantly, the poor women of the state have become active participants in the planning and implementation process of various anti poverty programmes. By participating in various income generating-cumdevelopmental activities, the morale and confidence of women become very high. Capacity of the poor women of the state in several areas has gone up considerably, status of women in families and community has also improved. Kudumbasree has gained national and international acclaim as an ideal and workable model of participatory development for eradicating poverty. It has proved without any doubt that women empowerment is the best strategy for poverty eradication. Women who were regarded as voiceless and powerless started identifying their inner power, their strength, opportunities for growth, and their role in reshaping their own destiny. The process of empowerment becomes the beacon light to their children, their families and to the society at large. It opens new vistas in development history.

References

1. Jacob John (2009), "*A study on Kudumbasree project* -A Poverty Eradication Programme in Kerala Performance, Impact and Lessons for other States" Kerala Development Society, (KDS-Delhi) May 2009.
2. Dr V P Raghavan, "Social Action, *Gender Equity and Empowerment:* The Case of Kudumbasree Projects In Kerala".
3. Dr V P Raghavan "*Micro-Credit and Empowerment*: A Study of Kudumbasree Projects in Kerala".
4. Dr V P Raghavan, "Livelihoods and empowerment: The Kudumbasree projects in Kerala, India – A new paradigm of participatory economy". Kerala Calling, January 2004 "Kudumbasree. A silent revolution".
5. Kudumbasree, State Poverty Eradication Mission Annual Administration Report 2009-2010.
6. Dr M A Oommen Committee Report on Kudumbasree.
7. Economic Review 2013, Kerala Planning Board.
8. Economic Survey 2014.
9. www.kudumbashree.org.

19

A Study on Constraints Faced by Elected Women Representatives under Panchayati Raj Institutions (PRI) in Empowerment Process, West Midnapore District, West Bengal

Ria Sarkar

1. Introduction

Perhaps no other species on earth, than women, command deification and glorification at one end, and confront subjugation and suppression at the other end (Boraian, 2008). In almost all societies in almost all periods of history women have been treated as men's inferiors. Typically, women have been barred from owning property, from employment opportunities, from holding offices and even from voting. This discrimination has often been embodied in laws and even more often enforced by rigid social customs.

The Indian society bears a unique social structure in the world, which has been oppressor of women folk in almost every sphere of life due to its denial of equal status to them since centuries. The patriarchal system of society forced the women to be confined in the four walls of their house and largely engaged in the household chores. The male-dominated society is often seen engaged in the purpose of serving male interests and the continuous subordination of women (Watane, 2011). In India, women constituting 48.46 per cent (Census of India, 2011) of the entire population have remained the most marginalized so far as the socio-political power structure is concerned. Unless equal social opportunities are extended to the female population, no political authority or society can usher in social, political or economic advancement.

The empowerment of women, especially rural women is crucial for the socio-economic progress of rural India and for involving women in the process of national development. Without the active participation of women at all levels of decision-making, the goals of equality, development and peace cannot be achieved. (Ambedkar and Nagendra, 2011).

Equal treatment to women in political life, to be meaningful and effective should start from the grass roots level. To provide training and practice in the process of decision-making, the rural democratic institutions are the ideal structures to begin with. For sustainable economic and social development to take place in any country, it is necessary that people participate in the political process. Unless specific conditions are met, women face multiple hurdles and find it difficult to participate in the political process that has hitherto been a male bastion. The reasons for this are gender specific. Women are less mobile than men are. They have domestic responsibilities, which puts limits on the time they can spend in such processes. There are historical prejudices. Consistent efforts will have to be made over a period of time to engender the political process and institutions and issues that are critical to this process (Vyasulu and Vyasulu, 1999).

Women's participation in the political process: Women as a whole have been under represented throughout India in both appointed and elected position; they have minimal power within parties; and they participate in elections as candidates and as voters with less frequency than men. The political participation of women has been limited due to various factors. The 73rd Constitutional Amendment Act (1992) to the Constitution of India is the milestone in the history of women empowerment in India. This ensured reservation of not less than one-third of the seats for membership as well as office of chairpersons in village, block and district level to be reserved for women.

Nature and extent of the problem The success of a democratic political system depends upon the nature and extent of the political participation among the citizens of the country irrespective of caste, colour, sex and religion. But, in India reality provides us a very discouraging picture. Indian women in general and the women of West Bengal in particular stand far away from the political world of the country in comparison of their male counterpart. Despite the widespread movement towards democratisation, women are largely under-represented at most levels of government, and have made little progress in attaining political power in legislative bodies. Political participation of women is limited due to various factors. And those who are elected face a lot of constraints in the process of empowerment. Empowerment process will be meaningful only when the constraints will be sorted out.

2. Rationale Behind the Study

With the 73rd Constitutional Amendment Act, 1992, significant changes were brought in the political scenario of the country with regard to women's participation in politics which ensured reservation of not less than 33 per cent seats for women in the three tiers of the Panchayati Raj Institution. But India had provided a discouraging picture with respect to political participation of women. Indian women stood far away from the political world of the country in comparison to their male counterpart. When the system was introduced, very few women contested and got elected. Those who got elected had to confront several obstacles and constraints that curbed their active participation in the political process. In most cases, they contested and participated influenced by their husbands, sons or other family members. Moreover a plenty of other factors restricted them from gaining empowerment in true sense even though they were elected.

So the question arises:

- What are the constraints that the Elected Women Representatives under PRI face which restrict them from executing their powers and gaining empowerment in true sense?
- What are the reasons behind these problems faced by the elected women members under PRI?

3. Objectives of the Study

With this background, this study "Constraints faced by Elected Women Representatives under Panchayati Raj Institutions (PRI) in empowerment process" has been taken up by the present researcher. This study has focused on all three tiers of the Panchayati Raj, with the following objectives:

Immediate Objectives:

- o To understand the constraints faced by elected women representatives under PRI.
- o To identify the reasons behind such problem.

Broader Objective:

- o To overcome the problems and make the process of empowerment meaningful and effective in the future.

4. Panchayati Raj Institution

Panchayati Raj means democratic decentralization. It ensures greater participation of people and more effective implementation of rural development programmes. There will be a Gram Panchayat for a village or group of villages, Taluk Panchayat / Block Panchayat/Panchayat Samiti at Block level and the Zilla Panchayat at the district level.

The passage of 73rd Amendment Act in 1992 by Indian Parliament became part of the Constitution in April, 1993 after many years of national discussion and debate. The Amendment required every state to pass its own Panchayat Act by April, 1994 and to hold elections by April, 1995.

5. The 73rd Constitutional Amendment Act, 1992

The Constitutional (73rd Amendment) Act, passed in 1992 by the Narasimha Rao government, came into force on April 24, 1993. It was meant to provide constitutional sanction to establish "democracy at the grassroots level as it is at the state level or national level". Its main features are as follows:

- The Gram Sabha or village assembly as a deliberative body to decentralised governance has been envisaged as the foundation of the Panchayati Raj System.
- A uniform three-tier structure of panchayats at village (Gram Panchayat — GP), intermediate or block (Panchayat Samiti — PS) and district (Zilla Parishad — ZP) levels.
- All the seats in a panchayat at every level are to be filled by elections from respective territorial constituencies.
- Not less than one-third of the total seats for membership as well as office of chairpersons of each tier has to be reserved for women.
- Reservation for weaker castes and tribes (SCs and STs) has to be provided at all levels in proportion to their population in the panchayats.
- To supervise, direct and control the regular and smooth elections to panchayats, a State Election Commission has to be constituted in every State and UT.
- The Act has ensured constitution of a State Finance Commission in every State/UT, for every five years, to suggest measures to strengthen finances of PRIs.
- To promote bottom-up-planning, the District Planning Committee (DPC) in every district has been accorded constitutional status.
- An indicative list of 29 items has been given in Eleventh Schedule of the Constitution. Panchayats are expected to play an effective role in planning and implementation of works related to these 29 items.

6. Panchayat System in West Bengal

In the West Bengal the PRI three tier structures was set-up under the Section 115 of the West Bengal Panchayat Act, 1973. The higher tier has the power of supervision over the lower tier. Gram Panchayat, Panchayat Samiti and Zilla Parishad are organically linked. Each tier has its own set of functionaries. For the interests of the weaker sections of the population, notably women, SCs and STs, an amendment in the Constitution of India took place in the year 1993. This 73rd and 74th Constitutional Amendments made it obligatory that one-third of the seats for membership as well as office of chairpersons of each tier must be reserved for women. This ensures the participation of women in local decision-making process.

Basic features of the Panchayats in West Bengal:

(a) Regular election since 1978

(b) Election based on party symbol in all three tiers

(c) State election Commission established in 1994

(d) Most of the members are from small and marginal farmers and landless families

(e) Sharing of responsibilities among all three tiers

(f) Direct accountability at all levels

(g) Institutional involvement at all levels

7. Current Status of Panchayati Raj Institution, West Bengal

The PRI system in the state comprises of 3351 Gram Panchayats, 333 Panchayat Samitis, and 17 Zilla Parishads and Siliguri Mahakuma Parishad.

8. Research Setting, Study Approach and Methodology

West Bengal is one of the 28 states where the Panchayati Raj Institution has been the role model. The three-tier PRI structure has set an example of perfect decentralisation.

Selection of district: Among the 19 districts of West Bengal, the West Midnapore district was selected purposively. The reason behind selection of this district is the recommendation of the Project Manager and Capacity building Manager of ISGPP Cell as this district comprises more women's political participation in rural governance than other districts.

Selection of Blocks: There are 29 blocks in the West Midnapore district. Out of these 29 Community Development Blocks, **Keshpur** and **Pingla** Blocks have been selected purposively. This selection has been made after consultation with the District Coordinator of ISGPP Cell, West Midnapore.

Selection of Gram Panchayats: Out of 15 G.Ps in the **Keshpur Block**, Golar, Sirsa and Keshpur G.Ps and out of 10 G.Ps in the **Pingla Block**, Kusumda, Gobardhanpur and Jalchak II G.Ps have been selected purposively on the recommendation of the ISGPP Cell, West Midnapore.

9. Sampling

Sampling method: Purposive sampling has been adapted to conduct the study. The Sampling has been done in the following stages:

- Purposive selection of the district from the state
- Purposive selection of the blocks from the district
- Purposive selection of the G.Ps from the blocks
- Purposive selection of EWRs in selected Gram Panchayats, Panchayat Samitees and Zilla Parishad
- Purposive selection of other male representatives and Government Officials

The study was undertaken in all the three tiers of the PRI system. The sample included EWRs at all these three levels. Besides, other male representatives and Government officials have also been included in the study.

Sampling Frame

Gram Panchayat (at village level)

36 EWRs from all the three tiers of PRI

6 other male representatives

4 other male representatives, 2 B.D.Os

39

Panchayat Samiti (at block level)

2 other male representatives, 2 Government Officials

Zilla Parishad (at District level)

Therefore, **Sample Size: 52** (EWRs: 36; other male representatives and Government Officials: 16)

Data Collection Instrument

After an extensive review, expert consultation and pretesting at the field, data collection tools were developed. Responses taken during pilot study also served as the basis for constructing the tools for data collection. Two separate **semi-structured interview schedules** were prepared- one for the EWRs and the other for male representatives and Government Officials.

Methods of Data Collection

- Primary Data Collection through observation, in-depth Interview and Case Study.
- Use of Secondary Data i.e., published books, reports, academic journals; research works newspapers and documents provided by ISGPP Cell, West Midnapore. Some information has also been collected from relevant websites.

Findings and Analysis of Data

A. Respondents: EWRs (n=36)

Majority of the EWRs fell between 34-49 years of age-group and were married. Most of them were housewives and all of them were literate though the levels of educational qualifications were varied.

Table 1. Reasons for joining

S.l. No.	*Reason for joining politics*	*Number of EWRs*			
		Zilla Parishad	*Panchayat Samiti*	*Gram Panchayat*	*Total*
•	Pressure from political party	1 (25)	5 (62.5)	16 (66.66)	22 (61.11)
•	Pressure from family members	-	1 (12.5)	4 (16.67)	5 (13.89)
•	Welfare of the people	3 (75)	2 (25)	4 (16.67)	9 (25)
•	To stay in power	-	-	-	-
Total		**4 (100)**	**8 (100)**	**24 (100)**	**36 (100)**

*Figures within parentheses are percentages.

Majority of the EWRs fell between 34-49 years of age-group and were married. Most of them were housewives and all of them were literate though the levels of educational qualifications were varied.

Nearly 61per cent i.e., 22 out of 36 of the respondents mentioned pressure from political parties as the reason for entering politics. Around 25 per cent of them mentioned that to help the rural poor and to serve the rural poor were the reason for joining politics. Only 13.89 per cent of them mentioned that there was strong pressure from family members to contest the elections. None of them had mentioned staying in power as the reason to enter politics.

From the table, it is evident that, three out of four (75 per cent) of the EWRs in the Zilla Parishad had mentioned welfare of the people as the main reason for them to join politics, whereas, out of eight EWRs in the Panchayat Samitis, five (62.5 per cent) of them and out of 24 EWRs in the Gram Panchayats, 16 (66.66 per cent) of them mentioned pressure from political party as the reason to join politics. This shows that most of the women representatives in the district took the decision to join politics on their own will and were more empowered because of their educational and political background compared to the women representatives at the block and village level. Most of them had themselves taken the decision to join politics with the urge to develop the masses. In case of the EWRs at the block and village level, majority of them had no previous experience in politics and had joined politics because of pressure from local political parties. All the parties are concerned with the game of numbers as majority alone ensures their control over the government at any level. This consideration determines their sole criterion for the selection of the candidates.

Table 2 : Length of stay in politics

Sl. No.	*Years of involvement in politics*	*Number of EWRs*			
		Zilla Parishad	*Panchayat Samiti*	*Gram Panchayat*	*Total*
•	Less than 5 years	-	1(12.5)	1(4.16)	2 (5.56)
•	5 years	-	3 (37.5)	19(79.17)	22 (61.11)
•	10 years	2 (50)	3 (37.5)	4 (16.67)	9 (25)
•	15 years	2 (50)	1(12.5)	-	3 (8.33)
•	20 years	-	-	-	-
•	Above 20 years	-	-	-	-
Total		**4 (100)**	**8 (100)**	**24 (100)**	**36 (100)**

*Figures within parentheses are percentages.

The above table reveals that out of 36 respondents, 22 of the women Panchayati Raj leaders (nearly 61per cent) were there in politics for the last five years. It meant that their initiation in politics started with contesting of the 2008 Panchayati Raj election. Nine of the respondents (25 per cent) mentioned that they were in politics for the last 10 years. Only threes of the respondents (nearly eigth per cent) stated their stay in politics for 15 years. It is worth-mentioning that two of the respondents (5.56 per cent) i.e., the Sabhapati of Keshpur Panchayat Samiti and the Pradhan of Gobardhanpur G.P. in the Pingla block had been in politics for less than five years as they were brought to power by the local political party after the change in political power in the mid of the five year term replacing the earlier candidates.

An overwhelming majority of the EWRs from the Gram Panchayats (19 out of 24 i.e., 79.17 per cent) had their initiation in politics only in the 2008 PRI election. They had no previous experience in politics and were there in politics only for the last five years. They were first-timers to the Panchayati Raj Institutions, whereas, in case of Zilla Parishad, the stay of all the members in politics was more than five years. They had experience in politics and most of them had political family background. Four EWRs at block level were in politics for more than five years.

Constraints faced by EWRs

Women in every sphere of life, in every society face a lot of constraints not only outside their houses but also within the four walls of their house. They are most vulnerable section of the society. They undergo hardships and obstacles in their daily lives. Women are the oppressed lot, they are depressed, deprived and are confronted by social, political and economic barriers. Women in the Panchayati Raj are no exception. They have to undergo a lot of constraints that restrict them from effectively executing their powers and carrying out their responsibilities.

In the context of the present study, the researcher has studied the constraints faced by the EWRs under PRI in all three tiers and the reasons behind these constraints. The constraints have been categorised under two broad heads.

(a) **Family Constraints** (b) **Constraints in work sphere**

Individual respondents were asked whether they faced the constraints. Those who answered positively were asked the reasons for the constraints. Options had been provided. (Multiple responses for the reasons of the constraints had been recorded. Different combinations of the reasons are possible as multiple responses have been recorded but the researcher has considered single reasons and not combined reasons for the purpose of interpretation.)

Family constraints faced by EWRs

Table (a) 1 : Difficult to manage household chores besides Panchayat works

Response	*Number of respondents*
Yes	28 (77.78)
No	8 (22.22)
Total (n)	**36 (100)**

*Figures within parentheses are percentages.

Out of 36 respondents, majority of the EWRs (77.78 per cent) found it difficult to manage their household chores alongside their office works. In this regard, it ought to be mentioned that, all the EWRs who gave positive response were married and were housewives. Eight of the EWRs (22.22 per cent) responded negatively. They mentioned that they did not find it difficult in carrying out their household responsibilities as their family members especially husband and children who were young enough to look after themselves and also helped her in household works. Of these eigth respondents four were living in their parental house with their parents and hence faced no such problem. Those 28 respondents who answered positively were asked the reasons for the problem, the result of which has been shown below.

(No. of respondents=28; Multiple responses were recorded from 28 respondents)

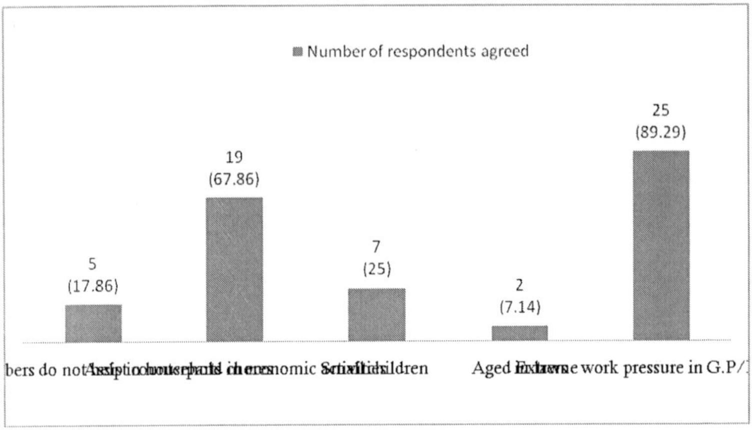

Fig.(a2). Distribution of respondents on the basis of reasons stated for difficulty in managing household chores.

*Figures within parentheses are percentages.

The above figure reveals that out of 28 respondents, 25 of them (nearly 89 per cent) admitted that because of extreme work load in Panchayat, they found it difficult to carry out their household responsibilities. They stated they had to spend the greater part of the day in conducting official works and had little time left for her family. A significant number of respondents (67.86 per cent) i.e., 19 of the respondents had to assist their husband agricultural activities. svean of the respondents had small children and had to invest a lot of time taking care of them. It also became unpleasant for them to leave their small kids and go to work. Only five of the respondents said that their family members did not help them in household chores, while, two of them had to take care and spend a lot of time for their aged in-laws.

Table (b1) : Non-cooperative attitude of family members

Response	*No. of respondents*
Yes	6 (16.67)
No	30 (83.33)
Total (n)	**36 (100)**

*Figures within parentheses are percentages.

When asked whether the women representatives got less support from their family members, majority of them (nearly 83 per cent) gave negative responses. They said they got full support from their family. Many even stated that it was because of the support of their family members that they were holding the posts. Only six of the respondents (16.67 per cent) answered positively to the question. All of them were married. These six respondents were considered for the next question, the result of which has been shown below.

(No. of respondents=6; Multiple responses were recorded from 6 respondents)

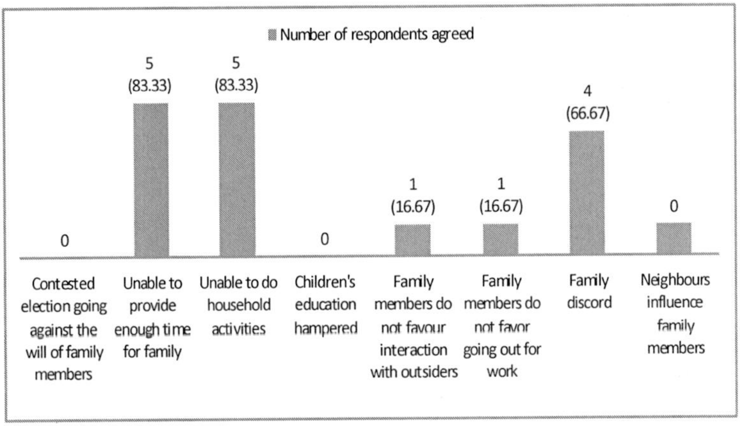

Fig. (b2) : Distribution of respondents on the basis of reasons stated for non-cooperative attitude of family member

*Figures within parentheses are percentages.

Out of these six respondents, five lived with their in-laws and one was compelled to leave her in-laws' house due to lack of support from them. The above figure reveals that out of six EWRs, five of them (83.33 per cent) stated that their family members did not support them because they were not able to provide enough time to the family as they had to spent greater part of the time in the office and doing official works. Same percentage of EWRs stated that as because they were unable to invest much time in household activities, their family members did not support them. Four out of the six respondents (66.67 per cent) considered that their going to work creates family discord so their family members opposed them. Only one of the six respondents (16.67 per cent) considered that unwillingness of family members to let her interact with outsiders as a reason for lack of support from her family members. Same percentage of respondents said that the other two reasons-family members did not favor going out for work and neighbours influence family members were reasons behind lack of family support.

Table (c1) : Family members did not give liberty for free movement for work purpose

Response	*No. of respondents*
Yes	11 (30.56)
No	25 (69.44)
Total (n)	**36 (100)**

*Figures within parentheses are percentages.

Out of 36 respondents, only 11 of them (30.56 per cent) said that their family members did not give them full liberty for free movement for work purpose whereas, rest of the respondents answered negatively to the asked question. These 11 respondents were asked the reasons for the constraint, the result of which has been shown below.

(No. of respondents=11; Multiple responses were recorded from 11 respondents)

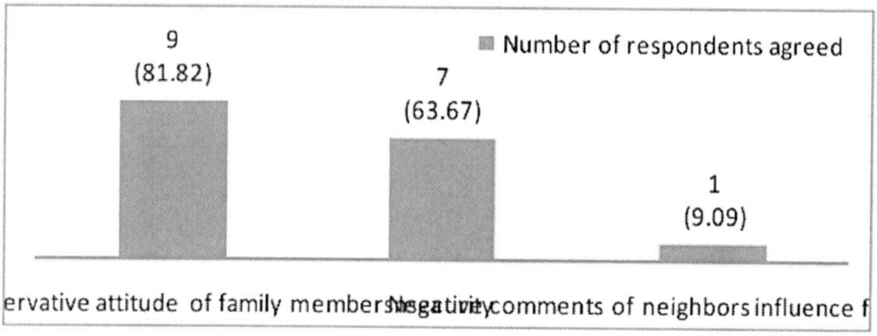

Fig. (c2). Distribution of respondents on the basis of reasons stated for not getting liberty for free movement from family members.

*Figures within parentheses are percentages.

Out of 11 respondents, 9 of them (81.82 per cent) held responsible the conservative attitude of their family members as the reason for not getting full liberty for free movement. Most of these EWRs were from rural areas and their families were very conservative. Conservative attitude of family members was the most important reason behind this constraint. Seven of the 11 respondents (63.67 per cent) stated that being women they were vulnerable and so their families were worried about their security. Only one of the EWR (9 per cent) stated that the negative comments of her neighbours were the reason behind the constraint. She added that, their negative attitude influenced her family members from restricting her from free movement to outside for work purpose.

Table (d1) : Family members did not allow going out for emergency works or meetings during night time

Response	*No. of respondents*
Yes	33 (91.67)
No	3 (8.33)
Total (n)	**36 (100)**

*Figures within parentheses are percentages

Majority of the EWRs (92 per cent) faced this constraint- their family members did not allow them to go out for any work during night time. It is worth-mentioning that among those who answered positively, married as well as unmarried women were present. Those respondents who answered positively were asked the reasons for the constraints, the result of which has been shown below.

(No. of respondents=33; Multiple responses were recorded from 33 respondents)

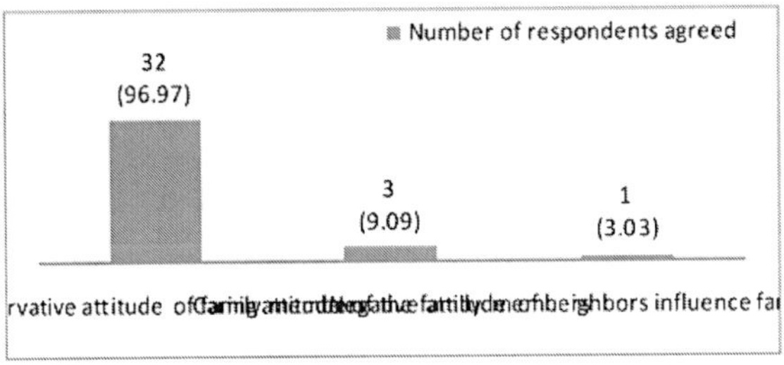

Fig. d2. Distribution of respondents on the basis of reasons stated by them for not being able to attend meetings during night time.

*Figures within parentheses are percentages

The figure reveals that out of 33 respondents, 32 of them (96.97per cent) regarded the conservative attitude of their family members as the reason behind the problem. Three of the 33 EWRs (nearly 9 per cent) considered the caring attitude of their family members responsible for this constraint. Only one of them stated that negative attitude of the neighbours influenced the family members for not allowing them to go out for any kind of work during night time.

Constraints faced by EWRs in work sphere

Table a1 : Difficult to understand and manage the duties and responsibilities of an elected representative

Response	*Number of respondents*
Yes	33 (91.67)
No	3 (8.33)
Total (n)	**36 (100)**

*Figures within parentheses are percentages.

To a question whether they found it difficult to understand the works, duties and responsibilities of an elected representative, the responses of the EWRs had been recorded in the above table. It is significant that out of 36 respondents, 33 of them (91.67 per cent) gave positive responses to the question. But it needs to be mentioned that all 33 said that they faced this problem only at the beginning. They stated that they could hardly understand their duties and found it difficult to handle their responsibilities when they were beginners. But with time, they had learnt, gathered experience and had become acquainted with it. Rest of the respondents (8.33 per cent) said that they had never faced this problem. It is worth-mentioning that out of these three respondents, two were post-graduate and one was a graduate. These 33 respondents who answered positively were asked the reasons for the constraint. Their responses have been shown with the help of the following diagram.

(No. of respondents=33; Multiple responses were recorded from 33 respondents)

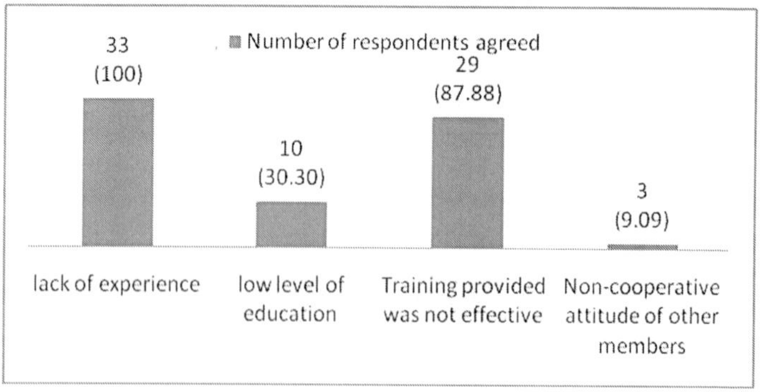

Fig. (a2). Distribution of EWRs on the basis of reasons stated by them for having difficulty in understanding and tackling the duties, assignments and responsibilities of an elected representative at the beginning

*Figures within parentheses are percentages.

Different combinations of the reasons are possible as multiple responses had been recorded but the researcher has considered single reasons and not combined reasons for the purpose of interpretation.

From the above diagram, it is evident that all 33 EWRs considered that because of lack of earlier experience in this field, it was difficult for them to understand and tackle their responsibilities at the beginning. 29 of them (nearly 88 per cent) mentioned that the training provided was not effective as they could hardly learn anything during the small-duration training. 10 of the respondents (30.30 per cent) considered their low level of education to be the hindrance, whereas, only three of them (9.09 per cent) held the non-cooperative attitudes of other male members of the Panchayat as the reason. All these three EWRs were the representatives from the same Gram Panchayat.

Table (b1) : Inhibitions in speaking in front of males and elders

Response	*Number of respondents*
Yes	5 (13.89)
No	31 (86.11)
Total (n)	**36 (100)**

*Figures within parentheses are percentages.

Nearly 14 per cent of the women Panchayati Raj leaders agreed that they felt hesitant to speak and express their views in front of male members and other elders. Majority of the respondents remarked that they had no such inhibitions. Those five respondents who answered positively were asked the reasons for the constraint. Their responses have been shown with the help of the following diagram.

(No. of respondents=5; Multiple responses were recorded from 5 respondents)

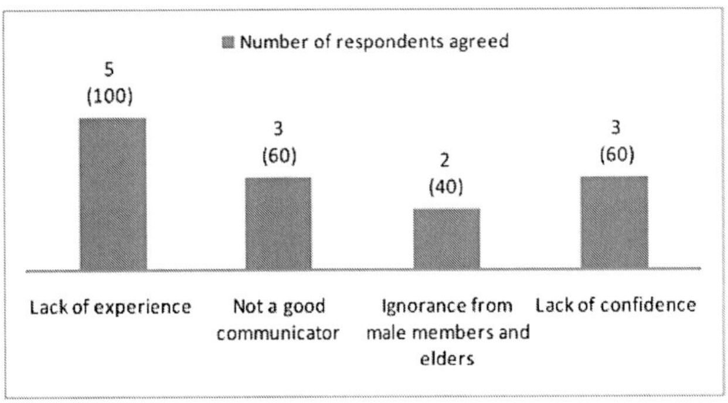

Fig. (b2) Distribution of EWRs based on the reasons stated by them for feeling hesitant to speak in front of males and elders.

*Figures within parentheses are percentages.

All five respondents considered lack of experience as the main reason behind their inhibition to speak in front of males and elders, whereas, 60 Per cent regarded lack of confidence to be the reason. According to them, they felt nervous to speak in front of male members. They feared they might say something wrong. three of the respondents believed that they were not good communicator. two of them stated that ignorance from male members was the main reason behind their interdict.

Table (c1) : Dependence on others for movement for work-related purpose

Response	*Number of respondents*
Yes	19 (52.77)
No	17 (47.22)
Total (n)	**36 (100)**

*Figures within parentheses are percentages.

The data reveals that 19 of the total number of respondents (nearly 53 per cent) agreed that they had to depend on their husband or on others to go to office or to attend meetings. Only 47.22 per cent stated that they faced no such problem. Of these 47.22 per cent, some of them knew cycling and had their own bicycles; some members at the block and Zilla level had been provided with vehicles by the Government. Those who underwent this constraint were asked the reason for it. Their responses have been shown with the help of the following diagram.

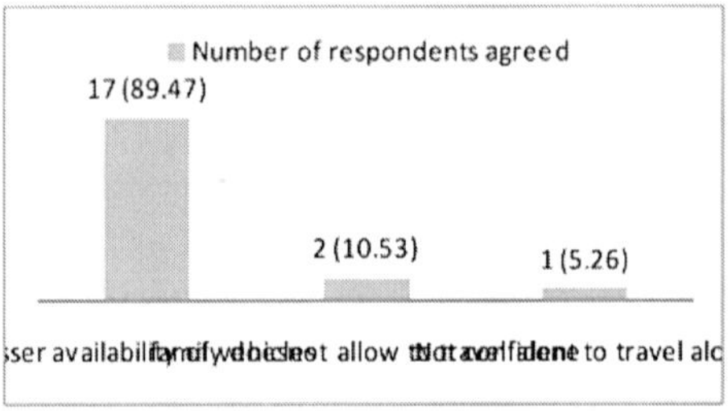

Fig (c2) : Distribution of respondents on the basis of reasons stated by them for dependency on others for movement.

*Figures within parentheses are percentages.

Of 19 respondents, 17 of them stated the unavailability of vehicles as the reason behind the constraint. West Midnapore is spread over a vast area. All the G.Ps and P.Ss surveyed were located in the interiors of the district. Very less availability of vehicles was a major problem in these areas. Two of them had mentioned that as their families did not allow them to travel alone and only one of them did not feel confident enough to travel alone and so had to depend on others.

Table (d1) : Lack of decision-making power

Response	*Number of respondents*
Yes	5(13.89)
No	31 (86.11)
Total (n)	**36 (100)**

*Figures within parentheses are percentages .

Majority (86.11per cent) of the EWRs said that they had decision-making power. Only 14 per cent of them agreed that they lack in decision-making power.

(No. of respondents=5; Multiple responses were recorded from 5 respondents)

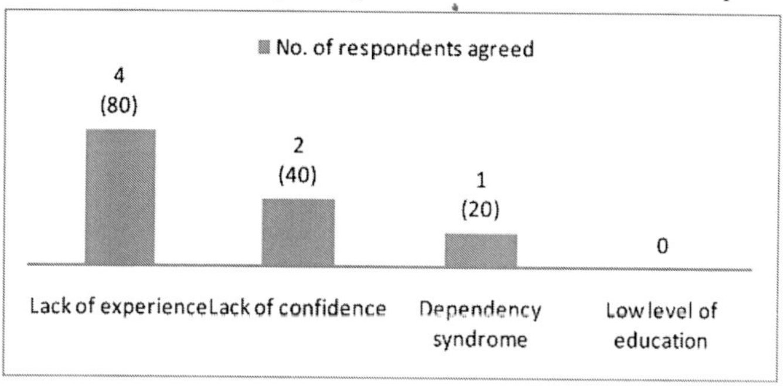

Fig (d2) Distribution of respondents on the basis of reasons stated by them for their lack of decision-making power.

*Figures within parentheses are percentages.

From the diagram, it is revealed that of the five representatives, majority (80 per cent considered their lack of experience in this field as the major reason for lack of decision-making power. 40 per cent stated that they did not feel confident enough to take any major decision on which lives of the villagers and their welfare were involved. They were not confident enough that decisions taken by them will benefit the people of their village. One of the respondent mentioned that since childhood she had always depended on others for taking any major decision and that had developed as a habit and so she could not any decision alone.

Table (e1) : Lack of support from male members

Response	*Number of respondents*
Yes	6 (16.67)
No	30 (83.33)
Total (n)	**36 (100)**

*Figures within parentheses are percentages.

Out of 36 EWRs, majority (30 i.e. 83.33 per cent) did not face any such constraint. Only six of them (nearly 17 per cent) responded positively to the asked question. They said that lack of support from the male members acted as the major constraint that hindered them from executing their power and responsibilities. It is worth-mentioning that out of these six respondents, four of them were from the same Panchayat. These six respondents who answered positively were asked the reasons for the constraint. Their responses have been shown with the help of the following diagram.

(No. of respondents=6; Multiple responses were recorded from 6 respondents)

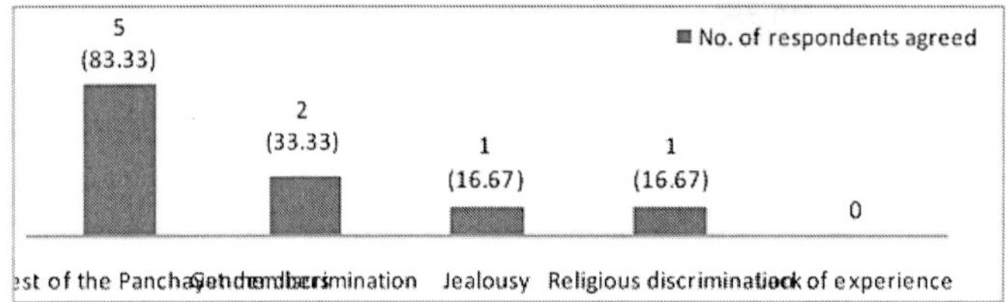

Fig . (e2). Distribution of respondents on the basis of reasons stated by them for lack of support from male members.

*Figures within parentheses are percentages.

Out of six respondents, five of them (83.33 per cent) mentioned that because of their own interests, the Panchayat members did not support them. They faced problems from other Panchayat members due to their self-motive; Panchayat members were exclusively guided by their personal interest. Various political and official issues were responsible for that. Two of them mentioned of gender discrimination and one of them mentioned jealousy to be the cause. It should be mentioned that EWR who regarded jealousy to be the reason was the Pradhan of Golar Gram Panchayat. She stated that as male members, they felt jealous that a woman was holding a superior post than theirs. One of the respondents from Gobardhanpur Gram Panchayat believed that as she was a Muslim, other Panchayat members did not support her. None of the members regarded their lack of experience to be reason behind getting less support from Panchayat male members.

Table (f1) : Not informed or invited to meetings

Response	*Number of respondents*
Yes	5 (13.89)
No	31 (86.11)
Total (n)	**36 (100)**

Out of 36 EWRs, only five of them (13.89 per cent) responded positively to the asked question. They complained that the male members often did not inform them about the meetings. The rest of the EWRs did not face any such constraint. These five respondents who answered positively were asked the reasons for the constraint. Their responses have been shown with the help of the following diagram.

(No. of respondents=five; Multiple responses were recorded from five respondents)

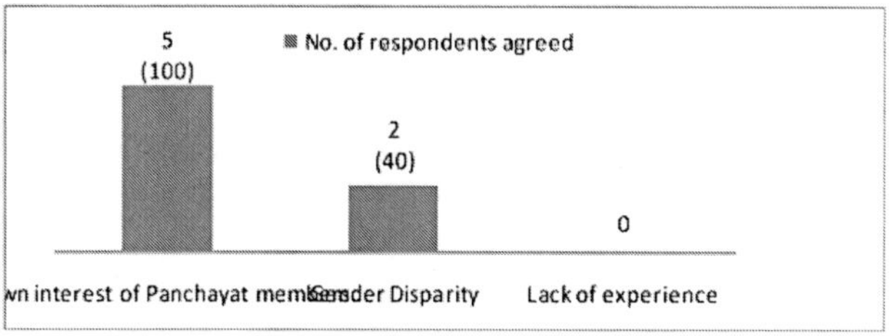

Fig. (f2). Distribution of respondents on the basis of reasons stated by them for not being invited to meetings.

*Figures within parentheses are percentages.

All five of the respondents said that because of their own interests, the Panchayat members did not invite them in important official meetings often. Various political and official issues were responsible for that. They faced problems from other Panchayat members due to their self-motive; Panchayat members were exclusively guided by their personal interest. Two of the EWRs (40 Per cent) regarded gender disparity as the major reason for not being invited to meetings. None of the members regarded their lack of experience to be reason behind not being invited to meetings.

Table (g1) : Not given freedom to express their opinions and take decisions

Response	*Number of respondents*
Yes	6 (16.67)
No	30 (83.33)
Total (n)	**36 (100)**

*Figures within parentheses are percentages.

Majority (30) of the respondents had complete freedom of expression in the meetings. They were not found meek or mute, they usually raised their point and view in the Panchayat meetings. Six respondents expressed that they were not free to put forth their view points and take decisions according to their will which they thought to be necessary. The reasons mentioned by them have been depicted in the following diagram.

(No. of respondents=6; Multiple responses were recorded from 6 respondents)

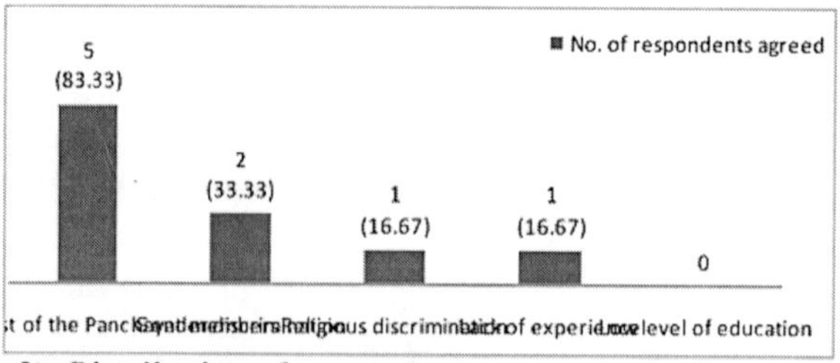

Fig. (g2). Distribution of respondents on the basis of reasons stated by them for not getting freedom to express views and take decisions.

*Figures within parentheses are percentages.

Out of six respondents, five of them (83.33 per cent) mentioned that because of their own interests, the Panchayat members did not support them. They faced problems from other Panchayat members due to their self-motive; Panchayat members were exclusively guided by their personal interest. Various political and official issues were responsible for that. Two of them mentioned gender discrimination. Gender disparity was found to be the major reasons for not entertaining their viewpoints as male members view points. One of the respondents from Gobardhanpur Gram Panchayat believed that as she was a Muslim, other Panchayat members did not entertain her viewpoints. So, religious discrimination was the cause. One of the respondents mentioned of lack of experience.

Table (h1) : Ignorance from villagers

Response	*Number of respondents*
Yes	4 (16.67)
No	32 (83.33)
Total (n)	**36 (100)**

*Figures within parentheses are percentages.

Majority (32) of the respondents faced no such problem. They were widely accepted by the villages. But only from the Kusumda Gram Panchayat, four members complained of ignorance from villagers.

(No. of respondents=4; Multiple responses were recorded from 4 respondents)

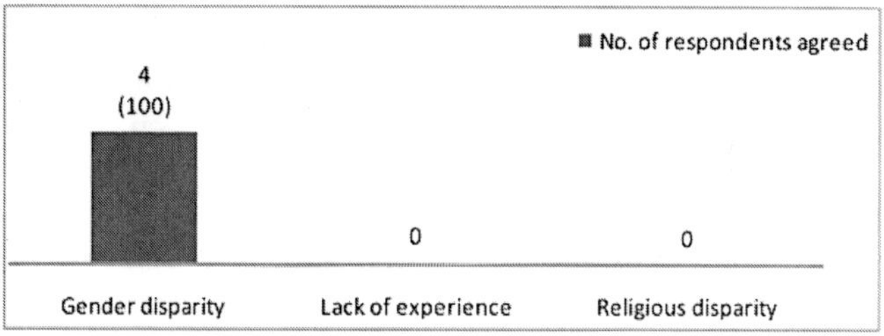

Fig. (h2). Distribution of respondents on the basis of reasons stated by them for ignorance from villagers.

*Figures within parentheses are percentages.

All four of the respondents (100 Per cent) considered gender discrimination to be the only reason as to why they faced ignorance from villagers. The villagers often refused to listen to them and hardly accepted their opinions. The villagers believed that as they were women, they knew nothing and were only holding the post out of reservation.

(i) Political constraints

Frequent political disturbances and other political issues were regarded as constraints by the EWRs that hinder them from implementing their responsibilities and working effectively. (Data could not be provided by the researcher).

B. Respondents: Other male representatives and Government Officials (n=16)

In the context of the present study, the views of other male representatives and Government Officials had also been considered. The study is mainly based on elected women representatives of rural local bodies. The focus was to explore the constraints faced by these women representatives during the execution of their duties and responsibilities. For that reason, it was very important to consider the views of the other male representatives and Government officials regarding the issue. Their views had been considered by the researcher as there were few barriers which were though not regarded as constraints by the EWRs themselves but people who worked with them considered these to be constraints like lack of decision-making power, lack of self-confidence, dependency on other members for taking decisions or for execution of duties.

All the respondents agreed that 33 per cent reservation was definitely required in the PRI system, especially in a country like India where women had been deprived from the decision-making process and had remained under-represented over the years. The reservation had enabled them to participate in the developmental and decision-making process and contribute to the development of rural India.

Table (a1) : Any advantage if a woman holds a post in the PRI

Response	*Number of respondents*
Yes	14 (87.5)
No	2 (12.5)
Total (n)	**16 (100)**

*Figures within parentheses are percentages.

Of 16 respondents, 14 of them (87.5 per cent) mentioned that there were advantages if a woman held any post.

Those who answered positively were asked about the advantages. Options had been provided. (Multiple responses had been recorded. Different combinations of the reasons are possible as multiple responses have been recorded but the researcher has considered single reasons and not combined reasons for the purpose of interpretation.)

(No. of respondents=14; Multiple responses were recorded from 14 respondents)

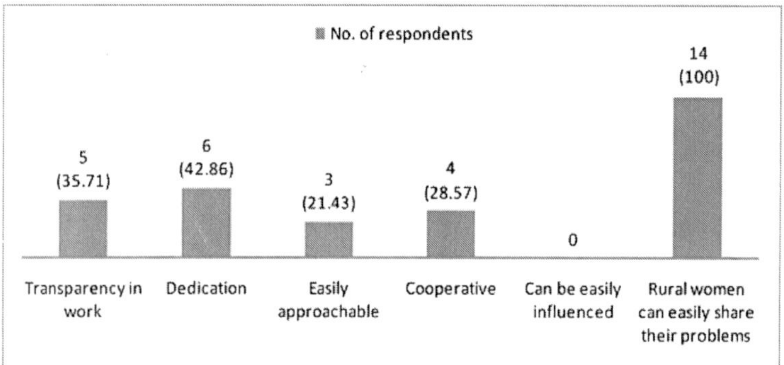

Fig. (b2). Distribution of respondents on the basis of advantages stated by them if a woman holds a post.

100 per cent of the respondents regarded that if a woman held any post in the PRI, rural woman would be able to approach them and share their problems easily, which they would not be able to with male members. Nearly 43 per cent of the respondents considered that women representatives were more dedicated than male representatives. 35.71per cent stated that if a woman held a post, there was more transparency in work as they are honest. Nearly 29 per cent and 21per cent considered that women representatives were easily approachable and were cooperative.

(b) Constraints faced by EWRs

When asked whether the EWRs face any constraint that restrict them executing their power, all the respondents agreed that being women, these representatives did face problems not only in the work sphere but also in their family which hinders their active participation. According to the respondents, the major family constraints faced by the EWRs which acted as stumbling block in the empowerment process included:

- Burden of family responsibilities
- Stereotype attitude of family members
- Over-interference of family members
- Lack of support from family members

One of the respondents opined that the greatest deterrent to women representatives is that they are women. A kind of patriarchal - male dominant social order is the building block to them.

All the male representatives and government officials opined that the women Panchayati Raj leaders did face innumerable number of problems during the execution of their responsibilities. These constraints have been pointed out:

- Indifferent attitude of official working system
- Lack of experience
- Illiteracy and low level of education of majority of the women elected to the PRIs
- Introversion due to lack of communication skills
- Lack of decision-making power
- Lack of self-confidence
- Lack of leadership qualities
- Dependency on other members for taking decisions or for execution of duties
- Lack of support from villagers
- Dependence on others for movement
- Lack of support from other Panchayat members

Majority of the respondents opined that 33 per cent reservation was definitely essential in the PRI system but the government should instruct political parties to select those candidates to contest elections who had minimum knowledge and experience in politics. They supported that EWRs should have minimum educational qualification for contesting election. Some of them even considered that if they were properly motivated and guided, then they could handle power and carry out their responsibilities better than men. Majority of the respondents opined that EWRs lack in decision-making power and leadership qualities and depend on her male colleagues for taking any decision though very few EWRs considered it to a constraint. Some government officials stressed on the process of capacity building through training. One of them believed that contact with outside world would make women more active in the political process. The reservation of women in such organisations alone will not help them to make decisions unless she becomes assertive.

Implications, Recommendations and Conclusion

Implications

Though the Indian Constitution guarantees equal rights for all citizens irrespective of their social and economic status, but in reality such provisions has remained in pen and paper for millions of economically and socially disadvantaged people in India like SCs, STs and women. In India, women are in much worst position than men not only in terms of sex ratio, literacy rate, work force participation, life expectancy. Empowerment of women in every sector-social, economic and political is one of the toughest challenges of the country. The researcher has experienced these constraints of women empowerment, especially political empowerment during the study.

In the context of the present study, the political empowerment of women is reflected through the constraints and problems faced by the Elected Women Representatives during the execution of their duties. The study has reflected that most of the respondents (nearly 61per cent) were comparatively new in politics and had their initiation only in the last 2008 election and the same percentage of respondents had joined politics due to pressure from political parties. This percentage was the highest among the women Panchayati Raj leaders at the village level. They were less experienced than the women representatives at the district level. The study had shown those EWRs who had joined politics willingly could implement their power, execute their duties and carry out their responsibilities more efficiently than those who had been compelled to join the political arena. It is worthy-mentioning that the EWRs at the Zilla level were more dedicated than the others at the block and village level. Most of the women representatives considered that the training provided to them after being elected were not sufficient. Level of education also played a vital role in this regard. Most of the EWRs (78 per cent) found it difficult to manage household chores besides Panchayat works. Conservative attitude of family members restricted them from attending meetings during night and from free movement for work purpose. Various other constraints like inhibitions in speaking in front of male members, lack of support from male members, not being informed about meetings were faced by some of the respondents in their work sphere. Various reasons were responsible behind it. Gender discrimination was found to be the cause for ignorance from villagers. Political disturbances had acted a major barrier.

All these shows that various problems and constraints existed that acted as stumbling blocks in front of these women Panchayati Raj leaders that hinders them from executing their power in true sense.

Recommendations

61.11per cent of the EWRs had their initiation in politics in the last 2008 election with no earlier experience. The situation recommended selection of candidates with minimum experience in politics.

Most of the women were from non-political background and 61.11per cent had entered into politics due to persuasion by local political parties. They should not be pressurised to join politics. Women who reluctantly entered into politics showed great maturity in outlook, enthusiasm, increasing political consciousness and increasing perception of their role and responsibility. It should also be taken into account that EWRs have minimum educational qualification for contesting election.

The study revealed that 87.88 per cent of the respondents agreed that the training provided to them was not effective as most of them were new-comers in politics and the short-duration trainings were not sufficient. Capacity building through training programmes is essential in this regard. Besides there is a need to train the women leaders at regular intervals to enable them to manage the responsibilities assigned to them in the Panchayats at all the levels. Training programmes incorporating skills, knowledge, issues and concerns of women, how to address them, how to organise, cooperate, participate, manage and build alliances, how to network with other women; s collectives, social practices adversely affecting women and how to deal with them, how information and knowledge is to be sought, stored and retrieved and how to maximise strengths and overcome vulnerabilities. It would also help to inculcate leadership qualities and decision-making power in these women representatives.

Contact with outside world would make these women more alert, updated and active in political process. Interaction with educated urban elected representatives should be encouraged.

These women Panchayati Raj leaders need and deserve state support, solidarity and networking with other women s organisations. Support must be given to women s local organisations and alliances. The women should also be encouraged to organise themselves. These EWRs face a lot of constraints not only in their work sphere but also from their family that restrict them from functioning effectively as EWRs. An important effort required for real empowerment of rural women is to bring about an attitudinal change in both men and women. The feeling that women are meant for household activities and rearing children needs to be transformed into a feeling of equal partnership of women and men. To inculcate this, they should be imparted education for bringing about social and political awareness among both.

Conclusion

Political empowerment of women is a slow process and is hard to achieve. Though, through reservation women are holding chairs in the political process but have not been able to be empowered in true sense and several reasons are responsible for it.

The researcher had concentrated her study on the constraints faced by the women elected representatives in the empowerment process. The present study disclosed that these women leaders in spite of holding powerful positions experience many constraints that hinder them from executing their powers and responsibilities and act as a stumbling block in the process of empowerment. To make the process of empowerment of women effective and meaningful, the ultimate objective would be to amputate and sort out these constraints.

References

1. Ambedkar, S. N., and Nagendra, S. (2011). *Women Empowerment and Panchayati Raj*. New Delhi: ABD Publishers, pp. 6-69.
2. Arun, R. (1996). *Role of Women in Panchayati Raj.* The Administrator, Vol. xii.
3. Biju, M. R. (2008). Women's *Empowerment, Politics and Policies.* New Delhi: Mittal Publications.
4. Boraian, P. M. (2008). *Empowerment of Rural Women: The Deterrents and Determinants*. New Delhi: Concept Publishing Company
5. Doshi, S. L., and Jain, P.C. (2004). *Rural Sociology.* Rawat Publications, Jaipur & New Delhi, pp. 329-344.
6. Dutta, S. K., and Ghosh, D. K. (2006). *Institutions for Development: The Case of Panchayats.* New Delhi: Mittal Publications, pp. 43-70.
7. Dutta, P. (1997). Political Empowerment of rural women in India. *Administrative Change*, Vol.xxiv, No. 2.
8. Ganguly, S. *Women in Gram Panchayats, State Institute of Panchayats* and Rural Development (SIPRD), Government of West Bengal.
9. Ghosh, D.K. (1995). Women Panchayat Members as Heads of Offices: A Study in West Bengal. *Journal of Rural Development,* Vol. 14, No. 4, p. 357.

10. Jain, S.P., and Hochgesang, T.W. (1995). *Emerging Trends in Panchayati Raj.* Rajendranagar, Hyderabad: NIRD.

11. Jain, D. (1996). *Panchayati Raj: Women Changing Governance.* Gender in Development Monograph Series, No. 5, UNDP, New York, September.

12. Joseph, V. (2011). *Capability of Elected Women Representatives on Gender Issues in Grassroots Governance.* New Delhi: Concept Publishing Company Pvt. Ltd., pp. 70-148.

13. Kaushik, S. (1995). *Panchayati Raj in Action: Challenges to Women's Role.* New Delhi: Friedrich Ebert Stifleeng.

14. Karl, M. (1995). *Women and Empowerment:* Participation and Decision-Making (Women and World Development Series). United Nations NGO Group.

15. Kaushik, S. (1993). *Women and Politics in India.* New Delhi: Vikas Publishing House Pvt. Ltd.

16. Kabeer, N. (2001). Reflections on the Measurement of Women's Empowerment- Theory and Practice, in: Discussing women's empowerment-theory and practice. Stockholm: Novum Grafiska AB.

17. Kumar, V. (2001). Panchayats and Water Scarcity. *Economic and Political Weekly,* Vol. xxxvi, No. 29, pp. 2752-53.

18. Kumar, A. (2006). *Indian Women in Politics.* New Delhi: Anmol Publishers.

19. Kumatakar, K. (1998). Governance and Representation: A Study of Women and Local Self Government. *Indian Journal of Public Administration,* XLIX (3).

20. Lal, S.K. (2005). *A Study of Issues and Challenges in Empowerment of Women through their participation in the Panchayati Raj Institution:* A Case Study of Allahabad District Of Uttar Pradesh. Delhi: The Women Press.

21. Lele, M.K. (2001). Local Government: Conflict of Interests and Issues of Legitimisation. *Economic and Political Weekly,* Vol. xxxvi, No. 51, pp. 4702

22. Manikyamba, P. (1989).*Women in Panchayati Raj Structures.* New Delhi: Gian Publishing House, pp. 80.

23. Mishra, S. (1997). Women and 73rd Constitutional Amendment Act: A Critical Appraisal. *Social Action,* Vol. 47, pp. 29.

24. Mondal, S., and Ray, G. L. (1999). *Social Research Methodology.* Kolkata: Kalyani Publishers.

25. Narayan, D. (2002). *Empowerment and Poverty Reduction.* Washington, DC: World Bank.

26. Nambiar, M. (2001). Making the Gram Sabha work. *Economic and Political Weekly,* Vol. xxxvi, No. 33

27. Pai, S. (2001). Social Capital Panchayat and Grass root democracy: Politics of Dalit Assertion in Uttar Pradesh. *Economic and Political Weekly,* 35(8): 649.

28. Pai, S. (1997). Women and Panchayati Raj: The Law, Programmes and Practices. *Journal of Rural Development,* 16(4): pp.15-18.

29. Panda, S. (1996). Emerging Pattern of Leadership among Rural Women in Orissa. *Indian Journal of Public Administration,* Vol. 42, No. 3-4.

30. Poonacha, V. (2001). Feminist Theorising and Politics. *Economic and Political Weekly,* Vol. xxxvi, No.29, pp. 3235.

31. Palanithurai, G. (2001). The Genre of Women leaders in local bodies: Experience from Tamil Nadu. *Indian Journal of public Administration.*

32. Rewadikar, N. (2010). *Gram Panchayat Leadership.* Jaipur, New Delhi: Rawat Publications, pp.161-177.

33. Samanta, R. K. (2005). *Empowering Rural Women.* Delhi: The Women Press.

34. Saxena, N. C. (2000). What is meant by people's participation: A note. *Journal of Rural Development.*

35. Singh, S. (2003). *Panchayati Raj and Women Empowerment.* New Delhi: Ocean Books Pvt. Ltd.

36. Sinha, N. (2000). *Women in Indian Politics: Empowerment of Women through Political Participation.* New Delhi: Gyan Publishing House.

37. Sridharan, D. (2009). (Ed) *Journey towards Empowerment.* New Delhi: Friedrich Ebert Stifleeng, pp. 8-17.

38. Sonalkar, V. (1999). An Agenda for Gender Politics. *Economic and Political Weekly,* Vol. xxxiv, Nos. 1 and 2.

39. Vyasulu, P., and Vyasulu, V. (1999). Women in Panchayati Raj: Grass-Roots Democracy in Malgudi. *Economic and Political Weekly,* Vol. xxxiv. No. 52.

40. Vats, S. (2004).*Women's Participation Rural Development.* Delhi: Abhijeet Publication, pp. 87-107.

41. Vidya, K.C. (1997). *Political Empowerment of Women at the Grassroots.* New Delhi: Kanishka Publishers, Distributors.

42. Watane, M.S. (2011). *Empowerment of Women: Panchayati Raj System.* Shodh Samiksha Aur Mulyankan, Vol. III, Issue 28.

43. The American Heritage Dictionary of the English Language. Fourth Edition. 2000.

44. The Harper Collins English Dictionary. Nineth, Edition, 2007.

Websites consulted: http://www.devactivism.org/2010/08/27/political-empowerment-of-women-in-rural-india/ Human Development Report, 2003 Indian Census Report, 2001 UN statistics

http://www.undp.org.in/webbook/Enlrg-spc-wmn-india.html

http://www.devakijain.com/pdf/jain_panchayatraj.pdf

http://www.paschimmedinipur.gov.in http://www.mapsofindia.com/maps/westbengal/districts/westmedinipur.html http://www.census2011.co.in/census/district/18-paschim-medinipur.html http://paschimmedinipur.gov.in/district/index.php

20

People's Participation and Decentralised Planning in Kerala A Revisit: Case Study of Two Village Panchayats

Dr. E. M. Thomas

1. Introduction

The introduction of decentralised planning in Kerala in the year 1996-97 was historic in the sense that, it was built upon the strong foundations of people's participation. In India, the need for effective participation or people in the decentralised planning process was echoed in the study reports of Ashok Metha Committee (1978), S.N. Mishra (1985), and Dant Wala (1986). The new system of planning, expected the people to " act as the watchdog of thc states activity,'' (J.D. Sethi 1990).

The Sen committee report, which is considered as the basic report responsible for the launching and building up of decentralised planning in Kerala, categorically emphasise people's participation as one of the fundamental principles of local planning. Hence, from the year 1996 - 1997, till now, (2013), Kerala has been in the forefront among all the other states in India , in the practice of local planning, with people's participation. Hence, it is high time to evaluate the extent and nature of people's participation as a process by which people, especially the disadvantaged people, influence decisions that affect them. (Bhavan Bhatnagar, 1992) In the opinion of Cerna (1993) in many developing countries, the need for popular participation in the implementation of plan projects emerged because of the following reasons: (a) the enormously expanding role of public sector in launching development projects without a commensurate improvement of the mechanisms for the public's involvement, (b) the growth of international aid which amplifies financial resources, scope and number of government programmes while increasing the distance between the programme's "Centre and periphery '' and (c) the traceability of recurrent failure in public programmes to alienation from their own intended beneficiaries". Moreover, as opined by Norman Uphoff (1992), Participation can be regarded both a means and as an end. People's taking responsibility for their own development is a better way to achieve improvement in economic and social conditions, it is more likely to be successful, more cost-effective and more suitable. It is also desirable because, it enlarges human talents and potential, the fulfillment of which is the most basic objective of development. The present paper is an attempt to study the various avenues for people's participation in the process of local governance and decentralised planning and the performance of various institutions to mobilise peoples participation at the time of launching of decentralised planning 1998–99 and now in the year 2012-13. The study also investigates the various problems in the mobilisation of the participation of people and recommends several suitable policy measures to tackle the problem effectively.

The study is based on the real experience of two village panchayats in Kerala; Viz. Aloor and Nattika, which belongs to Thrissur district. All the vital information regarding the topic had been collected mainly through direct personal interviews of various stake holders of decentralised planning. The minute's books of Grama Sabha meetings and other information were also used to collect reliable and accurate information.

Moreover, various published evaluation reports of decentralised planning, and other study reports were also used extensively to collect vital information regarding the issue of people's participation in the planning process of Kerala during the period from 1996-97 and 2012–13. It is a revisit by the author to the study area after a gap of 12 years. The paper is divided into three sections. The first part presents the various avenues for peoples participation and their performance during two time periods i.e, 1998-99 and 2012 –13, on the basis of the experience of two village panchayats. The second section presents the various problems in the mobilization of the participation of people and the third part suggests some important policy measures to enhance the degree of people's participation.

Section I

Decentralised planning programme in Kerala is based on the strong foundations of people participation. It is one of the basic principles of Decentralised, Planning in Kerala, as envisioned in the Sen (committee Report. In the words of Parameswaran (1999), who is one of the architects of people planning in Kerala, the main feature of decentralised planning in Kerala is the "assurance of mass participation in the development activities of the state".

The major avenues opened up for the participation of people, in the decsntralised planning process are (a) Grama Sabhas, (b) Neighbourhood Groups, (c) Development Seminar (d) Task forces/working groups (e) Beneficiary committee (f) Resource persons and (g) Voluntary contribution.

Grama sabha refers to a body consisting of all persons registered in the electoral rolls related to each ward of a panchayat. According to the eonstitutional Amendment Act, 1992, all the voters in the ward of a panchayat are supposed to attend the Grama Sabha meeting. The Kerala Panchayat Raj Amendment Act 1999 (Act 13) envisages clearly the powers and functions of Grama Sabha as follows.

(a) Assist the Panchayat in collecting valuable data and information which are essential for the preparation of development plans.

(b) Suggest the priorities for the preparation and implementation of development projects.

(c) Selection and ranking of individual beneficiaries for various beneficiary schemes.

(d) Support the panchayat in the implementation of development projects.

(e) Provide necessary assistance to the effective implementation of development projects in the form of voluntary service, money or material.

The Kerala Panchayat Raj Act (1999) clearly specified that, Grama Sabha's should be convened once in three months every year. The quorum for every meeting is specified as 10 Per cent of the total number of voters in each ward. Apart from the above mentioned powers and functions, the Panchayat Raj Act (1999) also envisages 14 other functions to Grama Sabhas. It includes various types of activities related to the provision of street light, water supply, village sanitation, maintenance of social harmony, assistance to beneficiary committees, and other related functions.

Devclopment seminars are organised at the panchayat level- Represstentatives of Grama Sabhas, elected members to the panchayat committee, expert committee members, voluntary workers, and implementing officers are the main participants of this seminar. The development seminars provide a forum for the mutual interaction between representatives from different wards of the Local Self Government Institutions (L.S.G.s I's). The views of different Grama Sabhas are finally coordinated and intesgrated in to one development report, at this seminar.

Task forces or working groups provide another area for peoples' participation. Such groups are formed at the conclusion of development seminars. Each task force will have 10 persons as members. Generally 12 task forces are formed in almost all L.S.G.I.'s. The task forces or working groups are generally related to the following subjects: Viz. agriculture and irrigation, fisheries, animal husbandry, education, health, sanitation, drinking water, industries, roads, energy, housing, culture, welfare of women, cooperatives, welfare of scheduled castes and scheduled Tribes, and resource mobiliation.

Resource person's forms the backbone of plan projects related to local planning. In the initial years of decentralised planning, three types of resources persons were trained by the government, viz. Key Resource Persons (KRP) who work at the state level, District Resource Persons (DRP) at the District level and local Resource Persons (LRP) at the panchayat level. Kerala launched decentralised planning during 1996-97 with the active cooperation of 600 KRP's, 15,000 DRP's and 100000 L.R.P's. In other words, these resource persons, made decentralised planning a reality in Kerala.

The flag ship institution of peoples planning was Beneficiary Committee. Almost all the development projects were undertaken and implemented by the members of various beneficiary committees. It was a dream, came true, to alleviate corruption from the rural development programme. Panchayats had freedom to assign the responsibility of a development project to any other agency or contractor, if and only if, they fail to form a beneficiary committee for the project.

People's participation in planning process becomes meaningful, when, they also start contributing money, material and manpower voluntarily for the completion of the project. Most often, panchayats fail to complete the construction of various infrastructure projects, due to the shortage of resources. Hence, when people themselves, come foreward, and contributes resources voluntarily for the project, the panchayat could, tackle the problem of scarcity of resources effectively.

Another, innovative attempt made by the government to attract more people, especially, retired people, to realm of local planning was the popularisation of the slogan.

"**Life after 55**". It means that, after retirement from government services, employees can start a new life, very active and productive life, by participating in the local development activities. Retired people are treasure houses of vast knowledge and practical experience.

Section II

The performance of the two village panchayats, in the mobilisation of people's participation, provides the real picture of Kerala's local governance today. The study is based on the experience of Aloor and Nattika village panchayats of Thrissur District. Aloor is situated in the midland area of Mala Block Panchayat, and Nattika is a coastal region panchayat of Thalikulam Block.

The extend of peoples participation in Grama Sabha meetings in Aloor and Nattika Grama Panchayat clearly indicates the approach of local population towards decentralised planning. Even though peoples, planning was initiated in the year 1996, it became properly institutionalised, only by the year 1999. Mean time, all the suspicions and initial troubles regarding the new institutions of planning were eliminated, and people began to participate in Grama Sabha meetings with the knowledge and awareness about its functions and scope. Hence this paper attempts to compare between the participation of people in Grama Sabha meetings during the year 1998-99 and 2012–13.

During the financial year 1998-99, both Aloor and Nattika panchayats convened two Grama Sabhas each. In Aloor, they convened their Grama Sabhas, during the month of August, 1998 and January 1999. In Nattika they conducted Grama Sabha meeting during month of August and December 1998. Like wise, Aloor Panchayat convened three Grama Sabhas during the year 2012-13, in the month of August and November 2012 and January 2013 respectively. Nattika convened two Grama Sabha meetings during the same period.

Details regarding the participation of people in Grama Sabhas in the two panchayats during the two time periods are given below in Tables 1(A) and 1 (B) and Tables 2 (A) and 2 (B):

Table 1(A)

Particpation of people in Grama Sabha meetings Aloor – 1998 – 99

Ward	*August 1998*		*January 1999*		*Total voters*	
	Number of parti-cipants	*Percen tage*	*Number of parti-cipants*	*Per-centage*		*Perce ntage Perce*
W1	63	3.38	55	2.82	1949	100
W2	125	5.88	90	4.24	2122	100
W3	149	7.71	136	7.04	1931	100
W4	162	7.79	126	6.06	2077	100
W5	119	6.14	70	3.61	1935	100
W6	118	6.09	84	4.33	1937	100
W7	106	7.26	86	5.89	1460	100
W8	220	12.05	165	9.04	1825	100
W9	120	5.45	144	6.54	2200	100
W10	156	7.38	86	4.07	2111	100
W11	129	6.34	59	2.90	2032	100
W12	134	6.21	70	3.24	2156	100
W13	157	7.98	114	5.79	1966	100
W14	178	9.45	93	4.94	1882	100

Source : Report Book of Grama Sabha – Aloor 1998-99

Table 1 (B)

Participation of people in Grama Sabha in Aloor 2012 – 13

Ward	*August Number of parti-cipants*	*Per-centage*	*November Number of parti-cipants*	*Per-centage*	*January Number of parti-cipants*	*Per-centage*	*Total Number of Voters as per electroal roll*	*Per-centage*
W1	130	9.37	134	9.75	140	10.07	1390	100
W2	102	7.76	132	10.04	132	10.04	1314	100
W3	113	7.60	113	7.60	114	7.65	1490	100
W4	107	6.44	203	12.22	179	10.77	1661	100
W5	153	10.28	153	10.28	156	10.49	1487	100
W6	133	10.49	126	9.95	129	9.87	1267	100
W7	133	11.00	110	9.01	120	9.94	1208	100
W8	123	10.01	121	9.86	122	9.94	1228	100
W9	131	10.01	108	8.33	135	10.41	1296	100
W10	130	10.35	102	8.13	135	10.75	1255	100
W11	147	10.45	151	10.78	151	10.73	1406	100
W12	159	10.45	153	10.09	165	10.89	1515	100
W13	173	9.85	97	5.51	175	9.95	1759	100
W14	146	8.98	148	9.91	167	10.27	1626	100
W15	142	7.55	85	4.51	175	9.31	1881	100
W16	139	8.57	55	3.40	134	8.26	1621	100
W17	97	9.95	97	9.95	97	9.95	975	100
W18	123	8.99	100	7.31	138	10.01	1369	100
W19	156	14.78	150	14.21	155	14.67	1056	100
W20	145	9.47	122	9.98	173	11.31	1530	100
W21	108	6.08	100	5.63	113	6.36	1776	100
W22	186	11.27	182	11.03	183	11.09	1649	100
W23	155	10.45	123	8.28	148	9.98	1482	100

Source : Report Book of Grama Sabha, Aloor 2012-13.

A comparison between the participation of people in Grama Sabha meeting in Aloor Panchayat during 1998 – 99 and 2012-13 as shown in Tables 2 A and 2B, reveals many facts. During the first period (1998-99) the participation of people, was comparatively higher in the meetings convened in August except in ward No. 9, than the second meeting organised in the month of January.

Another notable fact is the variation in the participation of people in different wards. In the second meeting, the participation of people declined from three digit number to two digits, in nine out of fourteen. In Ward No.I, participation of people remained at two digits levels during both months, August and January. Hence, it shows a decline in the interest of people to participate in Grama Sabha meeting. But during the financial year 2012-13; the trend has changed. During this period, the total number of wards also had been increased from 14 to 23. More over the participation of people in Grama Sabha meeting also increased to three digit numbers during the three Grama Sabha meetings except in three wards. Another notable feature is the participation of 10 per cent of the voters in each ward, in their Grama Sabha meetings. It is mainly due to the implementation of Kerala Panchayat Raj Act 1999 which declared the statory minimum attendance of 10 Per cent of the voters in Grama Sabha meetings. As a result all the elected panchayat members worked hard to mobilise local population to the venues of respective Grama Sabha meetings.

Participation of people in the Grama Sabha meetings in Nattika, can be observed from Table 2 (A) and 2 (B)

Table 2(A)

Participation of people in Grama Sabha Meetings -Nattika

Ward	*August 1998*		*December 1998*			
	Number of parti-cipants	*Perce-ntage*	*Perce-ntage*	*Perce-ntage*	*Total Number of Voters as perel-ectoral roll*	*Perce-ntage*
W1	378	23.46	115	7.13	1611	100
W2	136	8.82	216	8.82	1541	100
W3	189	14.62	152	11.76	1292	100
W4	80	5.66	10	0.70	1412	100
W5	149	11.39	126	9.63	1308	100
W6	96	7.98	177	14.71	1203	100
W7	155	8.76	244	13.80	1768	100
W8	52	4.32	138	11.49	1201	100
W9	153	11.67	243	18.53	1311	100
W10	153	9.75	204	13.05	1568	100

Source : Report Book of Grama Sabha – Nattika – 1998 –.

Table 2(B) : Participation of people in Grama Sabha meetings in Nattika Panchayat 2012-13

Ward	*August*		*November*			
	Number of participants	*Percentage*	*Number of Participants*	*Percentage*	*Total Number of Voters as per electoral roll*	*Percentage*
W1	168	11.88	177	12.51	1414	100
W2	132	11.2	140	10.23	1368	100
W3	125	9.41	136	10.24	1327	100
W4	136	9.68	137	10.20	1342	100
W5	131	9.65	145	10.68	1357	100
W6	153	9.99	155	10.12	1531	100
W7	145	9.92	138	9.43	1463	100
W8	158	10.23	160	10.34	1546	100
W9	155	10.00	157	10.12	1550	100
W10	147	1.20	148	10.30	1440	100
W11	142	9.58	147	9.92	1481	100
W12	131	9.78	138	10.31	1338	100
W13	177	12.92	177	12.32	1368	100
W14	182	11.71	189	13.96	1353	100

Source: Report Book of Grama Sabha – Nattika – 2012-13.

Similarly, Tables 2A and 2B reveals the pattern of people's participation in Grama Sabha meetings during two time periods 1998-99 and 2012-13. In Nattika Panchayat unlike Aloor the participation of people were comparatively high during the period 1998-99. They convened two Grama Sabhas during this period, the first in August and the second in December.Moreover, in almost all wards, participation of people was higher in the second meeting, compared to the first. But during the second period, 2012-13, the same trend of increasing participation, of people, could not be ensured by the panchayat.

Moreover the number of wards also has been increased in Nattika from 10 in 1998 – 99 to 14 during 2012 – 13. As in the case of Aloor panchyat, during the second period of 2012 – 13, in Nattika also participation of people in Grama Sabha meeting were just equal to the statutory minimum of 10 per cent.

Another notable feature is the comparatively high attendance of people in the Grama Sabhas of wards 1, 2 ,13 and 14. These wards are situated in coastal area, and the people living there are very poor people, whose only source of living is fisheries and other related activities. Hence, they are eager to understand and receive, the benefits assigned to them by the government, through the panchayat. So, this is the main reason for the comparatively high participation of people in their Grama Sabhas.

A comparative analysis of people's participation in Grama Sabha meetings during the two time periods of 1998-99 and 2012-13, reveals that, there is no remarkable increase in the number of people attending such meetings in both panchayats.

Several reasons were found responsible for the lack of interest and the consequent decline in the participation of people in the Grama Sabha meetings of Aloor and Nattika. A large number of people turned up to Grama Sabha meetings in the initial year, out of their curiosity to understand the meaning and importance of such meetings. After a short period of euphoria and enthusiasm, many people began to think that, Grama Sabhas had only very little to contribute towards the improvement in their living conditions. They began to conceive the concept of Grama Sabha as a programme for the poorest of the poor. So, a large number of people, stopped attending further Grama Sabha meeting.

Lack of awareness among the people, about the real importance of Grama Sabha is another reason. Coupled with these factors, the ignorance and lethargic attitude of the well educated and middle class people, also has caused a decline in the number of people in Grama Sabha meetings.

Another quite interesting factor is the response of beneficiaries of Schemes, like housing, sanitary facilities, cows, and so on. Once their grievances are resolved, most of them did not care to attend further Grama Sabha meeting.

Yet another set of rural people started attending Grama Sabha meeting in the initial years, fearing that, the absence from such meeting will prevent them from enjoying the services from the village panchayat. But later, they understood the fallacy of this belief, and began to keep away from Grama Sabha meetings.

Moreover, several educated people alleged that the quality of discussions held in Grama Sabhas was very poor, and hence they found it totally meaningless to spare time for such meetings. Another group alleged that, they went to grama Sabha meetings to discuss their problem with the various implementing officers. But many of them could not meet them due to the absence of officers in the meeting or the lack of time. The mismatch between the theory and practice of the ideals of Grama Sabha has also disheartened several initial enthusiasts. They felt that in theory Grama Sabha is the main center of power but in practice, it is not so. This paradox also had, kept many people away from Grama Sabha.

- **Development Seminar**

Development seminars are the venues for finalisation of various plan projects. These one day seminars are based on the Grama Sabha/Ward Sabha feed back of various plan projects. Moreover, these meetings are responsible for the proper integration of plan projects prepared at the ward level to one cohesive panchayat plan. So these seminars are very important. The experience of Aloor and Nattika Panchyats in organising development seminars during the two time periods, 1998-99 and 2012-13 will help to reveal the difference in the trends of people attending such seminars. It is evident from the following Table.

Table (3) : People's participation in Development Seminars of Aloor and Nattika Panchayats during 1998-99 and 2012-13

Participants	*Aloor*		*Nattika*	
	Year 1998-99	*Year* 2012-13	*Year* 1998-99	*Year* 2012-13
Representaives from Grama Sabhas	140	68	46	50
Elected representatives to the Panchayat committee	14	23	10	14
Members of expert com mittee and implem enting officers	13	13	13	10
Voluntary works	24	70	63	30
Employees of the panchayat	10	6	12	10
Male	111	90	80	70
Female	94	110	64	65
Total	**205**	**200**	**144**	**134**

Source : Official Records of Aloor and Nattika Village Panchayats.

The Table illustrates clearly the changes in the pattern of people attending development seminars. It is clear from the table that, the participation of people in development seminars is also declining. This decline is chronic in the case of representative from Grama Sabha meeting and voluntary workers. During the period 1998-99, all the development seminars had large number of workers of voluntary associations, particularly Shasthra Sahitya Parishad. But, the later years of decentralised planning witnessed the gradual withdrawal of parishad workers and other social workers from the local plaming process..

It is also evident from the table that, the status development seminars had been declined to the level of an official necessity rather than a vibrant body reflecting the development pulses of the people. The total number of people participated in the development seminars declined from 205 to 200 in Aloor and from 144 to 134 in Nattika Panchayat during the time periods 1998-99 and 2012-13 respectively.

At the same time, almost all the elected representative to the panchayat committee and implementing officer's attended the development seminars with out fail. Moreover, it is mandatory that, one-three of the total participants of development seminars must be women. This statutory condition also had been fulfilled in the two panchyats.

There are many reasons responsible for the decline in the number of people participating in development seminar as discussed below.

Several people participated in the first few development seminars enthusiastically, thinking that, some great changes are going to take place in their panchayats. But later they became so depressed, because of the in ability of panchayats to cater to the needs of the people.

The presence of excessive political interests in the selection of plan projects also, compelled many people to keep away from development seminars. Moreover, personal conflicts between members of various political parties attending development seminars, also prevented many people from attending such meetings anymore.

- **Task forces / working groups**

At the end of the development seminar, task forces or working guoups are constituted to prepare projects on the basis of the recommendations of the seminar. On an average almost all panchayats will have 11 to 12 working groups, related to various areas like agriculture, irrigation, animal husbandry industry, education, health, housing, women's welfare, public works, cooperation, energy and so on.

During the first period 1997-98, Aloor and Nattika had 11 and 13 working groups respectively. But after the launching of Kerala Development Plan, the number of working groups had been reduced to 10 each in both panchayats. Since the number of persons required for each working group is limited, ranging from 10 to 12. Both Aloor and Nattika panchayats could ensure participation of sufficient number of people in their working groups.

Another area of decentralised planning which requires peoples participation is related to the formation of expert committees and involvement of resource persons. In this regard, both panchayats had to witness drastic changes. It is evident from the Table (4), given below.

Table (4) : Participation of experts and Resource persons in the planning process of Aloor and Nattika panchayats during 1998-99 and 2012-13

	Year1998-99		*Year2012-13*	
	Aloor Number of partici-pants	*Nattika Number of partici-pants*	*Aloor Number of partici-pants*	*Nattika Number of partici-pants*
Members of monit orizg committee	7	13	8	8
People involved in the final preparation of plans	10	10	8	8
People participated in writing the development history	15	9	Nil	Nil
Participation of reti red prople	7	9	Nil	Nil
Key resource	1	2	Nil	Nil
District Resource persons	21	5	Nil	Nil
Local Level Res ource person	15	30	Nil	NIl

Source : Official Records of Aloor and Nattika Village Panchayats (1998-99, 2012-2013)

In the initial years of planning, a lot of people cooperated with the local bodies as experts and resource persons. During the period 1998-99, lot of people who retired from government service joined hands with the local bodies, in response to the much publicised slogan " Your life begins after 55". Aloor and Nattika could enjoy the services of svean and nine retired people respectively. Likewise both panchyats could mobilise the services of adequate number of Key resources persons, District resource persons, and local level resource person in both Aloor and Nattika. But the picture changed drastically in the second period of the present study, i.e., during 2012-13. This period is characterised by the absence of participation several categories of people, who were seriously engaged in the planning process of the above mentioned panchayats. It includes people who wrote the development history of the village panchayats, retired people, key resource persons (KRP's), District Resource persons (DRP's) and local level resource persons (LRPs). But , as mentioned in the report of the committee for evaluation of Decentralised planning headed by M.A.Oommen (March, 2009), here also, non expert members dominated the working groups.

Yet another high light of decentralised planning in Kerala is the facility for voluntary contribution of people in the construction works programmes undertaken by the local bodies. During 1998-98, both Aloor and Nattika could complete five and four projects respectively with the voluntary contribution of people. People contributed money for the construction of four ponds, four roads, one thodu, one Television Auditorium and one public health subcentre in Aloor Panchayat during the period 1998-99. Likewise in Nattika, one road, one bund, one colony, and three culverts were completed with the voluntary contribution of man power by the people. But during the period 2012-13, no projects were completed in both panchayats by using the voluntary contribution of people.

In the formation of Neighbourhood Groups, which consists of 40-50 families, both Aloor and Nattika could make tremendous progress. It is particularly true in the case of Nattika where, the number of NHGs increased from 45 in 1998-99 to 130 in the year 2012-13. In the case of Aloor the number of NHG's increased from 130 to 150 during the above period of time. This is mainly due to expansion of Kudumbasree programme, Mahatma Gandhi National Rural Employment Guarantee programme, (MGNREGP) and Ashraya Scheme.

In the case of beneficiary committees, the performance of both Aloor and Nattika are more or less similar. During the period 1998-99, Aloor and Nattika had several active beneficiary committees and they could thus complete 30 and 12 projects respectively, with their involvement. But during the period 2012-13, in both panchayats, real active beneficiary committees are substituted by "paper beneficiary committees". The actual works are done by professional contractors, under the banner of beneficiary committees. The lack of expertise, technology, machinery, raw material, and workers are the main factors responsible for the emergence of this trend in both panchayats. Since people are not coming forward to take up construction works, panchayats had no other option. Hence, it is meaningless to blame the panchayats for the active involvement of contractors in the construction works.

Section III

The revisit to the two villages to evaluate the levels of people,s participation, has taught several valuable lessons. The intense desire of the local people to participate actively in the process of development planning still remains as a distant dream. But, the authorities should learn lessons from their actual experience in mobilising the involvement of people in all the matters related to local development. Hence, the following policy measures may be adopted to increase people's participation in the various institutions of decentralised planning.

At present, many people consider Grama Sabhas as venues for the distribution of various beneficiary schemes to the poor people. As a result, a lot of people began to keep away from such meetings. This misconception must be changed by the authorities. Grama Sabha must be converted in to venues for very vibrant and dynamic discussions related to local planning. This may help to attract the welleducated and middle class people to Grama Sabha.

Another method is the practice of special Grama Sabha, to discuss some local issues. for example outbreak of some contagious diseases, advent of a new development project like a large scale industry, a new road, new irrigation project etc. As in the case of Kasturi Rangan Committee Report, Special Grama Sabha can be convened at each ward, to ward off the doubts of the people regarding the impact of the Report on the lives and livelihood of people living in the Geologically Sensitive areas of Western Ghat.

Sometimes, a little bit of compulsion is necessary for the public welfare. In the case of Grama Sabha meeting, if people do not turn up voluntairly, attendance in the meeting must be made compulsory by the panchayat.The authorities can insist everybody, to produce their certificate of attendance in Grama Sabha Meetings, to enjoy the services provided by the Panchayat. Thus, the denial of services by the Panchayat due to the failure of a citizen to attend Grama Sabha Meetings, at least once in a year may act as a stimulant for all to participate in such meetings.

The disappearance of beneficiary committees was a sad necessity in the rural Kerala. The unholy alliance between bureaucracy, politicians and contractors, is the main reason for the disappearance of Beneficiary committees from Kerala. The glory and importance of beneficiary committees can be regained through the formation of labour banks, and pooling of skilled labour, and experts, at the panchayat level. They should be made wellequipped through proper training and adequate support from the part of the panchayat.

Development seminar is another annual ritual performed in every panchayat in Kerala. The participation of people, in these meetings is also fast declining, mainly due to the failure of the panchyats to deliver. All the Grama Sabha representatives from various wards seldom think about the panchayat as one unit. The narrow outlook and vision of such members are serious bottlenecks to find solutions to development problems at the panchayat level. Moreover the failure of the panchayats to keep their promises, regarding development programmes also had resulted in the decline of peoples participations. Hence, deliberate effort from the panchayat executive committee is needed to alleviate the above mentioned problems.

Experts, resources persons and retired people are also chronically absent in the local planning process today. They had to leave from the scene because of several compelling situational, including deliberate avoidance. This loss of precious human capital should not be allowed to continue. Serious efforts from the part of the government is needed for including the above mentioned category of people in the planning process. Otherwise, the unholy triumvirate of the corrupt bureaucrats, politicians and contractors will turn the clock back and decentralised planning with peoples participations will be replaced by another form of perverted centralised planning. Hence, the authorities should ensure that, all the hurdles towards the enhancement of peoples participation in the local planning process are properly alleviated. What is needed is a strong dedication to the furtherance of the spirit of decentralised planning and political will.

In short, the revisit to the village panchayats of Aloor and Nattika after a period of thirteen years, teaches so many valuable lessons related to peoples participation. Grama Sabhas, in the two panchyats are struggling hard to ensure the patrticipation of the statutory minimum 10 per cent of the voters in each ward. Development seminars are suffering from a steady decline in the participation of people. Task force or working group members are active in both panchayats. The completion of plan projects with the help of beneficiary committees and voluntary contributions from people, still remains a distant dream. The active participation of Kudumbasree activists, and MGNREGP workers, are contributing much to the fast expansion of Neighbourhood groups in both panchayats. In short, even though decentralised planning in Kerala could not ensure maximum participation of people, the existence and perpetuation of various institutions of decentralised planning provides a ray of hope.

References

1. Sethi. J.D. (1990) "Power structure and Decentralisation" in K.S. Ramachandran (ed.) *Development Perspectives,* Vikas Publishing House, New Delhi.
2. Dant wala. M .L. (1986) "Rationale and Limited of Decentralized planning", in Dantawala M.L (ed) *Asian seminar on Rural Development;* Oxford and U.B.H. New Delhi.
3. Mishra, S. N. et.al (1984), "*Participation in Development*", NBO. Publisher, New Delhi.
4. Ashok Metha (1978), "Report on the committee on Panchayat Raj Institutions, Government of India, New Delhi.

5. Bhavan Bhatnagar, William Aubrey (ed) (199)" Participatory Development and the World Bank: potential for change" Book 183, World Bank Discussion papers, The World Bank, Washington DC,
6. Michael Cerna (1992) "The Building blocks of participations – Testing Bottom up planning" Book 166, World Bank Discussion Papers,. The World Bank, Washington DC.
7. Norman Uphoff (1992)"Monitoring and Evaluating popular participation in World Bank Assisted projects", Book 183, World Bank Discussion papers, Washington DC.
8. Parameswarn. M. P.(1999) "Decentralised Democracy in Kerala" (Malayalam) Kerala Shasthra Sahitya Parishad, Thiruvananthapuram.
9. Kerala Panchayat Raj Amendment Act (1999) (Malayalam) Superintendent of the Kerala Government Press, Thiruvananthapuram.
10. Report of the committee for Evaluation of Decentralised planning and Development (March 2009, M A Ommen committe), Kerala institute of Local Administration, (KILA), Thissur.

21

Local Goverance and Solid Waste Management in Kerala : Case Study of a Municipality in Kerala

Justin Thomas

1. Introduction

The launching of decentralised planning in Kerala on 17th August 1996 was an epoch making event in the development history of the state. The people's plan of Kerala has brought the fore the fundamental role of certain variables, basic to the success of the institutions of local self-Government which aimed at social justice and economic development. These variables include important initiatives at the micro level, a think tank at the state level, political and democratic consciousness of the citizens and above all, political will. Kerala had a combination of all these variables, in addition a fully literate population that was also politically aware (George Mathew, 2006). The theoretical, philosophical and economic foundation of decentralised planning in Kerala has been provided by the Sen Committee Report. The basic objectives of decentralised planning in Kerala are to promote local economic development with focus on employment and poverty reduction, reduction in gender disparities, integrated area development, upgrade the quality of basic services provided by local governments with special emphasis on health, education, water supply, sanitation including Solid Waste Management and care for the disabled, improve governance particularly with reference to the transperancy, peoples, participation and responsiveness and to bring about an organic relationship between transfered departments and local governments and bring in role clarity (Oommen M.A. 2009). Hence, it is clear that, Solid Waste Management is one of the major objectives of decentralised planning in Kerala.

This chapter is prepared on the basis of a study conducted in Irinjalakuda Municipality of Thrissur District, with the following objectives. (a). to study the present system of solid waste management, (b). to study the problems related to solid waste management and (c). to suggest some remedial measures to solve the problems associated with solid waste management.

Solid waste is a matter is in the wrong place, implying that, a material becomes waste only when specific owners ceasess to have a use for it (Trivedi , 1996).

According to Purushotam, (1991) Solid Waste relates to substances which are cheaper to be condemned than to make further use of it In short, solid waste is a mixture of organic and inorganic waste materials produced from domestic or commercial activities of the first user.

Municipal Solid Waste (Management and Handling Rules, 2000) states that, Municipal Solid Waste includes commercial and residential wastes included in municipal or notified areas in either solid or semi-solid form, excluding industrial hazardous but including treated biomedical wastes.

In Kerala, waste disposal is a very serious problem due to lack of land area and inadequate techniques as methods for their proper processing and disposal. As mentioned in the economic review (2004) urban solid waste is presently being disposed of unscientifically by dumping it in disposal yards. Such operations of open dumping results in unpleasant odour and air pollution, generation of leach ate polluting ground, surface water and fly, mosquito breeding.

The outbreak of diseases like chickengunia, and dengue fever in Kerala, are due to the unscientific handling and disposal of solid waste. In almost all the municipal areas, situations are same. The speedy growth of population, particularly urban population and the limited facilities for scientific waste disposal are the major problems of urban local bodies and the state.

Lack of financial resources, administrative inefficiency, improper choice of technology, and the irresponsible attitude of the general public towards waste management are the real problems in Kerala's Municipal areas.

2. Present System of Municipal Solid Waste Management in Kerala

In Kerala, the system solid waste management is extremely poor, except in certain pockets. The physical creation of municipal solid waste vary from place to place, depending on the geographical location, density of population, pattern of industrial development, number of hospitals , hotels and markets; In other worlds, the main sources of Municipal waste in Kerala are Houses, Hotels , Markets, Offices and Institutions, Hospitals and Road sweeping.

The most important methods of municipal solid waste management adopted in Kerala are the following:

(a) Land Filling : Land filling is the most widely used method of municipal solid waste management. It is a crude method. The landfills are also known as unstable digestors because it takes more than half a century to stabilise the Petrescible part of solid waste. It caused wastage of resources as results environmental impacts; like foul smell, breeding of mosquitoes and contamination of ground water.

(b) Incineration : It is another method of disposal of solid waste, all over Kerala, particularly in Municipal areas. Conventional incinerators burn municipal solid waste on moving grates in refractory lined chambers.This method is very popular in large cities due to the huge reduction of waste achieved during combustion emission control equipment to trap fly ash other sunder particles.

(c) Composting : Composting is natural degradation process. The composting processes stabilise the petrescible fraction of municipal solid wastes. Both aerobic and anaerobic composting processes are widely used in Kerala for the purpose.

(d) Vermi Compost : It is one of the most widely sought after method of composting. This method involves the stabilisation of organic waste through the consumption by earth worms. Moreover, the combined activity by earth worms and other micro-organisms, convert the biodegradable solid waste into high quality manure. This is preferred, due to its advantages like, high value of vermi compost in the market and the absence of environmental hazards like emission of poisonous gases and foul smell.

3. Clean Kerala Mission and Solid Waste Management in Kerala

In order to enable the local self-government to process the solid wastes, Governments of Kerala initiated a new wing called Clean Kerala Mission. Following are the main objectives of Clean Kerala Mission.

(a) To implement socially acceptable, technically feasible, operationally sustainable, financially viable and entrepreneur oriented waste management services.

(b) To enable the disposal of biomedical wastes through common facility approach.

(c) To improve the environmental conditions of the state through integration of various waste management activities –solid waste, sewage, waste water etc.

(d) To support the enforcement machinery and entrepreneurs drive for clean production and environmental management.

(e) To unleash the creativity and energy of communities, businesses and institutions to protect and improve the natural environment and to make environmental consciousness a preoccupation and cleanliness acts a habit to reverse any chance of ecological collapse.

Later by integrating the Clean Kerala Mission and Kerala Total Sanitation and Health Mission, Kerala Government constituted the Suchitwa Mission in the year 2008. This is the nodal agency for overseeing, advising and supporting sanitation activities of the urban and rural local self-governments in Kerala.

In short, the present methods of management of solid waste in the urban areas of Kerala are land filling incineration and composting. The nodal agency for facilitating and promoting waste management and sanitation development activities in the state is Suchithwa Mission.

4. Case Study of Irinjalakuda Municipality

The problem of waste management can be analysed on the basis of the experience of Irinjalakuda Municipality. Irinjalakuda is a municipality which was established on 2nd February 1936 which belongs to Thrissur District. The total geographical area of the municipality in 33.5 sq.km. with 41 electoral wards. The size of population is about 62,000 and the occupations of the people are agriculture, trade and industry.

Moreover Irinjalakuda Municipality received the 2nd prize in Kerala in the year 2009, for best performing municipality in the area of solid waste management. The main industries in Irinjalkuda are related to the production of soap, coconut oil, vessels and cattle feed.

The health and sanitation department of Irinjalakuda Municipality is headed by a health supervisor and assisted by one health inspector Gr.I, two health inspectors Gr.II, three junior health inspector grade I and six junior inspectors of Gr.II. Along with them there are 41 sanitary workers and 10 contingent workers and two units of Kudumbasree, called Cleansree and Hygenesree.

5. Composition of Solid Waste

The total quantity of solid waste generated per day in Irinjalakuda Municipality is composed of domestic waste, commercial waste, market waste, institutional wastes, bio medical wastes, wastes from streets and drains. The main sources of waste are houses, shops, slaughter house and educational institutions, government and semi government offices markets, and other public places. It is estimated that 5000 kg of waste is generated per day in Irinjalakuda Municipality.

6. Methods of Solid Waste Management

Wastes are collected, every day, directly by the sanitary workers from roads, shops, markets, hospitals, slaughter house, bus stand and other public places. The Kudumbasree workers collect wastes from houses directly.

7. Problem of Direct Collection of Solid Waste

The sanitary workers are divided in to different groups, their work start from 7 am and lasts till 1.pm. Hence, all types of wastes, including solid waste having radioactive effects are pooled together.

Another problem is the lack of protection against the dangers associated with the handling of radioactive E-waste. Most often these workers collect such materials by using their hands. They are ignorant about the hazardous effects of exposure to radioactive materials. These workers most often collect all types of solid waste manually and sometimes with pick axes. They seldom use protective devices like hand gear or glouse. Moreover there are only 74 community bins in the entire municipality to collect waste materials. It is quite inadequate. Due to lack of adequate number of collection bins, at suitable places, with proper spacing, wastes are dumped along road sides and open ground.

Street Sweeping

Traditional method of solid waste management, practiced in Irinjalakuda is sweeping of streets by sanitary workers.

- **Problems of sweeping**

The work schedule of these workers is not properly coordinated. As a result, all the streets and by-lanes are not swept properly. For many days, several areas may remain unswept. Busy streets and premise of temples, Busstand and market places, need sweeping at least two times a day. Moreover, sweepers keep away from duties during holidays. The authorities pay only very little attention towards the health problem of sweepers. So the sweepers who are exposed to all kinds wastes are easy preys to diseases like T.B, fever, and such other diseases.

Transportation of solid waste

Transportation of solid waste from the sources of collection to the final station of disposal, is another serious matter. The vehicles available in the municipality are quite inadequate to transport the solid waste. At present the transportation of waste is done in the municipality by using one Tipper lory, one Tractor trailor, One Pick up van and four hand carts. Moreover Irinjalakuda Municipality does not have any plants to process the solid waste.

Land Fill

Irinjalakuda municipality has 5.5 acre land for the purpose of landfill of solid wastes. But the problem related landfill are many. There are no collection layers, or protection from rag pickers. All types of waste including e-waste and infection bio-medical wastes are dumped together in the same area. It is the feeding ground of flies and rodents. Air pollution and problem of smoke due to the burning of waste is a constant problem to the people living in the nearby areas.

Every year, municipality make public declarations regarding the construction of a plant for waste processing, at the dumping site. But till now it remains a distant dream.

Facility for Production of Vermi Compost

The municipality has plans to promote vermi compost methods to do away with the problem of solid waste profitably. The major costs in connection with the proposed vermi compost production facility are construction of open trenches for discarding waste, collection of waste, construction of compound wall, construction of sorting room and office room. This project also could not be materialised even now.

Solid Waste Management – Practice:

The elected members of Irinjalakuda Municipality are quite aware of the problem of solid waste management and its consequent environmental hazards. It is evident from the published plan document of Irinjalakuda Municipality for the year 2012-13.

This document declares the following methods to do away with the problems related to solid waste management and related health hazards.

- Processing of wastes at the source of origin.
- Practice Biomathmitrism (the processing of bio degradable wastes at it source itself).
- Segregation of Bio degradable and non bio degradable waste.
- Plant for processing of solid waste.
- Mechanisation.
- Production of organic mannure.
- Afforestation.
- Development of infrastructure practices.
- Construction of a plant at the slaughter house in Irinjalakuda Municipal market to process solid waste.
- Start sanitary Engineering Division at the trenching ground.
- Provision of waste and electricity at the trenching ground.
- Purchase a new plot of land to dump degradable solid waste.

These are the proposals for effective solid waste Management, made by the elected members to the Executive Council of Irinjalakuda Municipality. At the same time the project proposal and the estimated, for the same period shows the nature of the paradox. It is clear from the following Tables (1) and (2)

Table 1

Category-wise/sector wise report 2012-13

(Solid waste management)

No.	*Name of Project*	*Total Amount (Rs)*
•	Slaughter House	16775
•	Evening Market	133429
•	Subsidy for solid waste management at source	8413550
•	Sanitary Equipments for radicals of mosquitoes	467610
•	Building a side wall for crematorium	200000
•	Water connection to the Trenching Ground	125000
•	Purchase of Vehicle for transportation of solid waste	60000
•	Construction of stock pit at the slaughter house	10000
•	Construction of slide wall around the slaughter house	260000

Source: Plan Document of Irinjalakuda Municipality -2012-13.

Table 2

Category-wise/sector-wise Report 2013-14

(Solid Waste Management)

No.	*Name of Project*	*Total Amount (Rs)*
•	Purchase of Sanitary Equipments, Eradication of Mosquitoes	357625
•	Subsidy for solid waste disposal at source	728850
•	Sidewall Crematorium Building	2900000
•	Incinerator Trenching Ground	150000
•	Stock pit construction waste water at Govt. Ayurveda Hospital	60000
•	Purchase of vehicle for transportation of solid waste	600000
•	Side wall – Trenching Ground	800000
•	Reconstruction of side wall slaughter house	9131
•	Thaliakonam Crematorium Side Wall	950000

Source: Plan Document of Irinjalakuda Municipality -2013-14.

A comparison between the category-wise report of the plan document of Irinjalakuda Municipality for the two consecutive years 2012-13, 2013-14 reveals the scope of decentralised planning in facilitating solid waste management. Out of the 12 project proposal suggested by the elected members eigth could not be materialised even now.

But the proposed projects for segregation of solid waste and recycling of waste, Mechanisation, production of organic manure and plant for processing solid waste are very important. In this regard the performance of the municipality is not satisfactory at all. It does not mean that; the municipality is back tracking from its avowed promises. The projects which were undertaken by the municipality and the fund allotted for them during the period 2012-13 and 2013-14 clearly indicate that, the municipality is very much interested and active in implementing projects for solving the problem of solid waste management.

The inability to implement several projects reveal the size and dimensions of the problem of solid waste management. The failure of the municipality to undertake several projects related to solid waste management are inefficient use of funds, lack of availability of land, lack of experts and lack of officers with social commitment to implement and supervise various projects

Even though there are many problems and drawbacks, Irinjalakuda Municipality could achieve several milestones in the area of solid waste management. As a recognition for their efforts in this field Govt. of Kerala, selected this municipality as the second best municipality in the state. This municipality is in the forefront of other LSGI's, in the process of disposal of waste at the sources of origin. For.example, all the waste in the market are supplied free of cost to the farmers residing within the radius of five kms, it has got two advantages :

- removal of solid waste from the market, and
- promotion of agricultural production through the supply biodegradable waste which farmers can vary effectively use in their farms.

Moreover the municipality is very strict to enforce the policy of processing of wastes from poultry farm, poultry shops, hospitals and industries within their own premises at their own costs.

Another very important and successful scheme introduced in Irinjalakuda is the night vigil programme to find out the people who deposit their wastes at road side and public places. The health workers during their regular patrol time, identify the register number of the vehicles used by the culprits to deposit their waste items at road side, and report the matter to the Road Transport Officer. Till now more than 40 such people were caught red handed and penalised by the municipality.

The segregation unit of Irinjalakuda is one of the best performing units in Kerala. They segragate the non biodegradable waste and collect the plastic materials which is sold to traders from Tamilnadu at a price. Every year municipality had to pay Rs 8, lakh as wages to the workers of the unit. The daily wages of the labour is working in the unit is Rs 377. But now Irinjalakuda Municipality has got a new project from the central government worth

Rs 5, Lakhs. Hence, it has been decided by the municipality to employ MGNREGA workers who receives Rs, 180 per day as wages, to do the work in the segration unit. Thus, the municipality expect to reduce the cost of solid waste management on the one hand and to provide more work days to the MGNREGA workers. Irinjalakuda is the only municipality, which had received the project in the state.

8. Policy Measures to Improve the Process of Solid Waste Management

On the basis of the study of the unique problem and prospects of Irinjalakuda Municipality in the field of solid waste management following policy measures are suggested.

1. *Effective utilisation fund:* In fact there is no scarcity for funds to implement solid waste management programmes. Both the Central and State Governments are composting each other to provide fund to LSGI's for this purpose. But, due to technical reasons, and laxity from the part of authorities funds could not be utilised properly in time. Most of the projects sanctioned by the governments are time bound projects. The inability to the municipality in this aspect should be corrected properly.

2. *Enhancement of the social commitment of staff member of health department:* This is very important, because in the case several projects, they remain incomplete only because of the lack of effective and timely intervention of the responsible officers.

3. *Conscientation of Students:* Training should be given to the school students regarding healthy ways of disposal of solid waste. They should be trained to make bio gas plants and preparation of vermi compost and other methods of converting the waste into useful things.

4. *Conscientisation of the general public.* The educated middle class, living in flats and villas are the main agents who deposit solid waste at road sides and public places. So governement should, with the active support of media, conscientise the general public regarding the health hazards they are creating in the locality.

5. *Fix a given percentage of plan fund for solid waste management:* Just like allotment of a fixed percentage of money for gender budgeting, in the case of solid waste management also a given percentage of the budgetary allocation should be assured every year. This will help the L.S.G.I's to implement various projects in the solid waste management section without the fear of scarcity of funds.

6. *Plastic processing and granule making units:* The use of plastic granules in the tarring works of public roads, open up new opportunities for the proper use of non biodegradable materials like plastic. Hence, plastic granule making units should be opened in every municipality.

7. *Regular sweeping of busy streets:* It is very essential for eliminating solid waste from busy street. Most often sweepers sweep straight only one time every day. This must be changed and it should be made compulsory to sweep busy streets and junctions two times a day.

8. *Intervention of municipal authority in the public places which were given by this municipality on auction for a given period:* Most often places like comfort stations were leased out to contractors by the municipality. In the case of the contractors, the ultimate goal is maximum profit rather than public welfare. So, the person who takes the public property like comfort stations on lease or rent, give less importance for the proper upkeep and maintenance of the asset. Hence, in such cases provision should be made for the timely intervention of government officials, to ensure that quality services are provided by the contractor.

9. *Ensure the cleanliness of the evening fish market:* The evening fish market of Irinjalakuda municipality is one of the most dirty and unhygienic places. Hence, immediate action should be made, to construct a biogas plant, at the evening market. More over the sweepers should be asked to sweep the fish market, at least in the evening time.

In short, solid waste management is a huge task, which is so difficult to handle. The nature of the problem is not an excuse for running away from the responsibility. The major problem of solid waste management faced by Irinjalakuda Municipality are insufficient utilisation of fundlack of land ,lack of transportation facilities, lack of technology and severe lack of committed officials. The decentralised planning process had helped the municipality to overcome many of its problems related waste management. The municipality can perform better in the future by overcoming hurdles posed by the problems discussed above.

References

1. George Mathew (2006), The peoples plan : Premise and Experience in Joseph Tharamangalan (ed) *Kerala : The panadoxes of public action and development, Orient longman.*
2. Oomen M. A. (2009) Report of the committee for evaluation of decentralised planning and development (M. A. Oomen) Government of Kerala, Kerala institution for local Administration KILA, Thrissur.
3. Trivedy P. R. Gurudeep Raj (1996), S*olid Waste pollution, Ashadeep Publishers.*
4. Purushotam Khanna,Vijay Kulkarni (1991), "Towards a waste utilisation policy in India," *Productivity*, Vol. 32 (4) Jan- March.

5. Municipal Solid waste, (Management and Handlling Rules (2000) Ministry of Environment and Forests Notification, Government of India (25th Notification).
6. Economic Review (2004), State Planning Board, Thiruvananthapuram.
7. The Official records of Irinjalakuda Muncipality.

22

A Study on Consumer Awareness Among Rural Households With Special Reference to Palakkad District

Savithri, K.B.

1. Introduction

The Process of development along with the expanding globalisation and liberalisation process has increased the number of consumer related issues. Consumer protection has earned an important place in the political, economic and social agendas of many nations. In India, the government has taken many steps including legislative, to protect consumers. Rural India is vast with unlimited opportunities. It accounts for about 74 per cent of the total population. The growing Indian population, particularly the middle class and the rural segments, present an opportunity to makers of branded products to convert consumers to branded products. The Indian rural market with its vast size and demand base offers a huge opportunity for investment. Rural India has a large consuming class. **"Go rural"** seems to be the latest slogan. Rural market simply means markets in rural areas. The rural folk are simple in living and very much culturally diverse. The major portion of rural population consists of low and middle income groups. We can see vast scattered markets in rural areas.

The slogan 'Jago Grahak Jago' has now become a household name as a result of the publicity campaign undertaken in the last four years. Through the increased thrust on consumer awareness in the XIth Five Year Plan, the government has endeavoured to inform the common man of his rights as a consumer. As part of the consumer awareness scheme, the rural and remote areas have been given top priority in Consumer Market.

All the people participate in the market either as consumer or seller or producer, any person who buys a commodity or service for direct use or ownership. I, you, we are all consumers when we buy a product or service. In free market economics, consumers dictate what goods are produced and are generally considered the centre of economic activity. Individual consumption of goods and services is primarily linked to the consumer's level of disposable income, and budget allocations are made to maximize the consumer's marginal utility.

Consumer awareness is the process of creating awareness in the minds of consumers about products and its related aspects. Consumer awareness can be achieved only through consumer education. Education is a lifelong process of constantly acquiring relevant information, knowledge and skills. Consumer education is an important part of this process and is a basic consumer right that must be introduced at the school level. Consumers by definition include all citizens who are, by and large the biggest group, who are affected by almost all government, public or private decisions. The most important step in consumer education is awareness of consumer rights. However, consumer education is incomplete without the responsibilities and duties of consumers, and this influences individual behaviour to a great extent. The main limitation faced by a rural consumer is the limited access to information about the products.

The study on Consumer awareness is of great significance nowa day's especially in Kerala being the largest consumer state. It is important to ensure that the consumers are well aware about their rights and various laws prevailing in the country to protect them. Many people are ignorant of their rights to get protected against the exploitation by so many others. So when there is a forum for such redress of grievances there seems to be no such exploitation by many; and become arare one.

2. Literature Review:

Dr P Jayasubramanian and A Vaideke (2012) conducted "A study on Consumer awareness and attitude towards consumer protection measures". They found that the consumer protection measures are not aware to general public because of lack of proper communication. So in this context it is necessary to say that information should reach to each and every individual consumer. It further reveals that government brings out lot of measures to protect consumer, but the consumers are not using it properly. Because of this the sellers remains as dominators of the market. So there is a need for a cooperative effort to protect the consumers from the consumers, business and government.

Jatinder Kishtwaria (2012) made a "eomparative study for consumer awareness among males and females of Kangsra district of Himachal Pradesh". In this study he says that Television is the main media for both the males and the females respondents which influenced in their buying and there existed a significant difference between the awareness level of the male and the female respondents regarding customer laws, male were more aware about the popular consumer technolo, gies than the female.

Suraiya Ishak and Nurfaridah M (2012) in their study "Impact of consumer awareness and knowledge to consumer effective behaviour" says there is a significant relationship between awareness and effective consumer behaviour. The result demonstrates that awareness is prior to effective consumers behaviours. While awareness leads to ignorant and up holding their rights against seller's frauds. The awareness of consumer's rights serve as soft-control mechanism aiming at creating more responsible business society.

Arivazhagan R and Geetha P (2011) conducted "A study on consumer awareness and satisfaction towards orange flavoured soft drinks in Tamil Nadu. They found that one of the yardsticks to measure the success of any brand or product is the quantum satisfaction in products. Every advertisement intends to communicate some message to create awareness about the brand or product and to create a desire to purchase. These advertisements in production and outside pressures create the consumption more difficult. Outside pressures become increasingly refind and harder to resist. It is necessary to the present generation to keep themselves well aware and active to be able to take the ultimate decisions in the market.

Aastha Khurana (2010) in study "Consumer awareness as a market approach" found that consumer awareness is about making the consumer aware of his/ her rights. It is a marketing term which means that consumers are aware of products or services, its characteristics and the other marketing P's (Place, Price and Promotion).

Mohammed Yaqoob Khan (2010) conducted a study on "Consumer awareness and protection in Indian context". In this study he found that consumer protection was given importance in the past. Kautilya's "Arthashasthra" mentions the protection of consumer's interests against exploitation by producers and sellers. Malpractices such as adulteration, overcharging and under weighting of goods were considered as punishable offenses. According to Indian ethos an ideal consumer is alert, responsible and environmentfriendly buys only when there is need, prevents herself/ himself from being cheated and knows his/ her rights and duties.

Rishikamella conducted "A study on consumer awareness in rural villages of Bhopal". He found that consumers are exploited in a number of ways in the market. They find themselves difficult to protect their interests. Sometimes traders indulge in unfair trade practices such as underweight, under measurement, adulteration etc.. Measures are – rules and regulations are required to protect the interests of consumer awareness should be made, and consumers should know their rights and duties.

Gupta M and Ogale N in their thesis "A study on consumer movement in India and it's importance" says that in India the consumer movement act as a social force originated with the necessity of protecting and promoting the interests of consumer against unethical and unfair trade practices like hoarding, black marketing, adulteration of food etc. gave birth to the consumer movement in organised form in the 1960's. Till the 1970's, consumer organisations were largely engaged in writing articles and holding exhibitions. They formed consumer groups to look in to the malpractices in ration shops and overcrowding in the road passenger transport. More recently India witnessed an upsurge in the number of consumer groups.

2. Objectives of the Study

- To study the purchasing habit of rural consumers in Palakkad district.
- To understand the consumer awareness about consumer protection, consumer rights and standardisation marks etc.
- To study the effect of advertisement on rural consumers.
- To understand the consumer awareness among rural households regarding consumer goods and study various habits of consumers in relation to the gender.

Palakkad district of Kerala state was selected for the study. The required data for study is collected by way of primary and secondary sources. Primary data is collected by way of questionnaire. The secondary data that was needed was collected by referring books, journals, internet etc. The study was conducted by administering the questionnaire among 60 rural consumers in Palakkad district by way of convenient sampling method. A detailed analysis is made by taking information from the questionnaire. The interpretations of the data are carried out by applying the statistical tools such as simple percentage method.

3. Data Analysis and Interpretation

Table 1 : Showing the Gender of the Respondents percentage

S.No.	*Gender*	*No. of Respondents*	*Per cent of Respondents*
1	Male	30	50
2	Female	30	50
Total		**60**	**100**

Source: Primary data.

Table 1: shows gender wise classification of respondents. 50 per cent of respondents are males and 50 per cent are females.

Table 2 : Age-wise elassification of Respondents

Sl.No.	*Age Group*	*No. of Respondent*		*Per cent of Responses*	
		Male	*Female*	*Male*	*Female*
1	15-25	-	4	-	13
2	25-35	14	16	47	53
3	35-45	6	4	20	14
4	45 & Above	10	6	33	20
Total		30	30	100	100

Source: Primary data.

Table 2 shows age-wise classification of respondents. Majority of the respondents i.e; 47 per cent of male respondents and 53 per cent of female respondents are in the age group of 25-35 .

Table 3 : The Annual Income Earned By The Respondents

Sr.No.	*Categories*	*No. of Respondents*		*Per centag of Responses*	
		Male	*Female*	*Male*	*Female*
1	Below 10,000	6	8	20	27
2	10,000-20,000	10	16	33	53
3	20,000-30,000	8	2	27	7
4	30,000-40,0000	2	-	7	-
5	Above 50,000	4	4	13	13
Total		**30**	**30**	**100**	**100**

Source: Primary data.

Table 3 shows in come -wise classification of respondents.Out of 60 the respondents the majority i.e. 33 per cent of males and 53per cent of females falls under the category of 10,000-20,000 income category.

Table 4: Examination of The Expiry Date of Items

Sl.No.	*Response*	*No. of Respondents*		*Per cent of Responses*	
		Male	*Female*	*Male*	*Female*
1	Yes	26	22	87	73
2	No	4	8	13	27
Total		**30**	**30**	**100**	**100**

Source: Primary data.

Table 4: shows response of the respondents in the examination of expiry date of items .Out of respondents 87 per cent of Male and 73 per cent of Female respondents examines the expiry date of the products bought. Male respondents are slightly more cautious in examining expiry date than Female respondents.

Table 5 : eross-checking of the weights of products items mentioned on the bought

Sr.No.	*Response*	*No. of Respondents*		*Per cent of Responses*	
		Male	*Female*	*Male*	*Female*
1	Yes	4	6	13	20
2	No	26	24	87	80
Total		**30**	**30**	**100**	**100**

Source: Primary data.

Table 5 shows response of the respondents' cross checking of the weights of products mentioned on the items bought. Out of the 60 respondents majority of the male and female respondents do not cross-check the weights of the products mentioned on the items. But, 13 per cent of male and 20 per cent female respondents are interested in cross-checking the weights of products.

Table 6: Checking of the Price of Goods Bought From Alternative Sources

Sr.No.	*Response*	*No. of Respondents*		*Per cent of Responses*	
		Male	*Female*	*Male*	*Female*
1	Yes	24	20	80	67
2	No	6	10	20	33
Total		**30**	**30**	**100**	**100**

Source: Primary data.

The results of table reveal that the respondents are duly interested in checking the prices of goods from alternative stores too. 80 per cent of male and 67 per cent of females are interested in gathering the information about the prices of products prevailing in the stores.

Table 7 : Check the M.R.P Before Buying the Product

Sr.No.	*Response*	*No. of Respondents*		*Per cent of Responses*	
		Male	*Female*	*Male*	*Female*
1	Yes	20	24	67	80
2	No	10	6	33	20
Total		**30**	**30**	**100**	**100**

Source: Primary data.

Table 7 shows that 80 Per cent of female and **67 Per cent of male** respondents checks the M.R.P. before buying the product.

Table 8: Satisfactory Level of Complaints Made to the Authority

S.No.	*Response*	*No.of Respondents*		*Per centage of Responses*	
		Male	*Female*	*Male*	*Female*
1	Yes	14	6	46	20
2	No	16	24	54	80
Total		**30**	**30**	**100**	**100**

Source: Primary data.

Table 8 shows 46 per cent of male respondents and 20 per cent of female respondents opinioned that there complains were treated to their satisfaction. The results of study enlightens that to a large extent the queries made by the customers are not treated to their level of satisfaction.

Table 9: Awareness of the Consumer Courts for Redressal of Grievances of Consumers

S. No.	*Response*	*No.of Respondents*		*per cent of Responses*	
		Male	*Female*	*Male*	*Female*
1	Yes	20	10	67	33
2	No	10	20	33	67
Total		**30**	**30**	**100**	**100**

Source: Primary data.

Table 9 shows 67 per cent of male respondents are aware of the consumer courts for redressal of these grievances; female respondents are having little knowledge about the consumer courts.

Table 10: Case of Filing of a Case in Consumer Court:-

S.No.	*Response*	*No.of Respondents*		*per cent of Responses*	
		Male	*Female*	*Male*	*Female*
1	Yes	0	0	0	0
2	No	30	30	100	100
Total		**30**	**30**	**100**	**100**

Source: Primary data.

The results of the study are so fascinating that neither the male nor the females had filed a case in consumer court.The table reveals that the respondents have no aggressiveness towards filing the case in the consumer courts.

Table 11: Awareness of the Procedure to File a Case in the Consumer Court

S.No.	*Response*	*No.of Respondents*		*per cent of Responses*	
		Male	*Female*	*Male*	*Female*
1	Yes	10	8	33	27
2	No	20	22	67	73
Total		**30**	**30**	**100**	**100**

Source: Primary data.

Table 11 reveals that more than half percentage of the consumers are not aware of the procedure to file a case in the consumer courts and a serious detect and measures should be taken to make them aware of the procedure to file a case in consumer courts.

Table 12: Awareness on the Right as a Consumer

S.No.	*Response*	*No.of Respondents*		*per cent of Responses*	
		Male	*Female*	*Male*	*Female*
1	Yes	18	18	60	60
2	No	12	12	40	40
		30	30	100	100

Source: Primary data.

Table 12: shows that Consumers should have knowledge about the rights to be exercised by him/her.

Table 13: Awareness About ISO and Other Standards Made by Government

S.No.	*Response*	*No.of Respondents*		*Per centage of Responses*	
		Male	*Female*	*Male*	*Female*
1	Yes	28	22	93	73
2	No	2	8	7	27
Total		**30**	**30**	**100**	**100**

Source: Primary data.

Table13: shows that 93 per cent of male and 73 per cent of the female respondents know about the ISO and other standards made by the governments.

Table 14: Awareness about the Taxation of Sticker Prices

S.No.	*Response*	*No.of Respondents*		*Per centage of Responses*	
		Male	*Female*	*Male*	*Female*
1	Yes	20	18	67	60
2	No	10	12	33	40
Total		**30**	**30**	**100**	**100**

Source: Primary data.

Table 14: shows that more than half of the customers believe the sticker prices to be taxed. The sticker price of the products makes them reliable and generates good faith in the health of the customer.

Table15 : Buying Decisions of the Respondents

S.No.	*Response*	*No.of Respondents*		*Per centage of Responses*	
		Male	*Female*	*Male*	*Female*
1	Price	12	8	40	27
2	Quality	12	14	40	46
3	Brand	4	-	13	-
4	Features	2	2	7	7
5	Warranty	-	6	-	20
Total		**30**	**30**	**100**	**100**

Source: Primary data.

Table 15: shows that 40 per cent of male respondents and 27 per cent of the female respondents make their buying decisions based on the prices of the product. 40 per cent of male and 46 per cent of the female respondents prefer quality of products while making the buying decision.

Table 16 : Awareness Selling Higher Than the M.R.P Is Illegal

S.No.	*Response*	*No.of Respondents*		*Per centage of Responses*	
		Male	*Female*	*Male*	*Female*
1	Yes	30	30	100	100
2	No	-			
Total		**30**	**30**	**100**	**100**

Source: Primary data.

Table 16 : shows 100 per cent of male and female respondents only know that selling higher than M.R.P is illegal.

4. Findings

- Majority of the respondents i.e, 47 per cent of male respondents and 53 per cent of female respondents are in the age group of 25-35.

- Thirty three per cent of males and 53 per cent of females falls under the category of 10,000- 20,000 income category.
- Out of total respondents 87 per cent of Male and 73 per cent of Female respondents examines the expiry date of the products bought. Male respondents are slightly more cautious in examining expiry date than Female respondents.
- Out of the 60 respondents majority of the male and female respondents do not cross check the weights of the products mentioned on the items. But, 13 per cent of male and 20 per cent female respondents are interested in cross-checking the weights of products.
- Eigthy per cent of female and 67 per cent of male respondents checks the M.R.P. before buying the product.
- The results of study enlightens that to a large extent the queries made by the customers are not treated to their level of satisfaction.
- Sixty seven per cent of male respondents are aware of the consumer courts for redressal of these grievances; female respondents are having little knowledge about the consumer courts.
- The respondents have no aggressiveness towards filing the case in the consumer courts.
- More than half percentage of the consumers are not aware of the procedure to file a case in the consumer courts and a serious detect and measures should be taken to make them aware of the procedure to file a case in consumer courts.
- More than half of the customers believe the sticker prices to be taxed. The sticker price of the products makes them reliable and generates good faith in the health of the customer.
- Ninety three per cent of male and 73 per cent of the female respondents know about the ISO and other standards made by the governments
- Forty per cent of male and 46 per cent of the female respondents prefer quality of products while making the buying decision.

5. Suggestions

- It is possible only through consumer education the consumer must be educated about the following aspects like what to buy, How much to buy, Where to buy, How to buy and How to Use.
- Local seminars must be conducted in rural areas to make the consumer aware about Consumer Protection Act, Various laws prevailing in the system, existence of consumer courts and various redressal measures etc.

- Consumer movements or consumer clubs must be organised under each Panchayath.
- Cable TV which is increasingly available in villages should be made better use for offering consumer information.
- Banners with slogans and appeals should be used in public places and on public buildings to create awareness among consumers.

6. Conclusions

Be an alert customer is the only remedy against being exploited by the sellers. Consumer awareness being the awareness of a consumer about the 4 Ps of Marketing mix, we can conclude that rural consumers are less aware about their rights and laws for protecting them. Only a low percentage of consumers take care regarding the manufacturing date, expiry date, label awareness etc. Many of them highly rely on advertisements to make their purchasedecision.The general awareness needed by a consumer like consumer rights, laws governing them, various redressal measures etc. are also lacking. So necessary measures have to be initiated by the government and concerned authorities to create awareness among consumers.

BIBLIOGRAPHY

Books

- Consumer Awareness and Information Needs Survey 2001 Bhattacharya D. K, Research methodology, Published by Excel Books 2004.
- Consumer behaviour, Leon G Schiff man.
- Marketing Research, Donald S Tull.
- Business & Economics reports.

Websites

- http://in.answers.yahoo.com
- http://www.consumerdaddy.com
- www.wikipedia.com
- http://business.gov.in
- Www. Ask.com

23

An Overview of Integrated Child Development Scheme (ICDS) on the Nutritional Status of Children in the Rural Areas of Kerala

Dr N. Karunakaran

1. Introduction

Integrated Child Development Service (ICDS) scheme is the largest national programme for the promotion of the mother and child health and their development, particularly in the rural areas of India. The beneficiaries include children below six years, pregnant and lactating mothers, and other women in the age group of 15 to 44 years. The package of services provided by the ICDS scheme includes supplementary nutrition, immunisation, health check-up referral services, nutrition and health and pre-school education. The distribution of iron and folic acid tablets and mega dose of vitamin A is also undertaken, to prevent iron deficiency anemia and exophthalmia respectively. The scheme rendered services mainly through workers at the rural village centre named "Anganwadi". Reduction in the prevalence of service grades of malnutrition and better utilisation of service of national nutritional anemia prophylaxis programme and national programme for prevention of nutritional blindness due to vitamin A deficiency are mainly focused by ICDS. This scheme is one of the important programmes in the country that aims at the holistic development of an individual. The reduction in prevalence of severe malnutrition is comparatively more significant in ICDS scheme. There has been an extensive improvement in the nutritional status of children living in rural and tribal areas, particularly those belonging to depressed sections of the community.

The ICDS scheme,which is the largest, programmes for promotion of maternal and child health and nutrition in India was launched in 1975 in pursuance of the National policy for children. ICDS is a multi-sectoral programme and involves several government departments and is coordinated at the village, block, district, state and central government level. The primary responsibility for the implementation of the programme lies with the Department of Women and Child Development at the centre and nodal departments at the states like social welfare, Rural Development, Tribal Welfare or Health Department or an independent department. It is one of the largest early child care programmes for improving the nutritional status of women and children by providing an integrated package of services to the beneficiaries.

Integrated Child Development Services is an integrated approach for the development of women and children from disadvantaged sections across the life style. ICDS programme was conceived in Kerala since 1975 with an integrated delivery package of early childhood services so that their synergistic effect can be taken full advantage of the scheme. The scheme targets the most vulnerable groups of population including children up to six years of age, pregnant women and nursing mothers belonging to poor families and living in disadvantaged areas including backward rural areas, tribal areas and urban slums. The identification of beneficiaries is done through surveying the community and identifying the families living below the poverty line.

The first ICDS project in Kerala was set up in 1975 at Vengara Block in Malapuram district under the first batch of projects launched in the country. At present there are more than 33000 Anganwadi centres functioning in 120 ICDS blocks in the state. The remaining 32 blocks have Balawadi centers set up by the State Government. The government has initiated steps to convert this Balawadicentres also into ICD Scenters. Out of the ICDS blocks in the state, 111 are in rural areas, one in tribal area and eight in urban areas. It is estimated that 10.32 lakh women and children in the State have benefited from this scheme. In 2012-13, the SNP programme under ICDS benefited nearly 8.55 lakh children in the age group of 0- 6 years and 1.68 lakh pregnant and lactating women. Nearly 4.4 lakh children in the age group of 3-6 years were benefited for pre–school education in 2012-13.

India which account for 46 per cent of India's children are under the age of three are underweight and highest percentage of undernourished children in the world (NFHS-3). Though the Health indicators of Kerala are higher, compared to other state in India, the situation of nutrition in critical sectors and areas of population does not portray a rosy picture. There is widespread prevalence of malnutrition in the form of underweight, low birth weight, wasting, stunting, anemia and other manifestations of micro-nutrient deficiencies among different age groups of the population as a whole. In the same way, children's nutritional status in Kerala has worsened in the seven years since NFHS-2 based on two of the three nutritional status measures. Children and adults are vulnerable to malnutrition because of low dietary intakes, infectious diseases, lack of appropriate care and inequitable distribution of food within household. Though Kerala is successfully implementing all nutrition oriented programmes of housing, sanitation and portable drinking water, the state could not achieve the nutritional level of best performing countries.

2. Objectives of ICDS

The main objectives of ICDS scheme are the following:

(i) To improve the nutritional and health status of children in the age of 0-6 years.

(ii) To lay the foundation for proper psychological, physical and social development of the child.

(iii) To reduce the incidence of mortality, morbidity, malnutrition and school drop-out.

(iv) To achieve effective coordination of policy and implementation amongst the various departments to promote child development.

(v) To enhance the capability of the mother to look after the normal health and nutritional needs of the child through proper nutrition and health education.

3. Features of ICDS

ICDS has some important and unique features which distinguish it from several other national programmes. These are as follows:

(i) It is a holistic approach for child development involving the active participation of mother.

(ii) It serves the extreme underprivileged communities of the backward and remote areas of the country.

(iii) It delivers services at Anganwadi right at the door-steps of the beneficiaries to ensure their maximum participation.

(iv) It comprises three essential components, which are nutrition, primary healthcare and education, delivered as a composite package of services to children and mothers.

(v) It utilises local women as honorary village level workers for the delivery of the package of services.

(vi) It works through a team approach, and members of the team include administers, professionals in service departments, academicians and voluntary workers.

4. Structure of ICDS

ICDS is a centrally sponsored programme implemented by the Department of Women and Child Development, Ministry of Human Resources Development of the Government of India; but the responsibility for its actual implementation rests with the State Governments. Under the Directorate of Social Welfare at the State level, ICDS projects have been set up in the blocks, with each block having one Anganwadi centre per 1000 population. At the block level the Child Development Project Officer is the official in-charge. There are supervisors who oversee the work at the Anganwadi centre in each of the project areas while the Anganwadi worker is responsible for the activities in each Anganwa dicentre at the unit level. There is a helper at each centre who provides assistance in the preparation of food and child-care.

Table 1 : Structure of ICDS

Category	*Department*	*Designation*
State-level	Directorate of Social Welfare	Director
Block-level	ICDS Project office	Child development project officer (1/5 supervisors)
Project-level Unit-level	ICDS Project office Anganwadi centre	Supervisors (1/5 AWS) Anganwadi workers (teacher) Anganwadi helper

Source: Official website of Govt. of Kerala.

The participation of the local community is considered an essential pre-requisite for the effective implementation of the ICDS scheme. For this purpose, it has been stipulated that the Anganwadi worker (teacher) attached to a centre should be a resident of the beneficiary area of that centre. It is also envisaged that a local people's committee should be constituted for the smooth functioning of each centre with the people's representative of the panchayath ward as its chairperson.

5. Services Provided through ICDS

The objectives are sought to be achieved through a package of services comprising:

- Supplementary nutrition
- Immunisation
- Health check up
- Referral services
- Pre-school non-formal education and nutrition and health education

Table 2 : Services provided by ICDS in Kerala

SERVICES	TARGET GROUP	SERVICE PROVIDING WING
Supplementary nutrition	Children below six years, pregnant and lactating mothers	Anganwadi worker and Anganwadi helper
Immunisation	Children below six years, pregnant and lactating mother	ANM/AWW
Health check-up	Children below six years, pregnant and lactating mothers	ANM/MO/AWW
Referral services	Children below 6 years, pregnant and lactating mothers	AWW/ANM/MO
Pre-school education	Children: 3-6 years	AWW
Nutrition and health education	Women: 15-45 years	AWW/ANM/MO

Source: Ministry of Women and Child Development, Govt. of India'.

The concept of providing a package of services is based primarily on the consideration that the overall impact will be much larger if the different service develop in an integrated manner as the efficacy of a particular service depends on the support it receive from related services.

6. Existing Monitoring System Under ICDS

Central Level

Ministry of Women and Child Development (MWCD) has the overall responsibility of monitoring the ICDS scheme. There exists a central level ICDS monitoring unit in the Ministry which is responsible for collection and analysis of the periodic work report received from the states in the prescribed formats. States have been asked to send the state level consolidated report by 7th day of every month about the existing status of the following six services.

(i) Supplementary nutrition

(ii) Pre-school education

(iii) Immunisation, health check-up and referral services

(iv) Nutrition and Health education

(v) Analysis and action

(vi) Number of ICDS project and Anganwadi centre

State Level

Various quantitative inputs captured through CDPO's/MPR/HPR are compiled at the State level for all projects in the state. Number of technical staff has been sanctioned for the state for programme monitoring. CDPO's/MPR capture information on number of beneficiaries for supplementary nutrition, pre-school education, field visit to AWC by ICDS functionaries like supervisors, CDPO/ACDPO, information on number of meeting on nutrition and health education and vacancy position of ICDS functionaries, etc.

Block Level

At block level, Child Development Project Officer (CDPO) is the in-charge of an ICDS project. CDPO's/MPR have been prescribed at block level. These CDPO's/MPR/HPR formats gave one to one correspondence with AWW's/MPR/HRR. CDPO's/MPR consists vacancy position of ICDS functionaries at block and AWC levels. At block level, no technical post of officials has been sanctioned under the scheme for monitoring. CDPO is required to send the Monthly Project Report (MPR) by 7th day of every month to State Government. Similarly CDPO is required to send half yearly progress report to state by 7th April and 7th October every year.

Village Level

At the grass-root level, delivery of various services to target group is given at the Anganwadi Centre (AWC). An AWC is managed by an honorary Anganwadi Worker (AWW) and Anganwadi Helper (AWH).

In the existing management information system, records and registers are prescribed at the Anganwadi level. The monthly and half yearly report of Anganwadi worker have been prescribed. The monthly progress report of AWW capture information on population details, births and deaths of children, maternal deaths, and number of children attended AWC for supplementary nutrition and pre-school education, nutritional status of children by weight for age, information on nutrition and health education and home visit by AWW. Similarly, AWW's half yearly progress report capture data on literacy standard of AWW, training details of AWW, increase/decrease in weight of children, details on space for storage ration at AWC, availability of health cards, registers, growth cards, etc.

7. Nutrition Status of Children

Malnutrition is undoubtedly the biggest public health problem in our country today. The economic condition of a vast majority of our population is so poor that they are not in a position to afford even the least expensive balanced diets. A number of nutrition and diet surveys carried out among adult population groups in various parts of the country have confirmed the existence of widespread malnutrition among the poor sections of our population. Children and women in the productive period appear to be the worst sufferer.

Several aspects related to the decline in under nutrition have been examined. It has been noted that young children belonging to special groups, namely, scheduled castes, scheduled tribes and backward communities, had all shown beneficial impact of ICDS on their nutritional status. Special multi-centric research studies at different intervals during the 39 years of ICDS had confirmed that the nutritional status of children in the ICDS project area was significantly better than that of their counterparts in areas without the benefit of the ICDS scheme. Thus, a study by the National Institute of Nutrition (NIN) had recorded better nutrition status of children attending ICDS Anganwadies as compared to children of the same village and similar socio-economic status not utilising the services of ICDS. There are multiple health and nutrition intervention factors in ICDS, which could have contributed to the decline in protein-calorie malnutrition. Food supplements providing 300 calories and 10-12 protein daily at the Anganwadi must have been a major contributing component.

A decade after ICDS was instituted; evaluation studies suggested that the decline in infant and early childhood mortality rates, observed in areas where ICDS was operational, was significantly greater than the decline reported in the national data of the sample registration scheme. Recent data confirmed these earlier findings and show lower neonatal, infant and early childhood mortality rates in ICDS covered populations as compared to the overall national data.

Studies carried out at NIN suggest that the psychological development of children attending the Anganwadi was better than those who had not. Further, school dropout rates were lower and the educational performance better in children who had attended the Anganwadi programme. According to the latest survey report of State Nutrition Research Centre; high degree nutritional deficiency is noted among the children in Palakkad and Wayanad districts and 42 to 48 per cent of students studying in 6th, 8th standards do not get sufficient nutritional food. A UNICEF investigation report on the recent infant deaths at Attappady says that 'Anemia in pregnant mothers and inadequate nutrition' are the main causes for the tragedy.

8. Challenges of ICDS in Kerala

(i) In appropriate, prior to 2005, ICDS assigned too much focus to children aged 4-6 years at the cost of younger children (0-3 years) who are at a more vulnerable stage in their development and where nutrition supplements have the most effect. Moreover states with the highest incidence of child under nutrition, malnutrition received the least funds and coverage under ICDS.

(ii) Poor physical infrastructure: more than 60 per cent Anganwadi centres had no toilet facilities. Lack of space within the premises for conducting outdoor and indoor activities such as games and songs adversely affect the delivery of non-formal pre-school education. Approximately 49 per cent of the AWCs had inadequate space for storage of materials.

(iii) Insufficient materials: approximately 44 per cent of the AWCs lacked pre-school education kits and about 37 per cent reported non-availability of materials, aids for nutrition and health education.

(iv) Inadequate supplementary nutrition and immunisation: the supply of nutritional supplements was irregular, with gaps in delivery ranging from one to seven months. Ready-to-eat supplements provided to pregnant and lactating mothers were less than the norm. Some AWWS reported that the number of children fully immunised was less than anticipated because of stiff resistance from certain section of communities resulting from inadequate awareness about the advantage of immunisation. Inadequate infrastructure, including shortage of AWCs and staff, also affected immunisation rates (Controller and Auditor General, 2005).

9. Recommendations

(i) Shift focus to changing behaviour: ICDS has focused on extending service to all blocks of the country and on providing supplementary nutrition with efficient attention to changing feeding habits of families and child care behaviours.

(ii) Community participation involving local communities in the delivery and monitoring of the scheme is widely held to be the best way to improve its performance. For instance, getting women from local self group to cook for children and pregnant and lactating mothers may ensure that the beneficiaries are provided through Anganwadies.

(iii) Popularising the programme and promoting gender inequality: the success of ICDS rests largely on communities accepting the services provided. Community up-take of ICDS services can be improved through awareness drives to raise consciousness of the community on issues related to women and children. In particular, discrimination against girl child, female foeticide, and infanticide is a problem that is prevalent in large parts of the country. To counter this, ICDS could incorporate awareness campaigns to attempt to encourage people to care for girls as well as boys.

10. Conclusion

India is a country suffering from over population, malnutrition, poverty and high infant mortality rates.In order to counter the health and mortality issues gripping the country there is a need for a high number of medical and health care experts. Unfortunately, India is suffering from a shortage of skilled professionals. Therefore, through Anganwadi system the country is trying to meet its goal of enhanced health facilities that are affordable and accessible by Anganwadi workers as better equipped than professional doctors in reaching out of the rural population. The Anganwadi provide nutritional service to children, pregnant, lactating women and adolescent girl in close coordination with the health service for improvement of health status and overall holistic development of children and other beneficiaries.

Malnutrition is highly prevalent among the poor communities in our country. The extent and severity of malnutrition however differ in various states and communities. Kerala has done exceedingly well in reducing the infant and child mortality. The infant mortality estimated to be 27 against the all-India average of 95, while mortality in children 1-4 year old is only 8/1000, against the all India figure of 24/1000. Through development, the nutritional indicators connected worth under-nutrition are very high especially among the marginalised communities. The analysis and results shows that the nutritional status of children belongs to the marginalised communities like

SCs and STs are very deplorable compared to the OBCs and other caste groups in Kerala.

References

1. Andrea Carlson, Ben Senauer (2003), *"The impact of the special supplemental nutrition programme for women, infant and child on child health*", American Journal of Agriculture Economics, Vol. 85, No. 2, pp. 479- 491.
2. Angus Deaton (2009), "*Food and nutrition in India: facts and interpretation*", Economic and Political Weekly, Vol. 44, No. 7, pp 42-65.
3. Anuradha Khati Rajivan (2006), "*ICDS with a difference"*, Economic and Political Weekly, Vol. 41, No. 34, pp. 3684-3688.
4. Aprajit Mahajan (2007), *"Child nutrition in India in the nineties"*, Economic Development and Cultural Change, Vol. 55, No. 3, pp. 441-486.
5. Arun Gupta and Jon E (2004), *"Infant and young child under nutrition; where lie the solution*", Economic and Political Weekly, Vol. 39, No. 49, pp. 5213-5216.
6. David Stifles (2006), *"The glass of milk subsidy programme and malnutrition in Peru*", The World Bank Economic Review, Vol. 20, No. 3, pp. 421-448.
7. Dipa Sinha (2006), "*Rethinking ICDS: A Right Based perspective*", Economic and Political Weekly, Vol.41, No. 34, pp. 3689-3694.
8. Geetha S (1996), "*Nutritional status of slum children of Mumbai: a socio-economic survey"*, Economic and Political Weekly, Vol. 31, No. 14, pp. 896-900.
9. Gopalan C (1995), *"Towards food and nutrition security*", Economic and Political Weekly, Vol. 30, No.52, pp. 134-141.
10. Jean Dreze (2006), "*Universalisation with quality: ICDS in a right perspective*", Economic and Political Weekly, Vol. 41, No. 34, pp. 3706-3715.
11. Jose Ignacio Anton (2010), "The *impact of remittances on nutritional status of children in Ecuador*", International Migration Review, Vol. 44, No. 2, pp. 269-299.
12. Kapil U (2002), *"ICDS Scheme: A programme for holistic development of children in India"*, Indian Journal of Paediatrics, Vol. 69, No. 3, pp. 597-601.

13. Katherine Tucker (1989), "*Household structure and child nutrition: a reinterpretation of income and mother's education*", Social Indicators Research, Vol. 21, No. 6, pp. 629-649.

14. Kristine Peterson (2009), "*Childhood under-nutrition: a falling global priority*", Journal of Public Health Policy, Vol. 30, No. 4, pp. 455-464.

15. Michele Gragnolati, Caryn and Monica Dads Gupta (2006), *"ICDS and persistent under-nutrition: strategies to enhance the impact*", Economic and Political Weekly, Vol. 41, No. 12, pp. 1193-1201.

16. Nair K R G (2007), *"Malnourishment among child in India: a regional analysis",* Economic and Political Weekly, Vol. 42, No. 37 pp. 3797-3803.

17. Nandini Nayak and Naresh C Saxeena (2006), "*Implementation of ICDS in Bihar and Jharkhand*", Economic and Political Weekly, Vol. 41, No. 34, pp. 3680-3684.

18. Patel R (2004), "*Impact of ICDS on pre-school children of urban slums*", Indian Journal of Paediatrics, Vol. 49, pp. 215-219.

19. Radhakrishna R and Ravi C (2004), "*Malnutrition in India: Trends and Determinants*", Economic and Political Weekly, Vol. 39, No. 7, pp. 671-676.

20. Ramachandhran K (2006), "*Impact of ICDS on infant mortality rate in India*", Indian Journal of Paediatrics, Vol. 2, pp. 157-158.

21. Samir Garg (2006), "*Grass root mobilization for children's nutrition rights*", Economic and Political Weekly, Vol. 41, No. 34, pp. 3694-3700.

22. Santhosh Mehrotra (2006), *"Child malnutrition and gender discrimination in south Asia"*, Economic and Political Weekly, Vol. 41, No.10, pp. 912-918.

23. Shanti Ghosh (2004), *"Child malnutrition*", Economic and Political Weekly, Vol. 39, No. 40, pp. 4412-4413.

24. Sundararamant (2006*), "Universalisation of ICDS and community Health workers programme: Lesson from Chhattisgarh",* Economic and Political Weekly, Vol. 41, No. 34, pp. 3674-3679.

25. Susan Evers and Alex WM. (1977), *"Social indicators of human nutrition*: *measures of nutritional status*", Social Indicators Research, Vol. 14, No. 2, pp. 185-205.

26. Tandon B(2000), *"Nutrition intervention through primary health care: impact of the ICDS project in India",* Bulletin of the WHO, Vol. 67, No.1, pp. 77-80

27. Tomoki Fuji (2010), "*Micro level estimation of child under-nutrition indicators inCambodia*", The World Bank Economic Review, Vol. 24, No. 3, pp. 520- 553.

28. Vandana Khullar (1998), "*Integrated child development services: A critique of evaluation techniques*", Economic and Political Weekly, Vol. 33, No. 10, pp. 537-545.

24

A Study on the Health Status of the Scheduled Castes, in Palakkad District, Kerala

Nisha, T.A.

1. Introduction

Health is a yardstick of one's well being. A healthy population is the most important resource of an economy because it is the most productive among different development alternatives. Economists judge health conditions of the people of a country by looking at the following indicators: Infant mortality, maternal mortality, life expectancy, nutritional levels, incidence of diseases, health infrastructure. As the country develops, its Infant mortality, maternal mortality and incidence of diseases decline. At the same time, life expectancy, nutritional levels and health infrastructure exhibits signs of improvement.

The widely accepted definition of health is that given by the World Health Organisation (1948) in the preamble to its constitution, which is as follows:

"Health is a state of complete physical, mental, and social wellbeing and not merely an absence of disease or infirmity." In recent years, this statement has been amplified to include the ability to lead a "socially and economically productive life."

2. Health and Economic Development

Jean Dreeze and Amarthya Sen (1996) viewed health from two aspects "health is wealth and also health creates wealth." The maxim that health is wealth highlights the increasing importance of health. Health is valued on its own; it is perhaps the supreme element of economic development.

- Health improvements results in declining child mortality and increasing life expectancy. High child mortality and low life expectancy can result in reduction in total labour supply.
- Low life expectancy is not conducive to development. Increase in life expectancy raises higher rate of collective saving and investment.
- Illness may lead to a decrease in learning potential. As a result, investment in education and human capital becomes less attractive.

Health and economic development are complementary to each other. High health status of individuals can stimulate economic development by raising productivity and efficiency. It is a multi-dimensional concept. Continuous illness and malnutrition in youth endangers mental functions and creativity. As a result attaining better health is considered to be a real challenge in front of the marginalised sections. Health and educational backwardness are the main reason behind their deprivation. Development of the marginalised sections especially, Scheduled castes are essential for the Sustainable development. So the present study concentrates on the health status of Scheduled castes in Palakkad district.

The study examines the health indicators of Palakkad district in general and scheduled caste in particular. The study is based on the secondary data only. The study includes the following health indicators: Crude Birth Rate, Crude Death Rate, Infant Mortality Rate, Maternal Mortality Ratio, Sex Ratio, Health Infrastructure, and Nutritional Status.

3. Review of Literature

K.R. Nayar (2007) examined the broad linkages between caste and some select health/health utilisation indicators. The health status and utilisation patterns of socially disadvantaged groups give an indication of their social exclusion as well as an idea of the linkages between poverty and health. Poverty and social exclusion are important socio-economic variables which are often taken for granted while considering ill-health effects. The linkages between caste and some health indicators show that poverty is a complex issue which needs to be addressed with a multi-dimensional paradigm.

D. Rajasenan, Bijith George Abraham and Rajeev B (2013) in their analysis highlights the disproportionate nature of socio-economic indicators within the tribes in Kerala owing to the failure of governmental schemes and assistances meant for their empowerment. The socio-economic variables, such as education, health, and livelihood have been augmented with SLI based on correlation analysis gives interesting inference for policy options as high educated tribal communities are positively correlated with high SLI and livelihood. Despite the government efforts in the area of healthcare, tribal communities still lack awareness of and access/affordability to modern healthcare. A disturbingly high percentage of the tribal population reportedly indulges in ill-health behaviours like alcohol and tobacco abuse. The situation takes a huge toll on the health status of backward communities. The ignorance of the severity of many health conditions and the problem of in-affordability to modern medical facilities expose them to health risks and eventually to high morbidity and mortality situations.

4. Data Highlights: The Scheduled Castes

The Scheduled Caste (SC) population of Kerala State is 3123,941 as per 2001 census constituting 9.8 per cent of the total population (31,841,374) of the State. The growth of SC population has been 8.2 per cent which is 1.2 per cent lower than the growth of total population (9.4 per cent) in 1991-2001. The State has a total of sixty eight (68) SCs and all have been enumerated at 2001 census.

The Scheduled Castes are overwhelmingly rural with 81.8 per cent residing in rural areas. Among the districts, Palakkad district has the highest proportion of SCs (16.5 per cent) followed by Idukki (14.1 per cent), Pathanamthitta (13.1per cent) and Kollam districts (12.5 per cent). Kannur district has the lowest percentage of SC population (4.1 per cent), preceded by Wayanad (4.3 per cent) and Kozhikode (7 per cent) districts.

Table 1

Scheduled Caste population in Kerala (2001 census)

District	*Percentage of Scheduled Caste population*
Palakkad	16.5
Idukki	14.1
Pathanamthitta	13.1
Kollam	12.5
Kozhikode	7.0
Wayanad	4.3
Kannur	4.1

Source: Census of India 2001.

5. Population - Size and Distribution

Out of 68 Scheduled Castes, Pulayan is the most populous caste with a population of 1,041,540 forming 33.3 per cent of the total SC population of the State. Cheruman is the second largest SC numbering 316,518. Five other SCs namely, Kuravan, Paraiyan, Kanakkan, Thandan and Vettuvan along with Pulayan and Cheruman constitute 77.7 per cent of the total SC population. Seven remaining castes, namely, Vannan, Chakkiliyan, Paravan etc. with population ranging from 40,070 to 90,962 accounts for 12.8 per cent and the remaining 54 SCs along with the generic castes constitute the residual 9.5 per cent of the total SC population.

District-wise distribution of the individual SC shows that Pulayan, numerically the largest caste, account for the highest proportion

(75.8 per cent) of total SC population in Ernakulum district, followed by Alappuzha and Kottayam (56.3 per cent) whereas Cheruman and Kuravan have the highest proportion in Palakkad (38.2 per cent)) and Pathanamthitta (35.5 per cent) districts respectively.

Table 2: Block-wise details of Scheduled Caste Colonies and number of families-2011

Sl. No	*Name of Blocks/Municipalities*	*No. of SC Colonies*	*No. of families*	*SC population*
1	Alathur block	378	5049	22336
2	Attappadi block	38	395	1453
3	Chittur block	283	402	16887
4	Kollengode block	282	4557	21027
5	Kozhalmannam block	413	6765	29105
6	Malampuzha block	210	3190	13673
7	Mannarkkad block	290	3568	15828
8	Nemmara block	286	4022	18306
9	Ottappalam block	466	5024	21448
10	Palakkad block	305	5012	21240
11	Pattambi block	294	3048	14149
12	Sreekrishnapuram block	320	3462	14569
13	Thrithala block	426	4654	20509
	Block total	**3991**	**49148**	**230530**
1	Chittur-Thathama nagalam (M)	46	623	2588
2	Ottappalam (M)	71	635	2644
3	Palakkad (M)	44	1028	4266
4	Shornur(M)	85	1049	4384
	Muni/corp. Total	**246**	**3335**	**13882**
	District total	**4237**	**52483**	**244412**

Source: Department of Economics and Statistics Kerala, Panchayath Level Statistics 2011 Palakkad.

Block-wise distribution of scheduled caste population is highest in Kozhalmannam block and lowest in Attappadi block as per the Panchayath Level Statistics 2011 Palakkad.

Table 3 : Vital Rates at a Glance- Kerala-2011

Districts	*Crude Birth Rate*	*Crude Death Rate*	*Infant Mortality Rate*	*Still Birth Rate*	*Maternal Mortality Ratio*
Thiruvana nthapuram	16.62	8.8	12.13	8.24	0.16
Kollam	14.18	7.33	2.62	2.06	0.16
Pathana mthitta	14.81	9.48	5.64	2.42	0.28
Alappuzha	10.93	7.68	4.39	5.01	0.34
Kottayam	14.35	9.15	9.24	7.53	0.28
Idukki	13.71	6.15	2.83	2.17	0.07
Ernakulum	14.39	8.55	8.22	4.77	0.29
Thrissur	17.88	8.92	8.48	4.33	0.21
Palakkad	**14.47**	**6.02**	**3.69**	**2.69**	**0.24**
Malappuram	22.28	4.68	4.60	2.99	0.15
Kozhikode	19.01	7.54	17.67	8.75	0.1
Wayanad	18.41	5.29	4.97	5.41	0.07
Kannur	20.16	6.75	6.03	5.17	0.16
Kasaragod	16.73	5.37	3.97	4.86	0.09
Kerala	**16.75**	**7.32**	**7.53**	**4.92**	**0.18**

Source: Department of Economics & Statistics, Annual Vital Statistics report – 2011.

As per the Annual Vital Statistics report – 2011 Malappuram holds first position in the case of CBR and last position in the case of CDR. In the case of IMR and Still Birth Rate, Kozhikode holds the first position. At the same time MMR is least in Kozhikode. Kollam is the lowest in the case of IMR and Still Birth Rate. Alappuzha holds first position in the case of MMR and last position in the case of CBR. CDR is highest in Pathanamthitta. In Palakkad MMR is higher than the state level.

6. Sex Ratio

The sex ratio of the total SC population at 1048 shows preponderance of females and is significantly higher than the national average of 936 for the total Scheduled Castes population as per 2001 census.

Table 4 : Sex Ratio of Scheduled Caste

Age group	*All SCs (India)*	*All SCs (Kerala) All SCs*	*Kuravan*	*Thandan*	*Pulayan*	*Cheruman*	*Kanakkan*	*Vettuvan*	*Paraiyan*
All Age	936	1048	1081	1067	1049	1048	1041	1037	1029
0-6	938	955	1001	975	949	946	936	941	959

Source: Census of India 200.

At the individual caste level, all the major SCs have sex ratio above 1000. Kuravan have the highest sex ratio of 1081 among the larger groups

The sex ratio among the SC children in the age group 0-6 years (955) is higher than that of the SCs at the national level. Among the major SCs, Kuravan have the preponderance of girl children with the child sex ratio of 1001 followed by Thandan, Paraiyan, Pulayan etc., whereas Kanakkan have registered the child sex ratio below the state and national averages.

7. Medical Institutions in Palakkad District

As regarding the medical institutions, three systems of medicine are considered – Ayurveda, Homoeopathy and Allopathic

Table 5 : Block wise details of Medical Institutions – Ayurveda as on 31-03-2011

Sl. no.	*Name of Blocks*	*Government hospitals*			*Government Dispensaries*		
		No.	*Beds*	*Doctors*	*No.*	*Beds*	*Doctors*
1	Alathur	1	20	2	5	0	5
2	Attappadi	0	0	0	3	0	3
3	Chittur	0	0	4	0	4	
4	Kollengode	0	0	0	7	0	7
5	Kozhalmannam	0	0	0	7	0	7
6	Malampuzha	0	0	0	7	0	7
7	Mannarkkad	1	30	3	4	0	4
8	Nemmara	0	0	0	7	0	7
9	Ottappalam	1	10	1	7	0	7
10	Palakkad	0	0	0	4	0	4

11	Pattambi	0	0	0	7	0	7
12	Sreekrishnapuram	0	0	0	7	0	7
13	Thrithala	0	0	0	5	0	5
	Block total	**3**	**60**	**6**	**74**	**0**	**74**
1	Chittur -Thathama nagalam (M)	1	20	3			
2	Ottappalam(M)	1	20	3			
3	Palakkad(M)	1	50	6			
4	Shornur(M)				1		1
Muni/corp. Total		**3**	**90**	**12**	**1**	**0**	**1**
District total		**6**	**150**	**18**	**75**	**0**	**75**

Source: Department of Economics and Statistics Kerala, Panchayath Level Statistics 2011 Palakkad.

We can see that the total numbers of Government Ayurveda hospitals are six and Government Ayurveda dispensaries are 75.

Table 6 : Block-wise details of Medical Institutions – Homoeopathy as on 31-03-2011

Sl. no.	*Name of Blocks*	*Government Hospitals*			*Government Dispensaries*		
		No.	*Beds*	*Doc-tors*	*No.*	*Beds*	*Doc-tors*
1	Alathur	0	0	0	4	0	4
2	Attappadi	0	0	0	4	0	4
3	Chittur	0	0	0	3	0	3
4	Kollengode	0	0	0	2	0	2
5	Kozhalmannam	0	0	0	4	0	4
6	Malampuzha	0	0	0	5	0	5
7	Mannarkkad	0	0	0	3	0	3
8	Nemmara	0	0	0	1	0	1
9	Ottappalam	0	0	0	6	0	6
10	Palakkad	0	0	0	4	0	4
11	Pattambi	0	0	0	1	0	1
12	Sreekrishnapuram	0	0	0	1	0	1
13	Thrithala	0	0	0	2	0	2
	Block total	**0**	**0**	**0**	**40**	**2**	**40**
1	Chitturthathamangalam(M)				1		1

2	Ottappalam(M)				1		1
3	Palakkad(M)	1	25	4			
4	Shornur(M)						
Muni/corp. Total		**1**	**25**	**4**	**2**	**0**	**2**
District total		**1**	**25**	**4**	**42**	**2**	**42**

Source: Department of Economics and Statistics Kerala.

Panchayath Level Statistics 2011 Palakkad

There is one Government Homeopathy Hospital and 42 government Homeopathy Dispensaries in Palakkad district.

Table 7 : No. of Allopathic Medical Institutions in Palakkad District

District Hospital	Specialt Hospital			Taluk Hospital	CHC	24×7 PHC	PHC	Others	Total
	W & C	Tribal	TB						
1	1	1	1	6	19	11	64	9	**113**

Source: Directorate of Health service.

8. Nutritional Status

The most dominant factor related to health transition in Kerala is low nutritional status due to low intake of food, cereals, proteins and carbohydrates. The National Family Health Survey III revealed shocking reality that Kerala represents 28.8 per cent of underweight children, 16.1 per cent wasted children and 21.1per cent stunted children. By considering the sound human development trends that existed in Kerala for the last few decades, the present nutritional picture is not attractive. Young children from scheduled tribes and scheduled castes are more likely to be stunted, wasted, and under weight than children from other castes/tribes. Total malnutrition is higher among women from scheduled castes and scheduled tribes than for women in the OBC group and women from other castes, but the differences are small. In all caste/tribe groups, most malnutrition is due to under nutrition.

As in conclusion the health condition of scheduled caste is far behind the state level in some of the indicators. The Maternal Mortality Ratio is higher than state level. The malnutrition among women is also alarming. So the government undertook a lot of measures to uplift them. Development of marginalised sections of the society especially Scheduled caste is essential for the sustainable development.

References

1. K.R. Nayar (2007), Social exclusion, caste and health: A review based on the social determinants framework. *Indian J Med Res 126*, pp. 355-363, Centre of Social Medicine and Community Health, Jawaharlal Nehru University, New Delhi, India.

2. D. Rajasenan, Bijith George Abraham and Rajeev B (2013), Health, Education and Employment in a Forward-Backward Dichotomy Based on Standard of Living Index for the Tribes in Kerala. *Journal of Economics and Sustainable Development,* ISSN 2222-1700 (Paper) ISSN 2222-2855 (Online), Vol. 4, No.7. www.iiste.org

3. Jayasree Paul (2014), Elective Course Health Economics EC6 E02. Calicut University Central Co-operative Stores Ltd.

4. Department of Economics and Statistics, Kerala.

5. Directorate of Health Services, Kerala.

6. Census of India 2001.

7. http://www.nfhsindia.org

8. WHO (1978). Health for All, Sr.No.1

9. Jean Dreeze and Amarthyasen. (1996), "Indian Development—Selected Regional Perspective. Studies in Development Economics Study Prepared by the World Institute for Development Economics Research of the United Nations. Oxford University Press.

25

Gender Disparity in Rural Poverty: A Sociological Evidences and Issues in Kerala

Jafar K.

1. Introduction

Poverty as a social phenomenongrapples with the human society today as more than 1 billion people in world, almost the half of the women, live in unacceptable conditions of poverty, mostly in the developing countries, substantially differing from region to region, from community to community, from one cultural system to another, and from one polity to another, and thus, it requires a socio-cultural analysis. Poverty as a complex, multidimensional problem, with origins in both the national and regional domains had historically persisted in different degrees and the ologically, culturally and politically perpetuated in the Indian territory. In the early 1950s, nearly half of India's population was living in poverty. Since then, poverty has been waning, though slowly, and today vast disparities between and within India's 28 states persist. With a gross national product (GNP) per capita of US$ 440 in 1999, India continues to have the highest concentration of poverty of any country, accounting for almost one-third of those with an income of less than one dollar a day. More than 360 million people—about 36 per cent of the population—live below the official poverty line; seventy-five per cent of them live in the rural areas.

Although there is a general consensus that the poor can be defined as those who are deprived of basic human needs required for their well being, there are different points of view on what exactly are these basic needs. The Indian Government equated poverty with the tangible dimensions of deprivation, i.e., lack of access to food, nutrition, clothing, shelter, water and basic education, and uses "food deprivation" explicitly to identify the poor from the non-poor (Planning Commission, 1979, 1993). However, the Human Development Report, 1997. brought out by the UNDP, questions such a narrow equation of poverty with material deprivation. It argues the need for broadening the definition of poverty to include Deprivation in terms of creativity, freedom, dignity, self-esteem and the respect of others (UNDP, 1997). Others, like Chambers (1998), draw attention to a few additional intangible Dimensions of deprivation: vulnerability, powerlessness and seclusion.

Poverty has been an ongoing phenomenon rural India. Rural poverty is a stuff of great concern for all sections of society, particularly to the academia. This study is an attempt to enquire in to the ramifications of poverty to rural women with a view to examine the prevalence and predicaments of gender issues in Kerala. The specific objectives of this paper are.

1. To elucidate the nature and extent of poverty among the rural women in Kerala.
2. To examine gender issues in rural poverty in Kerala.
3. To analyse gender disparity in rural poverty alleviation programmes Kerala.

This chapter, premised on the analysis of secondary data drawn from the census reports of India, throws light on the persistence of gender inequality in rural Kerala. Thus, the present paper attempts to inquire into the gender dimension of rural poverty by addressing the issues and conditions leading to disparity persisting among rural men and women in Indian society.

2. Gender Analysis of Rural Poverty

While it is widely acknowledged that women play decisive role in development, women perhaps are the poorest of even the poor in human society. This gender disparity gets doubly accentuated in the rural context in which women succumb to regional backwardness as well as backwardness among the poor. Rural women usually get engaged in home and farm activities. Women are the absolute decision makers in families where the male members migrate to cities better earning purpose. In fact, India, which is predominantly an agricultural country, cannot afford to ignore the women – the important segment of our rural population engage in farming, and hence on poverty alleviation and nation building.

Nonetheless, in rural society women are considered as poorest of the poor. Women constitute a significance section of Indian society and when more than two-third of the people live in rural areas, the same numerical strength of women live in rural areas. According to 2011 census, 36.09 crore women live in rural areas. The government of India, through five year plans, has introduced many programmes to eradicate poverty. However, poverty still continues to haunt the rural people of India.Women get less of the material resources, social status, power and opportunities for self – actualization than do men who share their social location. Rural women usually get engaged in home and farm activities. This force used to be utilised in planning, execution, monitoring, and assessment of poverty alleviation programmes for better results. Women are the absolute decision-makers in families where the male members migrate to cities better earning purpose.

Table 1

Gender-wise Rural-Urban Distribution of Population, Kerala, 2011

	Population	*Male*	*Female*
Rural	1,74,55,506	84,03,706	90,51,800
Urban	1,59,32,171	76,17,584	83,14,587
Total	**3,33,87,677**	**1,60,21,290**	**1,73,66,387**

Source: Census of India 2011-Provisional Population Totals–Rural and Urban Distribution.

3. Gender Development in Kerala

The regional and social group disparity in terms of income and human development is a concern in most developing countries. The National Human Development Report 2001 – India documented several dimensions of disparities in human development. Notable among them are the rural-urban, inter-State as well as within States in terms of districts. The report noted that "At the State level, there are wide disparities in the level of human development" (Government of India, 2002:4). The report underlined that while there has been improvement in the human development index and human poverty index during the 1980s, inter-State disparities have persisted. Within this national scenario, Kerala emerges as an exception because of its low disparity not only between rural-urban areas but also between different districts. Human Development Index: It goes without saying that Kerala continues to rank at the top among Indian States with respect to the human development index (as per 1981, 1991 and 2001 estimates), with continuous improvement. As already seen elsewhere, the human development of Kerala increased from 0.685 in 1991 to 0.773 in 2001 in the Human Development Index scale. What is remarkable here is the almost uniform distribution of the development within Kerala. To be more precise, as Table 2 shows, the district-wise human development indices of Kerala for 2001 all lie above 0.740. In fact, one district (Ernakulum) comes out with a HDI as high as 0.801. The low-rung lodger is Malappuram district with an index of 0.749, which itself lies far above the index compared with other regions in India. The hilly districts of Idukki and Wayanad are also in the same range as Malappuram. As already stated, what is striking nevertheless is that there is little variation in human development indices across the districts in Kerala. The coefficient of variation is negligible, around two per cent. Also, note that the component indices (of real per capita income, health and education) are distributed with minimum variability across the districts (though the distribution of the district-wise per capita income in terms does appear with higher variability). Some caution is necessary in the case of income, which as we discussed earlier, does not include remittances accruing especially to some districts in the northern part of Kerala. The low income indicated for

Malappuram district, which is an outlying district and thus raises the variability, does not take into account the significant amount of remittances accruing to that district. More than 40 per cent of the total international migration from Kerala is accounted for by this district alone. Thus, it seems safe to assume only marginal inter-district variability in respect of the income dimension. And, this strengthens our earlier argument that the overall situation is one of an absence of any significant disparity in human development between the 14 districts in Kerala. Viewed from an all-India context, this should be reckoned as a remarkable achievement.

TABLE 2:

District wise GDI and HDI 2001

Sl. No	*DISTRICT*	*GDI*	*GDI RANK*	*HDI*	*HD RANK*
1	THIRUVANTHAPPUAM	0.743	9	0.773	9
2	KOLLAM	0.764	6	0.787	6
3	PATHANAMTHITTA	0.765	5	0.795	3
4	ALAPPUZHA	0777	1	0.794	4
5	KOTTAYAM	0.765	4	0.796	2
6	IDDUKKI	0.742	11	0.754	12
7	ERNAKKULAM	0.775	2	0.801	1
8	THRICHUR	0.766	3	0.794	5
9	PALAKKAD	0.743	10	0.761	10
10	MALAPPURAM	0.689	14	0.749	14
11	CALICUT	0.730	13	0.781	8
12	WAYANAD	0.736	12	0.753	13
13	KANOORE	0.755	7	0.783	7
14	KASARGODE	0744	8	0.760	11
	KERALA	0.746		0.773	

Source: Human Development Report 2005, Kerala.

The committee, headed by noted economist Suresh Tendulkar, which has determined a new methodology for estimating the extent of poverty in India, has estimated that a little over one-third of Karnataka's population lived below the poverty line in 2004-05.

Table 3 : Proverty levels in South (in per cent)

State	*Rural*	*Urban*	*Overall*
Karnataka	37.5	25.9	33.4
Tamil Nadu	37.5	19.7	28.9
Andhra Prakash	32.3	23.4	29.9
Kerala	20.2	18.4	19.7
All India	41.8	25.7	37.2

Source : Report of the Expert Group to Review the Methodology for Estimation of Powerly, Manning Commission, December 2009

Karnataka maintains its status as the poorest among four southern States, according to the data on poverty recently released by an expert committee set up by the Planning Commission.The committee has revised rural poverty levels in India in 2004-05, from 28.3 per cent to 41.8 per cent, a significant upward revision.The committee established the poverty line for 2004-05 at Rs 417.8 per capita per month for rural Karnataka and at Rs 588.10 for urban areas of the State. (The poverty line implies a minimum consumption expenditure level required by a person to procure a standardised basket of goods and services to satisfy basic needs.) Significantly, the head-count ratio of people below the poverty line in Karnataka is far higher than in Andhra Pradesh, Tamil Nadu and Kerala. In fact, at 33.4 per cent, the poverty ratio is only marginally lower than the national average of 37.2 per cent in 2004-05. Kerala, a clear outlier among Indian States in respect of poverty levels, had a head-count ratio of 19.7 per cent. Karnataka's position is, in what would appear to be contrary to common perceptions of poverty, in fact closer to States such as Assam and Rajasthan, which are generally regarded to be poorer comparison of the committee's revised poverty data for 1993-94 and 2004-05 reveals two striking features of Karnataka's performance in poverty reduction. First, Karnataka has achieved the sharpest reduction among the southern states in the intervening period.The overall head age of count fell from 49.5 per cent in 1993-94 to 33.4 per cent in 2004-05. In particular, the head-count ratio in rural Karnataka declined from 56.6 per cent in 1993-94 (which in that year was higher than the national average head-count ratio) to 37.5 in 2004-05.However, despite this reduction in rural poverty, Karnataka has remained the leader (jointly, with Tamil Nadu) among south India states in the matter of rural poverty levels.

4. Gendered Poverty Issues in Rural Kerala

Gender Issues in rural Keralal issues pertaining to life, livelihood and health.Women get less of the material resources, social status, power and opportunities for self actualisation than do men who share their social location. This paper is summarising current thinking on the relationship between gender disparities in rural poverty, counting reflection on how their relationships have been articulated in development policy decision. Gender disparity is not only a phenomenon of poverty; there is an almost no correlation between per capita income and the gender disparity in health and education outcomes. So while the absolute level of health and education outcomes for girls is strongly related to economic conditions, the disparities between females and males are not.

5. Feminisation of Poverty

***Female-Headed Households and Women's Poverty*:** The term "feminisation of poverty" originated in the United States in the late 1970s, when it was discovered that the fastest growing type of family structure was that of female-headed households (Pearce, 1978). In addition because of the high rate of poverty among these households, their increase was mirrored in the growing numbers of women and children who were poor. Since the 1980s, study on the explosion of female-headed households and research into the social impacts and gender-specific effects of structural adjustment policies have led to increased attention to what has become known as "the feminisation of poverty". The perception is growing around the globe that poverty is becoming increasingly feminised, that is, that an increasing proportion of the world's poor are female. The typical definitions and measurements of women's poverty in the literature may be based on the conventional measures of household income and consumption, or on qualitative and quantitative measures of "entitlements" and "capabilities". The latter are captured by social indicators such as literacy, life expectancy, primary and secondary school enrollments, access to healthcare, maternal mortality rates, access to land or employment, wage differentials, time-use, average age at first marriage (or per cent teenage girls ever married or pregnant), fertility rates, the sex ratio, and the extent of prostitution. These social indicators, along with the more conventional definitions and measures of household income and consumption, capture what the UNDP terms "human development" or "human poverty". Human development is defined as the process of enlarging people's choices and opportunities through long life, health, and education. Human poverty is defined as "more than income poverty – it is the denial of choices and opportunities for living a tolerable life" (UNDP 1997, p. 2). The "dimensions of poverty"include a short life, illiteracy, exclusion, and lack of material means. These concepts are consistent with the WID/GAD framework, which seeks to elucidate the social, economic, and political positions of women by examining women's fertility, literacy, health, and educational attainment, access to employment, earnings, political participation, and legal status. Attention to progress or setbacks in social indicators is also important in tracking the state of women's "practical gender needs", or basic needs, and "strategic gender interests", or equality, autonomy, and empowerment (Moser, 1989). WID/ GAD specialists who research women's poverty and advocate solutions tend to combine an entitlements/capabilities approach with more conventional definitions and measures of poverty (see Beerier Feldman, 1992; Meer, 1994; Tanski, 1994; Bell 2004). As female-headed households and farms lag their male counterpart in their access to and ownership of most inputs, assets and services that are relevant for productive activities in rural areas. Education has seen important improvements in gender parity, with women even exceeding male attainment levels in some regions, but in most regions even in this area females lag behind. This biased distribution of assets damages not only women: it is also a hindrance to increased social welfare. A better distribution of assets across genders would improve overall well-being.The proponents of feminisation of poverty theory seem not only to be arguing that the incidence of poverty is increasingly severe among women than men, but also that some of the dimensions of women's poverty are different from that of poor men. So are the causes of poverty. Their ability to overcome poverty is much lower.

6. Feminisation of Agriculture

In broad terms, the feminisation of agriculture refers to women's increasing participation in the agricultural labour force, whether as independent producers, as unremunerated family workers, or as agricultural wage workers. Women work not only in the fields and pastures, but also in agricultural processing and packing plants. Katz (2003: 33-35) and Deere (2005: 17) provide more specific definitions for the feminisation of agriculture:

1. An increase in women's participation rates in the agricultural sector, either as self-employed or as agricultural wage workers; in other words, an increase in the percentage of women who are economically active in rural areas.

2. An increase in the percentage of women in the agricultural labour force relative to men, either because more women are working and or because fewer men are working in agriculture.

Agriculture can be an important engine of growth and poverty reduction. But the sector is underperforming in many countries in part because women, who are often a crucial resource in agriculture and the rural economy, face constraints that reduce their productivity.The agricultural sector in many developing countries is underperforming, in part because women lack the assets and opportunities they need to achieve their potential. Women represent a crucial resource in agriculture and the rural economy through their roles as farmers, labourers and traders, yet they face constraints – because of their gender – that reduce their productivity and retard progress on broader economic and social development goals.

Workforce participation rate, a useful measure of economic activity is computed as the ratio of total workers to the total population, expressed as a percentage. Census 2001 reveals that Kerala has the lowest workforce participation rate among females among all the major states in India. The total workforce in Kerala, according to the 2001 Census estimates is around 10.3 million out of which 7.8 millions are males and only 2.5 millions are females.

7. Feminisation of Malnutrition

As Planning Commission views "food deprivation" as the most hideous form of deprivation, consumption expenditure to meet the minimum calorie intake required for this, minimum food required to produce sufficient calorie energy in an adult for rural and urban environment fixed (about 2,100 for rural and about 2,400 for urban). Those not able to get this minimum are said to be below poverty line.

The unequal allocation of resources within households resulting in differential allotments of nutrition and healthcare that reflect the perceived inferior short-term and long-term value of females is one form of intra-household inequality. There are other forms of intra-household unequal distribution which do not necessarily lead to the "missing women" syndrome analysed by Druze and Sen., but which do result in a perpetuation of female disadvantage and vulnerability to destitution in extreme situations.

Adequate nutrition is an important factor in determining labour productivity. Nutrition is also linked to health because inadequate consumption of protein and energy as well as deficiencies in key micronutrients such as iodine, vitamin A and iron are key factors in the morbidity and mortality of children and adults. Marcoux (2002) and others have noted that a widely held belief in an anti-female bias in nutrition has been formed. However, there does not appear to be clear and systematic evidence to support this hypothesis. Women are generally considered vulnerable because of their energy and nutritional needs during pregnancy, lactation and menstruation as well as the impact of their nutritional status on their offspring. On the other hand, when they are not pregnant, lactating or menstruating their energy requirements are usually lower (typically 25 per cent less) than those of men, although they require the same amount or even more of many nutrients than men require (FAO, 2000; Webb, Nishida and Darnton-Hill, 2007).

8. Feminisation of Rural Indebtedness

The Poor Women's Bank : The Thrift and Credit Societies are formed with the objective of encouraging the poor women to save their meager means to widen the resource base of the NHGs. Women bring their little bit of savings when they come to attend the group meetings.This money is entrusted to the Community Volunteer, who in turn deposits it in the nearest bank. Each member is given an individual passbook.TheThrift and Credit Societies are considered as poor women's bank. The poor women, who were hitherto dependent on their men folk for every need and did not know the meaning of economic independence, have managed the impossible under Kudumbashree. Members can avail of loans to meet their urgent needs like medical treatment, purchase of school books and uniforms for children, to pay off their old debts, etc. It is interesting to note that more than 90 per cent of the savings in the thrift societies are given away as loans. The selection of beneficiaries, the rate of interest, the quantum of loans and the period of repayment, etc. are all decided and implemented by the women themselves. Since the decisions regarding the repayment of loans with the rate of interest are taken by the NHGs, the monitoring mechanisms are inbuilt and defaulting is rare. For the same reason the NHGs are also very considerate to genuine reasons of non-repayment and extensions aregiven. It is observed that 100 per cent (476 V P Raghavan Journal of Rural Development, Vol. 28, No. 4, October - December: 2009) repayments are ensured which are rare in banking history. The Thrift and Credit Societies becomes the largest informal bank in Asia.

Community Financial Management: Formati on of thrift societies and conduct of income generating activities have led to a large financial flow at NHG and ADS levels. This has necessitated proper maintenance of accounts and keeping records in a systematic way. So Poor Women activists were given proper training in 'Community Financial Management'. The strategies Kudumbashree aims at empowerment of women to become the active leaders rather than passive recipients.

Micro-finance Operations : Thrift and Credit Societies are set up at Neighbourhood (NHG) level to facilitate the poor and to avail of easy credits, which have now grown up to Informal Banks of the poor women at their doorsteps. Now, 10,687 Thrift and Credit Societies are in operation in the 58 urban areas enveloping the major 58 towns. In the rural segment, 1,45,674 Thrift and Credit societies are in operation covering all the 991 Village Panchayats in the State. Most of the Thrift and Credit Societies are capable of providing financial assistance to income generating activities. Through micro-finance operations, Rs 651.42 lakhs of thrift are raised and internal lending to the extent of Rs 1473.12 lakhs is provided.

The NHGs, which are able to avail of loans, are linked with banks under linkage banking programme of NABARD. Till date, 99,356 NHGs were upgraded and 71,702 of NHGs were linked with banks Rs 258.78 crore is distributed as loan to NHGs for internal lending and credit of Rs 32,281lakh flow through linkage banking. Linkage banking programme becomes an effective tool to augment resources of NHGs.

9. Poverty Alleviation

For the intention of betterment of women governments are introducing large number of policies in state and central level. Poverty alleviation schemes based on micro-credit system have been implemented in many of the developing countries in recent years. The Government of Kerala State in India has introduced a novel scheme of poverty alleviation based on micro-credit and self-help grouping. Paraphrased as Kudumbashree ('Prosperity of the Family'), the scheme aims at improving the living levels of the poor women in rural and urban areas. It seeks to bring the poor women folk together to form the grassroots organisations to help enhance their economic security. The project aims at removing poverty among rural women households through setting up of micro-credit and productive enterprises. The activities such as micro-credit and micro-enterprises under the scheme were undertaken by the locally formed Community Development Societies comprising poor women. The State Poverty Eradication Mission-Kudumbashree-launched by the Government of Kerala in India is a massive poverty eradication programme in contemporary history. It has proved without doubt that women empowerment is the best strategy for poverty eradication. Women, who were regarded as voiceless and powerless started identifying their inner strength, opportunities for growth, and their role in reshaping their own destiny. The process of empowerment becomes the beacon light to their children, their families and the society at large. It opens new vistas in development history. A new paradigm of participatory economics has been found emerging in "God's Own Country". Kudumbashree presents a unique model of participatory development, which can very well, be emulated by other developing countries. Rural poverty can be solved through a concerted effort by the State. Sustainable livelihood opportunities can be provided to the deprived and the impoverished by means of lending asset creating facilities. Women households are the cruel victims of deprivation and destitution. Therefore, any programme for poverty alleviation must aim at improving the living environment of the womenfolk. It is through creating livelihood opportunities for the women that they can be empowered, and the micro-credit and self-help groupings are a better means through which their living conditions can be improved. Poverty alleviation schemes based on micro-credit system have been implemented in many of the developing countries in recent years.

In all developing countries state actions are being reinforced in streamlining poverty alleviation programmes (Buckley,1996; Hulme and Mosley, 1996; Hussain, 1998). The institutional formations of various means are also invigorated for initiating schemes of poverty alleviation (470 V P Raghavan Journal of Rural Development, Vol. 28, No. 4, October - December : 2009) successfully. The Government of Kerala has introduced novel scheme of poverty alleviation based on micro-credit and self-help groups. Paraphrased as Kudumbashree (Prosperity of the Family), the scheme aims at improving the living levels of the poor women in rural and urban areas. It seeks to bring the poor women folk together to form the grass rootorganisations to help enhance their economic security. The project aims at removing poverty among rural women households through setting up of micro-credit and productive enterprises. The activities such as micro credit and micro enterprises under the scheme were undertaken occasionally from community Development Societies consisting of rural households. This Paper aims at examining the socioeconomic impact of the Kudumbashree projects on the rural and urban poor in salvaging from deprivation and creating gender equity.

Anti-Poverty Programmes under Kudumbashree: An Overview. It is the State Poverty Eradication Mission that has been paraphrased as Kudumbashree in local language, meaning 'prosperity of the family',which helps enjoy the economic opportunities by a good number of the poor womenfolk in rural and urban Kerala.The anti-poverty programme under Kudumbashree has been launched by the State Government of Kerala with the active support of the Central Government of India and the National Bank for Agriculture and Rural Development (NABARD) aiming at removing absolute poverty within ten years with the full cooperation of the local self-governments. Poverty is a multi-faceted state of deprivation. Hence a multipronged strategy alone can help eradicate poverty. The Mission of the Kudumbashree, therefore, states: To eradicate absolute poverty in ten years through concerted community action under the leadership of local governments, by facilitating organisations of the poor for combining self-help with demand led convergence of available services and resources to tackle the multiple dimensions and manifestations of poverty, holistically.

10. Recommendations

- Create opportunities for location precise micro enterprises development for diversifying sources of income of the rural poor.
- In order to wash the gap for rural – urban women with respect to their participation in the workforce we need cooperation from the males.
- Spreading of education level, not only literacy rate, at least up to secondary level among both categories of females are highly necessary. - Establishing new school in rural areas.

- Developing effective strategies for curtailing the formation and growth of new SHGs.
- Increased training in entrepreneurship and other relevant fields for the rural community.
- Poverty alleviation programmes which reduce better participation of the community and the poor.
- Media namely press, radio, TV, etc. should take parts in reducing gaps between rural – urban females.
- Empowering Women to Achieve Food - Security.

11. Conclusion

Elimination of gender disparity in rural poverty needed both macro as well as micro strategies. At the macro level a conscious choice has to be made to achieve pro-poor growth. This would mean that the attention should be on development of agriculture and in encouraging labuor absorbing industries, particularly small and village industries. Also a massive capacity building exercise needs to be taken up to enhance the capabilities of the poor. At the micro level a convergence of programmes, resources and services is called for. This can be achieved only through a demand led process, which means that the poor have to be organised and empowered to participate in the development process. In concrete terms it means setting up of micro enterprises, providing wage employment while creating rural infrastructure, targeting basic services and providing direct social security measures to the most vulnerable. Only such a concerted approach can tackle the multiple dimensions of poverty and their ratchet effect on the poor.

For implementation social change through gender development the most powerful instrument besides social awareness and voluntary community action would be economic empowerment. This economic empowerment will basically be achieved through the instrumentally of education and employment.The group dynamics have reasonably helped many members to overcome the feeling of low self-esteem and lack of confidence and empowered them.The findings of the study indicate there is a wide range gender disparities in rural poverty existing highly literate Sate like Kerala. The general backwardness of the area i.e., poor educational background, ignorance, adherence to traditional values etc. have hindered the pace of development. Poverty alleviation and gender development may be at stand still unless adequate policy measures are taken. If gender equality is indeed to be achieved, there is need to pay attention to the interest of women.

References

1. Sanyal, Tapati (1993) :*Inequalities Among the rural urban Females : Some reflections on Women Empowerment in Indian Economy . pp 147 -162* Ajithkumar , Sinha , New dimensions of Women Empowerment . (ed). Deep and Deep Publication, 2008. New Delhi.
2. Agarwal Bina, Jane Humphries and Ingrid Robeyns (2006*): Capacity Freedom and Equality: Amartya Sen.'s Work from a Gender Perspective*, Oxford University Press.
3. Jaya S, Anand,(1999), *"Self-Help Groups in Empowering Women: A Study of Selected SHGs and NHGs in Kerala".*
4. Chavan, Pallavi and R. Ram Kumar, (2002), " Microcredit and Rural Poverty- An Analysis of Emperical Evidence".
5. Sakiko Fukuda-Parr, *What Does Feminisation of Poverty Mean? It Isn't Just Lack of Income*, *Feminist Economics 5(2), 1999, 99–103*
6. Lastarria-Cornhiel ,Susana *Feminization of Agriculture: Trends and Driving Forces,*. November, 2006.
7. Deere, Carmen Diana. 2005. *The Feminization of Agriculture? Economic Restructuring in Rural Latin America (Occasional Paper 1). Geneva: United Nations Research Institute for Social Development.*
8. Y. D. Pujari, *Rural Indebtedness: Causes and Consequences*,,Vol. 1, Issue . 1 / February 2011, pp. 124-127.
9. M. A. Oommen, *Micro Finance and Poverty Alleviation: The Case of Kerala's Kudumbashree,* Working Paper No. 17, April 2008.
10. Jaya S Anand Workshop *Presented Paper on, Addressing Poverty Through Self-Help Groups: A Case Study of Kerala,* 6-8 December 2004 Kuala Lumpur, Malaysia.Government of Kerala, (1999-2000), *Kudumbashree Project: State Poverty Eradication Mission, Annual Report,* Local Self-Government Department, Thiruvananthapuram, and Kerala.
11. Census India 2011 provisional document' .
12. www.paho.or.
13. IFPRI http://www.ifpri.cgiar.org/2020/focus/focus06.htm

26

Death Rate and Infant Mortality Rate in Mysuru District: A Spatial Analysis

Sowmyashree K.L. and Pradeep Kumar

1.0 Introduction

Death rate is the basic component of population change and it is essential for population studies and public health administration. It is the significant indicator for population projections and life tables. There are various measures of mortality such as Crude Death Rate (CDR), Infant Mortality Rate (IMR) and Age Specific Mortality Rates (ASMR) etc. These measures are unevenly distributed in different regions. The refore, the level of death rate of a region shows the level of medical status.

Mysuru district is not exception from this pattern. There is a difference in the distribution of the death and infant mortality rate in Mysuru. However, these differences are not uniform among all the taluks; some taluks of the district having high death rate, some taluks are having less death rate depending on the regional availability of medical facilities. It is because of this it is essential to study the regional variation of the distribution of death rate in the district; it helps to find out the extent of deaths, which might give a suggestion to the planners and policy-makers to provide good and necessary policies and programmes.

Therefore, in this backdrop, the present paper is an endeavour to analyse the death and infant mortality rate in Mysuru district based on secondary data. The study covers Mysore district as a whole and taluks as units of analysis.

Here Death Rate means number of deaths per thousand people per year. Infant Mortality Rate means, the number of deaths of infants under one year old per thousand live births in a given year.

4.0 Study area

Mysuru (Mysore) district lies in the Southern Maidan (Southern Plateau) and it is in the southern most part of Karnataka State. Mysuru district forms a distinct land unit, besides being a cultural entity lying between 11°30' N to 12°50' N latitudes and 75°45' E to 77°45' E longitudes.

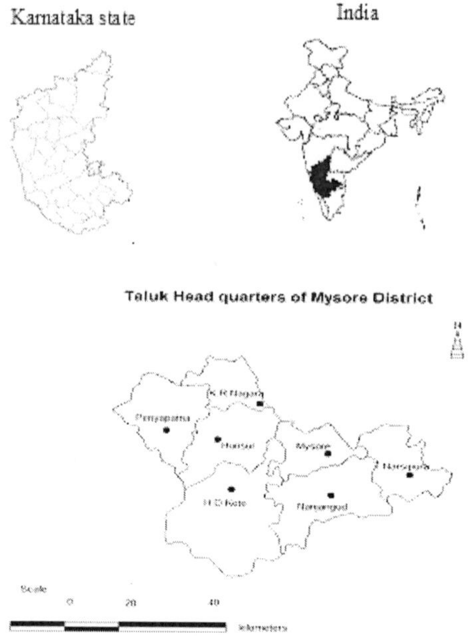

Map 1: Location of Mysuru district

Mysuru district covers an area of 6269 sq. km. that is, 3.29 per cent of the state's total geographical area. According to 2011 census the district having 29,94,744 population (male- 15,11,206 and female – 14,83,538) and sex ratio is 982. Physiographically, it lies between maiden and semi-Malnad range at an altitude of 610 meters from the mean sea level.

2.0 Objectives of the Study

The present study has been carried out with the following objectives,

- To examine the spatial distribution pattern of the death rate and infant mortality rate in Mysuru district.
- To compare the level of medical facilities with the pattern of death and infant mortality rate in the study area.

3.0 Data Base and Methodology

The present study is mainly based on secondary data collected from Mysuru District Statistical at a glance. Simple statistical technique like correlation has been used to find out the relationship between medical facilities with death and infant mortality rate. Tables, graphs are also used for data analysis.

Indicators of Medical Status:

Four parameters have been selected to show medical status, these are

X1 – Total Number of Hospitals

X2 – Total Number of Doctors

X3 – Total Number of Beds

X4 – Total Number of Medical shops

5.0 Discussion

5.1 The Pattern of Death and Infant Mortality rates in Mysuru District - A Comparative Analysis

The death rate is not uniform all over the district; there are regional variations. In this section it is attempted to show the pattern of death and infant mortality rate of the district.

Table 5.1 : The pattern of Death and IMR of Mysuru District

Taluks	*Death rate*	*IMR*
Periyapatna	4.42	10.98
Hunsur	4.98	7.50
K.R.Nagara	5.20	14.0
Mysore	2.25	8.80
H.D.Kote	4.18	15.60
Nanjangud	4.80	12.20
T.Narasipura	5.80	13.30
Total	**3.89**	**15.60**

Source: Mysore District Statistics at a Glance 2011-12

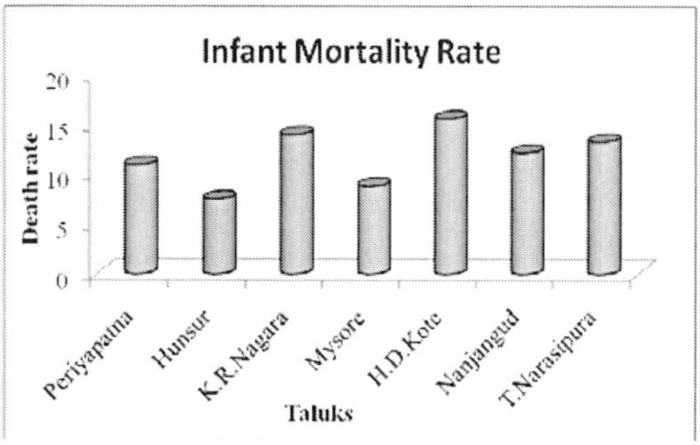

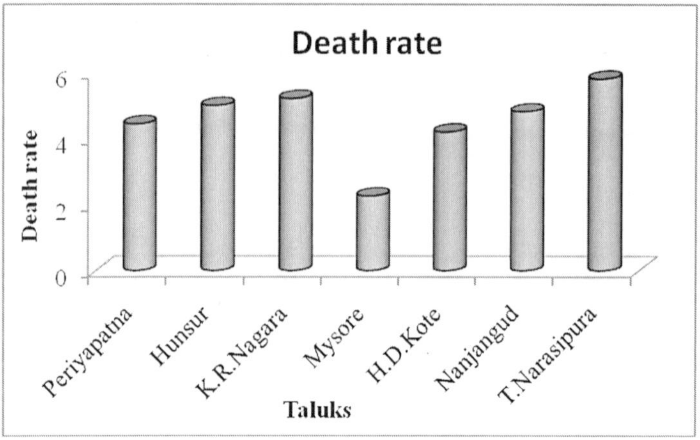

Graph 5.1 : The pattern of Death and IMR of Mysuru District

District Average

The Table 5.1 and Chart 5.1 depicts that, the district has 3.89 death rate and 15.60 is infant mortality rate. Mysuru (2.25 and 8.85) and Hunsur taluks (7.50 and 7.50) are having less death and infant mortality rate mainly because of the good medical facilities, whereas K.R.Nagara and T.Narasipura taluks are having very high death and infant mortality rate due to lack of medical facilities (Table 5.2). On the other hand Nanjangud and Periyapatna taluks are having medium level of death and infant mortality rate compared to other taluks of the district.

Table 5.2 : The Pattern of Medical Facilities in Mysuru District

Taluks	*Total No. of Hospitals*	*Total No. of Doctors*	*Total No. of Beds*	*Total No. of Medical shops*
Periyapatna	46	62	320	34
Hunsur	53	68	252	40
K.R.Nagara	49	66	262	41
Mysore	975	2167	6295	850
H.D.Kote	45	63	358	43
Nanjangud	82	135	318	33
T. Narasipura	53	64	212	37
Total	**1303**	**2625**	**8017**	**1078**

Source: Mysore District Statistics at a Glance 2011-12.

The significant point found out in the Table 5.2, Mysore taluk has very better medical facilities when compared to other taluks of the district, which led to less death and infant mortality rate, whereas H.D. Kote, K.R. Nagara and

T. Narasipura taluks are having lack of medical facilities, as a result of this death and infant mortality rates are high, whereas Nanjangud, Periyapatna and Hunsur taluks are having medium level of medical facilities in the district when compared to other taluks of the district.

3. Relationship between Death and Infant mortality rates and Medical status

The present section is an endeavour to find out the relationship between Medical status and death and infant mortality rates of the district. For this analysis, co-relation technique has been used.

Table 5.3 : Relationship between Death and Infant mortality rates with Medical status

Indicators of Medical facilities	*Relationship*	
	Death Rate	*Infant Mortality Rate*
Total Number of Hospitals	0.6	0.7
Total Number of Doctors	0.8	0.7
Total Number of Beds	0.5	0.2
Total Number of Medical Shops	0.4	0.3

It is evident from Table 5.3 that, there is a positive co-relation between medical status and death and infant mortality rates, where good medical facilities are available, there death and infant mortality rates are relatively less and vice versa. High positive co-relation found between death rate and total number of doctors (0.8). There is a moderate positive relationship between death rate and total number of hospitals (0.6), whereas less positive relationship between death rate and total number of medical shops (0.4)

On the other hand, there is a high positive relationship between infant mortality rate and total number of hospitals (0.7) and total number of doctors (0.7) respectively, whereas less positive relationship between infant mortality rate and total number of beds (0.2) and total number of medical shops (0.3).

Conclusion

It is clear from the analysis made above, H.D. Kote, T. Narasipura taluks are having high death and infant mortality rate, whereas Mysore taluk has less, which could be due to higher level of medical facilities in terms of availability of Hospitals, Doctors, number of beds and number of medical shops.

Recommendations

The findings of the study warrants that, government and non-government organisations should devise and adopt the appropriate strategies to increase number of medical facilities in those areas where the death and infant mortality rates are relatively high.

Reference

1. Manjunath Deshpande and Shanta B. Astige (2013), *Estimates of Mortality Indicators*: An Overview, Clobal Research Analysis, Vol. 2, Issue. 2.
2. Mysore District Statistical at Glance 2011-12.
3. National Institute of Medical Research (2012), *Infant and Child Mortality in India – Levels, Trends and Determinants*, New Delhi, India.

27

Pradhan Mantri Jan DhanYojana (PMJDY): A Myth about Financial Inclusion for Rural India

Rasananda Panda, Shailendra Patil, and Anushree Karani

For long, there have been talks of making rural India a part of discussion in economic development. However, there remains a yawning gap between plans made, actions taken and results achieved. The primary task of the governments over the years has been to free the farmers and small businesses from private moneylenders and make them economically self-sufficient and competent enough to run it and earn a living. The institutional credit stands at 58.7 per cent of total credit disbursed by organised institutions. In the wake of suicides by farmers in 2012, this became a glaring reality. Financial inclusion has been a part of policy-making. The RBI and policy-makers consider it as a three-way process. One, as making available, particularly credit services, to the vulnerable sections of society. Second, making available financial services to all activities within the country and third, a more balanced regional development in the sense that regional disparities in the availability of financial services must be eliminated. Following an exploratory–secondary data methodology and analysing from the recent economic history and present scenario, this paper explores the policies of the previous government, the reality of financial inclusion as it stands and the conspicuous agenda setting in the name of Pradhan Mantri Jan Dhanm Yojana (PMJDY) and whether rural India really stands to benefit out of it. The paper also discusses the success probability of the PMJDY in the presence of in frastructural bottlenecks.

On 15th August 2014, the Prime Minister announced the Pradhan Mantri Jan Dhan Yojana (PMJDY *henceforth*). The *yojana* aims at providing the households in rural as well as urban areas the access to banking facility- a bank account with a debit card from RuPay, access to credit, accident insurance, remittance and pension. It includes the direct transfer of funds of subsidy to the beneficiaries, an attempt towards preventing leakages. On the surface, it appears to be a game-changer. The common man has hailed it. However, the problems are deep-rooted. The PMJDY has stirred up the hornet's nest with criticism pouring in from the proponents of rural development, planners in financial sector and of course, from the opposition political parties each having their own reason. The rural sector rues about the lag in the delivery in the last mile. The banking and finance sector questions the viability and mammothness of the task at hand considering the fragile banking at the grassroots. While the Indian National Congress severely condemns it for the hype and hoopla around the scheme and not giving them the due credit for the work done on financial inclusion as the yconsider it as their brain child. (www.economictimes.indiatimes. com, 2014)

The attempt towards financial inclusion began way back in 1969 when the then Prime Minister, Indira Gandhi nationalised 14 banks. It enabled the reach of a bank into the hinterlands. It increased the bank deposits as the savings kept at home were now translated into bank deposits. It increased the investment rate from 13 per cent to 20 per cent in 1969-80. This not only helped the economy but the public sector banks (PSBs) as well (Mohan, 2014). However, in the 90s, servicing these small accounts proved to be cumbersome. They pushed up the operational costs. Coupled with bad loans, the net worth of these nationalised banks became negative requiring three major reforms now under consideration to resuscitate the PSBs – 1. Infusion of capital by the government (2 per cent of GDP) 2. Bank recapitalisation and 3. Listing the banks. In 1980, RBI formalised its direct lending policy in such a manner that, by 1985, 40 **per cent** of all banks lending go to priority sectors. Moreover, 25 per cent of this lending must go to individuals belonging to the weaker sections of society. Following the financial sector reforms in the 90s, the banks took structural measures as regards to reducing their operating cost etc. and thus undertook Voluntary Retirement Scheme for their employees. Under this scheme, a voluntary retirement package was offered to employees of the public sector banks. Banks implemented the package and relieved over one lakh employees during 2000-01. In the 10 years between 1996 and 2006, the banking system reduced its employee's strength by more than 10 per cent but increased its branch network by 6.3 per cent and increased the number of client accounts (deposits and advances) by 21.2 per cent. This is largely through technology and emphasis on quality lending. In 2005, for first time in India, the term financial inclusion featured when RBI, in its annual policy statement of 2005-06, urged banks to review their existing practices to align them with the objective of financial inclusion (Mehar, 2014).

The small bank deposits were a source of competitive advantage for the banks. These accounts did well over a period of time. Even after the financial crisis of 2007, the banks have stood strong. Overall, the nationalisation of banks proved to be a success. In the period between 2004 and 2012, metro cities saw a growth of 93.63 per cent in bank branches, urban areas by 72.12 per cent and 69.61 per cent in semi-urban areas. In contrast, new bank branches in rural areas - India's poverty-stricken heartlands - registered a measly 12 per cent growth. This is precisely the reason for which, the central bank issued directives that 25 per cent of the new bank branches should be opened in rural India.

With a focus on developing a comprehensive framework for financial inclusion and monitoring the entire process of financial inclusion, in September 2013, a committee was formed. The three member committee headed by Nachiket Mor* made following recommendations on financial services for small business and low income households: –

1. Assuming there will be successful implementation of Aadhar, the committee proposed that every adult should have a bank account by January 1, 2016.
2. It recommended abolition of waivers in loans and direct subsidies. It advocated the direct benefit transfer to the farmers.
3. It recommended the creation of Payment bank to facilitate services like credit, insurance and risk management products.
4. It aimed at withdrawing the permission to banks for pricing the farm loans.

The committee brought some bare facts to the fore. The findings revealed –

1. 90 per cent of small businesses are not associated with formal financial institutions.
2. For the country, overall, bank credit to GDP ratio is at a modest 70 per cent.
3. Currently, the share of institutional credit is 58.7 per cent.

Further as per the census households under institutional credit are as follows:

As per census 2001

	As per census 2001			As per census 2011		
House-holds	*Number of households availing banking service*	*Total number of houses*	*Per cent*	*Number of households availing banking service*	*Total number of households*	*Per cent*
Rural	41639949	138271559	30.1	9136980	167826730	54.4
Urban	2659063	53692376	49.5	53444983	78865937	67.8
Total	**68230642**	**19196335**	**35.5**	**144814788**	**2466926675**	**8.7**

Source : Financial Inclusion, Ministry of Finance. (Mor, 2013.

Post the submission of this report, political commentators and economists debunked it. Financial inclusion within two years was identified as a long shot considering the residue of the population (~ 41 per cent) to be covered. The report was criticised for its dependence on Aadhar. The report was also

* Nachiket Mor: Nachiket Mor is an Indian bank and is currently a member of the Central Board of the Reserve Bank of India.

chastised as a good academic work that lacked focus on last mile delivery despite the provisions mentioned. It was censured for outsourcing the services at the last mile. It was also criticised for not having water-tight provisions for client protection. (Sriram, 2013)

Several studies have been carried out in the past with respect to growth and development of the rural India with reference to rural financial institutions and their effectiveness in credit delivery and related benefits. But the purpose of this study is only to look into the fact that whether this scheme of financial inclusion in its current form will really work or it is a just an imitation of previous governments' financial inclusion initiatives providing an opportunity to the researchers to get an insight, compare and critically evaluate the scheme in its present form and be prepared to undertake further research as the scheme unfolds in later days as it is gaining the required media and governmental attention though not that much appreciation from bankers and experts in the financial services industry as seen in the public domain.

Objective and Methodology of the study

Following an exploratory – secondary data- research design, the study aims at finding out whether Pradhan Mantri Jan DhanYojana will really benefit rural India or it will be a myth only. The primary objective of exploratory research is to provide insights into and an understanding of, the problem confronting the researcher (Malhotra & Dash, 2009). Secondary databases used for the study are online internet, census data and other government publications which fall under the category of the computerised database and published secondary data.

The Pradhan Mantri Jan Dhan Yojana

The PMJDY was launched on August, 2014 with much fanfare. The main features are:

1. One bank account per household. The bank account will be coupled with a debit card from RuPay with an in-built life insurance of INR one lakh.
2. This INR one lakh cover will be ensured by National Payment Corporation of India (NCPI) which has inked a deal with HDFC Ergo to provide the amount.
3. Also, if the users register within the first 100 days from the launch of PMJDY, they will get an additional cover of INR one lakh which would be provided by New India Assurance, National Insurance, United India Insurance and Oriental Insurance Company.
4. INR 5000 ov
5. Overdraft facility for Aadhar-linked accounts.

The only distinguishing features of the scheme from that of the previous government (2009-2014) are: (1) including urban financial inclusion. (2) Easing the Know Your Customer norms with the use of Aadhar.(3) It proposes to address the lacuna in credit disbursement through the services of public sector banks (PSBs) and servicing the inactive accounts. (4) It talks about provisions for the Business Correspondent (salary of INR 5000). (5) Removing RBI from monitoring the scheme. *(Source: Pradhan Mantri Jan Dhan Yojana, 2014, Department of Financial Services , Ministry of Finance, Government of India)*

Work done by earlier governments

The question lies in how is the PMJDY different from the previous schemes on financial inclusion by earlier governments. Like Indira Gandhi, Modi also has relied on PSBs through Ministry of Finance to deliver the services. The scheme piggy backs on the existing infrastructure (Aadhar) and rules made by the previous government. It is a brilliant move by the Modi government to reap the benefits of the existing ground work and lay the foundation for an achievement that shall be under its name.

The current government has simply hard sold the scheme. This government also wants to empower rural India. Basically the inception and the subsequent adoption of this idea of the previous government are rooted in villages of the country. It aimed at serving the marginalised and disadvantaged sections of the society. When this government stresses on financial emancipation, it is worth noting the figures in rural India as indicated in table in page 2 above.They are much lesser than that in urban India. When PMJDY is extended to urban India, it is difficult to decipher what are they trying to achieve? Is it about simply creating world records of bank accounts opened? (Rama Kumar, 2014)

The previous governments had articulated their agenda on financial inclusion. However, there have been unwarranted policy interventions from the bureaucracy and the regulator that have botched the policy-making. During 1990 – 2010, the number of rural branches opened was far less than that opened in urban sector, semi-urban and metropolitan branches (Whither Financial Inclusion, undated). Since 2005, financial inclusion has been the corner stone of socio-economic programmes. The term 'financial inclusion' was commonly used post the budget speech of 2007-08 by the then Finance Minister where he defined it as, "the process of ensuring access to timely and adequate credit and financial services for vulnerable groups at an affordable cost". The government was committed to meet the cost of developmental and promotional interventions as suggested by Financial Inclusion Fund. Secondly, it established a Financial Inclusion Technology Fund. This was done to meet the cost of technology adoption. Over the years the mission financial inclusion has pivoted on leveraging biometric identification and mobile phone technologies to make it sustainable.

However, the point to be noted here is that the financial inclusion scheme under previous government was intensely focused on empowering rural India. It aimed at providing banking services to villages with population of or more than 2000. 73,000 such unbanked habitations were identified by the committee formed by the then Finance Minister, Pranab Mukherjee in 2011. The programme was named Swabhimaan and it not only provided banking services but also catered to financial literacy. By the end of 2012, this scheme successfully served 70,000 villages. It was done to keep them at bay from private moneylenders who used to loan at exorbitant rates.

In 2009, the government launched the Aadhar scheme under Unique Identification Authority of India (UIDAI)*. The aim was to reach out to the grassroots and be able to make direct transfer of funds. They believed in inclusion for which there was a need for valid identification. In the name of threatened national security, perceived separatist nature of the project and over-ambitious nature, the BJP who was in opposition then, opposed it. In 2013, the number of people registered under Aadhar was 46 crore. Shiva kumar, 2013.

Imitation in the name of Emulation

Aadhar and Direct Benefits Transfer (DBT) were big ticket reforms initiated by the previous government (UPA-II) that did not see the light of the day due to implementation bottle necks. Interestingly, in the most opportunistic turnaround of events, in September 2014, the current government endorsed the Aadhar-based DBT programmes including the provisions made for sanctioning LPG under Aadhar. In fact, during the launch, the PM urged the implementation of these Aadhar based roll-outs in 300 districts where the enrollment was more than 80 per cent. It now tries to further the Aadhar project by acknowledging that it avoids duplication, eliminates ghost beneficiaries and ensures better targeting. Now is this hijacking the agenda? (Tiwari, 2014)

PMJDY in a national mission on financial inclusion encompassing an integrated approach to bring about comprehensive financial inclusion of all the households in the country. Launched in August 2014, with a target to open 7.5 crore bank accounts by January 26, 2015; the scheme had met its objectives before deadline. It successfully registered more than 11.5 crore accounts by January 26, 2015 with INR 9000 crore being the deposits. The government rejoices in the figures as 51 per cent accounts are of women. The

---

*. UIDAI:Unique identification project was initially conceived by the Planning Commission as an initiative that would provide identification for each resident across the country and would be used primarily as the basis for efficient delivery of welfare services.

participation or the aforesaid inclusion of rural India under this scheme is 40 per cent while that of urban India is 60 per cent. (*Source: Pradhan Mantri Jan Dhan Yojana, 2014, Department of Financial Services Ministry of Finance, Government of India*)

The media has gone berserk post the republic day celebrations of this year. One can definitely notice the sheer timing of the ruling party to come in light every time during major events. In October 2014, prior to Maharashtra State elections, the central government took pride in opening five crore accounts within five weeks of launch. Be it Madison Square or Davos, the PMJDY created buzz. It gained lot of attention and the scheme is a definitely hit internationally though the efficacy of such schemes at the ground level is yet to be seen. (NDTV profit, 2015)

The government goes on to say, overall, public sector banks alone opened 9.11 crore accounts under PMJDY, followed by regional rural banks which opened about 2.01crore accounts. On the other hand, 13 private sector banks together opened just 37.58 lakh accounts. These figures for the private sector banks are so dismal that they account for just 3.4 per cent of the total accounts opened. The sting operation from *Tehelka* reveals even more ghastly details of this. The unwillingness of the private banks to serve people is clearly evident. These private players consider it a pain to handle such petty accounts as they deem fit not to consider this unsolicited burden in their ambitious growth-rate. It's a shame that government hasn't been able to keep a check on the private players. The discussion yet again hovers into the age-old grey are, is this a case of crony capitalism by the selected private bankers close to the government of the day. (Tehelka, 2015).

Hidden Reality

The scenario has only gone worse. People opened the bank accounts because of three significant features – (i) Overdraft Facility ; (ii) Life Insurance (iii) Accident Insurance. The government has simply played smartly here. Overdraft facility can be availed only after six months of opening the account. The initial overdraft amount is INR 1,000. It can be exceeded to INR 5,000 only after satisfactory performance. The grim reality is a big chunk of no-frill, low-income accounts either exist only on paper (the system of weeding out dead accounts in our banking institutions leaves much to be desired) or have sub-optimal use. These accounts offer no support to the working of the almost crippled system of working of the PSBs. No-frill accounts really amount to statistical inclusion because a very large number of these no-frill accounts (more than 80 per cent) are inoperative. This is also amply demonstrated by the fact that even though RBI suggested that overdraft facilities be given liberally to these accounts, only about 1.5 per cent of such accounts have enjoyed this facility.

The case of life insurance is more caustic. If one were to avail this service, the account holder has to transact within 45 days otherwise the life insurance service would cease to exist. Also, the insurance would be provided to only one person in the family with account opened between August 15, 2014 and January 26, 2015. People employed or retired from service in central or state government, state or public sector entities and the ones covered under Aam Admi BimaYojana will be excluded from PMJDY. The life insurance scheme would be provided to the earning member of the family only whose age should be between 15 and 59. So, what if the person aged 59 opened his account during this time? Also, if one is covered under one scheme, he'll have to choose between the existing one and the PMJDY. If this was the case with life insurance, accident insurance was not good either. The accident insurance would be effective until March 31, 2015 only. Extension would be considered only after deliberations. Similar is the case with encouraging plastic money. There is only one company producing RuPay* cards. Opening an account under PMJDY does not ensure you get a RuPay card. The issue at hand complicates even more when those limited number of people transact with small amounts because it is the bank that has to bear the expenses of ATM transactions. The government should have won accolades for this deceptive advertising! It carefully and categorically highlighted only the attracting points and camouflaged the *'conditions apply'* insidiously.

From the data it can be observed that, 5.9 crore out of 7.8 crore (close to 74 per cent) bank accounts opened by the end of November, 2014 were no-frills, zero balance accounts. The Census definition includes households with dormant bank accounts too. Studies show that about 50 per cent of the deposit accounts in the country are not operated at all. As a result, the actual extent of household-level financial exclusion is significantly higher than what the Census data show. These hard facts aggravate the problem of the dormant accounts. If they remain unused, it simply increases the burden on the overworked PSBs. Many have opened the accounts to get benefits of the scheme. Banks are already complaining about reduced business. Paucity of time to serve customers is a major worry. With so many underlying clauses, how will the banks function if they would simply be busy in answering the queries? (Tripathi, 2014) The nationalised banks handle pension accounts, MGNREGA accounts, gas subsidy and now the PMJDY accounts. Despite the working profit of close to 1.5 lakh crore in the last year, wage revision for these employees is still not considered under the pretext of provisioning-though

---

*. RuPay: RuPay, a new card payment scheme launched by the National Payments Corporation of India (NPCI), has been conceived to fulfill RBI's vision to offer a domestic, open-loop, multilateral system which will allow all Indian banks and financial institutions in India to participate in electronic payments.

the pay rise continue to happen at the ever-loss-making oil PSUs. The primary reason shoved into argument is the government has to account for losses encountered under loans. Now, here is the catch. Majority of these losses are because of government bonds. The unwillingness to open new branches or be it recruiting new staff has put massive strain on nationalised banks. The more we ponder, it only gets murkier. Do they really want these banks to exist? Or is it playing it in the hands of the private entities? (Daily Post, 2015) In addition, to put another argument, the PSBs in a way now has to serve all these small account holders in the name of financial inclusion under PMJDY and given the ticket size of these deposits and the services thereto, it will be increasingly difficult for the PSBs to concentrate on corporate and retail lending in a likely vibrant economy in the next three to five years and thereby may not gain much in their business but on the contrary their private sector counterparts with no such responsibility under PMJDY will make money from such lucrative business. In a way, is this government playing to the gallery of the private and foreign banks?

Inheriting infirmities

The mobilisation effort under PMJDY is undoubtedly unparalleled. In the wake of rise of moneylenders in the decade of 1991–2001 towards lending to rural and small business, the governments have expedited the formation of microfinance companies. However, the microfinance companies have not been able to replace the moneylenders and other such forms of credit with their slightly less usurious business model funded by venture capital and even the stock market.

The current government implanted the fact that it is the vision of the government to give one bank account per household in the country. However, targeting households is an old idea. It was mentioned in the report from Ministry of Finance on Financial Inclusion that "Banks have been advised that the service area bank in rural areas, and banks assigned the responsibility in specific wards in urban areas, ensure that every household has at least one bank account". So, this is an old provision that has been sanctioned and is like work in progress. Secondly, the hullabaloo around mobile banking is also an old provision as evident from the fact that National Payment Corporation of India has worked on a common Unstructured Supplementary Service Data (USSD) platform for all banks and telecommunication companies who wish to offer the facility of mobile banking using USSD based mobile banking. Thirdly, according to media experts, the Direct Benefit Transfers garnered such mileage after the announcement of PMJDY because people feared not availing funds on account of non-availability of bank account. This drew a lot of unbanked people to the PMJDY.

The Direct Benefits Transfer was initiated in January 2013. They were being rolled out in phases. The implementation of DBT involves three steps: opening the bank account, seeding the account with Aadhar and clearing the funds from the National Automated Clearing House – Aadhar Payment Bridge System. All this had already started since January 2013. Lastly, the banking reach is the most talked about. The scheme is not a one-size-fits-all solution. It could be good for pensions, MNREGA wages, etc. but it cannot be extended to food, education schemes. Shared ATMs for banks or the three per cent transaction fee are the proposed solutions but how practical are they? It should be noted that DBT is not a substitute for good governance. Inclusion is not about redistribution but creating additional responsibilities*.

How 'un-branched' banking failed?

The aim of PMJDY in a way was to introduce plastic money. However, transaction cost or cost of delivering small amounts of credit is very high. Several measures have been tried - group lending, lending through micro-credit institutions, business correspondents - all with an effort to reduce cost of delivering credit. This is the genesis of the idea of business correspondents (BCs). The concept of 'branchless banking' and providing banking services through BCs has been operational since 2006. BCs were appointed as intermediaries between banks and customers. The RBI took active steps to make this more professional and attractive. It permitted the appointment of 'for-profit' companies as BCs. A two per cent share of the total transfer was fixed as commission for BCs. Beneficiaries were to withdraw cash through BCs, who were to use Aadhar-enabled biometric devices or mobile phones to authenticate beneficiaries. Authentication errors recorded were in the range of 25-30 per cent. The direct bank transfer through BC model is a failure. It also failed because of corruption which eroded the accounts stealthily. The BC exploited innocent customers and extracted extra fees through unconstitutional means. The reasons cited were less commissions or salaries paid, less employees and tremendous workload. The measures taken to make them accountable are appreciable. The increase in wages and commission is one of the measures to make the inoperative ones active and bring in the efficiency by not wasting time in recruiting new BCs.(Basu, 2014)

During the last tenure of UPA government (2008 – 2013) it opened 17 crore no-frills bank accounts which directly remit government payouts like MNREGA. Many villages suffer from the bureaucracy and regulators' working that brings discrepancies in the system. With major PSUs associated with this project, banks are tempted by the two per cent commission that flows into their accounts on account of government funds being transferred into the

---

*. http://financialservices.gov.in/banking/Overviewofefforts.pdf

rural accounts. These banks were tempted to earn interests on the funds that were to be remitted. This is the first layer of the problem. Unpeeling it further, these banks turn to business correspondents to provide the last mile service by third party local organisations like Manipal Business Solutions, Fino, etc. They employed men and women to carry out the final transactions with the farmers in cash. Finally, the banks ran out of business because either correspondents embezzled the funds or they turned up late. Further, the private banks like Axis and ICICI have been roped in to provide the remittances online so that the process is better scrutinised. The government mandated these banks to clear the amounts within 15 days of completion. However, the reality is very different. There have been cases where the remittances haven't reached the recipients for more than two months.(Jain, 2014)

Bottlenecks may mar the success of PMJDY

Presently, the PMJDY faces problems on three fronts. First of all, pricing is a major challenge. The lower income groups are attracted to informal credit for following reasons: 1. Easy availability of credit 2. Returns on deposits (small amounts) tend to be higher.The organised finance doesn't have the liberty to price their products in such freewheeling manner, Secondly, delivery is another challenge that PMJDY faces. Delivery is by informal means by the business correspondents. The challenge is to develop a last-mile capacity to distribute products and ensure payments. Payment banks further complicate the issue. An effective model will be the one that provides best last mile services, is compatible to the entry of new players, the one with best back-end banks and insurance companies and a strong law enforcement mechanism. (Gokarn, 2014)

PMJDY may fully cater to the philosophy of inclusive growth. But no plan can work in isolation. Plan which cater to the needs of masses need infrastructural support. There are several bottlenecks which are associated with the success of PMJDY.

- **Telecom connectivity*:** Telecom connectivity in rural parts of India is ainfrastructural related question which needs urgent attention. It is very difficult for Bank Correspondent to work in the hilly and tribal areas where the telecom network is not reliable. Rural telecom penetration is only 44 per cent currently which need to be improved. Rate of penetration in rural areas is very low as compare to urban areas. The fact is though almost 70 per cent of Indian population stays in villages, less than 21 per cent of the total telephone connections are in rural areas. The success of PMJDY is a question in the absence of strong telecom connectivity.

*. http://timesofindia.indiatimes.com/india/Aim-to-reach-100-rural-tele-density-in-3-4-years-Telecom-secretary/articleshow/38558721.cms

· **Duplication of bank Accounts** : The fears of duplication of accounts have only made this problem worse. Raghuram Rajan, the RBI governor was vocal on criticising the duplication. He said, 'we don't want just numbers but the universality of it. It should be inclusive in real sense of the word'. Senior bank officials have also been critical of the haste in implementation of the idea. If there is a problem in strategising, things are bound to go haywire. The banks were given very little time to identify beneficiaries for this. It was necessary to avoid duplication.

· **Literacy and Awareness:** * Literacy and awareness are closely linked when we talk about socio-economic development. Latest data suggest that literacy rate among rural population is 67 per cent. Literacy can develop logical understanding and people can able to relate the PMJDY to their own growth and development only when the core message of financial inclusion reaches to them. The medium of reach is only education and awareness. There has to be awareness about Bank Correspondent for providing basic banking services, banking products available at BC outlets and RuPay Cards. Customers to be made aware that overdraft of Rs 5,000 to be provided in their account is a credit facility which needs to be repaid in order to get fresh limits and is not a grant. Customers also need to be aware about the proper utilisation of the overdraft facility in order to have a meaningful use of the scheme.

· **Other infrastructural bottlenecks:** Parts of North East, Himachal Pradesh, Uttarakhand, J&K and 82 Left Wing Extremism (LWE) districts in the states like Odisha, Chhattisgarh, Jharkhand, Maharashtra, West Bengal and Andhra Pradesh face challenges of infrastructure besides telecom connectivity. All households in such areas may not have been covered under the campaign. Another problem is availability of electricity. Nearly 40 crore people of the country still do not have access to proper electricity supply. Another fact is most of the villages in Bihar, Uttar Pradesh, West Bengal don't get power supply for days which highlight the pathetic condition in this matter. So the major challenge is to improve power generation, transmission and supply for social and economic development of the villages before thinking about providing a bank account to these people***.

Rural Connectivity is a key component of rural development in India. Rural roads are the virtual lifelines for the vast multitude residing in rural areas. However, even today, only about 60 Per cent of villages/ habitations in the country are connected by roads. Keeping in view the socio-economic

---

* http://www.newindianexpress.com/nation/Urban-rural-gap-in-literacy-rates-on-thedecline/2013/05/01/article1569601.ece

** http://www.niticentral.com/2014/06/25/power-supply-to-rural-india-a-pressing-concern-232244.html

benefits accruing from providing road connectivity to the villages, there is a need to impart greater thrust to providing road connectivity.

If seen from a larger philosophical view point, financial inclusion for the rural population without providing for the *bijli-sadak-pani* is a misnomer. In a way the PMJDY scheme may not have its desired success unless the infrastructural bottlenecks are addressed on a priority basis.

Conclusion

The financial inclusion has its existence since 1969.The earlier governments has set the pitch for the current ruling government to implement PMJDY. The efficiency of PMJDY which is an extension of *Swabhimaan* is based on Aadhaar. The implementation of Aadhar is linked to overall infrastructural development of the country in general and rural area in particular. Emphasis on education and awareness needs to be highlighted while discussing about the likely success of PMJDY for financial inclusion in rural area. Therefore, in the absence of infrastructural development, literacy and awareness –leave aside the reluctance of PSBs and RBI's own suspicion towards the scheme will the ruling government be able to achieve its missionary success as hyped for PMJDY or it will be another myth about financial inclusion in rural India.

References

(2014). Retrieved from http://articles.economictimes.indiatimes.com/2014-08-29/news/53362854_1_jan-dhan-yojana-upa-nda-government.

(2014, August 29). Retrieved from www.economictimes.indiatimes.com: http://articles.economictimes.indiatimes.com/2014-08-29/news/53362854_1_jan-dhan-yojana-upa-nda-government

(2013). *An overview on Financial Inclusion.* New Delhi: Ministry of Finance.

Basu, D. (2014, September 31). Retrieved from www.business-standard.com: http://www.business-standard.com/article/opinion/debashis-basu-narendra-modi-s-jan-dhan-what-s-new-114083100708_1.html

Daily Post. (2015, January 9). *PSU banks feel ignored.*

Gokarn, S. (2014, September 7). Retrieved from www.business-standard.com: http://www.business-standard.com/article/opinion/subir-gokarn-the-inclusion-triangle-114090700764_1.html

Jain, S. (2014, September 7). Retrieved from www.ndtv.com: http://www.ndtv.com/article/india/truth-vs-hype-jan-dhan-the-obstacles-and-opportunities-of-the-last-mile-587842

Malhotra, N. K., and Dash, S. (2009). *Marketing Research–An Applied orientation.* Delhi: Dorling Kindersley (India) Pvt. Ltd.

Mohan, T. (2014, September 2). *http://www.thehindu.com/opinion/lead/a-big-bang-reform-that-may-be-spot-on/article6370405.ece.*

Mor, N. (2013). *Committee on Comprehensive Financial Services for Small Businesses and Low Income Households.*

NDTV profit. (2015, January 21). Retrieved January 30, 2015, from http://profit.ndtv.com/: http://profit.ndtv.com/news/industries/article-jan-dhan-scheme-11-5-crore-accounts-opened-says-finance-minsiter-730127

(2014). *Pradhan Mantri Jan Dhan Yojana.*

Ramakumar, R. (2014, October 3). *Frontline.* Retrieved January 30, 2015, from http://www.frontline.in: http://www.frontline.in/the-nation/mirage-of-inclusion/article6412718.ece

Shivakumar, G.(2013, October22). Retrieved from www.thehindu.com: http://www.thehindu.com/news/national/aadhaar-not-approved-by-parliament-says-bjp/article5261575.ece

Sriram, M. (2013). *http://www.livemint.com/Opinion/rSlVyk6J9fqPMzj0H4yuxL/Why-the-Nachiket-Mor-committee-report-on-financial-inclusion.html.*

Tehelka. (2015, January 24). Retrieved January 30, 2015, from http://www.tehelka.com: http://www.tehelka.com/?p=230003

Tiwari, R. (2014, September 2). Retrieved from www.indianexpress.com: http://indianexpress.com/article/india/india-others/cashing-in-on-upa-schemes-nda-takes-them-a-step-further/

Tripathi, S. (2014, October). Retrieved January 2015, from Governance Now: http://www.governancenow.com/news/regular-story/jan-dhan-financial-inclusion-modi-idea-bank-account-for-all

Whither Financial Inclusion. Skoch eonsultancy Services.

Index

A

Aadhar
- And Direct Benefits Transfer (DBT), 388
- Card, 184

Aam Aadmi Bima Yojna, 390
Action Aid Report, 67
Agrarian
- Crisis, 42
- Economies, 51
- Reforms, 41, 42

Agreement on Trade Related Aspects of Intellectual Property Rights (TRIPS), 14, 17
Agricultural Credits, 81-115
- Demand for-, 101, 105
- Credit System, 102, 174
- Development in India, 81-100
- Economies, 66
- Employment, 46
- Export, 74, 105
- Labourers, 169, 229
- Operations, 81, 105
- Policies of India, 67
- Policies, 72
- Refinance Cooperatives (ARCs), 84
- Reform and Development Corporation (ARDC), 84
- System in Asia, 51

Agro-
- Based Resources, 13
- Industries, 106

AIDS, 43, 44
- Epidemic, 43

Al Khair Cooperative Credit Society, 202, 205
All India Rural Credit Review Committee, 84, 170
Andhra Pradesh Microfinance Institutions (Regulation of Money Lending) Ordinance, 197
Andhra Pradesh-Maharashtra, 94
Anganwadi
- Centres (AWC), 342
- System, 348
- Workers, (AWW), 30, 346, 348

Animal Husbandry, 32
Anti-Poverty Program, 41, 232, 373
Appellation of Origin (AOO), 13, 14, 17
Aravali, Oldest Mountain Ranges, 29
Armed Insurgencies, 45
Ashok Mchta Committee, 301
Asia, 35

B

Balwadi Centre, 342
Bangladesh, 194
Bangladesh—Nepal, 49
Bangladesh—Sri Lanka, 44
Banjara Handicrafts, 21
Bank Nationalisation, 173
Banking
- Commission, 1972, 170
- Regulation Act, 1949, 199
- System, 133, 176

Basic Saving Bank Deposits (BSBD), 184
Basic Savings-Bank Account, 196
Basmati Rice, 21, 74
Benevolent Loan (Qard Hasan), 201
Bharat Nirman Program, 40
Bhavanashree, 265

Bhore Committee, 142
Bihar—North East, 188
BIMARU States, 40
  Bihar, Jharkhand, MP, Rajasthan and UP, 40
BJP (Bhartiya Janta Party), 388
Block Panchayat, 273
BPL
  Card, 155
  Families, 213, 240
  In Karnataka, 367
Bureaucracy, 42

C

Cancer, 43
Caste System, 42
Centralised Planning, 315
Certified Seeds, 97
Cheap Foreign Food, 62
Chemicals and Pests, 62
Chickengunia, 318
Child Health, 143
  Factor Affecting-, 141-156
  In India, 143
  Policies and Programs, 143
Child
  Labour, 45, 53
  Labours, 144
Child Mortality, 149
China—Turkey, 20
Clean Kerala Mission, 319
Climate Change, 37, 48-52
  And Food Security Symposium, 51
Coastal Areas, 49
  Bangladesh—Sri Lanka, 49
Colonial Feudal System, 42
Commercial Banks (CBs), 82, 83, 84, 88, 89, 91, 102, 107, 109, 161, 166, 170, 172, 175, 176, 190
  Role of-, 86
Commercialisation, 166
  And Modernisation, 111, 114
  Of Resources, 13
Committee on Finance Inclusion, 195
Common Minimum Program (CMP), 233
Communication Technology, 114
Community
  Based Organisation (CBO), 53, 259
  Development Society, (CDS), 255, 257, 259, 260, 372
  Financial Management, 371
  Health Volunteer, 262
Compulsory Primary and Elementary Education, 53
Conservation of Land, 76
Constitutional Amendment
  (73rd), 272
  (73rd-74th), 255, 274
  Act, 303
Consumer
  Awareness, 329-339
  Among Rural Household, 329-339
  Market, 329
  Protection, 329
Cooperative
  Act, 106
  Banks, 88, 102, 170, 176, 177
Credit Structure (CCS), 83
  Movement, 54, 83
  Organisation, 16
  Societies, 175
  Societies Act, 1904, 83, 169
Cooperatives, 82, 83, 107
Credit
  Delivery System, 94, 111
  Markets, 167, 168

Unions, 94
Cropping System, 62
Cross Border Movement, 44
Crude Death Rate (CDR), 377

D

Dairy, 35
Development, 81
Darjeeling Tea, 13
Decentralisation
 And Privatisation, 119
 Of Professionals at Grass Root, 114
Decentralised
 Credit Planning, 84
 Planning, 301-316
 Program in Kerala, 302
Dengue Fever in Kerala, 318
Desertification, 52
Development
 Planning, 101
 Projects, 67
 Strategies, 40
Development Of
 Minor Irrigation, 76
 Rainfed Agriculture, 76
 Women and Children in Urban Areas, 257
 Women and Children in Rural Areas (DWCRA), 211, 212, 214
Dharwad Pedha—Tirupathi Laddu, 22
Direct Benefits Transfer (DBT), 392
Dispute
 Birbhum, 141
 Central Cooperative Banks, (DCCB), 83
 Idukki and Wayanad, 365
 Kannur, 355
 Malapuram, 342
 Mysuru, 377
 Palakkad, 223-229, 329-339, 361
 Planning Committee (DPC), 274
 Raipur MP, 170
 Settlement Mechanism, 14
 West Midnapore, 271-296
Diversification of Agriculture, 166
Doha Ministerial Declaration, 19
Droughts, 30, 52, 81, 94
Duggar, Dr NM, 31

E

Ecological Refugees, 67
Economic
 And Social Council (ECOSOC), 194
 And Social Infrastructure, 39
 Development, 30, 35, 40, 61, 161, 317, 353, 383
 Development of Rural India, 161
 Freedom, 39
 Growth, 36, 45, 65, 66, 117, 161, 231
 Production, 13
 Reform Policies, 65, 67
 Reforms, 231
 Theory, 22
 Welfare, 35
Economy, 13, 63, 108, 133, 153, 353
 Of India, 231
Education
 And Skill Development, 37, 117-131
 Life Long Process, 330
 Of Women, 156, 247
 Related Issues, 31
 System, 117, 119

Decentralisation and Privatisation, 119
Educational Institutions in India, 36
Elected Women Representation (EWR), 271-296
Employment
Assurance Program (EAP), 233
Generation, 31, 39
Structure in Kerala, 223-229
Structure in Kerala, Features, 224
Empowering Women, 245-254
Through Education, 245-254
Empowerment of Women, 271
Environmental
Degradation, 45, 62
Disaster, 49
Disaster and Climate Change, 48
European Union, 19, 20

F

Farm
Mechanisation, 81
Practices, 62
Farmers'
Size Group, 105
Suicides, 94
Farming System, 62, 65, 67, 77, 165
FDI In India, 65
Female
Headed Household, 368
Literacy, 248
Feminization of
Agriculture, 369
Malnutrition, 370
Malnutrition, Rural Indebtedness, 371
Poverty, 368
Financial
Exclusion, 103, 106-109, 112, 113, 133, 183-185, 195, 383-395
Inclusion
Defined, 183
For Rural Development, 183-191
In India, 183-191
Issues and Challenges, 188
Policies, 185
Institutions, 199
Literacy, 110, 189
Literacy Centres, (FLCs), 184, 185
Policies, 82
Sector Reforms, 169, 384
Services, 110
Technologies, 220
Fisheries, 35, 309
Five Year Plan
(1st), 142
(4th), 84
(5th), 142
(11th). 329
Flooding In
Bangladesh, 50
Pakistan, 49
Food
And Water Issues, 46
Corporation of India (FCI), 75
Crisis, 37, 47
For Work Program, 233
Insecurity, 40, 46, 47, 53
Management, 75
Safety Program, 233
Security, 35, 41, 62, 65
Free Movement for Work, 282
Functional Literacy, 39

G

Gandhi, Mahatma, 247
Gandhi, Mrs. Indira, PM, 384

Ganga
Basin, 29
Kalyan Yojna, 213, 214
Ganges And Brahmputra Rivers, 49
Gender
Development – Kerala, 365
Discrimination, 45, 110
Disparity, 317, 363-375
In Rural Poverty, 363-375
General Agreement on Tariffs and Trade, (GATT), 14
Geographical Indicators, (GI), 14-16, 18-22
And Rural Development, 23
In Foreign Jurisdiction, 25
Rights by State, 24
Global
Economy, 117, 231
Food Crisis, 54
Globalisation, 117-119, 193
And Liberalisation Process, 329, 339
Golar Gram Panchayat, 288
Good Registration Act, 1999, 20
Govt. of India Schemes, (GOIS), 36
Development of Women and Children in Rural Area (DWCRA), 36
Indira Awas Yojna, (IAY), 36
Integrated Child Development Scheme (ICDS), 36
Integrated Tribal Development Projects (ITDP), 36
Mahatma Gandhi National Rural Employment Guarantee Act (MGNREGA), 36
Pradhan Mantri Gram Sadak Yojna (PMGSY), 36
Rashtriya Sama Vikas Yojna, 36
Sampooran Grameen Rozgar Yojna (SGRY), 36
Gram
Panchayat, 277
Sabha, 274, 302-306, 307, 309, 310, 314, 315
Grameen Bank, 173, 194
Great Indian Desert (Thar), 29
Green Revolution, 47, 67, 84, 105

H

Handicrafts, 35
Haryali Kisan Bazaar (DCM), 185
Health
And Economic Development, 353
In Rural West Bengal, 141-156
Infrastructure, 353
Planning, 142
High Yielding Variety (HYV), 72, 74
Higher
Education, 118
Or Technical Universities, 119
HIV Technology in Agriculture Sector, 76
HIV/AIDS, 43, 44
Human Health Problems, 43
Hybrid Maize, 72, 76
Hydro-Meteorological Disaster, 48
Hydro-Power Generation, 49

I

Immunisation, 152, 344, 345
India, World Fastest Growing Economy, 231
India's
Development Policies, 67
Growth Story, 39
Population, 39, 363
Rural Credit Policy, 178

Indian
  Agriculture, 98, 99, 105
  Agriculture Sector, 61
  Community of-, 106
  Banking System, 173
  Constitution, 141
  Credit Market System, 175
  Economy, 61, 195, 232
  Employment Structure, 224
  National Congress, 384
  Poverty, 44
Indicators of Sources (IS), 13, 14, 17
Indigenous Seeds and Markets, 67
Indira Gandhi Canal, 30
Industrial
  Hazardous, 318
  Promotion and Policy, Department of-, 20
  Workers, 229
Industries, 61
Infant
  And Child Mortality, 142
  Mortality, 348, 353
  Mortality Rate, 142, 357, 377-381
In Mysuru District, 377-381
Information Technology, 118, 119
Information, Communication and Technology (ICT), 54, 113, 220
  And Digital Divide, 247
  Based Accounts, 184
  Enabled Banking Services, 185
  Strategies and Policies, 247
Infrastructure, 31, 49
Institutional Credits, 89, 91
Integrated Child Development Services (ICDS), 47, 141, 145, 147, 151-156, 341-349, 352
  Anganwadis, 346
  At Village Level, 346
  Features, 343
In Kerala, 344
  Objectives, 342
  Program, 156
  Program in Kerala, 342, 346
  Services Provided by, 344
  Structure, 343, 344
Integrated Rural Development Program (IRDP), 211, 214, 233
  Salient Features, 210
Intellectual Property
  Appellate Board (IPAB), 20
  Rights (IPR), 13, 14, 23
Interest
  Based Microfinance, 196
  Free Financial Services, 198
  Free Institutions, 200
  Free Microfinance, 198
  Free Microfinance Models in India, 201
  Free NIdhis, in Kerala, 201
Intergovernmental Panel on Climate Change (IPCC), 51
International
  Exhibition of Inventions at Vienna, 14
  Labour Organisation (ILO), 46
  Migration from Kerala, 366
  Year of Microcredit, 194
Internet Free Microfinance, 193
Iron
  And Folic Acid Tab, 341
  Deficiency, 341
Irrigation Management, 66
Islamic
  Banking, 193, 199
  Countries, 193

Finance, Principles of-, 199
Italy—Greece, 22

J

Jan Dhan Yojna, 187
Jawahar Gram Samridhi Yojna (JGSY), 233
Jawahar Rozgar Yojna, (JRY), 233
Job Opportunities, 225
Joint Family System, 42

K

Karnataka's Population, 366
Kasturi Rangarajan Committee Report, 314
Kerala, 223-229
 Decentralised Planning in-, 301-317
 Economy, 236
 Gendered Poverty Issues, 367
 Panchayati Raj Act, 307, 308
 Panchayati Raj Amendment Act, 1999, 303
 People's Participation-, 301-316
 Village Panchayats in-, 301-316
Kerala's Local Governance, 304
Kisan Credit Cards, 189
 Scheme (KCCS), 92, 94, 95, 196
Knowledge Oriented Markets, 118
Kudumbashree, 235, 250, 255-269, 315, 371-373
 Administration Plan, 263
 Formation of Women Collectives, 263
 Mission Focus, 261
 Need for Formation, 256
 Organisation, 263
 Programs, 267
 Project, 256
SHG Model Poverty Alleviation Program in Kerala, 255-269

L

Labour Markets, 46, 131
 Markets and Education System, 118
LAMC (Loan and Admittance of Members Committee), 204
Land
 Development Banks, 166
 Markets, 76,77
 Reform Policies, 72, 74
Landlords and Bureaucracy, 53
Lead Bank Scheme, 84
Leasing (Ijara) Facility, 200
Life Expectancy at Birth, 142, 353
Literacy, 36
 Rate, 294
Local
 Governance, 317-327
 Self-Government, 317
 Self-Government Institutions (LSGIs), 303, 325
Low Income Group, 195

M

Mahatma Gandhi National Rural Employment Guarantee Scheme (MGNREGA), 41, 190, 390, 392
 Beneficiaries, 235, 237
 Indicators of Performance, 234
 Workers, 325
Mahatma Gandhi National Rural Employment Guarantee Scheme (MGNREGS), 231-243, 313, 315
 Program for Inclusive Growth and Development, 231-243
Major International Conventions, (MIC), 17
 Lisbon Convention, 17

Madrid Conventions, 17
    Paris Convention, 17
Major Rural Self-Employment Projects, 208, 209
    DWCRA (Dev. Of Women and Children in Rural Areas), 209
    Ganga Kalyan Yojna, 209
    Integrated Rural Development Program, 209
Million Wells Scheme, (MW), 209
    NRLM (National Rural Livelihood Mission), 209
    SGSY, 209
    SITRA (Supply of Improved Tools for Rural Artisans), 209
    TRYSEM, 209
Male Dominated Social Order, 293
Malegam Committee Recommendations, 197
Malnutrition, 341, 346, 348
    Crisis, 67
    Impact of-, 44
Management Information System (MIS), 346
Manufacturing Skills and Traditions, 15
Marginal and Small Farmers, 99, 101
Market Failure, 16
Maternal
    And Child Health, (MCH), 341
Mortalitiy, 353
Mortality Rate, 142, 357, 360
Medical Institutions in Palakkad District, 358
Micro-Credit, 193, 194
    Program, 92
Microfinance, 92, 194
    Concept, 193
    For Financial Inclusion, 193-206
    And Rural Development, 193-206
    Internet Free, 193-206
    Institutions (MFIs), 94, 193, 196, 197, 197, 198, 200
    Operations, 265, 371
    Mid Day Meals Program, 47
Militarism, 45
Millennium Development
    Goals (MDGs), 142, 194
    Summit, 141
Million Wells Scheme, 213, 214
Mineral and Energy Resources, 13
Minimum Support Price (MSP), 75
Ministerial Conference, 19
Ministry of
    Commerce and Industry, 20
    Rural Development, 35, 40, 208
    Women and Child Development, 345
Minor Irrigation, 55, 81
Mirror Work, 21
Mobile
    And Internet Banking, 190
    Dispensaries, 30
    Phone Technologies, 387
Modern
    Agriculture System, 62
    Commercial Banking System, 193
    Industries, 225
    Technology, 91
Modernisation of Economy, 225
Modi, Narendra PM, 184
Mono-Cropping, 94
Monopoly Market, 166
Mother's Education, 153
Mudaliar Committee, 142

Muhammad Yunus, 194, 207, 221
Nobel Prize Winner, 194
Municipal Solid Waste, (MSW), 318
Management in Kerala, 318
Muslim
Countries, 193
Funds, 201

N

Narasimham Working Group, 169
National
Bank for Agriculture and Rural Development (NABARD), 83-86, 90, 94, 134, 161, 162, 169, 172, 178, 255, 260, 261, 266
Commission for Children, 145
Commission on Floods, 49
Economy, 118
Education, 119
Food Program, 67
Health Mission (NHM), 41
Health Policy, 142
Nutrition Policy, 145
Payment Certification, 386
Policy for Children, 143, 145
Population Policy, 142
Rehabilitation Centre, 145
Re Employment Guarantee Act, 2005, 31, 233, 239
Rural Employment Program, (NREP), 233
Rural Health Mission, 142, 144
Rural Livelihood Mission (NRLM), 219, 220, 221
Security, 388
Urban Health Mission (NUHM), 144
Nationalisation of Banks, 83, 195
Natural
Disasters, 51
Resources, 13, 35, 61
Navajat Shishu Suraksha Karyakram, 145
Nehru, Jawahar Lal, 161
Nepal—India, 51
Non-Banking Finance Corporation (NBFC), 197
Non-Governmental
Agencies, 35
Organisation (NGOs), 53, 56, 91, 94, 95, 113, 144, 163, 381
Nutrition Program, 43
Nutritional Status of Children—In Kerala, 341-349

O

Oil Resources, 13
Organic Manure, 324

P

Pakistan and Thailand, 167
Palakkad,
Agrarian District, 223
Occupational Structure, 228, 229
Working Population, 226
Panchayat
Committee, 303, 311
Samitis, 30, 273
Panchayati Raj, 41
Act, 303
Election, 278
Institutions (PRIs), 53, 271-296
System, 293
Leaders, 278, 293
System, 274
Panchayats, 40, 56, 246, 273, 301-303
Paris Convention (1883), 14
Patriarchal System of Society, 271
Planning, 301-316

Planning and Management, 54
Policies on Women Empowerment, 246
Policy
  Of Decentralisation, 41
  Of Reservation, 41
Planning, 232
Political
Participation, 246
Parties, 42, 43, 293
Poor Women's Bank, 371
Population in India, 47, 81
Post Office Banks, 190
Pothampally Ikal, 21
Poverty Alleviation, 76, 193, 196
  Program, 232
Pradhan Mantri
  Gramodaya Yojna (PMGY), 40
  Jan Dhan Yojna (PMJDY), 184, 190, 383-395
  Aims, 383
  Features, 386
Primary
  Agricultural Credit Societies (PACS), 83, 107, 161
  Health Centres, 142
Project Shakti (HUL), 185
Property Rights, 249
Public
  Distribution System (PDS), 47, 67
  Health Administration, 377
  Health Services, 44
  Sector Banks, 83, 384, 387, 389, 390, 391

Q

Quality Education, 119

R

Raghuram Rajan, Governor RBI, 184, 394
Rajasthan, 29
  And Gujarat, 207
  Largest State, 29
Rangarajan, Dr C, 195
Red Tapism and Corruption, 189
Referral Services, 344
Regional
Rural Banks (RRBs), 82, 83-85, 88, 102, 107, 161, 162, 166, 169, 170, 175-177, 239
  Act, 1976, 169
Rural Development Barriers, 36
Reproductive Child Health Program, 144
Revolving Fund, 212
Role of
  Agriculture Sector, 61-80
  Credit, 161
  Information Technology, 131
  NGOs, 196
Rural
  Banking, 106, 173, 178
  Community, 25
  Credit Institutions, 82
  Credit Market, 165-180
  Credit Policy, 177
  Credit Society, 103
  Credit System, 169
  Development Program, 36, 42, 304
  Development,
  Challenges and Barriers, 33-56
  Conceptual Framework, 37
  Explained, 35
  Program, 35
  Economy, 42, 82, 165

Economy of India, 231
Financial Institutions (RFIs), 111, 114, 166
Infrastructure, 241
Development Fund (RIDF), 85, 91, 99
Project, 91
Insurance, 190
Landless Employment Guarantee Program, (RLEGP), 233
People Issues, 30
Health Issues—Animal Husbandry, 30
Population, 81, 247
Self-Employment Programs, 207-221
Major Programs, 208
Treasures, 29
Unemployment, 232
Women
In Kerala, 364
Problems, 248
Removal of Backwardness, 252
Status and Power of-, 250

S

SAARC, Role of-, 56
Sarva Shiksha Abhiyan (SSA), 41
Scheduled Castes, 353-361
Colonies, 356
Kannaku, 355
Kurevan, 355
Health Status-in Palakkad District, 361
Paraiyan, 355
Population, 235, 357
In Kerala, 355, 356
Thandan, 355
Vettuvan, 355
Scheduled Castes/Tribes, 45, 235, 274, 294
And Minority Communities, 237
Communities, 213, 245
Scheduled Tribe, 360
Sector,
Agriculture, 111, 161, 161, 165, 223, 231
Agriculture, 46, 51, 61, 65, 68, 69, 72, 76, 77, 81, 83, 86, 91
Financial, 383
Industrial, 231
Microfinance, 196
Rural Development, 161
Services, 231
Unorganised, 232
Self-Help Groups (SHGs), 53, 85, 91-94, , 133-139, 190, 195, 238, 240, 374
In India, 133-139
Inclusive Growth, 133-139
SHG-Bank Linkage Program (SBLP), 93, 99, 134, 138, 139, 172, 196
Sen Committee, 301, 302
Sen, Dr Amartya, 251
SITRA, 213, 214
Skill
Development, 36
Formation and Infrastructure, 232
Small And Marginal Farmers (SMFs), 81, 82, 166
Smart Cards, 187
Social
And Economic Development, 44
Exclusion, 354
Group Disparity, 365
Justice, 40, 41, 63, 317
Reformers, 39

Security Program, 233
Structure, 271
    Welfare, 369
Socio-
    Cultural Issues, 248
    Economic
    Development, 36, 37, 117, 161
    Groups, 44, 157
    Infrastructure, 38
    Transformation, 40
    Economically Weaker Sections, 162
Solid Waste Management (SWM), 318, 320, 323, 324, 325
    In Kerala, 317-327
    Methods of, 320
    Practices, 322
South Asia, 37
South Asian
    Agriculture, 54
    Countries, 35
    Region, 46
South Malabar Grameen Bank, 239
Special Agriculture Credit Plans (SACP), 86, 95
Star Abhilasha Card, 187
State
    Commercial Banks (SCBs), 173, 174, 177, 184, 195
    Cooperative Agriculture and Rural Development Banks (SCARDBs), 83
    Cooperative Bank, 83
    Finance Committee, 274
    Poverty Eradication Mission, (SPEM), 255, 257
    Kudumbashree, 372, 373
Still Birth Rate, 357
Structural Adjustment Program, 67
Sub Sahara Africa, 36, 43, 44, 45
Suicides, 197
    By Farmers, 383
Sustainable
    Agriculture Development, (SAD), 61, 62
    Agriculture System, 62
    Development, 64
    Development in India, 61-80
    Development of Rural Economy, 165
Swaminathan, MS, Agricultural Economist, 42
Swaran Jayanti Shahri Rozgar Yojna (SJSRY), 233, 256
Swaranjyanti Gram Swarojgar Yojna (SGSY), 214, 219, 233

T

Taluk Panchayat, 273
Taluks, KR Nagara And T Narsipura, 380
Targeted Public Distribution System, (TPDS), 233
Technical
    Education, 118
    Skills, 46
Technological Changes, 66
Technology
    Adaption, 183
    In Agriculture Sector, 74
Tendulkar Committee, 101
Thar Desert, 29
Thrift Society, 371
Total Sanitation Campaign (TSC), 41
Tourism and Fisheries, 49
Traditional
    Community Based Practices, 31
    Knowledge, 29

Moneylenders, 197
Production System, 62
Transfer of Technology, 76
Transport System, 32
Transportation of Solid Waste, 321
Travancore and Cochin Literary, Scientific and Charitable Societies Registration Act, 1955, 255
Tribal Welfare, 341
TRIPS Agreements, 18, 19, 20, 21, 24
Trustee Partnership, 200
TRYSEM, 212, 214
Tuscany for Olive Oil, 15

U

UNICEF, 261
United Nations, 14, 194
Declaration of Rights of the Child, 143
Development Decade, 37, 368
Development Program, 363
ECOSOC, 194
Urban
Poverty Alleviation Program, 256
Self Employment Program, (USEP), 257
Urbanization, 246
US
National Intelligence Council, 44
Unemployment Role, 207
US—Uruguay, 20

V

Vermin Compost, 319
Village
And Cottage Industries, 38
Economies, 165-180
Panchayats, 371
Savings and Loans Association, (VSLA), 112
Vocational Training, 124, 129, 130, 131
Voluntary
Organisations, 250
Retirement Scheme, 384
Vyas, VS, 94

W

Water Conservation, 55
Welfare Programs, 141
West Bengal
Census, 2011, 141
Panchayat Act, 274
Women
Empowerment, 241
Role of New Media, 253
Of West Bengal, 272
Political Empowerment, 41
Representation, 271-296
Role in Development, 364
Women's
Agricultural Skills, 246
Economic Security, 249
Education, 251
In Rural Areas, 251
Empowerment in India, 246
Participation in Political Process, 272
Participation Rates, 369
Poverty, 368
Work Participation Rate (WPR), 227
World
Food Prices, 47
Health Organisation (WHO), 353
Intellectual Property Organisation (WIPO), 13, 14
Trade Organisation, (WTO), 14, 18, 19

Z

Zilla Parishad, 30, 274, 277